El Salvador

A Great Destination

El Salvador

A Great Destination

Paige R. Penland

with photographs by the author

The Countryman Press ✳ Woodstock, Vermont

FIRST EDITION

El Salvador: A Great Destination

978-1-58157-114-1

Interior photographs by the author unless otherwise specified
Maps by Erin Greb Cartography, © The Countryman Press
Book design by Bodenweber Design
Composition by PerfecType, Nashville, TN

Published by The Countryman Press, P.O. Box 748, Woodstock, VT 05091

Distributed by W. W. Norton & Company, Inc., 500 Fifth Avenue, New York, NY 10110

Printed in the United States of America

10 9 8 7 6 5 4 3 2 1

This book is dedicated to my aunt, Patricia Mouton, who dedicated her life to books. As an English teacher, president of the board of directors for the Syracuse (New York) School District, avid reader, and inspiration, she and my Uncle Steve taught me to respect good writing and love a great book.

Thanks so much Aunt Pat. I love and miss you.

EXPLORE WITH US!

This is the first edition of El Salvador: The Explorer's Guide. The book covers the entire country, at 21,040 square kilometers (8123 square miles), about the same size as New Jersey or Israel. It is bordered by Guatemala to the west and northwest, Honduras to the north and east, and the Pacific Ocean to the south.

PRICES

Remember that prices rise and quality fluctuates, businesses close and new options open, long before the guidebooks and Web sites have time to update their information. It's always worth asking fellow travelers and people working in the tourism industry about hotels, tour operators, taxi fares, and other information.

LODGING PRICE CODE

Cost of lodging is based on an average per-room, double occupancy rate during peak season, December through April. Note that peak surf season runs March through October, filling surf lodges opposite the usual Central American high season. El Salvador's 18 percent hotel tax and gratuities are not included; note that paying cash sometimes results in taxes being waived.

   Outside major cities, and particularly along the beaches, Ruta de las Flores, and El Pital Highlands, prices rise between 10 and 30 percent on weekends and holidays, when you should have reservations. The beaches get busy during the Christmas holidays and particularly Semana Santa (Easter Week), when hotels fill weeks in advance.

Inexpensive ($)	Up to $30
Moderate ($$)	$30 to 60
Expensive ($$$)	$60 to 100
Very Expensive ($$$$)	Over $100

RESTAURANT AND FOOD PURVEYOR PRICE CODE

Most restaurants offer a range of menu items, often including much less expensive set plates at lunch, or pricier steak and seafood dishes if you're in the mood to splurge. The following prices are based on the cost of a dinner entrée with a non-alcoholic drink, not including the recommended 10 percent tip, sometimes included in the bill. Meals served are abbreviated in the listings, breakfast (B), lunch (L), and dinner (D).

Inexpensive ($)	Up to $5
Moderate ($$)	$5 to 10
Expensive ($$$)	$10 to 20
Very Expensive ($$$$)	$20 or more

KEY TO SYMBOLS

While I've marked my favorite hotels, restaurants, and destinations with a ✪, you may find your tastes are different from mine.

Other symbols used include:

✎   The kid-friendly symbol appears next to hotels with special appeal for families.

☂   The umbrella symbol indicates businesses with pools.

♨   The hot water symbol denotes hotels with hot showers, though these may be heated with machines; see Bathrooms and Showers, later, for information on using them.

✳   The air-conditioning symbol appears next to hotels with climate control.

🚘   The gated parking symbol indicates gated or guarded parking. Most will allow non-guests to park for a small fee, space permiting.

"I"   The WiFi symbol denotes lodging that offer wireless Internet or data ports. Some luxury hotels charge a fee for Internet access, but most hotels offer free service.

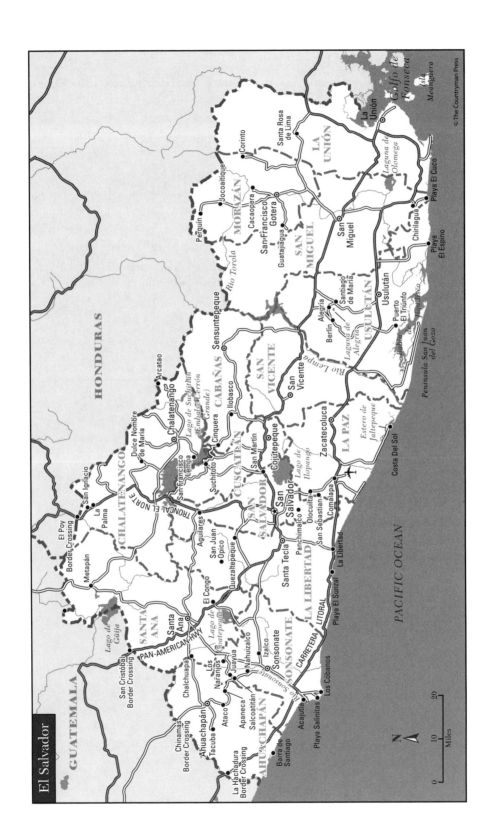

CONTENTS

MAPS

ACKNOWLEDGMENTS

I had an enormous amount of help on this book. Special thanks go out to my mom and stepfather, Wanda and Bob Olson, both of whom helped with research; my sister Beth Penland, who proofread and wrote the Literature and Music sections, and in Oak Ridge, Cher Morrison, Mark Quist, and Brittney Miller, who kept me going. Thanks also to Kim Grant, Lisa Sacks, Kermit Hummel, Erin Greb, Sandy Rodgers, Doug Yeager, and the crew at The Countryman Press, for believing in this project.

In El Salvador, special thanks go out to John Kim for helping me every step of the way, Fatima and Fatima, Alvero Calero (calerophotography.com) for his remarkable photos, Benoit Dagenais, Eric Keller, Eric Joo, Francesco Pilenga, Risa Fujimoto, Carolina Vides de Palomo, Dan the Man, Manolo González, César Magana, Robert P. Broz, Roque Mocan, Pascal Lebailley, FUNDAR, the Ministry of Tourism, and Omar Egan, Roberto Palomo, and Guillermo Nasser of La Charamusca (www.lacharamusca.net).

INTRODUCTION

The Mayans called it Cuscatlán, the Land of Precious Things. They must have been speaking of the magnificent volcanoes, today cloaked in coffee and cloud forests, so many filled with sparkling sapphire lakes.

Or perhaps they were referring to El Salvador's long, pearl gray beaches, which fringe its epic shore. While the waves are most famous—Punta Roca, El Sunzal, La Flor, Mizata—there's much more to be found along the Pacific. Massive mangrove wetlands and ceiba rainforests surround the starry bays, where sea turtles nest and migrating birds rest before continuing on their way.

Today, the Pacific is lined with great hotels, tiny fishing villages, and festive surf towns, though plenty of wilderness remains to enjoy. The mountains, as well, are home to Spanish Colonial cities, with their fine churches, food festivals, and cheerfully painted adobe homes, many now filled with art galleries and restaurants. The precious things are still revered, of course, and pretty tourist centers invite Salvadoran families and curious visitors to holiday next to hot springs, waterfalls, and rushing rivers.

And at the center of it all is modern, sophisticated San Salvador, a globalized business center overseeing the best highway system and infrastructure in Central America. In the shadow of its own iconic volcano, you'll find opulent malls, all-night discos, fine dining restaurants . . . and very poor neighborhoods.

Let me guess. This is what you've heard about El Salvador: These dangerous neighborhoods, the crime, and of course the Civil War. These are real, of course, and part of the Salvadoran experience.

Statistically, however, El Salvador is one of the safest countries in Central America for foreigners. As for the war, it ended in 1992, with the signature of the Chapultepec Accords. The "best negotiated ceasefire in history," this remarkable document laid the groundwork for rebuilding El Salvador's great cities, developing the excellent national parks system, and creating a notably peaceful, stable republic.

Optimistic and unpretentious, artsy and eloquent, Salvadorans are proud to welcome you to their little slice of paradise, even if some of the scars are still healing. The backdrop is astounding, crystalline crater lakes, magnificent volcanoes, and epic Pacific coastline. Within the landscape's fertile embrace a remarkable culture has arisen, so take time to enjoy the food festivals, murals, museums, and Mayan ruins. But you may find that your most memorable moments are one-on-one, enjoying the hospitality of people who are happy to have you here.

THE WAY THIS BOOK WORKS

San Salvador is the capital and transportation hub, within four hours of almost any destination in the country. It has El Salvador's finest hotels, restaurants, nightlife, and museums, and is a thriving business center, but is surrounded by wilderness escapes.

Most tourists head south to the Pacific Coast, which I've divided into two chapters. **The Western Beaches** are home to some of the best surfing waves in the world, and the sandy shores are lined with small towns, ports, and coral reefs. The chapter runs east (La Libertad, closest to San Salvador) to west, terminating at the Guatemalan border. **The Eastern Beaches** are perhaps prettier, with more swimming coves and lush mangrove estuaries, but they are considerably less developed. I've arranged this chapter from west (Costa del Sol, close to San Salvador) to east, ending at the Gulf of Fonseca and Honduran border.

Western El Salvador is well developed for tourism, boasting the bulk of the country's inland attractions, including Los Volcanes, El Imposible, and Montecristo-El Trifinio National Parks, as well as Coatepeque crater lake, and Cuscatlán's most important Mayan ruins. The major city is Santa Ana, but most travelers head to a string of artsy, appealing towns in the coffee-growing highlands of hot springs and waterfalls, collectively known as the Ruta de las Flores.

Suchitoto and the Artisan Route covers north-central El Salvador, centered on the beautiful Colonial town of Suchitoto, with beautiful hotels, restaurants, and art galleries. It makes a great base for visiting natural preserves, wildlife-rich lakes, volcanic Civil War battlefields, and the handicraft towns scattered throughout the rolling hills.

Eastern El Salvador, like the Eastern Beaches, is less developed but rewarding, centered on the city of San Miguel. Most visitors are headed to Ruta de la Paz and Morazán, with Civil War sites and developing eco-tourism. But the region's other volcano climbs, crater lakes, and handicraft villages are worth visiting as well.

EL SALVADOR FACTS AND FIGURES

Total Area: 21,040 square kilometers (8,123 square miles) Smallest in Central America; about the same size as New Jersey or Israel.

Land Measurements: Manzana (1.73 acres), hectare (2.47 acres), square kilometer (.39 square miles).

Population: 7,185,218, most densely populated country in Central America.

Type of Government: Democratic Republic.

Currency: U.S. dollar ($).

Time: GMT–6.

Electricity: 110 Volts AC/ 60Hz and 220 volts (US-style electrical plugs, but many have only two prongs; bring an adapter.)

Race: 90 percent Mestizo, 9 percent White, 1 percent Indigenous*.

Religion: 58 percent Catholic, 21 percent Protestant, 4 percent other, 17 percent no formal religious beliefs*.

Highest Point: Cerro El Pital, 2730 meters (8954 feet).

Nicknames: Guanacos/Guanacas (Salvadorans); Country with a Smile; Pulgarcito de America (Little Flea of America).

National Tree: El Maquilishuat.

National Bird: Torogoz.

National Flower: Izote.

*These figures are widely debated

WHAT'S WHERE IN EL SALVADOR

El Salvador is compact—not just small, but concentrated, with the best highway system in Central America streamlining travel. If you have the money for a rental car, you could easily surf world-class waves at dawn, finish climbing the country's tallest volcano by early afternoon, and be back to San Salvador in time for an upscale dinner and night of clubbing. If you pushed it, you could even squeeze in an ancient Mayan city.

There's a lot more to enjoy, and some of the country is much more difficult to visit; you could spend six months here and still not see it all. But you can comfortably visit a range of classic Central American attractions in just a few days: active volcanoes, cute Colonial towns, beach resorts, coral reefs, nesting sea turtles, hot springs, canopy tours, archaeological sites, and so on, all within a few hours of each other. It's convenient. Heck, if you're from the U.S.A., you don't even have to worry about the currency exchange.

That said, a little preparation goes a long way. Tourism is still developing, and remains largely geared to surfers and Salvadoran expatriates. A Spanish phrasebook is indispensable if you're planning to do much independent travel, and highly recommended even if you're not. Good maps are difficult to find outside the country, so you'll want to visit one of the excellent MiTur tourism offices here, and pick up some of their useful freebies.

ADDRESSES El Salvador uses a very convenient, efficient address system. Most freeways (*carreteras*) radiate out from San Salvador. Outside cities and towns, addresses are given at the kilometer (1 kilometer is .62 miles) mark from San Salvador on the freeway, most commonly designated by the major destination city. For instance, if your destination is 34

kilometers from San Salvador on the highway to Santa Ana, the address will be "KM34 Carretera Santa Ana." Highways between secondary cities are usually hyphenated, for instance, "KM27 Carretera Santa Ana-Ahuachapán" would be 27 kilometers from Santa Ana on the road to Ahuachapán.

The major road traversing Central America is the Pan-American Highway, which runs through El Salvador via Santa Ana, San Salvador, San Vicente, San Miguel, and Santa Rosa de Lima. The coastal highway is called the Carretera Litoral.

Most inland towns are designed using the logical, convenient Spanish Colonial grid. Cities and villages are usually centered on a town square usually referred to as the *parque central*, or central park. The main Catholic church and *alcaldía*, or mayor's office, are usually here, with most restaurants, hotels, banks, and grocery stores within a few blocks.

Streets are rarely given names, and are instead numbered. This is extremely useful, once you are used to it. *Calles* (streets) run east and west, while *avenidas* (avenues) run north and south. They are numbered from the point where the main calle and the main avenida cross, at the central park. Calles are designated *oriente* (east; often abbreviated Ote) and *poniente* (west, abbreviated Pte), depending on their relation to the main avenue. Avenidas, in turn, are designated *norte* (north) and *sur* (south), depending on their relation to the central calle.

All calles north of the park are given odd numbers (3 Calle Poniente, 5 Calle Oriente), those to the south have even numbers (2 Calle Oriente, 4 Calle Poniente). Avenidas work the

same way, designated with even numbers east of the park (2 Avenida Norte, 6 Avenida Sur) and odd numbers west of the park (3 Avenida Sur, 5 Avenida Norte).

This system breaks down somewhat in major cities, where important thoroughfares are often given names, and outlying neighborhoods (called *barrios* or *colonias*) don't quite match up with the central park. People are helpful, so you can always ask "*¿Dónde esta . . . ?*" (Where is . . . ?), followed by the address or name of your destination.

AIR TRAVEL El Salvador International Airport (SAL; 2366-9455; www.cepa.gob.sv/aies), also called Comalapa International Airport—but not San Salvador, The Bahamas (ZSA)—claims to be Central America's most modern airport. It is actually closest to the beach town of La Libertad (33 kilometers/20 miles), a $20 cab ride. A private cab to San Salvador (50 kilometers/30 miles) costs $25 to $30, but if you arrive before 5:30 PM, you can take the **Acacya Shuttle** (2271-4937; www.taxisacacya .com; 19 Avenida Norte #1117), which charges $5 to their offices downtown.

Unfortunately, San Salvador is often the most expensive regional airport; if you plan to spend time in Western El Salvador, consider flying into **Guatemala City La Aurora International Airport** (GUA; 502-2-600-311). Guatemala City is 181 kilometers (112 miles) from San Salvador, about four hours in international buses. If you're up for local buses, it's 122 kilometers (76 miles), also about four hours, to Ahuachapán, on the Ruta de las Flores.

Here are some destinations served from San Salvador:

American Airlines (800-433-7300; www.aa.com) Miami.

Continental (800-525-0280; www.continental.com) Houston and Newark.

Copa Airlines (800-359-2672; www.copaair.com) Managua, Nicaragua, and Panama City, with connecting service to San José, Costa Rica.

Delta Air Lines (800-525-0280; www.delta.com) Atlanta.

Mexicana (800-531-7921, www.mexicana.com) México City.

TACA (800-535-8780; www.taca.com) El Salvador's national airline serves Belize City, Cancún, Chicago-O'Hare, Dallas/Fort Worth, Guatemala City, Houston-Intercontinental, Lima, Los Angeles, Managua, México City, Miami, New York-JFK, Orlando, Panama City, San Francisco, San José, San Pedro Sula, Tegucigalpa, Toronto-Pearson, Washington-Dulles.

BATHROOMS AND SHOWERS If you stay at exclusively upscale hotels, bathrooms will have reliable hot showers and normal toilets, although you should *never flush toilet paper,* except in a very few places with special plumbing systems. If there's a wastebasket beside the toilet, that's where it goes.

Very few hotels have centrally heated water for showers. In warm areas, such as the beaches and tropical lowlands, even the mid-range hotels may offer only cool baths. In the mountains, hotels will often install electric water heaters on the shower, rather ominous-looking things with wires sticking out. Colloquially known as "suicide machines," these heaters require a delicate touch. Before turning on the shower, set the switch to the hottest setting, usually indicated with two blackened ovals. Turn on the water until you hear an electric hum, and give it a moment. The trick is to turn the water to the lowest possible flow while maintaining the hum, which usually will result in a lukewarm shower. When new, they work fabulously; three months later, not so much.

In very basic rural hostels and markets, you may run into bucket-flush toilets. The handle won't work, and there will be a large barrel of water with a smaller bucket nearby. Fill the small bucket, raise the toilet seat (if there is one), and pour about half a gallon of water into the bowl from chest high. Now you're flushing like a local.

CENTROS TURISTICOS One of the best ways to enjoy El Salvador is at a tourist center, family-friendly complexes of springwater pools and fairly epic water slides, surrounded by food stalls, playground equipment, and shady kiosks with hammocks. Some are quite simple, others astounding, with hot springs, hiking trails, waterfalls, crater lakes, archaeological sites, whitewater rafting, and even canopy tours. Admission is $1 to $5, depending on the attractions, and they're usually open from 9 AM to 5 PM daily, but may have lodging onsite. All are packed on weekends.

BICYCLES El Salvador's excellent road system includes wide, usually well-maintained shoulders with plenty of space for bicyclists, compared to other Central American countries, anyway. Highways are busy, and the volcanic landscape has tough hills, but serious bikers say this is a good place to ride. A few hotels rent bicycles, and many adventure tour operators offer mountain-biking trips.

BOATS Boat transportation is possible between several destinations on the Eastern Beaches; see that chapter for more information.

BORDERS Both border countries, Guatemala and Honduras, are part of the C4 (Central American Customs Union) treaty, which also includes Nicaragua. Thus, there are no stamps, entrance, or exit fees at overland borders.

Note that while it's legal and theoretically possible to take a boat from La Unión across the Gulf of Fonseca to Potosí, Nicaragua, no ferries or reliable captains were offering the trip at the time of research.

BUSES Public transportation usually involves refurbished Bluebird school buses, painted in festive colors and accented with neon piping, shark fins, Virgin Marys, football team logos, and prayers to God for safety, which even atheists will appreciate once they see how these guys drive.

There is no storage for large bags, so be prepared to put your backpack on your lap if buses fill. Keep an eye on your bags at all times, especially if someone tries to distract you. Most buses do not have rest rooms; plan ahead. Usually, you board the bus first, and once you're rolling, a young man comes around to collect the money. Buses usually run from about 4 AM to 6 PM.

There are several different classes of service, including *ordinarios,* which stop to pick up anyone along the highway; *directos,* which stop only at population centers; *exclusivos,* which run directly between destinations; and *especiales,* which have reclining seats and air-conditioning. Ordinarios leave more frequently, but for long haul trips, it's worth waiting for a better bus.

In many large cities, there is a main bus terminal. In most towns, however, buses leave from several spots around the city. I have done my very best to list accurate locations and schedules, but you can also check **Central America Bus Schedules** (www.horariodebuses.com), with suggestions for connecting buses, city maps, and other information. But it is always smart to double-check everything on the ground. Where is the bus to San Salvador? ¿Donde está el bús hacia San Salvador?

Useful Phrases: Where does this bus go? *¿A donde va este autobús?*

Does this bus stop in Usulután? *¿Se para este bús en Usulután?*

When does the bus for Perquín leave? *¿Cuándo hace el bús para Perquín departa?*

When will this bus arrive in Playa El Tunco? *¿Cuándo llegará este bús a Playa El Tunco?*

International Buses Several international bus lines ply the Central American isthmus. In general, they have reclining seats, bathrooms, and movies running on an endless loop. Make reservations at least a day or two prior to your trip, in person, as they need to see your passport. In general, they will not let you off between destinations, but ask ahead of time.

Autobus Fuente del Norte (2298-3275, 7891-4996; autobuses fuentedelnorte.com) Terminal del Occidente. Inexpensive buses to Guatemala City at 5 AM and 3 PM.

Comfort (2217-3300, 2217-3333; www.comfortpremium.com) Alameda Juan Pablo II and 19 Avenida Norte. Based at Hotel Puerto Bus, leaves for Guatemala City at 8 AM and 2 PM.

Herrera Najera (2223-4012) Terminal del Occidente. Budget buses to Guatemala at 6:30 AM, 7:30 AM, and 8:30 AM.

King Quality (www.kingqualityca .com) Luxury line has two San Salvador terminals, at Hotel Puerto Bus, Alameda Juan Pablo II and 19 Avenida Norte, convenient for early-morning buses, and at San Benito (2241-8702) on El Hipódromo Boulevard. Offers direct buses to Guatemala, Honduras, Nicaragua, and Costa Rica; see the Web site for schedules.

Pullmantur (503-2243-1300, 2243-2405; www.pullmantur.com) Avenida La Revolucion. Based at Sheraton Presidente, this luxury line does not allow children. Buses leave to Guatemala City at 7 am and 3 pm, and to Tegucigalpa, Honduras, at 2:15 pm.

Tica Bus (2243-9764; www.ticabus .com) Popular, reliable international line has two terminals in San Salvador, one in San Benito (2243-9764) on El Hipódromo Boulevard at excellent ✪ Mesón de María Hotel, and another downtown (2222-4808) on Calle Concepción #121 at grimy Hotel San Carlos. Buses run from the Mexican border to Panama City; the Web site has schedules. Hotel Mopelia in Playa El Tunco (Western Beaches chapter) has a Tica Bus reservations desk.

Transportes Mermex (2279-3676; www.transmermex.com.sv) Terminal del Occidente. Cheaper buses to Guatemala City at 9 AM and 1:30 PM.

Pickup Trucks *Camionetas,* or pickup trucks, are widely used because they are cheap, convenient, and go everywhere. If you're planning to explore less-developed regions, you'll probably have to take them in lieu of public buses. Basically, you just hop in the back of the truck and hold on; there are often guard rails so you can stand, which is more comfortable on unpaved roads, and allows them to pack everyone in like sardines.

CLIMATE El Salvador has two seasons. *Verano,* literally summer, but better translated as dry season, runs from November through April, and is hot and dry. Streams dry up, some trees lose their leaves (much like fall at higher latitudes), and you can count on sunny days. *Invierno,* winter, is the rainy season, when it rains most afternoons and evenings from May through October, with the heaviest rains in September and October. It's cooler, greener, and prettier, but carry an umbrella. The beaches and lowlands are warm—generally between 18 degrees Celsius (64 degrees Fahrenheit) and 32 degrees Celsius (90 degrees Fahrenheit), but temperatures can go to extremes in either direction. The coolest months are November and December, the warmest are March and April. The mountains, including the Ruta de las Flores, El Pital Highlands, and Morazán Department, can be chilly—it's been known to snow atop Cerro Pital. Unless you are planning to

spend your trip at the beach, bring long pants and a light jacket. If you plan to camp in the mountains, warmer clothes are recommended.

COMMUNICATIONS Public telephones are few and far between, and hotels often charge exorbitant amounts ($2–4) to make local calls. To use the few pay phones, you'll need a phone card, available in pharmacies. It's cheaper to buy a $10 cell phone and pre-paid chips, widely available at grocery stores and small shops. Or use your own; pre-paid SIM cards probably work with your phone. Systems operating in El Salvador include GSM 850, 900, 1900, and 1950. It's often cheaper to call the United States and Canada than make local calls, about 10 cents a minute. Local calls cost between 15 and 30 cents. Latin America and Europe run about 40 cents per minute.

Infocentros (www.infocentros .org.sv) is a nationwide chain of Internet shops offering inexpensive long-distance calls; check their Web site for locations, in most major towns close to the central park. Independent Internet cafés, which are everywhere, may also offer inexpensive digital

calls. Many hotels offer free wireless Internet; a few luxury hotels in San Salvador charge an extra daily fee. Free WiFi is also available at most malls, and at major chain restaurants including Pollo Campero, Coffee Cup, and Sushi Itto.

CRIME There is probably one aspect of El Salvador you've heard plenty about: Gangs. Foreigners make movies about them, take glorious black-and-white photos of them, and pen eloquent articles about them. Frankly, I think this type of notoriety just encourages them, so never mind. Here's what you need to know. There are two types of crime in El Salvador: opportunistic and organized (the gangs). As a tourist, opportunistic crime is your main worry. The main difference between opportunistic crime in El Salvador and elsewhere in Central America is that (1) it doesn't happen as often, and (2) when it does, it's more likely to involve guns. You probably already know the drill.

Always keep a close eye on your belongings, particularly in bus stations, beaches, and other public places. Your passport, credit cards, and other important documents belong in a money belt, which you should wear while in transit. Other-

wise, it stays in the hotel. Make photocopies of your passport to carry in a wallet with your day's spending money. If you are mugged, calmly and politely hand the wallet to the little crackhead, who will probably be armed.

When you need to take cash out of an ATM, do it in broad daylight, and stay alert. Don't flaunt your iPods, computers, cameras, and other expensive items needlessly. Don't use a computer bag; carry your laptop in a cheap daypack.

Beaches and most city centers are no-goes after dark. Ask at your hotel about current security issues. If you go out drinking, don't get too wasted, and don't accept open drinks from strangers. Always take taxis after dark in large cities. Just say no to drugs. And so on. But you already knew all that, right? So let's talk about the gangs.

El Salvador has a disturbingly high violent-crime rate, some 10 murders per day. But if you look at the statistics, these are almost all young Salvadoran men. You'll probably see gang members, with their tattoos, goatees, and Dickies. Since many were deported from the United States, they may even engage you in a friendly conversation in English. *Ese.*

Gang violence rarely affects tourists. Regardless, it's best to avoid gang-infested neighborhoods, which I have specifically mentioned at the beginning of each chapter. Most violence happens at night. Purchasing illegal drugs invites gangs into your life. Always trust your gut—if you feel like a situation is sketchy, get out quickly and calmly. If something does happen, above all, do not panic.

Salvadoran gangs model themselves after Italian mafias, and make their living by extorting business owners and bus drivers, which is where your paths might cross. If a business owner can't afford to pay, or refuses to do so, the gangs will threaten him or her. If a bus driver can't pay, gang members have been known to board buses and rob passengers as well. They will either charge everyone a fee, or simply take what they can. Gang members do not want to hurt tourists; that brings unwanted attention to their operation, and could cause the entire organization problems. But if you freak out, they may, too. So just chill.

Scared? Don't be. The vast majority of travelers have absolutely no problems in El Salvador. But being prepared is easy, free, and could come in handy if it's not your lucky day.

DIVING The most popular spot to dive is **Los Cóbanos**, the largest Pacific coral reef in Mesoamerica, with sunken ships, whales, sea turtles, and all sorts of coral and fish. Visibility is best November through January. A close second is **Laguna Ilopango**, a crater lake with 10 species of fish, sponges, crabs, and other wildlife, as well as boiling hydrothermic vents, just 30 minutes from San Salvador. There are a handful of other dive sites including another crater lake, Lago Coatepeque; the Golfo de Fonseca, with low visibility; and a coral reef near the surfing beach of Mizata, which is extremely dangerous because of fierce currents. El Salvador has small decompression chambers, but for full-sized problems, you'll need to be flown to Roatan Island in Honduras (400 kilometers/250 miles) in a special low-altitude plane.

Decameron Explorer (Oceanica; 2429-9097; www.decameron.com) All-inclusive resort next to Los Cóbanos organizes diving trips all over the country, resort dives, and PADI certification.

○ **El Salvador Divers** (503-2264-0961; www.elsalvadordivers.com, info@elsalvadordivers.com) 3a. Calle Poniente y 99 Avenida Norte #5020, Colonia Escalón. El Salvador's oldest dive company organizes diving trips, PADI certification, and other tours throughout the country. Staff speaks English, Spanish, and French, and can teach underwater photography, commercial diving, and underwater welding.

DRIVING El Salvador has the best freeway system in Central America, for the most part smoothly paved, intelligently designed, and well signed. Northern El Salvador, in particular Chaletanago and Morazán Departments, do have important secondary roads where a 4WD car is required.

Most rental-car companies are based in San Salvador, with offices in town and at the airport. There are a few others in La Unión, San Miguel, and elsewhere. The daily rate is deceptively inexpensive, $10 a day for the smallest cars, but insurance can cost four times that, and will not be included with your online reservations total. Contact your credit card company about supplemental coverage.

In general, you must be 25 years old and have a major credit card and valid driver's license (technically good for only 30 days after arrival) to rent a car. If you aren't 25, contact the offices directly to see if they'll make exceptions. You can rent a GPS system separately, through Q-soft (www.elsalvadorgps.com).

Carefully inspect tires, jacks, lights, and signals before signing anything,

and make sure all prior damage is recorded; while there is a tiny chance of getting carjacked, you're more likely to be ripped off by the rental company. Check all paperwork carefully as well, including the dates on your circulation card. Ask for another car if the first one isn't up to snuff.

You will be pulled over regularly at security checkpoints. Heavily armed officers will ask to see your driver's license, rental car agreement, and circulation card. This takes about five minutes and should be no problem. Gas stations are widely available in major cities and many smaller towns, but it's best to keep your tank half full at all times, just in case. Gas is denominated in gallons, (3.8 liters), and tends to be more expensive than in the United States, but cheaper than in Europe. The speed limit is 90 kilometers (56 miles) per hour on freeways and 40 kilometers (25 miles) per hour in cities, and strictly enforced. You must wear a seat belt. The police can confiscate your driver's license for minor infractions. Tickets are paid through your rental company, not on the spot. If you have an accident, you must call the police (84 for English) and your rental-car company's insurance.

Crime can be a problem. When driving in a city or crowded market area, keep your windows rolled up and doors locked. Avoid driving at night. Never allow anyone to approach your car at a deserted intersection. It's actually legal to run a red light if you feel threatened. *Always* use guarded parking, and don't leave anything visible in your car while it's parked, particularly overnight.

EMBASSIES AND CONSULATES
Most countries have embassies or consulates in San Salvador; you can

find a complete list at **Embassies Abroad** (www.embassiesabroad.com/embassies-in/ElSalvador). Note that the **Australian Embassy in Mexico** (www.mexico.embassy.gov.au) covers El Salvador, as does the **British Embassy in Guatemala** (2281-5555; ukinguatemala.fco.gov.uk; claims@gibson.com.sv) P.O.Box 242. **Embassy of Canada** (2279-4655; www.sansalvador.gc.ca) Roosevelt and 63 Avenida Sur, Centro Financiero Gigante, Colonia Escalón; open 8–4:30 Monday through Thursday, 8:30–1:30 Friday.

Embassy of France (2279-4016; www.diplomatie.gouv.fr) 1 Calle Poniente #3718, Colonia Escalón.

Embassy of Germany (2247-0000; www.sansalvador.diplo.de) 77 Avenida Norte and 7 Calle Poniente #3972, Colonia Escalón.

Honorary Consul of Ireland (2263 8236; gloria.olmedo@agrisal.com) Boulevard del Hipodromo #539, San Benito.

Embassy of Israel (2211-3434; sansalvador.mfa.gov.il) Centro Financiero Gigante, Torre B Piso 1163 Avenida Sur and Alameda Roosevelt; open 9–noon Monday through Friday.

Embassy of Japan (2528 1111; www.sv.emb-japan.go.jp) 89 Avenida Norte and Calle El Mirador, World Trade Center, Colonia Escalon; open 8:30–noon and 2–5:30 Monday through Friday.

Embassy of the U.S.A. (2278-6020; sansalvador.usembassy.gov) Boulevard Santa Elena, Final Antiguo Cuscatlán; open 8–3:30 Monday through Friday, until noon on Wednesday. Incidentally, this is the second largest embassy in the world, after the U.S. embassy in Iraq.

EVENTS Events listed in the Overview section are celebrated nationally, but each city has its own special celebrations and fiestas, listed in those chapters. If you can swing it, try to visit a village having its Fiestas Patronales, multiple-day parties that celebrate the town's patron saint. These aren't exclusively religious festivals, although there are special Masses and solemn processions, when townspeople carry an image of the saint or virgin around town. But they also might include indigenous elements, such as traditional dances and food, or in the case of San Miguel's famous Carnival, a month of absolute mayhem. Most have carnival rides, large markets, beauty queens, live music, and heavy drinking.

GAY AND LESBIAN TRAVELERS
Homosexuality is legal in El Salvador, and gays and lesbians may serve openly in the military. In 2007, a proposed constitutional amendment defining marriage as between a man and woman (which would have also prevented gay couples from adopting) was handily shot down in the legislature.

The current ruling FMLN party has also unsuccessfully supported anti-discrimination laws, with some politicians expressing support of gay civil unions and even marriage. While gays and lesbians cannot yet legally marry, they do anyway, complete with announcements that run in left-wing **La Pagina** (www.lapagina.com.sv).

That said, it's smart (as in most of Latin America) to refrain from being obvious about your orientation, particularly in rural communities. But there's a healthy gay and lesbian scene, particularly in San Salvador, as well as a handful of spots in Santa

Ana and Suchitoto, where you can feel comfortable out and about.

Log onto **Asociación Gay Salvadoreña** (asociaciongaysalvadorena.blogia.com), **Entre Amigos** (2219-3913; www.entreamigosgay .org), **El Savador Org** (www.elsal vadorg.com), **Lesbianas y Bisexuales** (lezzbi-sv.foroactivo.com) and **Gay El Salvador** (www.gayelsal vador.com) for Spanish-language information, as well as forums, events listings, and chat rooms.

GOLF There are two courses easily accessible to the public:

Hacienda El Campanario (2306-0623; www.haciendaelcampanario .com) KM46.5 Carretera La Libertad. This course doesn't earn raves, but it has an interesting terrain, a driving range, and classes, and it's convenient to the International Airport. The 18-hole green is $50 for tourists any time, $25 to $50 for nationals.

✪ **Las Veraneras** (2420-5000; www.veranerasresort.com) Playa Salinitas. Non-members can play this lush 7000-yard, 18-hole, par-72 course with dramatic water features, for $50. There's nice lodging as well, listed in the Western Beaches.

In addition, there are two pricey private clubs that offer reciprocity: **Club Campestre Cuscatlán** (2263-0281; www.clubcampestrecuscatlan .com), a narrow, challenging, 9-hole course on the side of a volcano; and **Club Salvadoreño de Golf Corinto** (2226-9111; www.clubsalvadoreno .com) in Lago Ilopango, an 18-hole, par-71 course that is excellent during rainy season.

HEALTH Though San Salvador and other urban areas have excellent infrastructure, much of the country is still

developing, and risk of tropical diseases is small, but real. Make sure that you have been vaccinated for hepatitis A and that your tetanus boosters are up to date. Hepatitis B vaccinations are also a good idea. The Center for Disease Control (http:// www.cdc.gov) recommends other precautions worth considering for visitors planning to spend long periods in rural, inland areas. Malaria is present in Central America, primarily on the Caribbean coasts of Honduras and Nicaragua, but is extremely rare in El Salvador. Dengue is another mosquito-borne illness, characterized by high fever and flushed skin, followed by severe body aches. It is also rare, but present, and there is no vaccine. If you begin showing those symptoms, definitely seek medical care. The best way to avoid either illness, not to mention itchy bites, is to use a DEET-based insect repellant (not readily available in El Salvador), which you should carry with you whenever exploring rural or wilderness areas. Many hotels have mosquito nets available at the front desk, so ask. In addition to DEET-based repellants, it can also be difficult to find contact solution and good sunscreen in El Salvador.

HOSPITALS AND CLINICS Just about every town has a health clinic that will treat walk-in patients inexpensively. Pharmacists can also diagnose and treat most common illnesses. Your hotel or any business can point you toward a good, and perhaps even English-speaking, health-care professional.

Bring your Spanish phrasebook (to describe your symptoms) and cash, as you'll need to pay up front. Most clinics do not accept credit cards. Some pharmacies do. Brand-name medication is often more expensive in El Salvador than the U.S.A., and may be difficult to find, so bring what you know you will need.

For more serious illnesses, you'll need to go to a hospital. Public hospitals providing high-quality care can be found in major cities including Ahuachapán, San Miguel, Santa Ana, and San Salvador. San Salvador has several better, more expensive private hospitals, worth the cost in an emergency. Most hospitals accept credit cards, but doctors' fees must generally be paid in cash.

San Salvador's best hospitals include **Hospital de Diagnostico** (2226-5111) Urbanización la Esperanza Segunda Diagonal #429; **Hospital de la Mujer** (2265-1212, 2279-1440; www.hospital-mujer.com) Calle Juan José Cañas and 81 Avenida Sur, Colonia Escalón, specializing in women's issues; **Centro Pediátrico** (2225-3688; www.centropediatrico .com.sv) Final Diagonal Luis Edmundo Vásquez #222, Colonia Médica, specializing in children's medicine; and **Policlínica Casa de Salud** (2288-4087; www.policlinica casadesalud.com) 4 Avenida Norte #3–5, Santa Tecla. For more information, log on to **Médicos de El Salvador** (www.medicosdeelsalva dor.com).

INTERNET RESOURCES There are dozens of useful Web sites about El Salvador; these are just a few favorites. Others are listed at the beginning of each destination chapter. Many are in Spanish only, but Google Translate makes them accessible to everyone.

✪ **Fundacion Clic** (www.clic.org .sv) Online magazine of art, technology, history, and culture has a wealth of information.

El Salvador Ahora (www.elsal vadorahora.com) Online travel and living magazine.

El Salvador Impresionante (www.elsalvador.travel) The Ministry of Tourism's official, bilingual site.

✪ **Guanacos Online** (www.guana cosonline.org) Big, messy, semi-bilingual site covers all things Salvadoran, with photos and listings.

Latin America Network Information Center (lanic.utexas.edu/ la/ca/salvador) Academic, government, and media links, plus several tourism-oriented Web sites.

La Prensa Grafica (www.la prensagrafica.com) El Salvador's newspaper of record is in Spanish.

Revue Magazine (revuemag.com) English-language magazine focuses on Guatemala, but both the Web site and monthly print edition have large El Salvador sections.

✪ **The Other El Salvador** (www .theotherelsalvador.com) Big site with bilingual information, photos, listings, and much more covering every aspect of El Salvador.

Visite El Salvador (www.visitel salvador.com.sv) Glossy, free, bilingual monthly has articles and information online.

Voices on the Border (voicesel salvador.wordpress.com) English-language blog covers social justice issues.

LODGING El Salvador's lodging is inexpensive compared to other Central American countries. Because most tourism is national, prices rise on weekends and holidays, particularly along the beaches, Ruta las Flores, and the El Pital Highlands. The surfing high season runs March through September, which can affect prices and availability of some beach hotels. Credit cards are widely accepted, but paying in cash often results in the 18 percent hotel taxes being waived.

Be aware that "motels," usually on the outskirts of town, with high walls to hide cars from prying eyes, are for couples and offer hourly rates. These aren't necessarily bad, and will certainly let regular tourists spend the night. Amenities may include in-room hammocks and bar service to your room.

This is a developing destination, and luxury lovers will find their options limited. San Salvador has the only true five-star hotels, all of them chains. Suchitoto has three wonderful boutique properties, while the beaches offer a few resort-style hotels, some quite nice, but most rather generic.

There is an enormous variety of very comfortable mid-range accommodations ($30–80) in most major destinations and cities. These generally have attractive rooms, modern hot bath (beach hotels may only have cool water), television, air-conditioning, and usually pools, restaurants, and pretty gardens. They may offer suites; note that these are usually larger rooms geared to families, often with kitchenettes, rather than more luxurious accommodations.

Budget travelers, you've found

your new favorite country. For $15–30, you can get clean, simple doubles with good beds, cable televisions, fans, private baths, and maybe even a pool. There's almost always something in the $7–10 range. Western El Salvador and the Western Beaches also have great backpacker hostels and surf shacks geared to international travelers, with dorm beds, shared kitchens, and a cool vibe.

Camping is more popular in El Salvador than elsewhere in Central America, and most national parks have developed campgrounds; some even rent tents. Many hotels will let you camp and use their facilities for about $5 per night.

MAPS Finding a good map of El Salvador outside the country is challenging. ITMB makes an **El Salvador Map** ($9.25), which is OK, but outdated and hard to read. Once you're here, MiTur has several useful maps, most of them free. They offer a good road map for US$1, worth it for drivers. The rental car companies have great free country maps as well.

The **Registro Nacional** (2261-8716) 1 Calle Poniente and 43 Avenida Norte, in downtown San Salvador, open Monday through Friday 7:30 AM–5:30 PM, has amazing maps, most more suitable for decoration or civil engineering than driving. You must bring a photo ID. The map office is upstairs. Detailed city maps run $12–18, departmental maps $10, and specialty maps $4–97.

MEDICAL TOURISM Spurred by Salvadoran-American doctors trained in the United States, as well as patients who return home for less expensive care, El Salvador is developing a solid medical tourism industry. **Export Salud El Salvador** (www.exportsalud.org) has information on doctors, hospitals, and popular treatments.

Quality is high at private hospitals, and treatment is very inexpensive by North American and European standards. Specialties include dentistry, orthotics, liposuction, breast implants, bariatrics, and fertility treatments. Several tour operators facilitate "medical tours," including lodging at hotels where nurses drop by for follow-up treatment.

MONEY El Salvador uses the U.S. dollar ($) as its legal currency. Euros are occasionally accepted, but in general, you'll need to exchange them at a major bank. British pounds and Canadian dollars can also usually be exchanged at banks, but rates are poor.

Nicaraguan, Honduran, and Guatemalan currencies should be exchanged at the border, as they are not accepted or exchanged anywhere else in El Salvador.

Large bills (including $20s and $10s) can be difficult to change outside major cities and tourist centers. If you plan to explore, carry plenty of small bills and coins.

Credit Cards Credit cards are widely accepted in major cities, and most places take American Express, Diners Club, Discover, MasterCard, and Visa. A few businesses only accept Visa. Call the credit card company before your trip to let them know you'll be in El Salvador, and ask for an international phone number to call in case of loss or theft. **Credit Card Services** (2206-4000, Spanish only) may also be able to help.

In rural areas and smaller towns, credit cards are rarely accepted. ATMs are available in many areas, and can provide cash advances on credit cards, if you have a four-digit PIN number. BAC is usually the easiest bank to arrange cash advances on foreign credit cards.

Debit Cards ATM machines can be found in most major cities, with HSBC, CitiBank, Scotia, and Banco America Central (BAC) the most likely to honor foreign cards. I've listed the locations of ATM machines throughout the book, but it's smart to always carry reserve cash. Fees are steep, around $5 per transaction, with a standard 3 percent currency exchange fee.

Travelers Checks A few businesses still accept travelers checks at poor rates, but in general, they are difficult to use and not recommended.

RAFTING Several of the adventure-tour operators offer whitewater rafting and kayaking, but the premier company is **Ríos Aventuras** (2279-3236; www.riosaventuras.com.sv). **Parque Acuático Apuzunga** (2483-8952; www.apazunga.com), in Metapán, Western El Salvador, also offers rafting trips on Class III Río Guajoyo.

RESTAURANTS AND FOOD PURVEYORS Salvadoran cuisine is easily the best in Central America. The national dish is the humble pupusa, a thick corn or rice tortilla usually stuffed with cheese, beans, *loroco* (an edible flower), and/or meat, served for 25 cents each everywhere in the country, starting around 4:30 PM. For El Salvador's other delicious dishes, check out the Food section in the History and Culture chapter.

The best places to sample Salvadoran cuisine are the many ✪ **Gastronomic Festivals** held throughout the country. The most famous is in **Juayúa** (why-YOU-ah), on the Ruta de las Flores, where dozens of stands set up every weekend, serving grilled rabbit, fresh ceviche, and local coffee, surrounded by diversions like a huge handicraft market, live music, and miniature train. But smaller, more traditional Gastronomic Festivals take place every weekend, all over El Salvador.

San Salvador has a range of international cuisine and fine dining restaurants, while **Suchitoto** and the **Ruta de las Flores** have several excellent options as well. Elsewhere, your choices are limited, with the best best restaurants (usually attached to hotels) serving delicious Salvadoran dishes and perhaps international cuisine, usually defined as pasta, pizza, and salads. At sit-down restaurants, you must ask for your check, as it's considered impolite to hand it to you right after your meal. Either say *"la cuenta, por favor,"* or use international sign language, holding an imaginary pen in the air and squiggling.

A gourmet experience runs $15 to $30, a solid meal between $5 and $10. Budget travelers can fill up at *pupuserías*, market stalls, and small eateries serving *comida a la vista* at lunch. Literally "food at sight," these are steamtable buffets where you can point at your choice of a dozen dishes, heaped on a plate for $2 to $4 per meal. El Salvador's cornucopia of fast-food chains will impress even U.S. citizens.

Vegetarians, if they're not too strict about animal fat, can survive on typical cuisine. *Casamiento,* or rice and beans, pupusas, and *comida a la vista* spots are good bets. San Salvador, the beach towns, Ruta de las Flores, and Suchitoto all have restaurants with more interesting meatless options.

In general, cooked food is safe to eat in El Salvador, even in the markets, but people with sensitive stomachs should be careful with salads and unpeeled fruit. Restaurants are theoretically more careful with preparation than are street stands. Tap water is not generally safe to drink. Most restaurants use filtered water, and bottled water is cheap and available everywhere.

SPECIAL NEEDS TRAVELERS
El Salvador has little specific infrastructure for travelers who are blind, deaf, or in wheelchairs. Some better hotels are fully equipped for wheelchairs—ramps, larger bathrooms, even pool access—but these are few and far between.

However, as with any country recovering from a major war, there are lots of locals in wheelchairs who get around fairly well. Makeshift concrete ramps have been poured in even the smallest towns, and many hotels have rooms that, while not specifically geared to wheelchair users, can be adapted with wooden ramps for access. I have described this type of access throughout the book as "challenging." Overall, El Salvador remains a destination for active, adventurous wheelchair users.

TAXES El Salvador has relatively low taxes, making this a better place to buy imported goods, such as cameras and electronics, than elsewhere in Central America. This also affects retirees, businesspeople, and other expatriates, who pay significantly less in taxes here than in, say, Costa Rica or Mexico. Hotels charge an 18 percent tax, which may be waived at smaller hotels for cash payment. A 13 percent VAT tax affects most items, except some basic goods.

TIPS El Salvador is a tipping country, and it's customary to leave a 10 percent tip at full-service restaurants (sometimes included with the bill, so check) unless service is terrible. Larger tips are appropriate at better restaurants and for exceptional service. Guides should be tipped at least a few dollars, as this is often their primary income. Tipping porters, maids, and other hotel staff is appreciated as well.

TOUR OPERATORS The fastest, easiest way to see El Salvador is with an organized tour. You don't have to commit to an entire vacation, as most offer day-trips to popular spots that may be time-consuming with public transportation, or difficult to organize on your own. Some specialize in adventure tours, such as whitewater rafting, rappelling, scuba diving, mountain biking, and even helicopter trips. Many arrange custom tours.

In addition to these, there are several excellent operators in Suchitoto and Western El Salvador; see those chapters for details. Most surf outfits offer other excursions; they're listed in the Western Beaches chapter.

Akwaterra (2245-2614; www.akwaterra.com) Adventure outfitter offers surfing, horseback riding, hiking, great lodging, and many other activities.

Avitours (2510-7619; www.avitours.com.sv) Hiking, biking, kayaking, and even skydiving are offered by this adventure operator, which also arranges the usual tours.

Cadejo Eco Adventures (2208-3115; www.cadejoadventures.com)

Operator offers surfing, mountain biking, sport fishing, scuba diving, hiking, and falconry.

Eco-Mayan Tours (2298-2844; www.ecomayantours.com) Long-standing operator still offers its popular Mayan Route tour, but also offers zip-lining, surfing, fishing, rock climbing, and medical tourism trips.

Enfi Tours (2533-7095, 2517-5494; www.enfitours.com) International company offers trips from Mexico to Panama in French, German, and English.

Eva Tours (www.evatours.com.sv) Offers the usual day-trips plus medical tours.

Guanatour's (2103-3814; www.guanatours-club.com) Specializes in rappelling, canyoning (rappelling down waterfalls), canopy tours, guided hikes, and camping.

Helicorp (2287-5005; 2295-5555; www.helicorp.com.sv) Offers helicopter tours.

Nahuat Tours (2257-4895; www.nahuatours.com) Well-regarded operator offers all the usual tours, as well as trips to little-explored Chalatanango and Morazán, with an emphasis on Civil War history.

Tamarindo Touring Company (1-888-882-8006, 317-818-6005 USA; www.tamarindotouringcompany.com) Top-notch adventure company owned by a former Jesuit priest, who served here during the 1980s, offers outdoor and cultural trips, as pricey packages or full-custom tours.

TOURISM POLICE The Salvadoran government offers free police escorts to all tourists, generally for hiking trails, but they can accompany you on any day-trip—and all you have to do is ask. This initiative has been incredibly effective combating El Salvador's famous security issues, and previous problems with muggings on trails have dropped to almost zero.

It's worth arranging escorts in advance, but often you can walk right into an office, close to most major hiking destinations, and see if an officer is available. There's usually someone on staff who speaks English, and operators at their **national offices** (2298-9982, 2298-9984) can provide English-language assistance. You are not allowed to tip, but providing lunch is certainly appropriate.

TOURIST OFFICES AND INFORMATION

The Ministry of Tourism (MiTur) and Salvadoran Corporation of Tourism (CORSATUR) run a handful of very useful tourism offices, which are well worth visiting. MiTur publishes several useful brochures and booklets, many available in English, and colorful, free tourist maps that are actually useful. Better country maps cost $1, worthwhile if you're driving. A bilingual **Traveler's Guide** ($12) has listings for better hotels, a good resource if that's your budget. Offices are generally open 8 AM–noon and 1–5 Monday through Friday, and usually 8 AM–noon and 1–4 Saturday and Sunday.

Elsewhere, the best places to find tourism information are hotels geared to international travelers, particularly backpacker hostels. In smaller towns, the place to go is the *Alcaldía,* or mayor's office. In department capitals, it's called the *Palacio Municipal.* These are city administration buildings, not tour offices, but they can usually point you toward local guides and guesthouses. They are almost always located on the central park, and open from 9 to noon and 2 to 5 Monday through Friday, sometimes Saturday morning. Staff generally speaks Spanish only.

Also close to the central park, you'll find the *Casa de Cultura,* or Cultural Center, with classes and workshops for residents. They may also have information about the area. MiTur offices include:

San Salvador (2243-7835, extension 165 or 166) Alameda Dr. Manuel Enruque Araujo, Pasaje y Edificio Carbonell 2, Colonia Roma. Take a taxi to the flagship MiTur office, with all the maps and brochures available. There's one at the **airport** (2339-9454, extension 164), but it's poorly stocked.

Puerto de La Libertad (2346-1898) KM34 Carretera del Litoral. Conveniently located at the entrance to town, it has information about the Western Beaches.

Ruta de Las Flores (2453-1082) KM70 Carretera CA-8, at the entrance to Nahuizalco. Inconvenient unless you have a private vehicle, but well stocked.

Suchitoto (2335-1739) Calle San Martín #2, central park. Right on the Central Park, they have good information and a handy, photocopied city map. A nearby Municipal Tourism Office arranges tours.

La Palma (2335-9076; cat.la palma.corsatur@gmail.com) Calle José Matias Delgado. Outstanding office right on the Central Park has information about La Palma, the El Pital Highlands, and destinations in neighboring Honduras.

La Unión (2604-0470) 6 Avenida Norte, Barrio San Carlos. Underfunded office has regional information.

USEFUL PHONE NUMBERS

Emergency: 911
El Salvador Country Code: 503
General Information: 114
National Operator: 110
International Operator: 120
Consumer Affairs (complaints about businesses): 910
Tourism Police: 2298-9982, 2298-9984
Fire Department: 2271-1244, 2243-2054
Red Cross: 2222-5155, 2222-5755
Immigration: 2221-2111
Office of Foreign Affairs: 2231-1000

VISAS AND FEES Entering El Salvador through the international airport requires a $10 visa, while the exit tax is $32. Your passport must be valid for six months beyond your intended stay. You are also required to possess an onward ticket, but in practice, this is rarely checked. Most visitors, including citizens of the U.S.A., Canada, Australia, and most Latin American and European countries, are granted automatic 90-day tourist visas. After your 90 days are completed, you must either pay to renew your visa for up to 90 more days, or leave the country for 72 hours. Unfortunately, the C-4 treaty means that Nicaragua, Honduras, and Guatemala do not count; you must leave the treaty zone. The closest destinations include Belize, Costa Rica, and Mexico.

For more visa information, log onto the Spanish-language **Ministerio de Relaciones Exteriores de El Salvador** (www.rree.gob.sv). The **Ministerio de Justicia y Seguridad Pública** (www.seguridad.gob.sv) has immigration information.

HISTORY AND CULTURE

NATURAL HISTORY

GEOLOGY Central America is a relatively new part of the world, its slender silhouette suspended above one of the world's most active fault lines by a string of volcanoes. These arise where the motionless Caribbean Plate and expanding Cocos Plate crash. As the ocean-soaked Cocos plate expands and moves eastward from the Middle American Trench, it is subducted beneath the Caribbean plate and melts, the steam carrying lava upward.

THE TOWN OF PANCHIMALCO, FAMOUS FOR ITS FESTIVAL OF FLOWERS, IS ONE OF THE FEW SALVADORAN CITIES WHERE THE NATION'S INDIGENOUS HERITAGE IS STILL DISPLAYED.

Alvaro Calero

The two most violent collisions between the plates happened between 130 and 65 million years ago, creating the **El Pital Highlands** (El Salvador's highest point: 2730 meters/ 8957 feet), **Montecristo-El Trifinio National Park,** and the **Department of Morazán**. Subsequent spreading has created more than a hundred known Salvadoran volcanoes, many of which you can climb, most notably the triumvirate at **Los Volcanes National Park**: mellow **Cerro Verde**; the naked cone of **Izalco**; and El Salvador's tallest volcano (2365 meters/7642 feet) **Ilamatepec**, Mother Mountain, most recently christened Santa Ana.

Other volcanoes include **Quetzaltepeque** (San Salvador), at El Boquerón Park just minutes from the capital; **Chichontepec** (San Vincente) and **Chaparrastique** (San Miguel) in Eastern El Salvador; and crater lakes such as **Coatepeque**, **Ilopango**, and **Laguna Alegría**.

32

THE CENTRAL AMERICAN ISTHMUS WAS ONCE AN ARCHIPELAGO OF VOLCANIC ISLANDS, MUCH LIKE THE GOLFO DE FONSECA TODAY.

By the middle of the Pliocene Era, about 3 million years ago, sediments— mixed with volcanic ash, creating El Salvador's black- and gray-sand beaches— collected around the archipelago, finally creating a viable land bridge between North and South America. This had two major consequences: It interrupted ocean currents and global weather patterns, plunging the planet into an ice age, and exposed species on both continents to unknown competition.

BIOLOGY The flora and fauna of the massive North and South American continents had been evolving independently for at least 100 million years, since the age of the dinosaurs, when the two continents were finally connected.

South America, once part of Australia, had developed a huge variety of marsupials, as well as coatis, giant sloths, and armadillos. In North America, hoofed grazing animals such as camels, deer, and three-toed horses were dominant, along with dogs, bears, and rhinos. Many species went extinct in the eons that followed, including most of South America's marsupial populations, and North America's camels and horses (their cousins, who had migrated to Asia during an earlier epoch, survived). You can see fossils displayed throughout the country, at **Museo de Historia Natural de El Salvador**, in San Salvador, **La Joya-Barranca del Sisimico Protected Area**, near San

EL SALVADOR'S VOLCANIC TOPOGRAPHY IS DISPLAYED ON A MASSIVE THREE-DIMENSIONAL MAP AT SAN SALVADOR'S CUARTEL EL ZAPOTE MILITARY HISTORY MUSEUM.

Vicente, with mastodon skeletons; **Via Roca Dinosaur Museum**, near Izalco; and **Aventura El Limo Parque Geotúristico**, near Metapán.

Today, there is a remarkable biodiversity on the isthmus, home to 7 percent of the world's species on only 1 percent of its landmass. El Salvador has somewhat fewer species than neighboring countries, as it is smaller and has only a Pacific coastline. Although El Salvador is Central America's most densely populated country, the population is concentrade in urban areas; during the civil war, cities represented safety, and many isolated homesteads were abandoned. Thus, there are huge tracts of secondary forest and other recovering wilderness, which the government is trying to conserve.

El Salvador's enormous range of altitudes and life zones, which include coastal wetlands, and humid tropical, dry tropical, premontane, and cloud forests, are home to many species, with 144 mammals, including sloths, anteaters, spider monkeys, agoutis, pacas, deer, possums, coyotes, 6 species of big cats, Baird's tapirs, dozens of bats, and many more. There are 130 reptiles and amphibians, including caimans, boa constrictors, and 4 kinds of sea turtle (green, olive Ridley, hawksbill, and leatherback) that nest along the gray-sand beaches. There are also 508 recorded bird species, including 310 breeding residents, 17 endemics, and 254 endangered species. Around 70 other bird species have been unofficially reported.

HISTORY

PREHISTORIC EL SALVADOR The oldest human artifacts in El Salvador are several caves emblazoned with paintings and engravings, most of them on the eastern side of the country. The most accessible site is Cueva de Santo Espíritu, which indicates human habitation for at least 8000 years; oral histories say they are far older. Petroglyphs, probably dating to between 1500 B.C. and 800 B.C., are found throughout the country, with examples at Lago de Güija, Parque Nacional El Imposible, and Cacaopera in Morazán.

By 1500 B.C., tribes of hunter-gatherers were beginning to embrace agriculture, creating small, permanent villages of perhaps 10 families living in wood-framed adobe huts. By 1200 B.C., they began building the stone cities surrounding modern-day Chalchuapa, with ties to the Olmec Empire (1400 B.C.–400 B.C.), based in Veracruz, Mexico. Trade routes stretched from the modern United States to Colombia during this period. Stone portraits discovered at **Tazumal**, and rotund female sculptures at **Hotel Santa Leticia** on the Ruta las Flores, are among the most artistic remains from this period.

THE MAYANS AND LENCAS The majority of El Salvador's most impressive archaeological sites were built by the Mayans (2000 B.C.–1524 A.D.) in the western half of the country, which they called Cuscatlán, "Land of Precious Things." Their cities were planned, with large, well-fortified plazas surrounded by stone buildings: Municipal palaces, pyramids, and ball courts, where teams would use their bodies to move a hard, rubber ball around a steep-sided field.

The Mayans were forced to evacuate Cuscatlán after the 260 A.D. eruption that created **Ilopango Lake,** just east of San Salvador. The disaster carpeted

Western El Salvador with a blizzard of ash, leaving the region uninhabitable for a century. After the Mayans returned, a smaller, but similar ash eruption in 640 A.D. eruption buried an intact Mayan village displayed at **Joya de Cerén Archaeological Park**.

Many of the Mayans who arrived after the Ilopango eruption are thought to have been refugees from Oaxaca, Mexico, fleeing Mayan oppression. There is linguistic evidence: Salvadorans still call themselves Guanacos (wah-NA-cos), sometimes translated as People of Oaxaca. Incidentally, Cuscatlán was the first Mayan polity to outlaw human sacrifice.

Modern tourists should note that Cuscatlán was a backwater, on the fringes of the empire. Thus its ancient stone cities are small and unimpressive compared to Mexico's massive ruins. Cuscatlán's relative isolation, however, helped it weather the Classic Mayan Collapse of 800–900A.D. While **San Andrés**, the Mayan administrative capital, was abandoned, other cities in the region thrived, including **Tazúmal** and **Casa Blanca**, by establishing peaceful trade connections to the Lenca states of Eastern El Salvador.

The Lenca are a little-studied people, presumably related to the Chorotegas of Nicaragua. Lenca archaeological sites are all located east of the Río Lempa, which apparently stopped the Mayan imperial advance. Most of their ruins are less developed for tourism than the flashier Mayan towns, but adventurous types

PETROGLYPHS, LIKE THIS DEPICTION OF A CHIHUAHUA, DISPLAYED AT THE GUZMÁN ANTHROPOLOGY MUSEUM IN SAN SALVADOR, ARE FOUND ALL OVER THE COUNTRY.

JOYA DE CERÉN, CALLED "AMERICA'S POMPEII," DISPLAYS A MAYAN CITY PRESERVED BENEATH 14 LAYERS OF VOLCANIC ASH EXPELLED IN 640AD.

can visit the archaeological sites at **Quelepa** and **Tehuacán**, or the town of **Cacaopera** in Morazán, with a museum of Lenca culture. Enormous **Cihuatán**, which displays both Mayan and Lenca architectural styles, was founded around 900 A.D., and some 25,000 people of both tribes lived there in peace.

Around 1200 A.D., after recovering from the collapse, the reinvigorated Post-Classic Mayan Empire violently re-incorporated Cuscatlán into the Tikal polity. Cihuatán was burned to the ground, and the Pipil-Mayans re-established political dominance over the region. This system was very much in place when the Spanish arrived. The best archaeological museum in the country is **Museo Nacional de Antropología David J. Guzmán** in El Salvador, but you'll find smaller museums all over El Salvador.

SPANISH CONQUEST By the time the Spanish conquistadors arrived in Western El Salvador, the indigenous peoples were without illusions. The Spanish had already defeated the powerful Aztec and Mayan capitals, often enslaving their new allies after the fact. The smallpox that would soon devastate the Americas, however, had not yet reached pandemic levels. The Maya Pipiles were strong, and knew they had nothing to lose.

They handily defeated the first poorly armed Spaniards, using thick cotton armor, stone-tipped clubs, and arrows. On June 8, 1524, Conquistador Pedro de Alvarado arrived in the port town of Acaxual, modern **Acajutla**, with 100 Spaniards on horseback, another 150 fully armed Spanish foot soldiers, and more than 5000 (perhaps as many as 20,000) indigenous troops.

Pipil commanders had prepared an ambush, with reinforcements hiding behind a hill above the battlefield. Alvarado sensed something suspicious, and feigned retreat. The Pipiles gave chase to lower, less defensible ground, and that's when the mighty Spanish-led military attacked. The brutal battle lasted 17 days, and though Alvarado received a crippling leg wound, the Spanish victory was complete.

Alvarado continued the conquest with a scorched-earth strategy, designed to destroy population centers where resistance could grow. They were met at every adobe gate by fierce Mayan citizen-soldiers, who battled them house to house, and many cities were never penetrated by military force.

In Eastern El Salvador, Lenca tribes led by Lempira, "Lord of Mountains," mounted another serious resistance. After seeing their powerful Mayan neighbors defeated, Lempira raised an army of some 30,000 troops, which met the Spanish in both direct combat and guerrilla ambushes. When Spanish armies approached, villagers would burn their fields to deny them food, preferring to starve than submit.

By the late 1530s, however, the smallpox virus was at full force. Between 30 percent and 60 percent of the population was dead within only a few years. The Spanish invited Lempira to peace talks. When he arrived, a Spanish officer shot him. The Lenca, exhausted, surrendered.

Following the warriors were Catholic priests, who brought tidings of their single God. Perhaps surprisingly, they were well received. Between the horses, guns, and smallpox, it may have seemed prudent to worship the winning team's deity.

SPANISH SETTLEMENT Though pockets of indigenous resistance remained (and would remain, until 1932), by the middle of the 16th century the Spanish were entrenched. Their first attempts to found the capital of El Salvador in 1525 and 1528, close to modern-day Suchitoto, were abandoned after repeated Maya-Pipil attacks. In 1545, displacing local farmers, they moved San Salvador to its present location, 12 kilometers (7 miles) from the still proudly indigenous city of Panchimalco.

The so-called Fourteen Families (there were probably many more) controlled almost every aspect of El Salvador's development and growth. These wealthy landowners built huge haciendas, harvesting crops for trade around the empire: cacao, cotton, indigo, henequen (an agave fiber), and balsam, the fragrant ingredient of soaps and medicines. This was so valuable that they named it Peruvian Balsam, to trick British pirates into sacking South America instead. In 1751, a new crop was planted in the mountains north of Sonsonate, coffee, which seemed to hold some promise.

Indigenous and mestizo workers as well as perhaps 1000 African slaves lived with their families in rented shelters on the haciendas, and were usually paid in coins (*fichas*) that could only be spent at the hacienda store.

The Spanish settlers built their first stone churches, massive monuments of a distinct Mudéjar style, in the important indigenous cities of **Caluco**, **Izalco**, and **Tacuba**. All of the churches were destroyed by the 1773 Santa Marta quake that famously leveled Antigua, Guatemala, but you can still visit their ruins.

INDEPENDENCE By the turn of the century, global politics were in flux. Enlightenment ideals were challenging such long-held assumptions as the divine right of kings and infallibility of the Catholic Church, inspiring democratic revolutions in the United States and France.

This was occurring even as Spain's royal whims were undermining the Salvadoran economy. European wars had led to an indigo blockade from 1798 and 1802, compounded by Napoleon's disruptive 1808 invasion of Spain. The Catholic Church, charged with seizing the haciendas of now bankrupt Salvadoran indigo and balsam growers—and awarding them to Guatemalan families—angered their traditional upper-crust allies.

In 1811, a group of Salvadorans, including the Aguilar brothers, San Salvador Vicar José Matías Delgado, and Bernardo and Manuel José Arce, began meeting in secret, calling for a democratic revolution of their own: Independence from Spain. The Guatemalan Captain General, José de Bustamonte, found out about the conspiracy and demanded the arrest of Manuel Aguilar.

A huge crowd gathered in San Salvador on November 5, demanding that the arrest be denied. Manuel José Arce stood up, and in the first Central American call for independence, declared, "There is no king, no tax, and no Captain General! We should only obey our Mayors!"

The independence movement quickly spread throughout El Salvador, but the cities of Santa Ana, San Vicente, and San Miguel did not heed its call. Unable to reach a critical mass for revolution, some conspirators joined forces with Guatemalan and Nicaraguan pro-independence factions. Others were incarcerated. By 1812, the rebellion had been shut down.

The repression that followed only solidified resistance to Spanish domination. For 10 years resistance groups organized, creating a parallel government with sympathizers among Spanish officials. And finally, on September 15, 1821, Central America declared independence from Spain.

CENTRAL AMERICAN REPUBLIC The decades following Independence were turbulent, as different groups tried to assert their dominance over Central America. The Mexicans went so far as to found the First Mexico Empire of Agustín de Iturbide in 1822, sending troops to conquer the newly liberated Central American isthmus. This failed, however, and five countries—El Salvador, Guatemala, Honduras, Nicaragua, and Costa Rica—formed the Central American Republic.

A network of bitter power struggles conspired to pull the young nation apart. Wealthy families were split, with Liberals demanding a federalist government like the United States, with considerable autonomy for member states. Their champion was Salvadoran hero **Manuel José Arce**, chosen as the Republic's first President, who abolished slavery and instituted democratic reforms.

Conservatives, made up of landowners and powerful businessmen, wanted a strong central government, with laws handed down from Antigua binding the entire isthmus. They pressured Arce into abandoning the Liberal cause, even as civil wars flared up across Central America.

Arce's presidency was then challenged by **Francisco Morazán**, a celebrated Honduran general and staunch Liberal, who—to the Conservatives' dismay—won Central America's general elections in 1830. Morazán enacted reforms that challenged both business interests and the Catholic Church, including freedom of the press, freedom of religion, and equality before the law. He also shrewdly moved the capital to San Salvador in 1934, far from Guatemala's powerful Conservatives.

The Catholic Church began spreading rumors that a cholera epidemic had been deliberately caused by Liberal politicians, helping set off several simmering indigenous uprisings, such as the **Nonualco Rebellion** in El Salvador's San Vicente Department and **Rafael Carrera**'s revolution in Guatemala. Combined with Conservative-led civil wars throughout Central America, this left the Republic weak and ungovernable.

U.S. politicians, themselves headed toward Civil War, took advantage of the Republic's 1840 collapse. Filibusterer (mercenary) **William Walker**, a U.S. veteran of the Mexican-American War who had declared himself President of Nicaragua in 1857, was offered payment from U.S. Southern politicians to conquer Central America and create five new slave states. He was handily defeated, however, by Costa Rican and Nicaraguan forces at the Battle of Rivas and by Salvadoran troops at **Puerto La Libertad**.

El Salvador, by now an independent republic, settled into the familiar Central American political pattern of authoritarian, militaristic presidents more or less chosen by Conservative landowners and legitimized with dodgy elections.

Despite the anemic democracy, El Salvador developed rapidly throughout the late 1800s and early 1900s, when coffee prices were soaring. With low shipping costs and almost no overhead thanks to a cheap Mayan labor pool, profits fueled a building boom responsible for some of El Salvador's finest architecture, most spectacularly displayed in **San Salvador** and **Santa Ana**'s city centers.

In 1929, however, the Great Depression ended the party with a global collapse in coffee prices. Hacienda owners laid off mostly indigenous workers, whose family farms had long ago been appropriated by these same powerful plantation owners and their compliant politicians. They had no land, and no work. Hunger set in.

THE PEASANT UPRISING As the Depression wore on, many of El Salvador's wealthy elite—who had always attached a higher status to lighter complexions and European features—began to embrace fascism. The peasants and Mayans, however, who had always lived in a more communal way, were inspired by the rise of communism in the newly founded Union of Soviet Socialist Republics.

Things came to a head in 1931. Farabundo Martí, a popular leftist leader who had worked with Nicaraguan revolutionary Augusto Sandino, had begun organizing unemployed coffee workers. Martí was sent into exile just before the fractious 1931 elections after his name was floated as a candidate for president. Coffee growers maneuvered a solid Conservative into office instead, but new President Arturo Araujo soon proved too weak and indecisive for their tastes.

In December 1931, they had Minister of Defense General Hernández Martínez stage a coup and seize control of the country. Though Martí's increasingly widespread protests had been largely peaceful, a January strike became violent. This was the excuse Hernández needed.

The response was planned, quick, and complete. By January 22, 1932, Martí's rebellion had been utterly crushed. Troops began rounding up peasants, including all Mayans, whether they had been involved in the uprising or not. Some 30,000 unarmed civilians were systematically executed and buried in mass graves, over a period of just weeks.

Hernández remained in power until 1944, when peaceful general strikes begun in Santa Ana forced him out of office; he was later assassinated. The survivors of his genocide remained undercover, however. They were forbidden to speak their native languages, and wisely eschewed traditional clothing in an effort to avoid further notice. This is why modern El Salvador seems to lack the rich indigenous heritage of Guatemala or Mexico. But it's still here, camouflaged in blue jeans.

Important Mayan towns that still embrace their heritage include **Izalco** and **Nahuizalco** in Eastern El Salvador, with colorful fiestas and traditional handicrafts, and **Panchimalco**, just south of San Salvador. In Eastern El Salvador, the town of **Cacaopera** remains a Lenca cultural center. Many of the handicraft towns around Suchitoto and along the Ruta de las Flores also display their indigenous heritage.

PERHAPS 30,000 COFFEE LABORERS, MOST MAYAN, WERE EXECUTED AFTER THE PEASANT UPRISING LED BY FARABUNDO MARTÍ.

CIVIL WAR Subsequent decades were marked by a succession of Conservative presidents, who stabilized the economy by creating one of the most socially stratified countries in the world. While wealthy Salvadorans enjoyed a lifestyle on par with any developed nation, a massive underclass was struggling for subsistence, without running water, electricity, or access to education.

At first, protests that began after the disputed 1972 presidential elections were peaceful. The government overreacted, however, sending in death squads to assassinate outspoken leaders. During this period, the Salvadoran government was notably supported by the United States, which provided military aid and officer training at the controversial School of the Americas.

As protests intensified, so did repression. In March 1980, government forces assassinated **Archbishop Óscar Arnulfo Romero**, an increasingly vocal proponent of Liberation Theology. This branch of Catholicism, frowned on by the Vatican, interprets the New Testament as a call for social and economic justice.

Romero was chosen as El Salvador's archbishop primarily because he seemed meek and compliant, unlikely to threaten the upper classes. The bookish theologian, however, quickly became a champion of the poor, defender of the oppressed, and proponent of democratic elections. His patrons were disappointed, and had him shot, while giving communion at Hospital La Divina Providencia in San Salvador. At his funeral, snipers fired into the huge crowds of mourners. This was the image that galvanized a revolution.

The previously disorganized left-wing resistance to the government met in Havana that May, and founded the Frente Farabundo Martí de Liberación Nacional (FMLN). With training and support from Cuba and Vietnam, the

CIVIL WAR BUFFS SHOULD BRING PHOTO ID TO MUSEUMS LOCATED ON MILITARY BASES, SUCH AS SANTA ANA'S MUSEO MILITAR GENERAL MAXIMILIANO HERNÁNDEZ MARTÍNEZ.

FMLN became a potent force, humiliating government troops at every turn. Unable to attack the guerrillas directly, the military began targeting civilians who (often unknowingly) sold rebels food and supplies.

For the first half of the war, the government deliberately massacred civilian populations, most famously at **El Mozote** in Morazán, but throughout the country. A memorial with the names of some 25,000 dead and disappeared can be visited at **Parque Cuscatlán** in San Salvador. There are dozens of museums across San Salvador where you can learn more about the conflict as well.

The official point of view is perhaps best summarized by the words of Domingo Monterrosa Barrios, commander of the feared Atlactal Batallion, emblazoned above the Civil War exhibit at San Salvador's excellent **Museo de la Historia Militar-Cuartel el Zapote**: THIS IS A WAR FOR PEACE, FOR THE FUTURE OF ALL SALVADORANS. Other museums, on active military bases in Ilopango, Santa Ana, and San Miguel, argue this side as well, alongside polished collections of guns, bombs, and materiel.

The FMLN has a very different story, told by guides at the **El Mozote Memorial**, and battlefields of **Guazapa Volcano** and **Cinquera** near Suchitoto. A republic without democracy, they will argue, where politicians serve only a wealthy minority and elections are ignored, cannot stand.

Based in the small mountain town of **Perquín**, Morazán, in Eastern El Salvador, the rebels mounted their resistance. Atrocities were committed on both sides. In the end, 12 years of Civil War left some 75,000 dead and millions more refugees, sending a Salvadoran diaspora to every corner world. Finally, behind Perquín's **Museo de la Revolución**, the 1992 Chapultepec Peace Accords were signed.

EL SALVADOR TODAY Called the "best negotiated ceasefire in history," the Chapultepec Accords laid the groundwork for what has turned out to be a notably stable, peaceful, democratic republic. Salvadorans pride themselves on being a hard-working people, and before the ink was dry on the peace treaty, they had begun the arduous task of rebuilding.

In towns like **Suchitoto**, artists and writers began organizing cultural festivals and rebuilding theaters. In the countrysides, left-leaning communities formed cooperatives to rebuild farms, homes, and churches, often with help from Christian missionaries, NGOs, and groups like the Peace Corps.

Business leaders, many of whom fled during the war, began returning home, firing up old factories and bringing their golf buddies down to see the possibilities. Other Salvadoran expats kept working in the U.S.A. and elsewhere, sacrificing new cars and bigger houses to send their paychecks home; remittances still represent about 15 percent of all Salvadoran income.

The conservative Alianza Republicana Nacionalista (ARENA), until recently the ruling political party, invested heavily in infrastructure: rebuilding cities, guaranteeing free education through high school, and paving the best highway system in Central America. They kept taxes low, signed every free trade agreement handed to them, put El Salvador on the U.S. dollar (and allowed the U.S.A. to open a military base, despite being blocked by Congress, ahem) and transformed their war-torn country into Central America's business center.

THE CHAPULTEPEC ACCORDS, WHICH ENDED THE CIVIL WAR IN 1992, WERE SIGNED HERE, IN THE SHADE OF A MANGO TREE.

This strategy has been, in many ways, successful, as evidenced by Central America's highest average wages and relatively booming economy. However, El Salvador is ranked the 18th most economically iniquitous country in the world, with a Gini Index rating of 52.4; without going into detail, that basically means a few families still own almost everything, most families get by on less than $200 a month, and there's no middle class.

It seems like déjà vu all over again. But this time, rather than returning to the cycle of revolution and repression that characterized 1932 and 1980, an obviously much-needed change in national strategy has been initiated peacefully. In March 2009, following free and fair elections, Mauricio Funes was sworn in as the first left-wing president in Salvadoran history. Hardly a fire-breathing liberal, the former journalist was an avowed independent until becoming the FMLN presidential candidate.

MOST OF EL SALVADOR'S FAMILIES LIVE ON LESS THAN $200 PER MONTH, IN SIMPLE ADOBE HOMES WHERE YOU MAY WELL BE INVITED TO RELAX FOR A WHILE.

His slogan was "A Safe Change," with proposals centered on universal health care, rather than radical land reform. Venezuelan President Hugo Chavez pointedly skipped Funes' inauguration, while Brazilian President Lula and U.S. Secretary of State Clinton were both mentioned in the speech. ARENA politicians arrived with fake smiles and polite applause, politics as usual—which is better than some of the alternatives. A year into office, he enjoys an unprecedented 80 percent approval rating.

And the average person? If you speak some Spanish, you'll hear plenty of opposing viewpoints about El Salvador's economic and political situation, peppered with of gossip about which politician stole what. But you'll find that when they're hamming it up for the cameras, people from across the political spectrum pose the same way, flashing a peace sign.

CULTURE

LITERATURE Hard working, efficient, and optimistic, Salvadorans are a dream to work with and a pleasure to know. The Salvadorans are storytellers, and thanks to their eventful history, they have had no shortage of tales. While there were always writers, El Salvador's literary traditions bloomed with the Spanish Romantics of the 1800, with over-the-top poets like Juan José Cañas (1826–1918), who also wrote the National Anthem.

They oversaw the rise of Liberalism and Modernism, helping found El Salvador's first university (1841) and library (1870), stocked with classical Greek texts and offering an environment where students and historians would begin to put together true written histories of the country.

Writers like **Francisco Gavidia** (1864–1955), after criticizing El Salvador's florid poetic traditions, began writing more profound narratives with indigenous and modern themes. The result was what is now considered a true Salvadoran style, wrought with emotion, sarcasm, and often delivered in bite-sized stories and poems rather than drawn out tomes.

Álvaro Menén Desleal (1931–2000), a journalist and quirky character who held diplomatic posts in Europe, published strange sci-fi microtexts and parables that lamented the dehumanization of society. Desleal and his contemporaries, including **Roque Dalton** (1935–1975), were members of a literary group called *Generacion Comprometida*, or Committed Generation, which sought social change to better the lives of the poor.

Dalton was recognized as a revolutionary poet, saying that "Politics are taken up at the risk of life, or else you don't talk about it." His life was one of adventure, miracles, and political intrigue, complete with earthquakes, prison breaks, military training, and rumors of plastic surgery so he could sneak home after being exiled. Such exploits have become a hallmark of the Salvadoran literary tradition.

MUSIC Like El Salvador's writers and poets, its musicians have an independent streak. Classical composers such as Victor Manuel López Guzmán (1922–93) incorporated pre-Columbian rhythms into his string compositions, conjuring visions of the national landscape.

Gilberto Orellanna Jr. (1939–) was the first to incorporate electronic techniques to achieve stark contrasts between good and evil, followed by **Angel Duarte** (1952–), considered a radical experimentalist in music composition.

Classical music has long had a home in El Salvador. In 1875, the **Philharmonic Society of El Salvador** was founded, replaced in 1910 by the **National Orchestral Society** and later the **National Symphonic Orchestra**, founded by the German Paul Muller in 1922. The first Salvadoran conductor, **Alejandro Muñoz Ciudad Real** (1902–91) organized public performances, giving everyone a taste of the arts.

Today, the **El Salvador Opera** (www.operaelsalvador.com) is on a mission to be recognized as the premier destination in Central America for live theater, variety shows, and opera. They develop artists' talent, work with local children, and produce professional performances.

As for popular music, turn on the radio and you'll find a mix of influences from Cuba, Mexico, and Colombia, as well as plenty of classic rock. Hip-hop and reggaeton groups have a growing influence on the music scene, embracing the storytelling ethos of the Salvadoran literature. Have a listen at **El Salvador Rap** (www.elsalvadorrap.com).

FOOD Salvadoran cuisine is arguably the best in Central America. The national dish is the humble *pupusa,* a thick corn or rice tortilla, freshly grilled and usually stuffed with cheese, beans, *loroco* (an edible flower), and/or meat, although dozens of fillings, both sweet and savory, can be found. They are usually served with *salsa roja,* a slightly spicy red sauce, and *curtido,* a vinegary cabbage and carrot salad.

But that's just the beginning of the wonderful dishes on offer here, all of which can be found at El Salvador's splendid weekend **Gastronomic Fairs**. The most famous takes place in the town of Juayúa (why-YOU-uh), where thousands of people pack streets lined with food stalls, artesanías, and live music every Saturday and Sunday. These festivals are held all over the country, however, with each town cooking up its own special recipes.

Desayuno (Breakfast) Salvadorans often begin their day with the *desayuno tipico,* or typical breakfast: *casamiento* (rice and beans), or refried beans; *platanos* (sweet fried plantains, a type of banana), *huevos* (eggs) prepared *fritos* (fried) or *picados* (scrambled with onions and peppers, you can also say *revueltos*), and a cup of coffee.

Bebidas (Drinks) *Atole:* A sweet, hot corn beverage of Mayan origin.

Cebada: A sweet beverage made with native seeds and milk.

Chilate: Atole with cacao, traditionally served in a morro-shell bowl.

Horchata: A sweet rice beverage.

Licuados: Fresh fruit juices, blended with ice, water, sugar, and sometimes milk.

Entraditas/Bocas (Appetizers) *Ceviche:* Raw fish, shrimp, calamari, etc., cooked in lime juice.

Cokteles: Seafood cocktails.

Chicharrones: Fried, fatty pieces of pork, perfect with a beer.

Chirimol: Diced tomatoes, onions, and peppers.

Chorizo: Sausage.

SALVADORAN CUISINE IS CENTRAL AMERICA'S FINEST. CHOOSE BETWEEN THE MARISCADA, SOPA DE PATA, CHICHARRONES, OR CUIJADA. OR TRY ONE OF EACH.

Montuca: Large travel tamale made with fresh corn.

Salpicón: Salad, usually with beef, cheese, avocado, and fruit.

Ticuca: Tortillas stuffed with refried beans and an egg, cooked in banana leaves.

Yuca frita: Fried manioc.

Fruits and Vegetables *Anonas:* Sweet, soft, greenish fruit with a custard consistency.

Camote: Sweet potato, sometimes served fried with syrup.

Izote: The national flower, elephant yucca, is often cooked with scrambled eggs. *Loroco* and *pitos* are two other edible flowers.

A HEARTY, TYPICAL SALVADORAN BREAKFAST USUALLY INCLUDES BEANS, CHEESE, FRIED PLANTAINS, SCRAMBLED EGGS, AND A STACK OF THICK CORN TORTILLAS.

Jocote: Small fruit with a large pit, eaten both hard and green, and when softly ripened to orange.

Marañon Japones: Red, pear-shaped fruit with a very light, refreshing taste, also called *manzana de agua.*

Pacaya: Bitter palm flowers, usually batter fried or pickled.

Paterna: Large, woody pod filled with seeds wrapped in a fuzzy, edible coating.

Sopas (Soups) *Sopa de frijoles negros:* Black bean soup, sometimes with an egg cracked in it.

Sopa de gallina India: Chicken and vegetable soup (the chicken is sometimes served on the side, with bones intact) is a popular weekend dish.

Sopa de pata: Rich "cow foot" stew can be messy.

Mariscada: Creamy, tomato-based seafood stew, with shrimp, fish, mussels, crab, and even lobster, usually served with the bones, heads, and shells intact.

Mains *Chiles rellenos:* Breaded, deep-fried peppers stuffed with meat and vegetables.

Churrasco: Grilled meat platter.

Gallo en chicha: Chicken stewed with dried fruit and fermented corn.

Garrobo: Iguana, usually roasted.

Panes: Hot submarine sandwiches, often made with marinated chicken or turkey and served at street stands.

Preparations Often, you'll be asked how you'd like your chicken, fish, or meat dish to be prepared.

Al ajillo: In garlic sauce.

Al vapor: Steamed.

En algüaihste: In a fantastic sauce made of ground seeds.

Encebollado: Smothered in onions.

Dulces (Sweets)

Every town has a *panadería,* or bakery, selling regional specialties.

Chilate con nuégados: Deep fried balls of yuca, corn, and other starches, served with sugarcane syrup and a bowl of *chilate,* a spiced corn drink.

EACH REGION HAS ITS OWN TYPICAL PAN DULCE, OR SWEET BREAD, ALWAYS AN INEXPENSIVE AND TASTY WAY TO START THE DAY.

Quesadillas: Not like the Mexican version at all, this is more like a rich pound cake made with soft, fresh, unsalted cheese.

Rigüas: Sweet, grilled corn cakes, sometimes stuffed with beans.

Rellenitos de plátano: Fried ripe plantains served with cream and sugar.

Semitas: Fruit tarts; a *semita de piña* is a pineapple tart.

Tamales de elote: Sweet corn tamales.

NATONAL CELEBRATIONS

January: New Year's Day (January 1) Most businesses close.

Día de la Paz (January 16) Holiday commemorates the 1992 signature of the Chapultepec Peace Accords, which ended the Civil War.

March or April: **Semana Santa** (one week before Easter) Holy Week runs the entire week prior to Easter, filled with special Masses, processions, passion plays. Many inland businesses close Thursday through Sunday, when everyone goes to the beach; hotels are often reserved weeks in advance. Izalco, Sonsonate, and Suchitoto have particularly elaborate festivities. This is not the easiest time to travel, so plan ahead.

May: **Labor Day** (May 1) Many businesses close.

Día de la Cruz (May 3) Day of the

YOU MUST TRY A PUPUSA, THE SALVADORAN NATIONAL DISH. THOUGH USUALLY MADE WITH CORNMEAL, HERE IN OLOCUILTA THEY'RE PATTED INTO A TASTY RICE-FLOUR MASA.

Cross is celebrated with mass pilgrimages up tall mountains once sacred to indigenous populations, which are now topped with crosses.

Mothers Day (May 10) Restaurants are packed.

June: **Fathers Day** (June 17)

Teachers Day (June 22)

August: **Feast Day of El Salvador del Mundo** (August 1–6) El Salvador's patron saint and namesake, the Divine Savior of the World, has its biggest blowout in San Salvador, with parades, fireworks, special Masses, processions, and parties all week. The rest of the country enjoys a somewhat subdued version of events, often traveling to visit family or spending time at the beach.

September: **Independence Day** (September 15) Celebrates Central America's 1821 independence from Spain with marching bands, parades, fireworks, and plenty of flag waving.

October: **Día de la Raza** (October 12) Christopher Columbus's arrival in the New World is celebrated with mixed emotions.

November: **Día de los Difuntos** (November 2) During the Salvadoran version of Day of the Dead, families decorate graves with flowers, cook special foods, and pass the night in cemeteries with loved ones here and gone.

Primer Grito de Independencia (November 5) In 1811, long before the rest of Central America was ready to revolt, Father José Matías Delgado made the First Cry of Independence from Spain.

National Day of the Pupusa (Second Sunday in November) Celebrations are held throughout El Salvador in honor of the nation's favorite snack.

December: **Fiesta de la Virgin de Guadalupe** (December 12) Some businesses close.

Christmas (November 25) People decorate their homes with huge, elaborate *nacimientos,* or model manger scenes. Many businesses close for Víspera de Navidad, or Christmas Eve, and families head to midnight Mass, then open presents that night, before going to sleep. Christmas Day is relaxed, with many businesses closed but some restaurants opening midday.

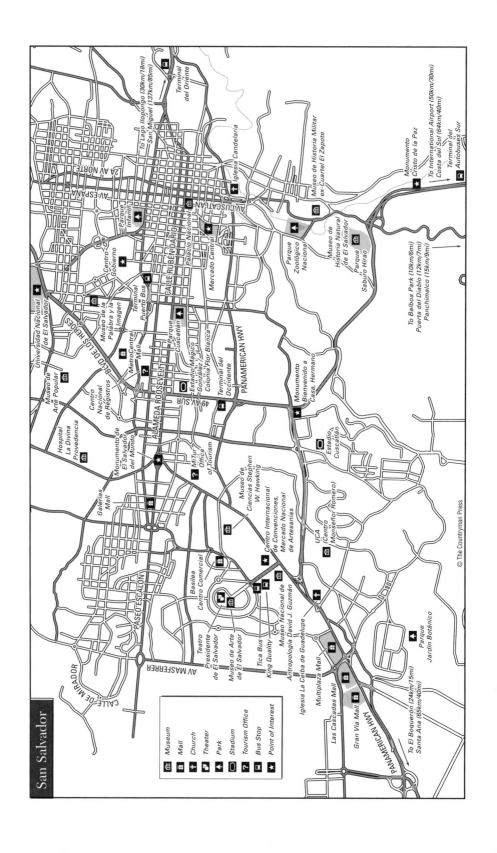

SAN SALVADOR

HEART OF THE NATION

In the shadow of Quetzaltepeque volcano, San Salvador's metropolitan sprawl hums with the lives of some 1.6 million people. This is the second largest city in Central America, a business hub, and the cultural, political, and geographical heart of the nation.

The capital is a place of glittering wealth and intractable poverty, fantastic museums, fine dining, and fabulous nightlife, and neighborhoods where you should never, ever go. You can visit the chaotic city center, with the city's most impressive architecture and monuments, cloaked in a sea of market stands and bus fumes; or head to the opulent malls and upscale districts on the edges of town.

Despite San Salvador's densely populated expanse, you're only minutes away from impressive parks, a crater lake, and **Panchimalco**, a still proudly Mayan village in the mountains, with views all the way to the sea.

Named for *El Divino Salvador del Mundo*, the Divine Savior of the World, this city has had its share of tough times—between the earthquakes, eruptions, and wars, little is left of the original 1545 Colonial capital. It is a modern city, particularly the high-rise hotels and upscale shopping districts of **San Benito** and **Paseo Escalón**, in the **Zona Rosa** district, but even poorer neighborhoods (if not the shanty towns) have impressive infrastructure, by Central American standards.

San Salvador can be overwhelming, but it has plenty of safe and attractive neighborhoods that you can enjoy on a human scale, and some real cultural gems, if you like museums and architecture. Imagine fine dining, five-star accommodations, and dress-to-impress nightlife, as well as cheap hotels, *pupuserías,* and artsy bars and galleries catering to students and hipsters on a budget.

Because it is at most four hours to just about any destination in the country, some short-term visitors make San Salvador their base for day-trips and tours. Most operators listed in the What's Where chapter have offices in town.

Alvaro Calero

SAN SALVADOR'S CITY CENTER BOASTS SOME OF THE MOST BEAUTIFUL ARCHITECTURE IN THE COUNTRY, MOST BUILT DURING THE COFFEE-BOOM YEARS OF THE EARLY 1900S.

Crime While El Salvador's crime rate is often overstated, big city rules *definitely* apply here in the capital. Some tourists seem unnerved by the security guys (and gals) in front of almost every business, packing huge guns. Stop worrying—they are your friends, and as long as they are around, you are totally safe.

Gang activity is largely confined to outlying neighborhoods with little to interest the casual tourist, particularly Soyapango, Apopa, and San Marcos. Upscale neighborhoods, such as Escalón and the Zona Rosa, are heavily patrolled and safe. The Metrocentro area, Calle Abad, and National University district are also fine, though you should stay alert and avoid walking around with valuables, particularly after dark. Downtown is fine by day, but best avoided after dark.

GUIDANCE Concultura (2281-0100; www.concultura.gob.sv) Edificio A-5, Plan Maestro Centro de Gobierno. The Ministry of Culture can provide information about museums, archaeological parks, and other activities; the Web site has events listing for the entire country.

✪ MiTur Tourist Bureau (2243-7835 ext 165 or 166) Alameda Dr. Manuel Enrique Araujo, Edificio Carbonel 2, Colonia Roma; open Monday through Thursday 8–5, Friday 8–4, closed weekends. Though it's out of the way, it's worth taking a taxi to this stocked tourist office, with a great selection of useful maps, booklets, and brochures, most of them free.

Politur (2298-9984, 2298-9982, 84) Alameda Araujo, Edificio Carbonel. El Salvador's Tourism Police can provide police escort on day-trips, and English-language assistance.

GETTING THERE This is the transportation hub of the nation. San Salvador is not a particularly good

ONLINE RESOURCES
San Salvador Online (www.sansalvador.gob.sv) Government site has an excellent directory of tourist sites with Spanish-language information and photos.

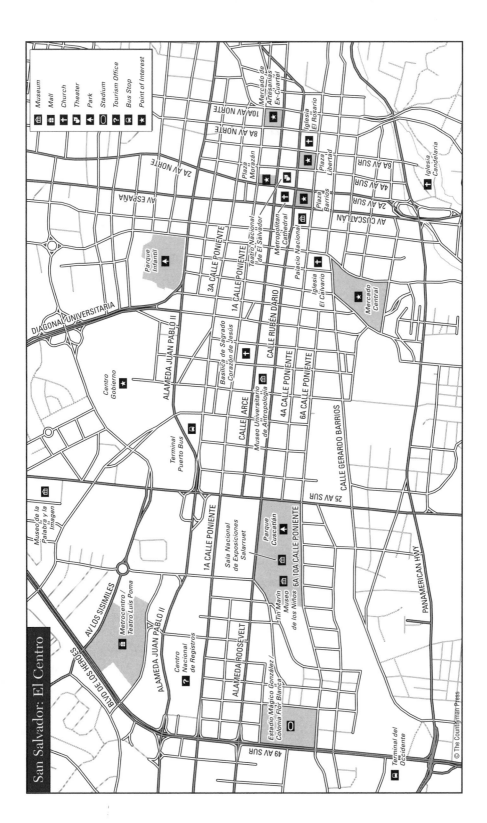

San Salvador: El Centro

Museum
Mall
Church
Theater
Park
Stadium
Tourism Office
Bus Stop
Point of Interest

Mercado de Artesanías Ex-Cuartel
10A AV NORTE
8A AV NORTE
Iglesia El Rosario
Plaza Morazán
2A AV NORTE
Iglesia Candelaria
Plaza Libertad
6A AV SUR
AV ESPAÑA
4A AV SUR
Teatro Nacional de El Salvador
2A AV SUR
Metropolitan Cathedral
Plaza Barrios
AV CUSCATLÁN
Parque Infantil
Palacio Nacional
3A CALLE PONIENTE
1A CALLE PONIENTE
Iglesia El Calvario
Mercado Central
CALLE RUBÉN DARÍO
DIAGONAL UNIVERSITARIA
ALAMEDA JUAN PABLO II
Basílica de Sagrado Corazón de Jesús
4A CALLE PONIENTE
6A CALLE PONIENTE
Centro Gobierno
CALLE ARCE
Museo Universitario de Antropología
CALLE GERARDO BARRIOS
Terminal Puerto Bus
25 AV SUR
Museo de la Palabra y la Imagen
1A CALLE PONIENTE
Sala Nacional de Exposiciones Salarruet
Parque Cuscatlán
6A 10A CALLE PONIENTE
AV LOS SISIMILES
Metrocentro / Teatro Luis Poma
Tin Marín Museo de los Niños
BLVD DE LOS HÉROES
ALAMEDA JUAN PABLO II
Centro Nacional de Registros
ALAMEDA ROOSEVELT
Estadio Mágico González / Colonia Flor Blanca
PANAMERICAN HWY
49 AV SUR
Terminal del Occidente

© The Countryman Press

walking city, although the upscale neighborhoods around Escalón, San Benito, and the Zona Rosa are safe on foot, and there's no other way to explore the chaotic downtown. You'll more than likely end up at one of the huge malls, with some of the city's best restaurants and nightlife.

Comolapa International Airport is about 50 kilometers (30 miles) south of downtown, and all international buses leave from San Salvador. These are covered in the What's Where chapter. There are three major bus terminals serving the entire country, located on the outskirts of town; it's a $5 cab ride between them.

GETTING AROUND The **city center**, built around the National Cathedral and Plazas Libertad and Morazán, is home to the city's most important historic architecture, **Parque Cuscatlán**, and several museums, all surrounded by a makeshift sprawl of market stalls and traffic jams. It's a mess, but worth exploring.

Due north are the residential neighborhoods between **Metrocentro Mall**, **Boulevard de Los Heroes**, and **Calle San Antonio Abad**, with inexpensive restaurants, mellow hotels, relaxed nightlife, and a few small but excellent museums.

West of downtown are the wealthy neighborhoods of **San Benito**, **Escalón**, and the **Zona Rosa**, with five-star hotels, upscale dining, glittering malls and boutiques, fabulous clubs, and the city's best museums.

By Car: Navigating San Salvador in a car is no picnic, but major roads are generally broad and well signed. Side streets and even some main roads are often oneways, may lack signs, and don't follow the logical Spanish grid outside the city center. A good city map is indispensable, one is usually provided by the rental car company. Most rental companies offer drivers, but it's cheaper and easier to hire a taxi for the day.

Driving at night is not recommended, and you should always keep your windows rolled up when moving slowly, particularly in areas with pedestrians. Carjackings are rare but do happen. Never let anyone approach your vehicle at a deserted intersection—it's actually legal to run a red light if you get nervous (but look both ways first!). Even if you have a rental car, take a taxi for evenings out.

By Rental Car: Most rental car companies are based in San Salvador, with offices in town and at the airport. For more information about renting a car, see the Transportation section in What's Where. These are just a few in-town options:

AutoRent Central America (2526-9322; www.autorentcentralamerica.com) Boulevard Constitución and Calle al Volcán. Delivers to your hotel, and rents cell phones. **Avis** (2261-1212; www.avis.com) 43 Avenida Sur #127. Also has an **airport location** (2339-9268). **Budget** (2263-9777, 2264-3888 Escalón; www.budget.com.sv) Calle El Mirador y 85 Avenida Norte #648. Solid company also has an **airport location** (2339-9942; aerobudget@intercom.com.sv). **Inter-Price** (2259-8000, 818-285-2828 USA; www.interprice.com.sv) Avenida Olimpica, #5-A. Also offers private tours and chauffeur service. **Thrifty** (2263-7799; www.thrifty.com) Calle Circunvalación #304, San Benito. Has a good reputation. **VM Rent-A-Car** (2317-3559; vm_rentacar@hotmail.com) Final 35 Avenida Norte, Reparto Santa Fé #3. Locally owned.

By Intercity Bus: San Salvador is the nation's transportation hub, with three major bus terminals on the outskirts of the city. Some buses also leave from the city center, but it's easier for most tourists to use the terminals; if you're staying downtown, ask about this option at your hotel.

Terminal de Occidente Well-organized terminal on Boulevard Venezuela serves all of Western El Salvador. In addition to the major tourist destinations listed here, buses serve **Armenia** (208), **Juayaque** (105), **San Cristóbal** (498), **San Julian** (203), and other towns. **Ahuachapán via Santa Ana** (202) Every 15 minutes; connecting buses serve **Tacuba**, **El Imposible National Park,** and the **Guatemalan border. Metapán and Montecristo-El Trifinio National Park** (19) Every half hour. **La Libertad** (102) Every 10 minutes; buses pass outside the station. **San Juan Opico via Joya de Cerén** (40, 108) Every 15 minutes. **Santa Ana via San Andrés Archaeological Park** (198, 201, 22) Every 10 minutes. **Sonsonate** (16, 17, 205) Every 5 minutes; connecting buses serve **Ruta de las Flores**, and **Los Cóbanos**, **Salinitas**, and **Barra de Santiago** beaches.

Terminal de Oriente Chaotic terminal on Alameda Juan Pablo II serves eastern destinations including: **Berlín** (303) 6 AM, 8 AM, 11 AM, 1 PM, 3 PM; connecting buses serve **Alegría. Chalatenango** (125) Every 10 minutes. **Dulce Nombre de María** (124) Every hour. **El Poy (Honduran Border) via La Palma** (119) Every 30 minutes; connecting buses serve the **El Pital Highlands. Guazapa via Cihuatán Archaeological Park** (117) Every 10 minutes. **San Miguel** (301) Every 10 minutes, connecting buses serve **Perquín. San Sebastian** (110) Every half hour. **San Vicente via Cojutepeque** (116, 511) Every 10 minutes. **Santa Rosa de Lima** (206) Every half hour. **Sesuntepeque via Ilobasco** (112, 181) Every hour. **Suchitoto** (129) Every 15 minutes; connecting boats serve **Chalatenango. La Unión** (304, 446) Every 30 minutes.

Terminal del Sur Dusty and disorganized, this small bus lot is due to be remodeled. **Costa del Sol** (495) Every 10 minutes. **Puerto El Triunfo** (185) 9 AM, 11 AM, 12:30 PM, 1:30 PM, 2 PM. **Usulután via Jiquilisco** (302) Every 10 minutes; buses leave across the street from the main lot, and can drop you off at the entrance to Jiquilisco, with regular connecting buses to Puerto El Triunfo. **Zacatecoluca** (133) Every 10 minutes.

By City Bus: San Salvador has a good, inexpensive, easy-to-use city bus system, but this is probably best for people with some Spanish and a sense of adventure. Buses become crowded at rush hour, and there are safety concerns (see Crime, What's Where chapter). They run from about 4 AM until 8 PM, but should be avoided when it's dark or if you're carrying valuables.

Useful routes include **Bus #30B**, between Galerías Mall, the San Benito rotunda, and Metrocentro; **Bus #34** between Metrocentro and San Benito; **Bus #52**, which plies Paseo Escalón; and **Bus #44** from Boulevard de Los Heróes to UCA and Terminal Occidente.

By Taxi: Clearly marked yellow cabs are safe, and congregate at taxi stands scattered every few blocks around the city; ask anyone (*"Taxi?"*) to point you in the right direction. Your hotel can call a cab as well.

There are no meters; you are charged a "set rate" according to how many "zones" you cross, with a minimum fare of $3 to $5. If you hail a cab on the street, they will try to overcharge you, but you'll usually get a fairer price at taxi stands.

Taxis are cheaper if you hire them for more than four hours, more if you're headed outside the city. If you find a driver you like, take his or her card; rates drop and service improves with repeat business.

✴ To See

This wasn't the Spaniards' first choice for their capital; it was only after annoyed Maya-Pipil Indians forced them out of a more stable spot, close to Suchitoto, that they built San Salvador here, in Acelhuate, Valley of the Hammocks. So named for the region's regular earthquakes, not to mention volcanic eruptions (most recently destroying the city in 1917) and mudslides (most recently destroying the suburb of Tecla in 2001), there's not much, if anything, left of the original 1545 village.

The heart of San Salvador is always rebuilt with style, however, and there are several fine plazas, monuments, museums, and important buildings. Many boast the frilly architecture of the coffee-boom years of the late 1800s and early 1900s, while others are much more modern. The neighborhood remains one of the nation's largest markets, thus the beautiful architecture is swamped with chaotic food and clothing stalls, with the fumes of congested traffic wafting through.

Though disorienting and disorganized, this area isn't particularly dangerous during the day—there are people all about—though you should be careful of pickpockets. It's best avoided at night, unless there are special events on.

EL CENTRO The historic center is based on the 1888 ✪ **Metropolitan Cathedral** (2271-2573; Calle Darío and Avenida Romero); most recently rebuilt in 1952, with Byzantine, Romantic, Naïf architecture. The artwork on the façade is by El Salvador's most famous painter, **Fernando Llort**, whose colorful, naïve work is symbolic of the nation. Inside is the image of the Divine Savior of the World, donated in 1546, and several other notable pieces. Most movingly, this is the final resting place of **Archbishop Oscar Romero**.

It overlooks **Plaza Barrios**, named for three-time President General Gerardo Barrios, depicted in a 1909 sculpture on horseback. On the west side of the plaza is the 1911 **Palacio Nacional** (2281-5860; Avenida Cuscatlán and 4 Calle Poniente), a stately, marble, neo-Classical structure. The statues of Christopher Columbus and Queen Isabella, outside, were donated by the Spanish government in 1924.

On the south side of the plaza is the 1870 **Biblioteca Nacional Francisco Gavidia**, most recently rebuilt after a 2001 earthquake. It contains books and newspapers dating to the 1400s, including a first edition of *Don Quixote*.

Three blocks east of Plaza Barrios is remarkable ✪ **El Rosario Church** (4 Calle Oriente and 6 Avenida Sur) completed by architect Rubén Martinez in 1965. Though it looks a bit like an airport hangar from the outside, its soaring interior, bathed in colored beams of light, is transcendent. The original church dated to 1810, and several prominent Salvadorans are buried here, including the three Aguilar brothers who started the Independence Movement of 1811.

It's next to the original city center, **Parque Libertad**, with the 1811 **Monument to the Próceres**, honoring the three voices of independence: Joseph Matias Delgado, Juan Manuel Rodriguez, and Manuel José Arce. It is surrounded by excellent examples of coffee-boom architecture, including the 1888 Art Deco ✪ **Portal de la Dalia**, now a billiards hall.

IGLESÍA EL ROSARIO'S NON-TRADITIONAL ARCHITECTURE HAS CREATED ONE OF THE MOST BEAUTIFUL SPACES IN SAN SALVADOR.

Six blocks east of the plaza is San Salvador's oldest church, 1660 **Iglesia El Calvarío** (6 Calle Oriente between 5 and 3 Avenida Sur), a Gothic beauty most recently rebuilt in the 1950s, but with several original altars. Six blocks south of the plaza is 1816 **Iglesia Candelaria**, a tiny church near the busy intersection of Avenida Cuscatán and the Panamericana, perhaps the original site upon which San Salvador was founded.

Two blocks north of Plaza Barrios is **Plaza Morazán** (2 Avenida Norte and Calle Delgado) and the **1917 National Theater**, Central America's first. The French Renaissance-meets-Federalist façade, and ornate interior with a dome painted by Carlos Cañas, are agreeably over-the-top. In the plaza, an 1882 statue honors **General Francisco Morazán**, President of the short-lived Central American Federation.

If you continue north to Calle Arce, you'll find the ornate 1901 ✪ **Basílica de Sagrado Corazón de Jesús** (2222-8606; basilicasagradocorazon.wordpress.com; Calle Arce #810), another good example of the ornate sheet-metal construction popular during the coffee boom.

Farther north to the major thoroughfare of Alameda Juan Pablo II and Avenida Norte is **Casa Dueñas** (2259-0917; academia@historia.org; Alameda Juan Pablo II y 9 Avenida Norte #425) rising to stately Art Nouveau heights next to the modern government complex. It once served as the U.S. embassy. Next door is the 1892 **Parque Infantil** (North 3rd Avenue and Alameda Juan Pablo II) or

Children's Park, with an array of playground equipment and cute miniature train.

If you aren't tired yet, you could return to Calle Arce and head a kilometer west to **Parque Cuscatlán**, with food stands, soccer courts, two good museums, and the ✪ **Monumento a la Memoría y la Verdad**, a polished granite wall engraved with 25,000 names of those killed or missing during the Civil War.

OTHER BUILDINGS AND MONUMENTS **Plaza del Salvador del Mundo** (Alameda Roosevelt and Boulevard Constitución) In a large, rather pretty traffic island, this tiny park holds two emblematic statues: 1942 Divine Savior of the World, Jesus standing on a globe, and Archbishop Oscar Romero. At the Civil War's bloody peak, in 1986, San Salvador was hit by a 5.7 earthquake that killed some 1500 people, and toppled El Salvador de Mundo, shattering Jesus on the ground. Shortly afterward, the government and guerrillas resumed peace talks.

Just about every other major traffic rotunda has an amazing monument, too, most impressively the 1995 **Monumento a la Paz** (San Marcos, Carretera Costa del Sol), a classical winged sculpture cast from molten weapons used during the Civil War. The **Monumento Hermano Bienvenida a Casa** (Calle Monseratt and Autopista Aeropuerto), *Welcome Home, Brother,* is an abstract piece erected in 1994 to honor Salvadorans who work abroad, and selflessly send their paychecks home. You'll see it as you arrive from the airport.

You could also stop by **Hospital la Divina Providencia** (www.divinaproviden ciahospital.org; Avenida Rocio), the working hospital just off Bulevar Constitución where Archbishop Romero was assassinated. You can see his room, where a few of his belongings are displayed.

MUSEUMS A new city museum was poised to open in Santa Tecla while this book is still on the shelves, in their century-old former prison; ask about it.

THE MONUMENT TO MEMORY AND TRUTH IN CHAPULTEPEC PARK LISTS THE NAMES OF SOME 25,000 DEAD AND DISAPPEARED DURING THE CIVIL WAR.

✪ **Museo de Arte de El Salvador (MARTE)** El Salvador Museum of Art (2243-6099, 2243-1579; www.marte.org.sv) Final Avenida La Revolución, Colonia San Benito. $1.50 adults, $.50 students, children younger than 8 free, Sunday free. Open Tuesday through Sunday 10–6. Even the sculpture fronting this museum, *Monumento a la Revolución* (but better known as *El Chulón, The Naked Guy*) is extraordinary, an enormous mosaic of a man reaching skyward, with Volcán San Salvador rising behind. The museum itself is an apt monument to the finest work this fantastically artistic country has produced: Raúl Elas Reyes, Muriel Hasbún, Valera Lecha, Camilo Minero, Dagoberto Nolasco, and modern painters like William Chilin. Their work is displayed in white, high-ceilinged indoor space. More sculptures are outside, in the Jardín de las Artes. This collection is outstanding by any standards, but surrealism fans will come away especially satisfied.

Museo de Arte Popular (2274-5154; www.artepopular.org) Avenida San José #125. Admission $1. Open Monday through Friday 10–5, Saturday 10–6. North of Metrocentro, this kaleidoscope of colorful handicrafts is an indispensable introduction to the traditional *artesanías* of El Salvador. You'll see the finest examples of *tejidos,* or handwoven cloth, of Panchimalco; *miniaturas,* the miniature ceramic figures of Ilobasco; and the gold filigree jewelry of Zacatecoluca. And there's much more. This is a must for collectors planning to explore El Salvador's crafts.

PLAZA DEL SALVADOR DEL MUNDO DISPLAYS CHRIST AS THE SAVIOR OF THE WORLD, AND ARCHBISHOP OSCAR ROMERO AS THE VOICE OF HIS PEOPLE.

Museo Nacional de Aviación Ilopango (2250-0070, ext. 1119) KM9.5 Boulevard del Ejército. Admission $1 adult, 25¢ child. Open: 8–noon and 2–5 Wednesday through Sunday. Closed: Monday and Tuesday. Halfway between San Salvador and Lago de Ilopango, this museum is worth the trip for aviation and war buffs. It was Central America's first international airport, opened in 1940, but became an air force base in 1976; bring photo ID. A soldier, who may speak English, leads the 45-minute tour of exhibits, such as a map and timeline of the 1969 Football War, though your guide will be offended if you call it that. Here, you'll learn that it is properly called the War of Legitimate Defense, and while set off by riots at a Honduras-El Salvador World Cup qualifying match, actually concerned the abuse of undocumented Salvadoran workers in Honduras. Other exhibits cover El Salvador's first air force, Salvadoran inventor Herman Varon, who improved plane-mounted machine guns, and plenty of old engines, bombs, flight simulators, Civil War murals, and even planes and helicopters, out on the tarmac.

Centro Monseñor Romero (2210-6675; www.uca.edu.sv/cmr) Admission: Free. Open: 8–noon and 2–5 Monday through Friday. On November 16, 1989, six Jesuit priests, their housekeeper and her young daughter, were murdered by federal troops here on the Universidad Centroamericana (UCA) campus. The priests were espousing Liberation Theology, a branch of Catholicism that interprets the New Testament as a call to help the poor and liberate the oppressed. Exploitative capitalism is considered a sin, peaceful political activism a responsibility to God. The Salvadoran government considered that a little too close to communism for comfort. The Jesuits, including UCA rector Ignacio Ellacuria, were asleep when soldiers stormed the building. Federal troops tortured the priests, then shot them execution style. Four of their bodies were left on the lawn for students to discover. Their personal effects and very graphic photos (this is *not* for children), are displayed here, as are those of other civilian victims. There are usually guides available. Take Bus #44 from Metrocentro to the UCA campus.

Museo de Ciencias Stephen W. Hawking (2223-3027; www.museodeciencias elsalvador.org) Calle La Reforma No. 179, Col. San Benito. Admission: $1.15 adult, 55¢ child. Open: 10–4 Monday through Saturday. Closed: Sunday. Small museum in a converted home is filled with Spanish-language exhibits and hands-on experiments designed to teach biology, physics, astronomy, and other branches of the sciences. It's obviously done on a budget, but the information is actually pretty sophisticated, though clear and simple enough for kids. The museum also runs all sorts of workshops and classes; check the Web site for more information.

Museo de Historia Natural de El Salvador (2270-9228) Final Calle Los Viveros, Parque Saburo Hirao. Admission: $1. Open: 9–5 Tuesday through Sunday. Closed: Monday. This graceful, wooden home has a subtly different aesthetic than many others built during the heady days of the coffee boom. Original plantation owner Saburo Hirao arrived here in the late 1800s from Japan, and today the Asian-accented architecture of his residence is a natural history museum surrounded by Japanese gardens. The museum is designed for kids, with several rooms tracing the region's geological development, with mineral samples, fossils, and models. Different niches describe the various ecosystems of El Salvador.

✪ **Museo de la Historia Militar–Cuartel el Zapote** (2250-0000) Calle los Viveros, Barrio San Jacinto. Admission: Free. Open: 9–noon and 2–5 Tuesday through Sunday. Closed: Monday. This fascinating museum is an operating military base; bring photo ID. A soldier guides you through half a dozen trailers that tell the tale of El Salvador's bloodiest moments, from the official perspective. The first displays date to the1820s, of polished guns and cannons used to defeat Spain. Later, President Maximiliano Hernandez Martínez, perhaps better known for the slaughter of 30,000 indigenous coffee workers in 1932, is celebrated for modernizing the army, founding the central bank, and building roads. Weapons and paintings follow El Salvador's military through history: Berettas, Uzis, Colts, Vickers, Brownings, and Hotchkiss, as well as radios, uniforms, and other materiel. The Civil War exhibit is surreal. One side of the room has scores of guerrilla weapons, from the USSR, Yugoslavia, Vietnam, Belgium, East Germany, and elsewhere. On the other, those used by federal troops: from the United States, Israel, West Germany, and so on. Not one gun was manufactured in El Salvador. You'll also see Plaza de la Sobrenia Nacional, with an enormous monument containing the ashes of President Manuel José Arce. And finally, an awesome, huge, three-dimensional map of El Salvador, its dramatic topography labeled with cities, rivers, and volcanoes.

✪ **Museo de la Palabra y Imagen** Museum of the Word and Image (2275-4870; www.museo.com.sv) Avenida 27 Norte 1140, La Esperanza. Admission $1. Open Monday through Friday 8–5, Saturday. 8–2. Closed Sunday. Close to Metrocentro, this cool, artsy, lefty museum offers thought-provoking and creative displays. Some, like the cavern painted with replicas of El Salvador's finest prehistoric painting, are basically installation art pieces. Another cave was a model of Radio Vencermos, the FMLN's mobile revolutionary radio station during the 1980s. Exhibits about Salvadoran writers and artists change every six months; they sell a nice selection of books, indy magazines, and videos, which they'll play by request.

Sala Nacional de Exposiciones Salarrué (2222-4959) Parque Cuscatlan. Admission: Free. Open Tuesday through Sunday 9–noon and 1–5. This small art museum, conveniently located on Parque Cuscatlán, is named for writer Salvador Efraín Salazar Arrué (1899–1975), founder of the *narrativa costumbrista* school of Latin American folk narrative. The ever-changing displays are culled from public and private collections of El Salvador's best painters. It probably isn't worth a special trip, but if you're already down here, drop by.

Tin Marín Museo de los Niños (2271-5147, 2271-5122; www.tinmarin.org) Calle 6a Poniente, Parque Cuscatlán, Central San Salvador. Admission: $2; Reptilandia 50¢; Planetarium $1. Open: Monday through Friday 9–5; Saturday and Sunday 10–6. Also on Parque Cuscatlán, this is an excellent place for kids, a colorful wonderland with activities for everyone from toddlers to preteens. Different areas offer basic science demonstrations, model marketplaces (including a modern supermarket next to a traditional farmers' market) and a walk-through volcano. For small extra fees, you can also visit the **Planetarium**, with Spanish-language shows running throughout the day, and **Reptilandia**, with 22 species of snakes and lizards. Get there right when it opens for feeding time.

Museo Universitario de Antropología (2275-8888 ext. 8836; www.utec.edu .sv/mua.html) Calle Arce and 17 Avenida Norte #1006. Admission: Free. Open: 9–noon and 3–5 Tuesday through Friday, 9–noon Saturday. Closed: Sunday and Monday. This historic, neo-Rennaissance mansion dates to the coffee boom of the early 1900s, as does most of the neighborhood. Today it is managed by the Universidad Tecnológica de El Salvador (UTEC), which has opened a museum displaying some 300 artifacts tracing 20 centuries of Salvadoran history. The most important pieces are a rare, polychrome Sallu vase, dating to the Late Classic period (600–900 AD), and a jade mask probably imported from Mexico. Typical costumes, farming tools, and pottery from Santo Domingo and Ilobasco are also on display. One room is dedicated to beloved Salvadoran musician Pancho Lara (www.pancholara.com), who wrote the popular song "El Carbonero," with guitar, suits, sunglasses, and personal effects donated by his family.

✪ **Museo Nacional de Antropología David J. Guzmán (MUNA)** (2243-3750; www.munaelsalvador.com) Final Avenida la Revolución, Colonia San Benito. Admission $1 Central Americans, $3 other visitors. Open: Tuesday through Sunday 9–5. Closed: Monday. Although Cuscatlán, a polity of the Mayan Empire that once covered Western El Salvador, was something of a backwater, its artifacts are in many ways more interesting than those found at flashier sites in Mexico and Guatemala. El Salvador has a much more diverse heritage, with large populations of less militaristic Lenca in the east, Cotzumalhuapa in the southwest, and much older cultures who were painting caves and carving petroglyphs perhaps 8000 years ago. This museum, arguably the country's best, does the finest artifacts left in the country justice, with elegant, easy-to-understand exhibits. Jade jewelry and finely crafted obsidian pieces are highlights, as are expressive ceramic figures and huge incense burners, many of the most impressive from little explored Cihuatán. There are also rooms dedicated to the Spanish and Independence eras. Guided, 90-minute tours for groups of up to 30 people are free with reservations; guides speak English and possibly other languages, so ask. A research library, pricey art gallery, and free stamp museum are onsite as well. The gift shop has an interesting selection of hard-to-find books of Salvadoran history, culture, and literature, most in Spanish.

✳ To Do

NIGHTLIFE San Salvador has the best nightlife scene in the country. The hottest spots, believe it or not, include **Multiplaza Mall**, with trendy restaurants at Las Terrazas, and clubs like posh ✪ **Envy** and lounges such as **Bliss**, **Live**, and **My Way**; and the **Gran Vía Mall**, with nightclubs including El **Alebrije**, **Llenya**, and **Republik**. Also check **Musica El Salvador** (www.musica.com.sv) to see what's on.

Calle San Antonio Abad Calle Abad is the hipster strip, with clubs and cafes geared to the university crowd.

Bar El Arpa Irlandés (2225-0429) Avenida A #137. Just off Calle Abad, behind Nash, this popular Irish pub has a great student and expat scene; check their Facebook page for events.

Café La 'T' (2225-2090) 2233 Calle Abad. Bohemian spot with revolutionary posters, good coffee, and lefty vibe.

✪ **La Luna Casa y Arte** (2260-2921; www.lalunacasayarte.com) Calle Berlin 228. Funky gallery and bar on a quiet side street has contemporary art exhibits, live music (ranging from European ska to Mexican mariachi to Salvadoran heavy metal), and cool bathrooms. The food is good, there's a coffee shop, and movies and other events as well.

GLEAMING GRAN VÍA MALL IS JUST ONE OF SAN SALVADOR'S OPULENT SHOPPING CENTERS, PACKED WITH NIGHTLIFE, FINE DINING, UPSCALE SHOPPING, AND OTHER AMUSEMENTS.

Zona Rosa

Code (2223-4770) Boulevard de Hipódromo. Best dance floor in El Salvador.

Foro Discoteca Boulevard del Hipódromo #243. Hot disco fills up with well-dressed 20-somethings by midnight or so; and **Elements**, sort of the same scene.

La Enoteca (2279-1607) Boulevard de Hipódromo #243. Sleek and modern wine bar specializes in Italian vintages, and also offers steak, pastas, and a tasty tiramasu. It's a great date spot.

Lipps (2263-6258) Paseo Escalón #5146. San Salvador's finest strip joint has 80 live performers, waitresses in Catholic schoolgirl outfits, and admission includes a very large beer.

Bingo Marbella Paseo Escalón between Avenida 73 and Avenida 75 Sur. Open 1 PM–3 AM daily. Escalón's own little casino has machine gambling.

La Taberna Beer Garden (2264-2262) 79 Avenida Norte and 9 Calle Poniente. Open noon to 2 AM. Loud music and beer for $2 per liter, including your choice of 40 different *bocas,* or bar snacks.

✪ **La Ventana** (2263-3188; laventanacafe@yahoo.com) 83 Avenida Norte and 9 Calle Poniente, Plaza Palestina. Cozy German-themed bar and gallery is known for its cutting-edge art, big breakfasts, hefty Continental cuisine, and full bar including foreign wines and German beers. Cool crowd.

Zanzibar (2279-0833; www.zanzibar.com.sv) Centro Comercial Basilea, San Benito. Young Salvadoran crowd enjoys live bands, deep-fried bar food, and occasional cultural activities, like fire dancing.

Gay and Lesbian El Salvador's gay and lesbian scene revolves around a cluster of clubs near Juan Pablo II and 58 Avenida Norte. **Gay El Salvador** (www.gayelsalvador.com) and **El Savador Org** (www.elsalvadorg.com) have more information.

Body Club (2257-1963; www.bodyclub1.com) Calle los Abetos # 17, Colonia San Francisco, San Salvador. Open noon–10 PM daily. More than just a sauna, this friendly spot has gardens, pools, and screens independent and gay-themed movies.

Millenium Prolongación Juan Pablo II. Open 9 PM–4 AM Thursday through Saturday; cover $4–6, free on Thursday. Small, popular club.

Scape (www.scapedisco.com) Centro Comercial Juan Pablo Segundo. Open 9 PM–2 AM Thursday through Saturday; $5–10 cover. Huge bar and disco is the epicenter of all things gay and lesbian, with live DJs, drag shows, movies, and classic disco. Close by are mellower bars catering to the scene, including **Amazonas**, **Icon Bar**, and **Zeus**.

Streepers Club (2269-5590) 1 Calle Poniente #30-38, 50 meters (55 yards) from Capillas Memoriales. Across from Scape, this straight-friendly club has live entertainment and dancing. Next door, **Lady's Night Club** has a similar vibe.

THEATER Teatro Presidente de El Salvador (2243-3407) Avenida de la Revolución. The largest theater space in El Salvador hosts national and international theater and events. Try to catch the Opera de El Salvador (www.operael salvador.com).

El Teatro Luis Poma (2261-1029; www.teatroluispoma.com) Metrocentro. You might not expect to find such an elegant theater space in a mall, but hey, it's San Salvador. Quality plays, many of them cutting edge, are offered; check the Web site for schedules.

Teatro Nacional El Salvador (2222-8760; tito.murcia@concultura.gob.sv) Calle Delgado and 2 Avenida Norte. Overlooking Plaza Morazán, this French Renaissance masterpiece is Central America's oldest theater, and its dramatic and ornate interior hosts regular performances for as little as $1.

✳ Green Space

NATIONAL PARKS AND OTHER PROTECTED AREAS There are several parks within an hour of the city center. You could also arrange a night tour of the city cemetery with **Necrotour Historic Los Ilustres** (2510-7625, 7319-9279; info@elsalvadorturismo.com.sv) US$15, by reservation only, with ghost stories and highlights from Salvadoran history.

Balneario Los Chorros 20 kilometers (12 miles) west of San Salvador on the Panamericana. Admission: 80¢. Open: 8–5 daily. El Salvador's oldest Centro Turistico surrounds this beautiful complex of pools. It offers developed areas featuring slides, fountains, and playground equipment, and a more natural area, where waterfalls streak the cliffs set into the side of Periquera Volcano. It's cheap, beautiful, and convenient, which means it is packed on weekends.

Jardín Botánico La Laguna (2243-2013, 2243-2012; www.jardinbotanico .org.sv) Urbinazación Industrial Plan de la Laguna, Antiguo Cuscatlán. Admission: $1 adults, 60¢ children. Open: Tuesday through Sunday 9–5. Closed Monday. Hidden within a jungle of factories and food-processing plants is a truly unexpected oasis of peace and green. This was once a proper crater lake, but it drained away after an 1873 earthquake. When the industrial park was developed, some of it reappeared. In 1978, the Laguna Botanical Garden opened, with wheelchair-accessible trails through lush, shady gardens, quiet ponds and small waterfalls, experimental gardens, and all sorts of rare and beautiful plant life. It's also a research laboratory and library; there are some 5000 books, journals, and videos, and an herbarium with more than 27,000 specimens from all over El Salvador.

○ **El Boquerón** (2243-7835 ext. 165 San Salvador) Final, Carretera Volcán de San Salvador. Admission: $1. Open: 8–5 daily. Soon to be declared a national park, this fantastic volcanic complex atop the triple peak of Quezaltepec, better known as San Salvador Volcano, opens onto a huge, deep crater, called El Boquerón (The Big Mouth). The last eruption was in 1917, when it destroyed much of the city, creating a smaller crater within its profound depths. At the park entrance, there is a beautiful botanical park just grazing cool premontane altitudes, with ferns, bromeliads, orchids, and easy trails along the crater's edge. Serious hikers can arrange guided hikes with police escort (2305-6478) in advance, to the bottom of the crater or a nearby lava field. Unfortunately, there's no public bus here. Bus #103 from Santa Tecla drops you off a steep 2 kilometers (1.2 miles) from the park entrance. There are several restaurants, cafés, and lodges surrounding the summit, a popular weekend escape for city dwellers. These include:

Boa Vista Café & Grill (2278-3481, 7091-8703; bvistacafe@gmail.com) KM20.5. $$. Cash only. Closest to the park, this cool (literally) spot serves grilled rabbit, great coffee, and spectacular views of Picacho, the highest peak.

Cajamarca (2226-8981; eventoscajamarca@gmail.com) KM22.5 Carretera Volcán de San Salvador. In a coffee plantation accented with pretty gardens, a comfortable, whitewashed, adobe rental home sleeps up to four amidst art and antiques. There's a Colonial-era chapel built of rock onsite.

Jardín Ecológico Café del Volcán (2306-2001; cafedelvolcan@intera.com.sv) KM20 Carretera Boquerón. $. Cash only. Enjoy typical Salvadoran food in colorful gardens, with views of Volcán San Salvador.

Café y Restaurante Miranda (2298-4577; www.cafemiranda.com.sv) Open 8–5 Wednesday through Friday, 8–7 Saturday and Sunday. $$$. AE, MC, V. Misty mountain views are served alongside excellent fajitas, churrascos, pastries, and their rich coffee, grown right here. There's also a free **Museum of Coffee**, with machinery dating to the 1800s and archaeological artifacts; and a **Canopy Tour** ($25) with more than 1000 meters (3280 feet) of cables.

Las Orquideas (7930-7435) KM27. Open 11–4 Saturday and Sunday. $$. Cash only. Coffee finca offers trails, Salvadoran and international cuisine prepared with local, often organic ingredients, and a full bar; there's sometimes live music.

Café Volcán and Jardín (2306-2001) Open 9–6 Wednesday through Friday, 8–6:45 Saturday and Sunday. $$–$$$. AE, MC, V. Sitting on 2 manzanas (3.5 acres) of gardens threaded with kid-friendly trails, this upscale spot serve great Salvadoran cuisine in a fairly fabulous dining room.

Lago de Ilopango About 30 kilometers (18 miles) east of San Salvador. Just past the capital's surburban sprawl is an almost pristine crater lake called Ilopango, Place of Abundant Corn. Cradled in sheer volcanic walls, it covers 72 square kilometers (28 square miles), and is 248 feet deep at the center. Dive operators can take you to see deep fissures in the crater walls, with underwater geysers and "more fish than the Caribbean." Or, you can just come hang out, and perhaps take a boat ride to see the Cerros Quemados, or Burnt Hills, volcanic islands that formed after a series of earthquakes in 1879 and 1880. Pilots used them as target practice during the Civil War, and you can still find bullets. To get here, take Bus #15 (every 15 minutes; 40¢) from the Palacio Nacional (Calle 9 Poniente and 1 Avenida Norte) to Apulo. The best beach is at the Turicentro.

Finca Buena Vista Restaurant (2372-5770; www.fincabuenavistarest.com) Calle Cerro de las Pavas, Cojutepeque. L, D. $$–$$$. AE, MC, V. On the other side of the lake, in Cojutepeque, this spot has lake views, swimming pools, and Salvadoran food.

Club Savadoreño de Golf Corinto (2226-9111; www.clubsalvadoreno.com) Private club has a golf course, sailing club, and plush lodging, but is generally for members only.

Mirador 70 (2295–4768) Lago Ilopango. L, D. $$$. This restaurant, well signed from the highway, specializes in lake fish and views. They also have simple accommodations.

El Salvador Hostel (7472-6838; www.elsalvadordivers.com; info@elsalvador divers.com) Brand-new hostel ($) operated by El Salvador Diving caters to scuba aficionados, but anyone can stay. It has two dorms sleeping four each on sturdy bunk beds, and there's one private room, just meters from the lake. There's a communal kitchen, and they arrange tours.

Turicentro Parque Acuatico Apulo (2222-8000) KM16.5 Cerretera a Corinto. Admission 80¢. Open 8–5 daily. Sprawled along the lakeshore, this turicentro has the usual pools and slides, plus a cute collection of restaurants overlooking safe swimming areas on the lake, where pretty boats vie to take you out.

JUST HALF AN HOUR FROM SAN SALVADOR, LAKE ILOPANGO OFFERS RURAL RESPITE—BOATING, SCUBA DIVING, RELAXING—IN THE SHADOW OF CHICHONTEPEC VOLCANO.

PANCHIMALCO

On the Planes de Renderos, close to the Puerta del Diabo, is the mountain town of Panchimalco. It is known for 1725 Santa Cruz de Roma church, El Salvador's finest remaining Colonial building; a fierce defense of its Mayan culture, considered (along with Izalco in Western El Salvador, and Cacaopera in the East) one of the last indigenous centers in the country; and serving the best corn pupusas in El Salvador, with views to the sea.

The name means Site of Flags and Shields, and these sheer granite cliffs are certainly a defensible position. When the Spanish arrived at San Salvador in 1545, its previous residents fled here. Though weekends are always quite colorful, with live music and handicraft stands, the very best time to visit is during one of Panchimalco's marvelous fiestas, such as the Flower and Palm Fronds Fair in May.

You can always stop by the **House of Salvador Salazar Arrue** (2280-5538; Avenida Salarrué, close to Fatima Church), one of El Salvador's greatest writers; the **Casa Taller Encuentros** (2280-6958), school and gallery of contemporary artist Miguel Angel Ramirez; and **Abbi Pupusería** (2280-8856; KM10.5, road to Panchimalco; B, L, D; $; cash only), where they once grilled a two-meter (six-foot) diameter pupusa for a Guinness World Record.

JUST OUTSIDE SAN SALVADOR, YOU CAN SCALE THE CLIFFS OF PUERTA DEL DIABLO, WITH VIEWS TO THE SEA.

Hotel Vista Lago (2273-7677, 2283-8317, 7729-2694; murias.caballero@integra .com.sv) Lago Ilopango. Sitting pretty 300 meters (1000 feet) above the lake is Ilopango's best hotel and restaurant, offering fish dishes and rooms with private cool bath. You should make reservations, as it's not always open. Follow the signs to Turicentro Apulo.

Parque Zoológico Nacional (2270-0828) Calle Modelo, Colonia Minerva. Admission: 59¢. Open: 10–4 Wednesday through Sunday. This popular little zoo is actually quite nice, shaded by large trees and stands of giant bamboo, with relatively humane enclosures for about 120 Salvadoran species and several exotics, including lions and elephants. The aviary section is outstanding, and there are three "monkey islands" surrounded by a lagoon. It is packed on weekends.

Planes de Renderos Only 12 kilometers (7.4 miles) south of San Salvador, this cool, clean escape from the city has two excellent parks, and is home to the colorful community of Panchimalco.

Balboa Park (2280-8206) KM12, Planes de Renderos. Admission: Free, 69¢ to park. Open: Daily. This much-loved 70-acre park is filled with meandering trails through the trees, bamboo, and coffee, with hidden picnic spots, playgrounds, soccer fields, and skateboard ramps. There are a few simple restaurants near the entrance, and what may be the cleanest public bathrooms in Latin America. From San Salvador, take bus #20 from Mil Cumbres at the corner of Avenida 29 de Agosto and 12 Calle Poniente (continues to Puerta del Diablo) or Planes de Renderos microbuses from the minibus terminal at Calle Calvario and Avenida Cuscatlán.

✪ **Puerta del Diablo** (No phone) KM14 Planes de Renderos. Admission: Free, parking $1. Open: Daily. About 2 kilometers (1.2 miles) uphill from Balboa Park is a truly spectacular geological phenomenon: two enormous granite plugs carpeted in cool, damp ferns and bromeliads, rising side by side to incredible views. Steep hikes carved step by step into the stones offer vistas to Lake Ilopango, the Pacific, and over San Salvador. Trails are clear and easy to follow, but lack railings; simple food stands are set up at the base. Some tour operators offer rappelling. Just up the hill, **Albaclara Restaurant and Park** (2101-3186; www .parquealbaclara.com; KM12.8; $$–$$$; AE, MC, V) opens on weekends, with a good restaurant, horseback rides, a small canopy tour, and a *mariposario*, or butterfly garden.

✴ Lodging

There are scores of hotels in San Salvador, ranging from flawless five-star chains to grimy downtown hovels, with a huge number of mid-range options scattered around the city. These are all great choices, but there are many other recommendable hotels in town, and most have Web sites.

Most top-end lodging and mid-range hotels are found in the safe, prosperous neighborhoods of **San Benito**, the **Zona Rosa**, and **Paseo Colón**, close to great dining, shopping, and nightlife options. It's safe to walk around at night, and convenient to many museums and malls.

Another cluster of solid budget and mid-range hotels is located close to **Metrocentro**, most on **Calle Los Sisimiles**. They are convenient to downscale dining and artsy nightlife options, as well as a couple of great museums and Central America's largest mall. It's a fairly safe neighborhood as well.

Just north of the Sisimiles strip, west of the **Universidad Nacional** and north of **Calle San Antonio Abad**'s strip of hip bars and cafés, is another cluster of good budget and mid-range hotels in a quiet residential neighborhood.

The busy **city center** isn't the best place to spend the night, as it's dangerous after dark and always congested. But there are a few recommendable spots close to the Puertobus Terminal. A better bet for urban explorers is a group of hotels in **Colonia Flor Blanca**, next to Estadio Magico Gonzalez, a quiet residential area close to downtown that was the city's best address in the 1960s. The money has migrated to the Zona Rosa, but it's still a pleasant, relaxed neighborhood.

Zona Rosa, San Benito, and Paseo Escalón

Upscale Zona Rosa and the safe, strollable, surrounding suburbs boast the city's best selection of luxury and mid-range properties, fine dining, charming boutique hotels, and even a few cheapies. These are just a few of my favorites.

✳ 🚗 "1" **Casa de Huéspedes Australia** (2224-3931; josecaballer 003@hotmail.com) Calle 1 Poniente 3852, Colonia Escalón. $. AE, MC, V. Handicap Access: Challenging. The lowest rates in Escalón can be found

at this rambling property, featuring different-sized rooms with mismatched furniture and pretty gardens. Some are small, fan-cooled, and stuffy, with shared bath, others are larger with air-conditioning, private bath, and TV.

✶ ✳ 🚗 "1" **Hostal Lonigo** (2264-4197; www.hostal-lonigo.com, info @hostal-lonigo.com) Calle El Mirador #4837. $$. Handicap Access: Challenging. AE, MC, V. B&B has both character and comfort, with 19 nicely decorated (if a bit frilly) rooms of different shapes and sizes; #16 has windows onto the interior gardens. Most are small, with good furnishings and color schemes, cable TVs, telephones, and tiny desks. There's a small, pretty pool in the gardens, and a full breakfast is included.

✶ 🛏 ✳ 🚗 "1" **Hotel Marela** (2263-4931, 2211-3432; www.hotelmarela .net, vista_marella@123.com.sv) Calle Jeán José Cañas and 83 Avenida Sur 5. $$$. AE, MC, V. Handicap Access: Challenging. With a spray-on stucco façade and 53 clean, cookie-cutter, US-style rooms, this is a professional operation. Rooms have two double beds, cable TV, and all the modern amenities, plus a small pool and gym.

🛏 ✳ 🚗 "1" **Hotel Mariscol** (2298-2844; www.hotelmariscal.com, hotel mariscal@integra.com.sv) Paseo Escalón #3658. $$–$$$. AE, MC, V. Handicap Access: Challenging. For more than 50 years, this excellent hotel has offered spotlessly clean, very pretty (if pleasantly outdated) rooms that are surprisingly peaceful, despite the busy location next to Galerías Mall. It's popular, so make reservations. Rooms are rambling and air conditioned, with cable TV, telephone, and other comforts. Suites

LUXURY IN THE CAPITAL

There are several luxury chain hotels in San Salvador, each offering beautiful rooms with all the amenities: Fantastic bedding involving goose down and Egyptian cotton, perfect bathrooms with hairdryers and phones, executive levels with free newspapers and drinks, huge TVs, daily fees for WiFi, rooms outfitted for wheelchair users, fabulous onsite restaurants and bars, business centers, pools, gyms, and so on.

Courtyard Marriott (2249-3000; www.marriott.com) Gran Via Mall. $$$$. AE, MC, V. San Salvador's newest luxury property is located adjacent to opulent Gran Via Mall, with many of the city's finest dining and nightlife options. It's gorgeous, with a great staff, lovely outdoor pool (and waterfall), elegant furnishings, and an unbeatable breakfast buffet.

Hilton Princess (2298-4545; www.hotelesprincess.com) Avenida Magnolias y Boulevard del Hipodromo, San Benito. $$$$. AE, MC, V. From the moment you enter the stately, opulent lobby, with its fluted columns, mahogany accents, and marble floors, you feel fabulous. The 206 predictably perfect rooms are decorated with a soothing palette, and there's a tiny pool, a very complete gymnasium, and a small spa.

Hotel Intercontinental (2211-3333; www.ichotelsgroup.com) Boulevard de Los Heroés #544. $$$$. AE, MC, V. Away from the Zona Rosa crowd, and across from Metrocentro Mall, the Intercontinental has character, with a small pool, huge gym and sauna, onsite spa, and fantastic sculpture by Fernando Llort in the lobby. There are four classy restaurant/bars: Faisa do Brasil, serving skewers of meat alongside an enormous salad bar; Tequila's, a casual Mexican place offering 60 brands of tequila; Vertigo, a sleek martini bar serving Italian food; and Tanoshi, a Japanese restaurant. Business lunch dilemma, solved!

have two bedrooms and kitchenettes. Breakfast is included and service is outstanding.

Hotel Mesón de María (Tica Bus) (2243-0442; hmesonde maria.com, hmesondemaria@gmail.com) Boulevard Hipódromo, Casa #301, San Benito. $. Handicap Access: No. AE, MC, V. If you're taking Tica Bus, spend your first or last night in safe, friendly San Benito at this cute hotel, with clean, basic rooms (fan or air-conditioning), private bath, cute gardens, a small eatery, and great sorbet shop downstairs. Tica Bus also has a downtown terminal and hostel, grimy **Hotel San Carlos** (2222-4808; Calle Concepción 121; $; cash only), but it's only a bit cheaper and not nearly as nice.

🛵 🏌 🛎 ❄ 🚗 "¶"
Radisson Plaza
(2257-0700; www
.radisson.com;
radisson@hotels
al.com) 89 Avenida
Norte y 11 Calle
Poniente, Colonia
Escalón. $$$$. AE,
MC, V. With its
excellent pool, airy
and elegant lobby,
Colonial-style

THE LOBBY OF THE REAL INTERCONTINENTAL DISPLAYS
A WROUGHT-IRON MURAL BY ARTIST FERNANDO LLORT.

details, and 195 beautiful rooms, it's easy to see why some travelers prefer
the 50-year-old grand dame of the luxury scene. Service is fantastic, there's
a small spa onsite, and transportation to area malls and restaurants is free.
It's connected to the World Trade Center and Japanese Embassy.

🛵 🏌 🛎 ❄ 🚗 "¶" **Sheraton Presidente** (2283-4000; www.sheraton.com;
sansalvador.presidente@sheratonpresidente.com.sv) Avenida Revolución.
$$$$. AE, MC, V. With a great location in the Zona Rosa, next to the MARTE art
museum, this fine choice has splendid volcano views, a better-than-average
pool, spacious rooms and suites (get one with a terrace), and an onsite spa.
It's also where amateur historians will want to stay, the site of a 28-hour civil
war siege, where rebels (who may have been trying to kidnap the OAS Secretary General, but were probably just after the breakfast buffet, seriously),
accidentally trapped 12 Green Berets on the fourth floor before slipping away,
setting off a media circus in the USA and humiliating President Cristiani.

🏌 🛎 ❄ 🚗 "¶" **Hotel Mirador Plaza**
(2244-6000; www.miradorplaza.com,
reservaciones@miradorplaza.com)
Calle El Mirador and 95 Avenida
Norte #4908. $$$. AE, MC, V. Handi-
cap Access: Challenging. Plush, busi-
ness traveler-friendly local alternative
to the big chains has an impressive
lobby, elegant artwork, gym, pool, and
large, well-appointed rooms (some

fully equipped for wheelchairs) with
wide-screen televisions, excellent
beds, security boxes, telephones,
modern baths with real hot water, and
soothing color schemes.

🛎 ❄ 🚗 "¶" **La Posada del Angel**
(2237-7171; www.hotellaposadadel
angel.com, laposadadelangel@
integra.com.sv) 85 Avenida Norte
#321, Colonia Escalón. $$–$$$. AE,

MC, V. Handicap Access: Challenging. This elegant, artsy gem of a hotel is decorated for culture tourists, with handcarved beds covered in gorgeous Guatemalan *telas*, original Salvadoran art, and beautiful gardens fronting a fine patio. Standards are high, service is excellent, and each of the spotless rooms has cable TV , private bath, and includes a full breakfast. They rent laptops and cell phones, and also have a business center. Make reservations.

✪ 𝆑 🛏 ❋ 🛏 "𝕀" **Suites Las Palmas** (2250-0800; www.hotelsuiteslaspalmas .com.sv, ventas@suiteslaspalmas .com.sv) Boulevard El Hipódromo, San Benito. $$–$$$. AE, MC, V. Handicap access: Yes. One of the best properties in the city, this locally owned hotel offers just about everything the five-star chains do at a better price, close to several good restaurants and nightlife options. The high rise has a rooftop pool with Jacuzzi, and the gym and complimentary breakfast area also have fantastic views. There are several types of tastefully decorated, jewel-toned suites, described in English on the Web site. All are large, with huge TVs, telephone, excellent bedding, and real hot water; some have tubs. The more expensive rooms could include full kitchens and terraces (recommended) with views over the city and volcano. There's a great bar, restaurant, and coffee shop onsite, and they can arrange tours, some quite adventurous, all over the country, perhaps stopping at their sister hotel in Suchitoto, Posada Suchitlán. Make reservations during the week.

🛏 ❋ "𝕀" **Villa Castagnola Hotel** (2275-4314, 2275-4315/17; www.hotel villacastagnola.com, info@ hotelvilla castagnola.com) 1 Calle Poniente 3807, Colonia Escalón. $$. AE, MC, V. Handicap Access: Challenging. Beautiful 1950s mansion next to Galerías Mall is now a lovely family-owned bed and breakfast, offering six elegant, high-ceilinged rooms with great beds, telephone, cable TV, pale tiles, heavy curtains with wrought-iron accents, interesting art, private hot bath, and excellent service, which give this mid-range option a rather luxurious feel. A small second-story terrace offers great views to San Salvador Volcano, and a continental breakfast is included.

🛏 ❋ 🛏 "𝕀" **Hotel Villa Florencia** (2221-1706, 2271-0190; www.hotel villaflorencia.com, centroinfo@hotel villaflorencia.com) Avenida la Revolución #262. $$. AE, MC, V. Handicap access: Challenging. Across the street from MUNA, this delightful bed and breakfast has Colonial flavor and modern amenities, with fine ceramic-tiled common areas, beautiful handcarved furnishings, and original art and lovely ceramics that add to the ambiance. The onsite café is divine.

Metrocentro and Calle Los Sisimiles

This strip of inexpensive hotels is walking distance from Metrocentro Mall, scores of chain restaurants, and the artsy entertainment options in the university district. It's a fairly safe neighborhood, but stay alert and take big city precautions when transporting valuables or at night.

🛏 ❋ 🛏 "𝕀" **Hotel Las Flores** (2261-1946; hotellasflores@hotmail.com) Avenida Sisimiles #2955. $. Cash only. Handicap Access: Challenging. The cheapest spot on the strip is sparsely decorated, with dark, air-conditioned rooms, private hot bath, computers for guests, and nice gardens out back.

♨ ✳ 🛏 "ᵀ" **Hotel Grecia Real** (2261-0555, 2261-0577; www.greciareal.com, greciareal@hotmail.com) Avenida Sisimiles #2922. $$. AE, MC, V. Handicap Access: Challenging. The theme is ancient Greece meets Las Vegas, with Doric columns, voluptuous statues, faux marble, and gauzy curtains. The pool is small but clean, and rooms simpler than the lobby suggests but just fine, most with air-conditioning, hot showers, and cable TVs.

♨ ✳ "ᵀ" **Hotel Happy House** (2260-1568; www.hotelhappyhouse-elsalvador.com, hotelhappyhouse@hotmail.com) Avenida Sisimiles #2951. $. AE, MC, V. Handicap Access: No. Simple and sweet, this is my favorite cheapie on the strip, with clean, spacious rooms (some are a bit dark, though), new mattresses, cable TVs, desks, and a computer for guests to use.

🍴 ♨ ✳ 🛏 "ᵀ" **Hotel Miramonte** (2280-1820, 2260-1880; www.hotelmiramonte.com.sv) Calle Talamanca #2904. $$–$$$. AE, MC, V. Handicap Access: Yes. This four-story hotel provides modern, mid-range amenities in several classes of clean, acceptable rooms with cable TV, and hot bath; the pricier rooms have refrigerators and/or terraces. There's a pool in the parking garage and computers for guests.

✪ ✐ 🍴 ♨ ✳ 🛏 "ᵀ" **Hotel Villa Real** (2260-1579, 2260-1665; www.hotelvillarealelsalvador.com, villarealsv@netscape.net) Calle Sisimiles #2944. $$. AE, MC, V. Handicap Access: Challenging. This adorable spot was designed with Colonial style and modern amenities, all archways and flowery courtyards that have been spotlessly whitewashed with deep

blue trim. It's pretty classy for a mid-range place, and often hosts NGOs and aid groups, which give it high marks for service, security, and cleanliness; they can arrange group tours, transportation, and meetings in the glassed-in, third floor meeting room, with great views. All 17 sunny rooms are simple but perfect, with cable TV, real hot water, top-notch mattresses, fans and air-conditioning, telephone, desks, framed prints on the walls and Hummel figurines in the halls. They rent a beach house near La Libertad.

Universidad Nacional, Calle Antonio Abad, and Jardines de Morazán

"ᵀ" **Hotel Balché** (2226-9936; www.alameda.com; jgiovanni.cabrera@gmail.com) Boulevard Universitario #2032, between Avenida 37 and 39. $. Cash only. Handicap Access: No. Right on the bus line, this convenient option is homey, with surprisingly nice furnishings in seven spacious rooms with cable TV and private hot bath. There's a computer for guests.

"ᵀ" **International Guest's House** (2226-7343, 2225-0132; i_guesthouse@yahoo.com) 35 Avenida Norte #9. $. Credit cards: No. Handicap Access: No. Relaxed and sprawling, this 15-room guesthouse is artsy, revolutionary, and cheap. Rooms are large, clean, and over-filled with beds; all have private hot bath and some have TVs; there's a computer for guests (US$1 per hour). There are lots of communal hangout spots, brimming with socialist literature, including owner Tirso Canales books, including *Schafick Hándel por la Senda Revolucionaria* and *Ciudad Sin Memoría*. Breakfast is included, and there's a scruffy garden out back.

♨ ⁙ **Hotel Tazumal House** (2235-2506; www.hoteltazumalhouse.com, gerencia@hoteltazumalhouse.com) 35 Avenida Norte #3, Reparto Santa Fe. $$. AE, MC, V. Handicap access: No. Bright colors, artesanías, and a great complimentary breakfast make this beauty stand out in a crowd. Rooms are excellent, with new beds, telephone, and desk; two have shared bath, saving you $5 a night. Very nice.

🗡 ⁙ ⁙ **El Torogoz** (2275-4860; www.suhogarfueradecasa.com; eltrogoz@telesal.net) Final 35 Avenida Norte 6-B. $$. AE, MC, V. $$. Handicap Access: Challenging. Acceptable mid-range option has clean rooms with huge windows, cable TVs, air-conditioning, and fans. There's a complimentary breakfast.

Downtown

The Centro is crowded, congested, and none too safe at night. But there are a few decent options close to the King Quality bus terminal.

⁙ ⁙ **Hotel Bella Vista** (2221-5178; edwinhernanbarcenas@ymail.com) Calle 3 Poniente, half block from Puertobus. $. Cash only. Handicap Access: Challenging. The cheapest spot close to Puertobus has fancooled rooms with cable TV, telephone, private bath, and the lingering smell of cigarettes. Three rooms have air-conditioning, and there's complimentary coffee.

♨ ⁙ ⁙ ⁙ **Hotel Puerto Bus** (2217-3300, 2217-3333; www.hotelpuertobus.net) Alameda Juan Pablo II and 19 Avenida Norte. $$. AE, MC, V. Handicap access: No. In the same building as the King Quality/Comfort Line bus terminal, this business hotel is convenient if you've got an early bus, and is actually pretty nice. All of the clean, modern, tastefully furnished units come with cable TV, refrigerator , telephone, and full breakfast.

✪ ⁙ ⁙ ⁙ **Hotel Villa Florencia** (2221-1706, 2271-0190; www.hotelvillaflorencia.com, centroinfo@hotelvillaflorencia.com) Calle 3 Poniente 1023, half block from Puertobus. $. Handicap Access: Challenging. This beauty is too good for the gritty downtown, with Colonial style—dark-wood vigas, handcarved columns, spiral staircases, antique furnishings, fresh flowers—and great security. Rooms are all very pretty, if basic, and vary in size, shape, and amenities. All have private bath and cable TV, air-conditioning is a few dollars extra.

Colonia Flor Blanca

This quiet residential area is convenient to downtown, Parque Cuscatlán, and Estadio Magico Gonzalez.

🗡 ⁙ ♨ ⁙ ⁙ **Hotel Alameda** (2267-0800; www.hotelalameda.com.sv, hotelalameda2005@yahoo.com) Alameda Roosevelt and 43 Avenida Sur #2305. $$. AE, MC, V. Handicap Access: Challenging. Rising to five aging stories above the smoggy main drag, this old hotel was once a pretty swish spot. There's a pool, WiFi in the lobby, a recommended restaurant, **La Mansión** (B, L, D; $$–$$$) and a smoky, dimly lit bar. Threadbare rooms are carpeted in industrial blue gray, with cable TVs, telephones, room service, good beds, and views. The top-floor suites even have Jacuzzis.

⁙ ⁙ **Hostal La Portada** (2298-6558; 7883-2700; www.hostalelsalvador.com, hostallaportada@yahoo.com) 8a Calle Poniente 2326, between 43 and 45 Avenida Sur. $. V. Handicap Access: Challenging. Special: Dentist office onsite. One of the best deals in town, this super cute, Spanish-tiled hostel has just seven adorable rooms, all with high ceilings, big windows, and private bathrooms, including machine-heated showers. It's not plush, but there's a dentist office geared to foreigners onsite, where you can get your teeth cleaned. Or, just hang out in the small yard and enjoy cheap Salvadoran eats in the onsite cafeteria. They also operate Beach Lodge La Parlama in Barra Salada (see Western Beaches), near a sea turtle nesting ground.

☗ ❋ 🛏 "🍴" **Hotel San Mateo** (2298-3825; www.hotelsanmateo.com; hotelsanmateo@gmail.com) Calle Caracas #20-H, Colonia San Mateo. $$. AE, MC, V. Handicap Access: Challenging. In a nearby residential neighborhood, convenient to the Terminal del Occidente, this comfortable guesthouse has sunny rooms decorated in cool pastels, cable TV, hot bath, continental breakfast, and an onsite dental office.

☗ ❋ 🛏 "🍴" **Villa Serena** (2260-7544/(503) 2260-7545; www.central america-smallhotel.com, hotelvilla serena1@integra.com.sv) Colonia Flor Blanca, 4a Calle Poniente #2323. $$. AE, MC, V. Handicap access: Challenging. This is just one in a citywide chain geared to business travelers on a budget. All are thoughtfully decorated, with murals, plants, fountains, and rocking chairs. Compact, cheerful rooms come with desks, complimentary cell phone, minifridge, and cable TV, and some with kitchens and private terraces. The other two Villas Serena are located in the Zona Rosa, **Villa Serena San Benito** (2237-

7979; www.pequenoshoteles.com; Curcunavalación #46), which costs $10 more than the other two, but has the better location next to MARTE; and **Villa Serena Colonia Escalón** (2257-1937; www.hotelvillaserena.com.sv; 65 Avenida Norte #152), near Plaza Las Américas.

Airport
Monte de Oro (2339-9683) KM38 Autopista Comalapa. $. AE, MC, V. Handicap Access: Challenging. If you want to stay close to the airport but can't swing the Quality Hotel below, this nicer-than-average love motel has clean rooms, great beds, private cool bath, and hourly rates that might work out nicely if you've got an early flight. Upstairs rooms are much better.

✪ ✐ 🔑 ☗ ❋ 🛏 "🍴" **Quality Hotel Real Aeropuerto El Salvador** (2366-0000; www.realhotelsand resorts.com, quality.sal@realhotelsand resorts.com) KM40.5 Autopista al Aeropuerto Internacional. $$$$. AE, MC, V. Handicap access: Yes. Perfectly presented hotel offers every major chain amenity in flawless, if somewhat sterile, environs. Creature comforts include an excellent pool complex, onsite ATMs, full gym, tennis courts, conference rooms, tour operator, business center, and WiFi for a daily fee. Service is professional, with neatly uniformed staff, many of whom speak English, guiding you to comfortable minisuites that come with refrigerator/minibar, microwave, coffeemaker, fabulous bedding, large-screen cable TV, and complimentary breakfast buffet, among many other amenities. Master suites are larger. Los Balcones has a different themed buffet every night—Mexican, seafood, pasta bar, etc.—which is good, because there's nothing else out here. An airport shuttle is included, and it's $25 for a cab into San Salvador.

Elsewhere in San Salvador

⚖ ❄ 🚗 ⁱↂⁱ **Arból de Fuego** (2275-7065; www.arboldefuego.com, hotel@arboldefuego.com) Avenida Antiguo Cuscatlán #11c Colonia La Sultana. $$–$$$. AE, MC, V. Handicap Access: Challenging. In a safe, quiet neighborhood close to UCA, this hotel has pretty gardens and simple but comfortable rooms with colorful bedspreads, desks, and fresh flowers every day.

🖋 ⚖ ❄ 🚗 ⁱↂⁱ **Hotel Beverly Hills** (2505-9999; www.hotelbeverlyhills.com.sv, ventas@hbh.com.sv) Calle Llama del Bosque Poniente #17, Antiguo Cuscatlán. $$$–$$$$. AE, MC, V. Handicap Access: Yes. Upscale business-class hotel close to the U.S. embassy has rooms and suites that are almost plush, with all the amenities you'd expect at this price.

MULTIPLAZA MALL'S LAS TERRAZAS IS PACKED WITH FINE DINING OPTIONS, SUCH AS TUMBAO, SERVING TASTY CUBAN-FUSION CUISINE.

🖋 ⚖ ❄ 🚗 ⁱↂⁱ **Hotel Casino Siesta** (2283-0100; www.hotelsiestaelsalvador.com, info@hotelsiesta.com.sv) Final Boulevard Los Próceres. $$$. AE, MC, V. Handicap Access: Yes. On the ring road close to the Multiplaza, this spot has great rooms, a big pool, and packages that include a welcome cocktail, buffet breakfast, and $20 coupon for the onsite casino.

⚖ 🚗 ⁱↂⁱ **El Portal de las Colinas Santa Tecla** (2287-2544) 4 Calle Poniente #4–5, Santa Tecla. $–$$. AE, MC, V. Colonial-style budget B&B has simple, fan-cooled rooms with private bath that open onto a lovely little patio surrounding very pretty gardens. Breakfast is included.

✴ Where to Eat

El Salvador has a great dining scene, with many of the world's major cuisines represented at elegant, upscale restaurants and popular budget spots. Paseo Escalón, the San Benito Rotunda, and Boulevard Los Heroés all have dozens of options, including a neon-lit collection of fast food restaurants to rival any in the world.

In addition to your favorite international chains, look for **Mister Donut** (www.misterdonut.com.sv), a bakery serving cheap Salvadoran cuisine; **Cebollines** (www.cebollines.com), a great family-style Mexican chain; **The Coffee Cup**, El Salvador's answer to Starbucks, but with much better coffee; and **Pollo Campero** (www.campero.com), a fried chicken joint with an almost religious following.

DINING OUT ✪ Alo Nuestro

(2223-5116; alonuestro@integra.com.sv) Calle La Reforma, San Benito.

$$$$. Cuisine: Salvadoran fusion. Serving: L, D. Closed Sunday. AE, MC, V. Handicapped Access: Challenging. Reservations: Recommended. This refined restaurant in the heart of the Zona Rosa, with a formal dining room lit by candles and delightful chandeliers, is considered the best in El Salvador. The ambiance is rather formal and romantic, the cuisine decidedly gourmet, created with the freshest Salvadoran ingredients and prepared using international techniques. Presentation is creative and elegant, the wine list complete, and food outstanding. The menu changes frequently, but the delicate soups and gourmet tamales are a good bet for starters, before moving on to perfectly marinated steak and perhaps tilapia in a rich pepper sauce, served over grilled vegetables. The desserts get raves.

Restaurant Basilea Grill (2223-6818; www.restaurantebasilea.com) Bulevar del Hipódromo, San Benito. $$–$$$. Cuisine: International. Serving: L, D. AE, MC, V. Child's Menu: Yes. Handicapped Access: No. Reservations: Yes. Ladies who lunch come to this popular, rather posh, Zona Rosa institution for its creative, beautifully presented salads—perhaps the sesame-encrusted chicken salad, with an Asian vinaigrette—and other light meals, such as the grilled eggplant focaccia sandwich, red pepper quiche, or macadamia-coconut fish in a ginger and curry sauce. There are heftier dishes as well, including pizzas, homemade pastas, and the famous desserts.

Restaurant Casa de Piedra (2280-8822; www.casadepiedra.com.sv) KM8.5 Carretera a Los Planes de Renderos. $$. Cuisine: Mexican, Salvadoran. Serving: L, D. AE, MC, V. Child's Menu: Yes. Handicapped Access: No. Reservations: Recommended on weekends. This is a classic destination in the mountains of Planes de Renderos, a popular spot for families escaping the city, with stunning city views, playground equipment, and live music some nights. Rock House Restaurant serves simple fare such as nachos and tacos, and nicer dishes such as sea bass grilled *al ajillo* (in garlic butter), and shrimp sautéed in whiskey. It has a very full bar.

Kamakura (2263-2401) 93 Avenida Norte, Colonia Escalón. $$–$$$$.Cuisine: Japanese. Serving: L, D. Closed Sunday. AE, MC, V. Handicapped Access: Challenging. Reservations: Yes. Fine Japanese restaurant specializes in fresh sushi, prepared several different ways; the tuna tataki deserves a special mention, as does the seaweed salad. In addition, there are other excellent Japanese dishes, including tempura, yakisoba, ramen, and teriyaki. There's even a good value special at lunch.

✪ **Mai Thai** (2210-4763; www.mai thailounge.com) Las Terrazas, Multiplaza. $$–$$$. Cuisine: Asian Fusion. Serving: L, D; closes 4 PM Sunday. Closed: Monday. AE, MC, V. Handicapped Access: Challenging. Reservations: Yes. Popular, atmospheric restaurant and nightspot attracts a sophisticated crowd with its Thai-influenced pan-Asian cuisine and exotic cocktail menu. Lighter fare includes salads, such as papaya and mint shrimp, or enjoy appetizers such as the *bolsitas picantes,* steamed, spicy meatball dumplings made of pork, shrimp, and mushroom. Several stir fries, curries, and seafood dishes round out the menu. Also at Multiplaza, the same restaurateur, Jaime E.

Castro, operates **Tumbao** (2243-2883; L, D; $$–$$$; AE, MC, V), a sleek Cuban fusion restaurant with a creative martini menu. Check out the cozy jazz and cigar bar, with cool art, specialty rums, and Cuban *porros.*

La Pampa Argentina (2298-5817; www.lapampafranchise.com) Bulevar del Hipódromo, Centro Comercial Las Palmas, San Benito. $$–$$$. AE, MC, V. Cuisine: Argentine. Serving: L, D. Handicap Access: Challenging. Reservations: Evenings. Within the rustic adobe walls of this well-regarded steakhouse, you'll enjoy outstanding Argentine-style churrasco, or grilled meats, as well as several excellent steak cuts. Lunch brings in businesspeople; dinner has a more romantic vibe, when you might indulge in their excellent selection of Chilean, French, and Spanish wines. There are a handful of other locations around town, as well as in San Miguel and Santa Ana.

Pasquale Pasta e Pizza (2263-1693 reservations; 2283-4545 delivery; susanam@integra.com.sv) Paseo Gral Escalón #3931. $$$. AE, MC, V. Cuisine: Italian. Serving: L, D. Handicapped Access: Yes. Reservations: Yes. Recommended Italian eatery with indoor seating and pretty gardens does it right, from the candle-lit antipasto bar with a dozen different appetizers to their exceptional wine list. Try the *calamari a la Romana* or *prosciutto crudo con mozzerela.* Wood-fired pizzas and the *spaghetti de pescatore,* with lobster and other seafood, are also great. Many ingredients come from Italy, and they also have a deli selling imported Italian meats, cheeses, sauces, canned goods, olive oils, and alcohols, including grappa and limoncillo, as well as their own fresh pasta and bread.

El Sapón Tipico (2298-3008; www.elsapontipico.com) Avenida La Reforma, Colonia San Benito. $–$$. AE, MC, V. Cuisine: Salvadoran. Serving: L, D. Handicapped Access: No. Reservations: No. The Big Typical Soup specializes in soups, from modest, such as *sopa de pato* (cow foot soup), to extravagant, like the delicious *mariscada,* a cream-based seafood stew. They also serve exotic Salvadoran dishes: *garrobo* (iguana), *conejo* (rabbit), and *cazuco* (armadillo), are just a few choices. It's a homey spot, with an open-air cement dining room set with cheerfully decorated tables. There's another branch near Metrocentro, (2260-2671, Avenida las Palmeras #130), near Pops.

✪ **Los Tacos del Paco** (2260-1347) Avenida Los Andes 993. $. AE, MC, V. Cuisine: Mexican, Poetry. Serving: 11:30 AM–3 PM; 5–10. Handicapped Access: Challenging. Reservations: No. Sustenance for your body and soul is on offer at this artsy outpost hidden in the fast-food wasteland around Metrocentro. Just off the main drag, Paco's serves more than a dozen types of tacos alongside outstanding salsas, *sincronizadas* (tortilla sandwiches), *molletes* (toast topped with beans and cheese), and other treats in the hip courtyard filled with art and flowers. Come by Wednesday for a poetry slam at 7 PM, book readings Thursday evenings, and live music (sometimes with a cover) Friday at 8 PM. Because "Man does not live on tacos alone," there's a cool bookstore featuring local writers and poets.

La Valentina (2264-1808) 3 Calle Poniente #5328, Escalón. $$$. AE, MC, V. Cuisine: Mexican. Serving: L, D. Handicapped Access: No. Reservations: Recommended. This fine-dining Mexican restaurant has a romantic ambiance, with fountains, candles, murals, and excellent service. The focus is on the cuisine of Oaxaca, especially savory *moles,* a rich, complex sauce that can have more than 30 ingredients and take a week to prepare. Start with one of their *ceviches,* raw fish "cooked" in lime juice. Other Mexican classics are well prepared and attractively presented, making for a fine evening out.

Voila (503-2263-1539; voilarestaurant@yahoo.com) 3a Calle Poniente 5241, Colonia Escalón. $$–$$$. AE, MC, V. Cuisine: French. Serving: L, D. Reservations: Yes. El Salvador's finest French cuisine comes courtesy of chef and Voila owner José Roberto, classically trained in Lyon, France. After years on the French food scene, he returned home to open this romantic restaurant, serving a short menu of creative cuisine. While many items are quite classic—the pates get raves—they also do a bit of Salvadoran-French fusions, with special attention on the chocolate desserts.

ASIAN Restaurant Beijing City (2275-5563) Calle Lamatepec #16. $. Cash only. Long before the Metrocentro area became chain-restaurant row, this spot was was serving huge plates (order half a portion) of seafood stir-fries, vegetarian dishes, even Peking duck, cheap. It has a huge TV, a full bar, and lots of cheesy red décor.

✪ **Minh's Cuisine** (2264-7246; minhscuisine@yahoo.com) Plaza Masferrer, Avenida Masferrer and 7 Calle Poniente. L, D. $$–$$$. AE, MC, V. Tucked away in a little strip mall, this Thai and Vietnamese restaurant serves up some of the tasiest food in San Salvador, including pad Thai, pho, and plenty of vegetarian dishes. Beer and wine are served.

Pabellón Coreano (2278-3169) Avenida El Boquerón #37, Jardines de Merliot. L, D. $$–$$$. Excellent, authentic Korean cuisine in unpretentious surroundings.

Yong Fong Supermercado Oriental (2287-0389) Paseo Escalón and 77 Avenida Sur #3949. The city's best Asian grocer has everything you need.

BAKERIES Le Croissant (www.lacroissantelsalvador.com) B, L, D. $. Local chain sells its excellent pastries and breads in **San Benito** (2243-2280; Avenida La Capilla #261), **Escalón** (2224-2865; 1 Calle Poniente #3883), Gran Vía, and Multiplaza.

Dulces Albanés (2263-8570) Surcursal Escalón, 85 Avenida Norte. B, L, D. $. Cash only. Sweets shop and bakery has been turning out homemade Salvadoran-style treats for almost a century.

San Martín Multiplaza, Comercial Paseo Escalón. B, L, D. $. Cash only. Turns out delicious loaves, good pastries, sandwiches and snacks.

CAFÉS Los Olivos (2245-4221; www.olivoscafe.com) Avenida Magnolias y Boulevard del Hipodromo, San Benito, Zona Rosa. B, L, D. $$. WiFi. Wheelchair access. Attached to the Hilton Princess, serves Chinameca coffee, light meals, and good wines.

Shaw's (2223-0959; www.shaws.com.sv) Centro Comercial Basilea. B, L, D. $–$$. This chain is known for its chocolate and pastries, but also serves light meals.

ITALIAN Al Pomodoro (2264-0017; al.pomodoro@yahoo.com) Paseo Escalón #3952. L, D. $$–$$$. AE, MC, V. Though not as atmospheric as Pasquale, this smaller, more subtly elegant Italian favorite offers outstanding thin-crust pizza, handmade pastas, and excellent desserts, alongside one of the country's best wine lists. Delivers.

Il Buon Gustaio (2245-1731) Calle Loma Linda 327, San Benito. L, D. $$–$$$. AE, MC, V. Another contender for the "best Italian in town," this cozy, romantic spot with gardens serves classic Italian cuisine amidst fine art, with a good wine list.

PERUVIAN Inka Grill (2230-6060) 79 Avenida Sur. L, D. $$–$$$$. AE, MC, V. Lima-based chain serves quality cuisine, including *chaufa*, Chinese-Peruvian fusion, in Inca-themed environs.

Roberto Cuadra Cocina Peruana (2263-2413; www.robertocuadra.com .sv) Calle El Tanque #130, 99 Avenida Norte. L, D. $$–$$$. AE, MC, V. Formerly known as Café Café, this pretty eatery offers the finest seafood (you must try the *ceviche*) and beautifully presented Peruvian classics, including *causas* (sculptural potato salad) and *aji de gallina* (chicken in a rich yellow pepper sauce). There's another branch in Ataco, open weekends only, and a cooking school.

SALVADORAN Note that there are two tiny towns just south of San Salvador claiming pupusa supremacy: **Panchimalco**, known for its corn pupusas, and **Olocuilta**, the *cuna* (cradle) of rice pupusas. Serious pupusa connoisseurs may find it worth the pilgrimage.

Abuelita Celia (2225-7247) 37 Avenida Norte 10. $. Cash only. Open daily. Convenient to the National University, pupusería and tamale shop serves a Sunday *chilate y nuégados*, deep-fried yuca and cornmeal donuts served with sugarcane syrup and spiced *atole* in morro-shell bowls.

El Café de Don Pedro (2260-2011, www.elcafededonpedro.com) Avenida Roosevelt and 39 Avenida Norte, Colonia Flor Blanca. B, L, D. $. AE, MC, V. For half a century, this citywide chain has been serving good, inexpensive típica, with other locations in Soyopango, El Trébol, and Ciudad Merliot.

✪ **Las Cofradías** (2264-6148) Calle Mirador. L, D. $$. Two blocks from the Radisson, this restaurant offers award-winning comida típica.

Típicos Margoth (2263-3340; www .tipicosmargoth.com) 77 Avenida Norte. B, L, D. $–$$. Popular local chain also specializes in typical food; try the *rigüas*, sweet corn turnovers with bean filling.

STEAKHOUSES Faisca Do Brasil (2211-3333) Boulevard Los Heroés. L, D. $$$. AE, MC, V. Brazilian steakhouse at the Hotel Intercontinental serves skewers of perfectly prepared meat, sliced right at your table, accompanied by a salad bar.

✪ **Hacienda Real** (2243-8797; www .hacienda-real.com) KM8 Panamericana. L, D. $$–$$$. AE, MC, V. Huge, self-consciously rustic steakhouse close to Multiplaza is known for its parilladas (grilled meat plates), sausages, fajitas, and Texas-style barbecued ribs.

Restaurante Tucson (2278-8822) Gran Vía Mall. L, D. $$–$$$. AE,

MC, V. Polished steakhouse gets high marks for its aged beef and international dishes.

VEGETARIAN Estancia Natural (2102-2549; www.estancianatural.com) Centro Comercial Plaza Bernal, Avenida Bernal. Serves Salvadoran specialties such as pupusas, Middle Eastern salads, and other international dishes. Many products are organic.

Kalpataru (2279-2306) Avenida Masferrer 127, Colonia Escalón. L, D. Closed Sunday. $–$$. AE, MC, V. This sunny space, filled with greenery, is San Salvador's oldest vegetarian restaurant and health food store, with daily specials and a steam-table buffet.

Koradi (2221-2545) 9 Avenida Sur and 2 Calle Poniente. B, L. Closed Sunday. $. Cash only. Relaxed cafeteria-style eatery in the city center has a steam-table buffet with lots of soy.

Shen Zhuan Restaurant Taiwanes (2243-0424, 2533-6428) Avenida Revolución #5, Colonia San Benito. L, D. $–$$. AE, MC, V. Unassuming spot serves Taiwanese-style vegetarian dishes in cheerful, lacy surroundings. The best deal is the *plato del día,* with rice, soup, two veggies, and a drink for $4.

✳ Selective Shopping

MALLS El Salvador loves its spectacular assortment of malls, a cultural quirk of a less safe and stable past when security issues were of utmost importance.

Basilea Centro Comercial (2279-0833; www.ccbasilea.com) Boulevard del Hipódromo, Colonia San Benito, Zona Rosa. Lush, plush little open-air mall houses a handful of treasures, including colorful shops like **Book Marks** (www.bookmarks.com.sv), a bookstore with mostly Spanish titles; **Fuscia**, with Indian and hippy clothing, **Nahanche** (2245-2945 nahanche.net), with top-quality Salvadoran arts and crafts, and **Zanzibar** (2279-0833; www.zanzibar.com.sv), as well as **Basilea Restaurant**.

Galerías (2245-0800; www.galerias.com.sv) Paseo Escalón 3700. This fabulous mall built around a 19th-century mansion houses L'Occitane en Province, Benetton, Cartier, MAC, and other upscale shops. There's also a post office, **Cinépolis Theater** (www.cinepolis.com.sv), and a pretty chapel for San José.

Gran Vía (2273-8111;www.lagranvia.com.sv) Calle Chilitupán and the Pan-American. This marble-paved outdoor mall with artistic fountains and upscale stores is sort of mind-blowing. The opulent walkways are lined with some of the city's best nightlife and dining, a five-star Marriott, a **Cinemark Theater**, miniature golf, and much more.

Metrocentro (2257-6000; www.gruporoble.com) Avenida Sur and Boulevard Los Heroés. The biggest mall in Central America sprawls across several city blocks in a chaotic collection of stores, restaurants, cafes, movie theaters, grocers, and much, much more.

Multiplaza (2248-9800; www.gruporoble.com) Avenida Jerusalén and the Panamericana. This glittering option offers more than 250 stores ranging from mundane to chic, as well as some of the city's finest bars, restaurants, and discos. There is also a movie theater, department stores, live music, and the biggest SuperSelectos in town.

MARKETS Mercado Ex-Cuartel Centro. Monday through Saturday 7:30–6, Sunday 7:30–3. In a former military barracks, this huge, kitschy souvenir market can help you get your gift shopping done, cheap. Everything from fine handmade crafts to cheesy T-shirts is covered.

Mercado Municipal de Antiguo Cuscatlán Jardines de La Hacienda, Santa Tecla. This fantastic market is relatively clean and well organized, with stalls selling everything from fresh fruit and flowers to piñatas and shoe repair. There are several excellent food stands; try **Mariscos y Cocteles** (2278-5377; B, L, D; $; AE, MC, V) toward the back of the market, specializing in seafood.

Mercado Nacional de Artesanías Alameda Araujo, next to the Fería Nacional. Close to the Gúzman Museum, this collection of handicrafts stands offers just about every sort of Salvadoran craft.

CLOTHING Boutique de Clemen (2224-4014) 1 Plaza Boulevard del Hipódromo, Colonia San Benito, Zona Rosa. Upscale women's clothing store specializes in cocktail dresses and formal wear.

✪ **Botas El Charro** (2271-0648; www.botaselchorro.com) 71 Avenida Norte and 1 Calle Poniente. Across from Gallerías Mall, this great shop sells beautiful handcrafted leather boots, all made in El Salvador, for $50 to $150 a pair, as well as belts, holsters, mariachi outfits, and more.

GALLERIES 123 Gallery (2275-9856; marcovalencia.net) Avenida La Capilla 258, Colonia San Benito. Shows the dreamily realistic landscapes of artist Marco Valencia, and many other artists.

El Arból de Dios (2263-9206; arbol dedios@integra.com.sv) Calle La Mascota and Avenida Masferrer. Founded by famed Salvadoran artist

SAN SALVADOR'S MERCADO MUNICIPAL DE ANTIGUO CUSCATLÁN IS ALWAYS A FESTIVE SPOT FOR LUNCH.

Fernando Llort, it offers arts and crafts in his signature, brightly colored naïve style, as well as a great onsite café.

Galería Espacio (2223-4807; espacio@navigante.com.sv) Calle Reforma #209, San Benito. Classy gallery features El Salvador's best artists.

La Pinacoteca (2223-2808; www .lapinacoteca.net) Boulevard El Hipódromo #305, Zona Rosa. Displays cutting-edge modern art.

Sala de la Miniatura (2274-5154) Avenida San José 125. Innovative Ilobasco ceramicist María Dominga Herrera began making the art town's signature *miniaturas,* ceramic miniatures, in the 1920s, and her shop still carries the finest.

SOUVENIRS Axul (2263-3447) 79 Avenida Norte #420. Shop specializes in textiles, but also tin work, wood, and ceramics.

Arte Maya Pipil (2223-6640; www .artemayapipil.com) Boulevard del Hipodromo No. 129, close to Redondel Brazil, Colonia San Benito #129. Top-notch crafts store offers high-quality artesanías in the Zona Rosa, at prices that match.

Nahanché (2260-3603; www.na hanche.net) Metrocentro Mall, Boulevard Los Heroes. Closed Monday. High-quality selection of tradi-tional souvenirs can be found at Metrocentro Mall, Multiplaza Mall, and Centro Comercial Basilea

✳ Special Events

All of the national holidays are celebrated with special aplomb in the capital.

May: **Festival of Flowers and Palms** (First Monday in May) Panchimalco throws one of El Salvador's most famous fiestas as rainy season begins. The Virgin Mary is carried through town, her passage hailed with palm fronds threaded with beautiful flowers.

August: **Fiesta de El Salvador del Mundo** (August 1–6) El Salvador's patron saint and namesake, Jesus Christ The Savior of the World, has its biggest blowout in San Salvador, with parades, fireworks, special Masses, a procession of El Salvador del Mundo borne by 25 strong men, and all-night parties that run for at least a week. When the statue is unveiled, many people fall to their knees. The rest of the country enjoys a somewhat subdued version of events, often traveling to visit their families or spending time at the beach.

September: **Fiesta del Señor de Santa Cruz** (September 13–14) Panchimalco's second-most important fiestas are also worth seeing.

Western Beaches

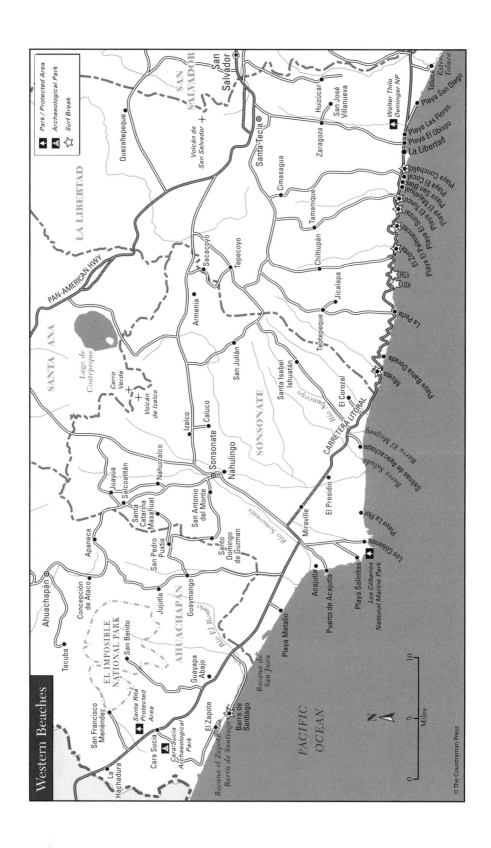

Western Beaches

Legend:
- ◀ Park / Protected Area
- 🏛 Archaeological Park
- ☆ Surf Break

Ahuachapán

Tacuba

La Hachadura

San Francisco Menéndez

Concepción de Ataco

Apaneca

Juayúa

Salcoatitán

Santa Catarina Masahuat

Nahuizalco

San Pedro Puxtla

Santo Domingo de Guzman

Jujutla

Guaymango

Guayapa Abajo

San Benito

Santa Rita Protected Area

EL IMPOSIBLE NATIONAL PARK

AHUACHAPÁN

Cara Sucia

Cara-Sucia Archaeological Park

El Zapote

Barre de Santiago

Bocana el Zapote

Barra de Santiago

Bocana de San Juan

Río El Rosario

Río El Naranjo

PACIFIC OCEAN

Playa Metalío

Acajutla

Puerto de Acajutla

Playa Salinitas

Los Cóbanos

Los Cóbanos National Marine Park

Playa La Flor

Miraville

El Presidio

El Cóbanos

Barra de El Masguey

Salinas de Ayacachapa

Barra Salada

SONSONATE

Sonsonate

Nahulingo

San Antonio del Monte

Caluco

Izalco

San Julián

Armenia

Santa Isabel Ishuatán

El Corozal

Río Banderas

Río Sonsonate

CARRETERA LITORAL

Teotepeque

Jicalapa

Chiltiupán

Tamanique

Mizata

Playa Bahía Dorada

La Peña

K61

El Zonte

Playa El Sunzal

Playa El Tunco

Playa El Majahual

Playa San Blas

Playa El Cocal

Playa Conchalío

La Libertad

Playa El Obispo

Playa Las Flores

Walter Thilo Deininger NP

Playa San Diego

Toluca

Estero Toluca

San José Villanueva

Huizúcar

Zaragoza

Santa Tecla

Cimasagua

Tepecoyo

Sacacoyo

San Salvador

SAN SALVADOR

Volcán de San Salvador

Quezaltepeque

LA LIBERTAD

PAN-AMERICAN HWY

SANTA ANA

Lago de Coatepeque

Cerro Verde

Volcán de Izalco

Río Amacuyo

N

0   5   10 Miles

© The Countryman Press

WESTERN BEACHES

CATCHING WAVES AND RAYS

There's a reason why the West Coast is El Salvador's most popular destination: the epic surfing waves, among the best in the world, that crash on these gorgeous shores. Even during the Civil War, surfers couldn't resist their allure and kept coming, undaunted by guerrillas and gangs.

Today, this is El Salvador's most developed destination for international tourists, its endless shady coves and pearl gray sands lined with surf bars, relaxed resorts, and upscale ecolodges, sea turtle sanctuaries, canopy tours, and deep sea fishing and dive outfitters.

But the vibe has remained the same, Bob Marley and big swells that roll in from the south with a hollow roar, curling with a famed consistency around long, delicious rides. And though this coast is now being "discovered" by less adventurous travelers, plenty of sweet spots still remain.

Begin in the port of **La Libertad**, its long fishing pier covered with colorful boats. The fishermen unload their catch every cool, golden morning, as surfers paddle out to greet the day. To the west are the reliable waves of **Playa La Paz**; east is **Playa El Obispo**, with a scruffy tourist malecón, serving cheap seafood to day-trippers. You could continue east several kilometers, to palm-fringed **Playa Las Flores** and the endless swimming beaches of **Playa San Diego**.

But most head west. The next batch of beaches also boast good waves, **Cochalío**'s sandy breaks, and then the prized surf of **El Cocal** and **Playa San Blas**, with a few surf lodges that offer everyone access to the deep gray shore. Next is the ramshackle Salvadoran vacation town of **Majahual**, with a good swimming beach.

The most popular stops for international travelers are the colorful little beach towns of **El Tunco** and **Playa Sunzal**. Even if you're not a surfer, it's a good place to ease into your Salvadoran adventure, where other travelers can tell you about the scene. Continuing west, more waves await in the fishing village of **El Palmarcito** and the flashy resorts of **Playa El Zonte**.

Tourists thin as the *Carretera Litoral,* the Coastal Highway, climbs to blufftop viewpoints and through tunnels carved into the headlands, past a few more developed spots. **Bocana La Perla** has a simple spot to surf, then **Playa Mizata**'s fickle but famous waves.

After that, however, you reach the **Sonsonate Beaches**, most famously **Salanitas** and **Playa Los Cóbanos**, home to all-inclusive resorts, coarse golden beaches, a quiet fishing village, and a spectacular coral reef.

The major port town of **Acajutla**, where the Mayans made their last stand against the Spanish fleet, doesn't have much for the average tourist, but it's safe to explore before continuing west, to the nation's last and least traveled shores.

Playa Metalío is a Salvadoran escape, with a few hotels and swimming beaches. Then last, but not least, are the long, smoky gray sands of **Barra de Santiago**, a peninsula and mangrove estuary that's home to basic guesthouses, sea turtle nesting sites, and one excellent ecoresort.

Crime The popular, touristed surf beaches of Western El Salvador do have crime issues, but they aren't really gang related. The main problem is opportunistic crime: Never leave belongings unattended on the beaches, and be careful with your cool new friends.

The Port of La Libertad, once notoriously sketchy, has cleaned up its act, with more security and a police presence. Regardless, it's best to avoid the town center and dark beaches at night.

CEVICHE DE COLORES, FISH "COOKED" IN LIME JUICE WITH ONIONS AND PEPPERS, IS A LA LIBERTAD SPECIALTY.

GUIDANCE MiTur La Libertad (2346-1898; cat.lalibertad@gmail.com) KM34.5 Carretera Litoral. Open 8–4 Monday through Friday, 9–1 Saturday and Sunday. At the entrance to Puerto La Libertad, across from the Texaco gas station, this tourist office covering the Western Beaches can recommend hotels, give you bus schedules, provide maps, and turn you on to area tours.

FUNDARRECIFE (2417-6817; www.elsalvadorexperience.com, casadelsol@integra.com.sv) Los

ONLINE RESOURCES
All these are in Spanish; surf sites (see Surfing) have more English information.

Acajutla Tourism (turismoacajutlense .blogspot.com) Tourism information, well, community gossip, online.

Cara Sucia Online (www.carasucia.8m.com) Basic information about the town.

✪ **Puerto La Libertad** (www.puertolalibertad.com) Big site with lots of tourist information, photos, an events calendar, and complete, ranked listings of La Libertad hotels and restaurants.

Cóbanos Village. In the heart of Los Cóbanos, offers tourist information and organizes tours.

GETTING THERE The Western Beaches are a snap, with one main road—the Carretera Litoral—and great bus service between La Libertad and Los Cóbanos. Beaches farther west, sometimes called the Sonsonate Beaches, are less accessible, with poorer bus connections and roads, but worth the effort.

By Car: The CA-2, better known as the Carretera Litoral, is a smoothly paved highway that hugs the incredible shoreline almost until Acajutla, turning inland just before the Los Cóbanos turnoff. Beach towns generally are small, easy to navigate, and well signed from the Litoral. Acajutla is more difficult to navigate, but there's little here for tourists, and it's easily bypassed. Particularly in the town of La Libertad, it's worth investing in guarded parking. There are at least two public lots.

By Public Buses: Public transport is excellent along the beaches of La Libertad Department (up to Los Cóbanos). Several lines ply the Litoral, and you can just hail one on the highway. All will happily carry your surfboards. The hub is La Libertad, with regular service to San Salvador and Zacatecoluca. These can drop you off on the highway to connect with buses to Costa del Sol.

For the beaches of Sonsonate Department—Los Cóbanos, Barra de Santiago, and Mizata, as well as the inland town of Cara Sucia—it's easiest to go through the city of Sonsonate, covered in the Western El Salvador chapter.

For convenience, I've listed Sonsonate's beach connections here. Buses from La Libertad can drop you on the highway to catch Los Cóbanos buses, if you don't want to backtrack to Sonsonate. Hotel Mopelia in Playa El Tunco has a Tica Bus desk, reserving international buses that leave from San Salvador.

La Libertad: Most buses leave from Calle Gerardo Barrios and 4 Avenida Norte:

FUNDARRECIFE IN LOS CÓBANOS WORKS WITH AREA ALCALDÍAS (MUNICIPAL GOVERNMENTS) TO PRESERVE THE BEACHES AND CORAL REEFS.

San Salvador (102) Every 15 minutes.

Sunzal (102A) 5:20 AM, 5:50 AM.

Tamanique (La Paz, Conchalio, San Blas, El Cocal, Tunco) (187-A) Every hour.

Playa Las Flores (11L) Microbuses leave throughout the day.

Other buses leave from 4 Avenida Norte and 1 Calle Oriente:

Chiltiupán (La Paz, Conchalio, San Blas, El Cocal, Tunco, Sunzal) (192A) 7:10 AM, 9 AM, 11 AM, 1:10 PM, 2 PM, 3:30 PM.

Comalapa (187) every 15 minutes.

La Perla (La Paz, Conchalio, San Blas, El Cocal, Tunco, Sunzal, Zonte) (192) Every hour.

Sonsonate (287) 6:15 AM, 1:45 PM.

Teotepeque (La Paz, Conchalio, San Blas, El Cocal, Tunco, Sunzal, Zonte) (192B) 10:10 AM, 2:30 PM.

Zacatecaluca (540) 5:25 AM, 7:50 AM, 8:50 AM, 12:10 PM, 3:05 PM, 4:20 PM.

Others leave from 4 Avenida Sur, next to the Polideportivo:

Playa San Diego (signed) Every 30 minutes.

Majahual–Sunzal (signed) Every 15 minutes.

Sunzal: San Salvador (102A) 5:20 AM, 5:50 AM.

Tamanique (La Paz, Conchalio, San Blas, El Cocal, Tunco): La Libertad (187-A) 65¢; 6:30 AM–5 PM, every hour.

San Salvador (102-A) 66¢; leaves Sunzal at 5:20 AM, 5:50 AM, passing Tamanique 5:30 AM and 6:08 AM; returning from San Salvador at 6:55 AM, 7:37 AM, 2:20 PM, 3:52 PM.

Sonsonate: Taxis outside the terminal can take you to Los Cóbanos or Salinitas ($20).

Acajutla (252) Every five minutes.

Barra de Santiago (285) 10 AM and 4:30 PM, returning at 4:30 AM and 11:30 AM.

Los Cóbanos (257) Every half hour.

Frontera La Hachadura via Cara Sucia (259) Every nine minutes.

La Libertad (287) 3:45 PM.

Mizata (281) Ten buses daily.

San Salvador (205) Every 10 minutes.

✸ To See

Though most of this shoreline is only recently developed—historically, neither the Spaniards nor Mayans cared to build their cities by the Pacific—the two major port towns bookending the more famous beaches are truly ancient. There are no museums to memorialize their fascinating stories, but they're worth relating nonetheless.

La Libertad was once called "Tepeagua," "Big Hill" in the Mayan tongue. Small boats, as today, set out to find fish, which was salted, dried, and carried to the mountain cities.

The Spanish were unable to develop the port, what with the pirates sailing all about. Nervous conquistadors even resorted to trickery to protect the coast's most important commodity, the fragrant sap of the balsam tree, still used in soaps and shampoos. They called it Peruvian balsam, though it was produced here. The pirates sailed southward and El Salvador's orchards survived; you can still see them at Finca San Jorge (see Mountain Lodges, later).

After independence from Spain, the port was renamed "Freedom," La Libertad. In 1824, the young republic began developing the protected waters properly, building an important commercial port used for shipping balsam, coffee, indigo, and other products.

In 1857, it was the site of an important naval battle against William Walker, a Tennessee mercenary hired by pro-slavery elements in the U.S. government to overthrow Central America. He never got past the Salvadoran Navy. La Libertad's first steel wharf was opened in 1870, and it was the nation's most important port, until ceasing commercial operations in 1976.

Puerto Acajutla Today, this is the country's most important port town, but remains a bit difficult for tourists to explore. There's plenty to enjoy, however, including a monthly Gastronomic Festival in the Botanical Garden, and a lively pier scene, with a few restaurants and bars.

Its history is fascinating and bloody, the scene of the Spaniards' single toughest battle in Central America. The Mayan polity of Cuscatlán had bitterly and successfully resisted the Spanish invasion for years, despite their superior numbers and weapons. Then, on June 8, 1524, conquistador Pedro de Alvarado arrived in the port town of Acaxual, Acajutla's old name.

The Pipil troops were prepared; they'd seen the galleons coming, and were ready with an ambush. A few units, with an entire army hidden behind them, watched from atop a hill as 250 fully armed Spaniards, 100 horses, and more than 5000 (perhaps as many as 20,000) indigenous Mexican troops disembarked. Alvarado sensed something suspicious, and instead of climbing to meet them, feigned retreat. The Pipiles and all their hidden troops gave chase to lower, less-defensible ground, and the mighty Spanish military attacked. The brutal battle lasted 17 days, and though Alvarado received a crippling leg wound, the Spanish victory was utter and complete.

In the 1830s, as coffee was quickly becoming El Salvador's most important crop, a need arose for a western port, close to the coffee-growing highlands. Acajutla, still a fishing town, was rapidly developed, and a major commercial pier was inaugurated in 1938. The town grew wealthy as

TAKING IT EASY IN PLAYA EL TUNCO.

trade increased with the construction of railways across Panama and Nicaragua, which brought goods and gold prospectors on a quicker route from the United States' East Coast to the California shores. In 1961, it was modernized yet again, and by 1975, its facilities were the finest on the Central American Coast. La Libertad shut down commercial operations the following year.

✳ To Do

CANOPY TOURS KM 29 Canopy Tour KM29 Carretera La Libertad. Admission $15. This 13-cable canopy tour can be booked by special arrangement through any hotel close to La Libertad.

CENTROS TURISTICOS Parque Acuatico El Sunzal (2533-8718) KM43 Calle Litoral. Entry $3/1.50 adult/child. Just north of the coastal highway, between Playa El Tunco and El Sunzal, this smallish water park has slides, sprays, playground equipment and cheap eats for the whole family.

Montaña Acuatica Park (2301-6135; www.lamontanaacuaticapark.com) KM27.5 Carretera de La Libertad, at the Zaragoza exit. Natural spring water-filled pools with water slides and playground equipment are surrounded by ranchos with hammocks, basketball courts, camping areas, and views over the Grand Canyon of Zaragoza.

La Libertad Centro Deportivo Entrance to Puerto La Libertad. Admission 25¢. The outdoor La Libertad Sports Center has basketball courts, skateboarding ramps, and other facilities.

DIVING AND SNORKELING Los Cóbanos (see National Parks) is the largest coral reef on the Central Pacific, and every surf operator in the country offers diving here; they're all based in San Salvador, so see that chapter for listings. Los Cóbanos Village Lodge, the Decamaron, and Los Veraneros (see accommoda-

FÚTBOL, OR SOCCER, IS THE NATIONAL SPORT, PLAYED ANYWHERE AND EVERYWHERE THAT KIDS CAN FIND A BALL AND GOALPOSTS.

LOS CÓBANOS VILLAGE'S COLORFUL FISHING FLEET IN THE SUNSET.

tions) can all organize diving excursions once you're here. **FUNDARRECIFE** (2417-6817; www.elsalvadorexperience.com; casadelsol@integra.com.sv), around the corner from Los Cóbanos Village lodge, offers snorkeling excursions.

Playa Mizata has another coral reef, but dangerous currents and huge waves make it almost impossible to explore.

FISHING While the Eastern Pacific Coast is perhaps better known for its fishing (see that chapter's Fishing section for more general information), the Western Beaches have plenty of fish in the sea, giant snapper, snook, barracuda, yellowfin tuna, mackerel, and roosterfish in dry season; and dorado, mahi-mahi, wahoo, and yellowfin tuna in rainy season.

The best beaches for organizing artisanal fishing trips with local captains (you'll need to do this in Spanish) are Puerto La Libertad and Los Cóbanos. Local hotels can help. Or, do it with serious fishing boats and equipment with **Fish El Salvador** (503-7899-1818; skype leve1976; www.fishelsalvador.com; mahimahi@fishelsavador.com; Los Cóbanos). Owner Luis Villanova puts down anchor next to the Central Pacific's largest coral reef with excellent fishing year-round.

NIGHTLIFE Many hotels in and around La Libertad can arrange Nightlife Tours to San Salvador.

La Libertad While you might expect this to be a nightlife hotspot, your choices after, say, 8 PM are a few very downscale local bars—not recommended for most tourists, and the rest of you should be careful.

There's also the sparkling new **Complejo Turistico**, just west of the pier, inaugurated just three months prior to research. With its white-tented roofs, breezy patios, and gleaming chrome furnishings a la South Beach, this spot was already filling up with fairly upscale seafood restaurants and bars, one of them open till 11 PM.

El Tunco This relaxed surf town has the best nightlife on the coast, which isn't saying much. Hot spots come and go; ask around.

Bam Bar (see Where to Eat) Surfers and backpackers congregate over the estuary to enjoy a cold beer.

Bar La Guitarra (see Lodging) Festive hotel-bar near the village center sometimes has live music.

✪ **Kayu Surf Bar** (2389-6135) KM44 Playa El Sunzal. B, L, D. $$. A short ride up the coast, and well worth the effort, this is the West Coast's prettiest spot for a few brews (or cocktails involving Red Bull), as well as great hamburgers and nachos. Operated by plush Paraiso Azul Resort, it overlooks one of El Salvador's sweetest stretches of sand, also renting boards and organizing surf and adventure tours. Enjoy beach access, free movies, and more.

Zip Pop Disco (7971-4602) KM42 El Tunco. Open 5 PM–4 AM Tuesday through Saturday. Mayan-themed bar and restaurant has two floors and a big dance floor, murals, DJs, and live music. They also serve simple vegetarian dishes—pastas, veggie burgers, hummus—and seafood.

QUAD AND MOTORCYCLE TOURS Mototour El Salvador (7729-0188, 7894-9466, 7887-9058; www.mototourelsalvador.com) About 15 minutes from La Libertad on the Coastal Highway. Motorcycle and Quad tours include road trips and dirt trails, ranging from $60 to $85 per day, per person. They also rent motorcycles.

SURFING It's no secret that El Salvador offers some of the best waves in the Americas, the coast crashing with uncrowded rights (and at least one left). Local guides and international operators offer rentals, lessons, packages, and tours for every budget. And with a few exceptions, you won't have to fight for your rights, as El Salvador remains well off the beaten path. For now.

Water is warm, so you won't need a wetsuit, though you may want to bring a rashguard for UV protection and jellyfish, and booties for some of the rocky breaks and sea urchins. There's never been a shark attack in modern history, so no worries there. Public buses on the West Coast happily transport boards. If they break, **Hospital de Tablas,** the Surfboard Hospital (7944-3632; entrance to Playa la Paz), in La Libertad may be able to patch things up.

El Salvador's surf may be the most consistent in the world, but it does change with the season. Beginners will have the best luck from November to February, with great weather, small waves (usually 2 to 4 feet), and fewer irritated experts hogging the swells. But, it can flatten out for a week at a time, particularly in late January and early February. March brings in big, consistent waves from the Southern Hemisphere, as well as surfers from all over the world. Conditions are sunnier until May, when rainy season begins, but swells reach 6 to 12 feet through October. Here are some of the biggest waves:

Punta Roca: Considered the best wave in Central America, this long, hollow barrel works best at 4 to 15 feet, offering 300-meter (328-yard) rides, but can get shallow on the rocks at low tide. Booties are recommended.

La Paz: Just inside Punta Roca, this easily accessible wave is usually best for beginners, but can get big when the lineup is right.

Conchalío: This long, hollow barrel with a sandy bottom is one of El Salvador's best beach breaks, a great option on small days.

La Bocana: Rivermouth break and the country's only consistent left gets crowded with territorial locals on weekends, but those hollow waves roll in all week long. There's a powerful right here as well.

La Bocanita: Serious beach break with strong currents is a local favorite, and for experienced surfers only.

El Sunzal: Consistent, long rides reaching 300 meters (328 yards) have a fast takeoff and clean walls. Easy access mean this right gets crowded at times, but this deep-water break is great, best for long boards at high tide, short boards at low. Nearby, Sunzalito is a fast beach break for experienced surfers.

El Zonte: Hollow right with a sandy bottom is a popular spot with easy access and waves for every level—but beginning surfers should ask about conditions, and avoid it if it's crowded.

Palmarcito: Point break with a mostly sandy bottom is great for beginners.

K59: Boat access only (the beach is gated off by a mansion farm) this short, hollow right-hand point break has a rocky bottom and almost no crowds

K61: Empty, peeling right isn't always working, but at medium to low tides, it becomes one of the best waves in the country for experienced surfers.

Mizata: Inconsistent, isolated swell actually forms different waves, an A-frame beach break, a rivermouth break, and a point break; usually at least one is working, and when it's on, this is one of the best surf spots in the country.

Barra de Santiago: At the western border with Guatemala, the tip of this peninsula has decent surfing, good for beginners.

SPAS Vydiananda Yoga (7736-1713; www.somosyoga.com; melisaoli@gmail .com) Arrange an appointment at one of several hotels from Playa El Tunco through K59 for private yoga classes, several different types of massage, and other holistic treatments.

SPANISH SCHOOLS El Salvador Spanish Schools (7051-4171, 413-374-0159 USA; www.salvaspan.com) Offers Spanish classes in La Libertad (2346-0228) and El Sunzal (2441-4948), with another campus in Santa Ana. Surf, dance, and cooking lessons, among many other activities, can be arranged.

Mango Wald (7731-2224; marcowiech@yahoo.com) Playa El Sunzal. Six-room surf lodge offers Spanish and German classes, as well as surfing lessons.

Spanish, Surfing, and Sun (7269-9831; knibalsurf@hotmail.com) Playa El Tunco. Private teacher can come to your hotel.

Study Spanish and Surf (www.studyspanishandsurf.com) International organization has a campus in La Libertad; it's currently not operating.

SURF TOURS

Just about every hotel on the coast can help you arrange lessons, find boards to rent, or hook you up with a tour, often your best budget option. Many international operators, including **Baja Surf Adventures** (www.bajasurfadventures.com), **Quiksilver Tours** (quiksilvertravel.com), and **Surf Express** (www.surfex.com), offer pricey packages to El Salvador. However, there are plenty of local operators who know the swells best.

Akwaterra (2245-2614, 7888-8642 English; www.akwaterra.com) Plaza Basilea, San Salvador. Top-notch tour operator runs Las Olas (see Lodging) as well as surf and adventure tours all over the country.

Epic Surfing Adventures (7890-4751; www.epicsurfingadventures.com) Based at Mizata Surf and Miraflores (see Eastern Beaches chapter), it offers tours and lessons.

El Salvador Surf Camps (7238-6362, 7927-0757; www.elsalvadorsurfcamps .com) KM44 Playa El Tunco. Offers lessons and custom tours all over Central America, as well as at their QI-X Rancho surf lodge.

K59 Surf Tours (7894-9466, 2300-5490; k59surftours.com) K59 Litoral. Based at K59 Surf Villas, it offers packages and tours all over the country.

Olas Permanentes (2510-7621, 2237-7658; www.olaspermanentes.com) Operates surf camps in El Zonte and El Espino, and organizes tours all over the country.

Quiver Surf (2223-0807, 7892-2866; www.quiversurfworld.com) Playa El Tunco. Operator based at beautiful Hotel Tekuani Kal rents boards, arranges lessons, and offers tours all over the West Coast.

Sunzal Surf Company (7731-4848, 2389-6337; www.sunzal.com) Playa El Tunco. Based at Sunzal Surf shop, local operators offer rentals ($15/day), lessons ($30), day-trips, fishing excursions in a 31-foot Bertram Sportfish, and more.

✳ Green Space

NATIONAL PARKS AND PROTECTED AREAS On the western edge of the country, **El Imposible National Park** offers incredible hiking and camping opportunities, with easy access from Barra del Santiago and Los Cóbanos.

Note that most surf operators, listed later in this chapter, also offer day-trips to the Ruta de las Flores and natural attractions of Western El Salvador. Check their Web sites, or ask at your hotel, for more information.

Surf La Libertad (7810-0421; www.surflalibertad.com) 4 Calle Poniente, Playa La Paz, La Libertad. Based in La Libertad, this Salvadoran-owned and -operated company offers tours all over the country.

Surf Libre (2615-9235, 7729-5628; www.surflibre.com) KM42 Playa El Tunco. Based at relaxed Hostal La Sombra ($) in El Tunco, offers lodging, lessons, surf tours, and packages.

Surf Travel El Salvador (7927-0757, 7238-6362; www.surfestravel.com) KM36 Litoral, Playa El Cocal. Offers custom surf treks and other tours, and lodging at some of the best surf lodges in the country.

Tortuga Surf (7888-6225, 2298-2986; www.elsalvadorsurfer.com) KM43 Playa El Tunco. Roberto Gallardo operates a very pretty mid-range surf lodge in El Tunco and offers several bilingual tours and packages, including some budget trips.

Villa Siguapilapa (7210-9781; www.surfelsal.com) It offers surfing, diving, and combo packages, plus lodging at two beautiful private guesthouses.

WITH FOUR AWESOME BREAKS OFF A BEAUTIFUL BLACK-SAND BEACH, PLAYA SUNZAL BRINGS OUT SERIOUS SURFERS INTENT ON TESTING THEMSELVES IN THE SUN.

Los Cóbanos National Marine Park (2417-6817; www.elsalvadorexperience .com, casadelsol@integra.com.sv) Playas Los Cóbanos. El Salvador is home to the largest Pacific coral reef in Central America, stretching some 21,312 hectares (82 square miles) off the Los Cóbanos shore. The coral is anchored to an archi-pelago of volcanic rocks, black and barely visible above the small waves, cast forth 250,000 years ago in the massive eruption of Ilamatapeque Volcano. These reefs have drawn more building material into their embrace, such as the SS *Douglas,* that set out one sunny February day in 1890 to carry coffee from Acajutla to Germany. Today, it is an undersea museum, with a 7-meter (35-foot) engine tower, jutting up from a mass of rusted winches and equipment, now covered with sea life.

From November to February, when visibility is highest, conditions are perfect for scuba divers, though you can take your chances all year-round. Every dive operation in San Salvador (see that chapter for listings) offers the trip. Scores of fish species, sting rays, medusas, urchins, three types of lobster, and during September and October, nesting green, olive Ridley, and leatherback turtles all populate this deep blue world, where migrating pilot whales relax and fisherman make their living.

The fragile reef is managed by several different national and international groups, who work through **FUNDARRECIFE**. Their offices are two blocks from Los Cóbanos Village Lodge, with a small museum and gift shop, and several guided tours, currently in Spanish only.

Fauna Marina (October to March; $37) Popular three-hour snorkel tour offers the chance to see dozens of species of fish and coral, as well as whales, turtles, dolphins, rays, and other sea life.

Barco Chirrigón (October to March; $23) This 2.5-hour snorkel tour visits the coral-encrusted remains of the SS *Douglas.*

Coral Tour (year-round; $12) A good choice if you want to get wet but visibility is low. You can still get up close and personal with the coral reef.

Caminata Interpretiva (year-round; $7 per person) A three-hour wilderness hike explains more about the region.

Liberacíon de las Tortugas (year-round) Visit Carey Sea Turtle Nursery in Playa El Flor, and if the timing is right, you can help release the adorable babies into the sea.

Santa Rita Protected Natural Area (2411-1280)

KM117, Carretera La Hachadura; 6 kilometers (3.5 miles) northwest of Cara Sucia. Admission: $3. Open: 8 AM–3 PM. The lush tropical lowlands along the Río San Francisco, northwest of Cara Sucia, are protected for several reasons: to maintain the rare semi-humid rainforest ecosystem, to protect the all-important watershed, and most adorably, to protect lots of cute caimans, or crocodiles. *Cocodrylus acutus*, which grows up to 2 meters (6 feet) in length, is relatively rare in El Salvador, but more than 200 of them reside here. The best time to visit is in dry season, when water levels drop in the expansive lagoons, shrinking the toothy creature's habitat. An easy trail has been built on platforms above the swampy area that allows safe viewing and scary photo ops; pets are not allowed, and small children should be kept under strict observation.

Other exotic wildlife include the tropical gar fish, often called a living fossil as it exists, unchanged, since the time of the dinosaurs. Hachadura buses pass close to the entrance.

Walter Thilo Deininger National Park (2345-5684; 2222-8000 reservations; www.corsatur.gob.sv/ingles/deininger.htm) 4 kilometers (2.5 miles) east of La Libertad. Admission: $1; parking 50¢. Open: 7–4. This pretty park preserves a

slender slice of coastal countryside, some 732 hectares (1047 acres) of pristine subtropical and dry tropical forest, criss-crossed with well-maintained trails that offer a glimpse of the rich ecosystems that carpeted more than 70 percent of El Salvador.

As the cool green of winter rainy season gives way to the dry, brittle summer, many key trees lose their leaves. Four of the parks' six streams are usually completely dry by the end of December, when wildlife is much more easily seen. Deer, coyote, anteaters, ocelot, *garrobo* (iguana), and *tepezcuintle* (agouti) are a few of the 25 species of mammals, 27 of reptiles, and 115 of birds, many endangered.

There are four trails, ranging from a short 2.5-kilometer (4-mile) loop that takes in the Enchanted Cave; the Poza El Salto, for swimming; and a mirador (viewpoint) close to the entrance, where you can see kilometers of achingly beautiful coastline. Very ambitious hikers can do the steep, 8-kilometer (5-mile) trail into the mountains. You must hire a local guide. Reservations are highly recommended, although you can usually just show up and find someone to take you around. Bring a picnic lunch to enjoy in the botanical garden. Groups can arrange camping in advance.

To get here, either catch Bus #187 to Comalapa or #540 to Zacatecoluca from La Libertad, or pay $4 for a taxi.

Archaeological Parks Cara Sucia (No phone) 3 kilometers (1.8 miles) south of the Litoral. Admission: Free. This should have been an important archaeological site, a city marking the southernmost outpost of the Cotzumalhuapa culture, based in Chiapas, Mexico, and northern Guatemala. The city was probably founded in about 500 B.C., with inhabitants briefly abandoning the site after the 260 A.D. Ilopango eruption. Only about a meter of ash fell on this far-off site, so they returned shortly afterward and simply swept the center clean. From 650 A.D. to 950 A.D., it was a thriving Cotzumalhuapa town, until the resurgence of the Post-Classic Mayan Empire. Pipil troops rushed into the region, burned the place, and occupied it until 1524. That's when the Spanish arrived, and destroyed it again.

THE MAGNIFICENT ARTWORK OF THE COTZUMALHUAPAS BECAME SO COLLECTIBLE, THAT THE CARA SUCIA ARCHAEOLOGICAL PARK WAS LOOTED AND ALL BUT DESTROYED IN THE 1980S.

The site, rediscovered in the 1800s, became famed worldwide for its incredible artistry. Excavations unearthed some of the most beautiful artifacts ever discovered in El Salvador, including the iconic Jaguar Disk displayed at the Gúzman Museum in San Salvador. And the many thousands of other graceful ceramic and stone pieces uncovered here? Lost.

In one of the great tragedies of Central American archaeology, this site, protected prior to the Civil War, was systematically raided by local families during the chaos of the 1980s. They pockmarked the site with clumsily dug holes, extracting pieces for the international underground collector's market, and destroying everything else. The site's 20 known structures—pyramids, ball parks, and plazas—were all but leveled in the free-for-all, which inspired a 1987 international treaty forbidding such nefarious trade. Today, the site, though well signed from the Litoral (there's no public transport), has almost no infrastructure and little to see. Guards can let you in, but there are no guides through the unimpressive remains, being reclaimed by the dust and grass.

✳ Lodging

El Salvador's West Coast is the best-developed region in the country for international tourists, with all-inclusive resorts, flimsy surf shacks, luxurious lodges, and simple hotels geared to Salvadoran families.

Many hotels for Salvadorans offer two prices, a normal 24-hour rate, and a half-day rate, popular with Salvadoran day-trippers, usually 9 AM–6 PM, and 6 PM to 9 AM. Note that surfing is best March through October, when surf lodges fill and rates rise opposite the normal Central American high season.

La Libertad

La Libertad proper is 32 kilometers (about 20 miles) south of San Salvador, where dozens of budget hotels (many more than are listed here; look around) and surf shacks cluster close to the pier and waves, interspersed with a few decent mid-range options.

The town is centered on a pier where you can buy fish as they're being unloaded from brightly painted boats. To the west is the new Complejo Turistico, with relatively upscale dining and drinking; to the east is the older, agreeably scruffy Tourist Malécon and Playa Obispo, with cheaper ceviches and beer. A short walk brings you to famous Playa la Paz, with great waves and several hotels.

⚓ Brisas del Mar (7815-1778) Playa la Paz. $. Handicap Access: Challenging. Very basic rooms with private cool bath come with hammocks.

ƒ ✳ ⚓ Hotel Malecón (2346-1369) 2 Calle Oeste. Playa Obispo. $$. MC, V, AE. Handicap Access: Challenging. Acceptable mid-range spot right off the tourist Malecón, has a pool and long water slide on grounds populated by garden gnomes. Rooms are small, but open onto a spacious porch.

ƒ ♨ ✳ 🚗 "❢" Hotel Pacific Sunrise (2526-7000; www.hoteleselsalvador .com, reservaciones@hoteleselsalvador.com) Carretera Litoral and Calle El Obispo. $$. AE, MC, V. Handicap Access: No. The most comfortable hotel in La Libertad proper is hard to miss, right at the intersection of the Carretera Comalapa and the Litoral. It offers 30 smallish, antiseptically clean rooms with cable TV, air-conditioning, real hot-water modern bath, and great ocean views from the doubles and family-sized suites with dining area. Singles overlook the huge pool and mountains. There's an open-air restaurant (B, L, D; $$) with very full bar.

ƒ ♨ ✳ La Posada de Don Lito (2335-3166; ravalos@turbonett.com) 5 Avenida Sur, Playa La Paz. $$. AE,

MC, V. Handicap access: No. Solid choice right on the waves, offers worn but comfortable rooms with private bath. It's nothing fancy, but clean with nice color schemes, wood accents, and cool tile floors, all fronted by a shady porch hung with hammocks and a small but well-maintained pool.

❋ **Hotel Renacer** (2352-9323) 4 Calle Poniente, Playa la Paz. $. Handicap Access: No. Four freshly painted cinder-block rooms on the breezy second floor of this simple comedor are a great deal, with new beds and private cool bath. Air-conditioning costs $10 more.

❋ **Hotel Surf** (2101-1755, 7926-3654; netodueñas@yahoo.com) Across from the Complejo Turistico. $. Handicap Access: No. Basic hotel in an old strip mall has huge rooms, thin mattresses, mismatched furnishings, and an eclectic hangout area with hammocks and couches beneath an arched roof. For $10 more you get air-conditioning and cable TV.

Playa San Diego

Playa San Diego is just 6 kilometers (3.7 miles) east of La Libertad proper, served by Bus #80 and #11L (or a US$4 taxi ride), with a long, gorgeous swimming beach, and a few lodging options.

𝄎 **Hostal El Roble** (7252-8498, 2301-6060; elrobleelsalvador.blog spot.com; el roble_elsalvador@yahoo .co.uk) Calle 1. $. Cash only. Handicap Access: Challenging. A complimentary drink welcomes you to this excellent hostel geared to international travelers, with good dorms and a couple of private rooms surrounding a swimming pool. They rent bikes, boards, tents, and offer a community kitchen and basic meals.

🛏 ❋ 🚗 ⁇ **The Laughing Pelican** (7126-8179; 250-240-6606, Canada; www.thelaughingpelican.com, cjra@ shaw.ca) Playa San Diego. $$$$. MC, V, AE. Handicapped Access: Yes. Canadian-operated beachfront bed-and-breakfast is on a beautiful stretch of beach just 10 minutes from La Libertad. Colorful, comfortable, homey rooms come with buffet breakfast, happy hour drink, and more. There's a wellness center onsite, offering massages, hypnotherapy, and other holistic treatments, as well as special packages. Several tours are offered, with a percentage of profits going to help local kids.

𝄎 🚗 **Rancho Alcimar** (7001-5253) Calle 1. $–$$. Cash only. Handicap Access: Challenging. Three tiny but clean, fan-cooled rooms have double beds, shared cool bath, large pool, restaurant service, and dogs. English-speaking owner José Hernandez arranges fishing trips and more.

🚗 ❋ **Rancho Bungalows** (2345-5721) Calle 1. $$. Cash only. Handicap Access: Challenging. Basic, family-run hotel with pleasant gardens has threadbare doubles with air-conditioning and private cool bath, and more spacious bungalows with two bedrooms and rusty kitchens.

𝄎 🚗 ❋ **Rancho San Cristóbal** (7423-8123) Calle 1. $–$$. Cash only. Handicap Access: Challenging. Sturdy, air-conditioned cement rooms surround an overgrown courtyard and pool.

Playa Conchalío

North of La Libertad 5 kilometers (3 miles) is quieter Playa Conchalío, with a long, broad, pale gray beach.

𝄎 🚗 **Entre las Olas** (7955-3760) Boulevard Conchalío and Calle

Almendrera. $. Credit Cards: No. Handicap access: No. This fading beauty offers a breezy second-story mirador with wonderful views, perfect for a seafood dinner, or nap in the hammock. The 18 small, fan-cooled rooms with private cool baths and soft beds are clean, if a bit musty, and surround a pretty courtyard with palm trees and a little pool.

El Cocal and San Blas

✐ ☾ ♨ ✳ ㊙ ⁀ᵀᵀ **Punta Roca** (2346-1753, 2335-3261; www.puntaroca.com.sv, waves@surfingelsalvador.com) Playa Cocal, San Blas. $$$. MC, V. Handicap Access: Yes. This well-known surf lodge, right on the waves, lives up to its reputation. The manicured grounds surrounding four fine pools, offer several levels of accommodations and one of the best seafood restaurants on the coast. The thatch-roofed bungalows are all nicely outfitted with air-conditioning, cable TV, hot water bath, and good art, and the three enormous family suites will sleep five. They arrange surfing excursions all over the coast, as well as tours to the region's top inland sites.

✪ ♨ ✳ ㊙ ⁀ᵀᵀ **Sol Bohemio** (7887-6241, 7887-6241; www.solbohemio.com, godosal@telesal.net) Playa San Blas. $. AE, MC, V. Handicap Access: No. Charming and artsy, this beautifully constructed lodge in the village of San Blas is, indeed, a delightfully bohemian spot. Polished natural wood details, décor involving batik, seashells, river rocks, and bamboo, and ceramic tiles give rooms character. Some are small, but comfortable, with new beds, private baths, and cable TVs; for $10 more you get air-conditioning. Less expensive rooms

overlook the grassy grounds, others are larger and right on the waves.

☾ ♨ ✳ ㊙ ⁀ᵀᵀ **Tropical Surf Lodge Hotel** (2346-2024, 2208-3101; www.tropicalsurflodge.com, reservaciones@tropicalsurflodge.com) Playa El Cocal. $$$. AE, MC, V. Handicap Access: Challenging. This lodge has wonderful rooms, with high ceilings and pleasant paint schemes, outfitted with amenities including cable television, alarm clock, and complimentary cell phone. All rooms include access to the pool, Jacuzzi, pool table, and restaurant, as well as an open kitchen. Or enjoy the good restaurant onsite, serving Salvadoran classics and seafood, overlooking a fine little pool; a second-floor mirador has great ocean views. In addition to surf safaris and the usual regional tours, they offer guided hikes to swimming holes and haunted Cueva la Vaca (Cow Cave) in Playa Plateada.

Playa El Mahajual

This scruffy town on a safe swimming beach is popular with Salvadoran families, though its chaotic expanse of ramshackle shops, thatch-roofed restaurants, and open-air pupuserías might not appeal to you. If you'd like to enjoy a more authentically Salvadoran destination, however, it's cheap.

✐ ☾ ✳ ㊙ **El Pacifico Hotel and Parque Acuático** (2310-6504; www.hotelelpacifico.com, hotelelpacifico@hotmail.com) KM40.5 Carretera Litoral. $–$$. AE, MC, V. Handicap Access: Challenging. Yes, the rooms are tiny and perhaps overpriced, but very clean and heavily air-conditioned, with cable TV. And you're really here for the water park right at your door, with five massive pools, huge water slides, kinetic playground equipment, and a great little **restaurant** (B, L, D;

$$) serving fresh seafood, salads, and lots of fruity cocktails and beer. Day-trippers can visit for $3/2 adult/child.

✪ ⚡ ❋ 🚗 **Hotel and Restaurant Santa Fe** (2310-6508 Litoral, 2345-5327 beach; www.hotelrestaurante santafe.com, juanraarias_44@hotmail .com) Playa El Mahajual KM40.5. $–$$. AE, MC, V. Handicap Access: Challenging. The Santa Fe has two buildings, one right by the beach that costs a few dollars more, and the original on a bluff above town, perhaps five minutes to the shore. They make a stab at New Mexican style, with smooth adobe exteriors accented with a few perfunctory vigas. Rooms aren't fancy, but have slightly New Mexican décor, cable TV, two good restaurants and a guitar-shaped pool.

Playa El Tunco

This is a classic beach town, though the rocky beach doesn't invite swimming. Surfers, however, paddle out to iconic "El Tunco," a supposedly pig-shaped rock providing the perfect backdrop to La Bocana's waves.

✪ ⚡ ❋ "†" **Casa Miramar** (2389-6153; hotelcasamiramardeltunco @hotmail.com) KM41 El Tunco. $–$$. Cash only. Handicap Access: No. Great blufftop spot overlooks the town and waves from a hammock or small pool, with good, air-conditioned rooms, private bath, and shared kitchen.

⚡ ❋ 🚗 "†" **Hotel La Guitarra** (2389-6398; www.surfingeltunco.com, info@ surfingeltunco.com) KM42 El Tunco. $–$$. Cash only. Handicap Access: No. This laid-back lodge, built of river rocks and imbued with a guitar theme, is a relaxed spot with excellent bar and lounge area for playing some pool, having a beer, or surfing the net between sets. The 23 rooms are cool and soothing, with tie-dyed bed-spreads, new mattresses, and private cool baths, but no TVs; pay a few dollars more for air-conditioning. The pool is outstanding, the vibe tranquil, and the soundtrack Bob Marley.

🚗 "†" **Hotel Mangle** (2389-6126; rocasunzal@hotmail.com) KM42 El Tunco. $. AE, MC, V. Handicap Access: No. Operated by plush Roca Sunzal across the street, this very basic, relaxed surf shack has dorms

EL TUNCO IS NAMED FOR THE UNUSUAL ROCK FORMATION JUST OFFSHORE, SUPPOSEDLY SHAPED LIKE A PIG

and private rooms, some with shared bath, a community kitchen, and mangrove views.

 ⨍ ❄ 🛏 "I" **Hotel Mopelia** (2389-6265; www.hotelmopelia_salvador.com) KM42 El Tunco. $–$$. Cash only. Handicap Access: No. Enclosed grounds and great pool are surrounded by several basic but attractive little cabañas with hammock-strung porches, some with private bath. There are two good restaurants onsite, one with a daily special and WiFi, the other with gourmet pizza.

"I" **Papaya's Lodge** (2389-6231; www.papayalodge.com; papayadeltunco@hotmail.com) KM42 Playa El Tunco. $–$$. Handicap Access: Challenging. Overlooking the estuary, this basic surf lodge is known for quality lessons and tours; the attached surf shop rents boards. The dorm beds and simple rooms, some with private bath, don't boast any frills, but there's a shared kitchen and great hangout spot in the mangroves.

⨤ ⨍ ♨ ❄ 🛏 "I" **Roca Sunzal** (2389-6126; www.rocasunzal.com, rocasunzal@hotmail.com) KM42 Carretera Litoral, Playa El Tunco. $$$–$$$$. AE, MC, V. Handicap Access: Challenging. This fairly upscale surf spot snagged the very best spot on the beach: Right in front of El Tunco, where you can watch the waves of La Bocana break. Even if you don't stay, dine in their popular, slightly overpriced **restaurant** (B, L, D; $$–$$$), with those great views, full bar, and excellent seafood, steak, and Salvadoran dishes. Double rooms are simple, though outfitted with air-conditioning, Claro TV, modern hot baths, and safety boxes. Seven new suites, however, are quite luxurious and spacious, with quality furnishings and a sitting area.

The grounds are tidy, with two big pools, and they organize tours and surf lessons.

Roots Camping (7349-4461; fruboza@hotmail.com) KM42 El Tunco. $. Cash only. Super basic spot offers camping in rickety tree houses for $4 a night, $3 if you bring your own tent.

✪ ❄ "I" **Tekuani Kal** (2389-6388, 2389-6387; www.tekuanikal.com, info@tekuanikal.com) KM42.5 Calle Litoral, Playa El Tunco. $$$. AE, MC, V. Handicap Access: No. On a bluff overlooking El Tunco, this is a beautifully crafted hotel, filled with art and muted jewel tones reminiscent of a Rothko painting. There are only six rooms, with remarkable views, lovely tiles, and colorful Guatemalan spreads on the low, Zen-style beds. They're simple, with cool water bath, but the waterfall fountain and private porch make it seem much nicer. The rather elegant **restaurant** (B, L, D; $$–$$$) serves gourmet Salvadoran, such as *garobo en iguashte,* iguana in pumpkin seed sauce, or lobster in coconut and cashews. Breakfast is included, as is guest use of the *temazcal,* a therapeutic steam room. Be sure to check out their bar, Los Siete Venados, designed to look like a local cave, with stars.

 ⨍ 🛏 "I" **Tunco Lodge** (2389-6318; www.tuncolodge.com; tuncolodge@gmail.com) KM42 Playa El Tunco. $–$$. MC, V. Handicap Access: Challenging. Large, ceramic-tiled, freshly painted rooms have good beds and better art, including cool driftwood sculptures that adorn the hammock-strewn patios. Room #8 is like staying in a treehouse. The common area has a shared kitchen, small library, couches, cable TV, fine pool, and a computer for guests.

Playa Sunzal

With four breaks and soft sands on a perfect beach, it's no surprise it's home to some of the finest lodging on the coast. Also check out La Curva de Don Gere (Where to Eat).

⊘ ⌀ ⛱ ❈ 🚗 "🍴" **Paradizo Azul Resort** (2389-6135; www.paradizo azul.com, paradizoazul@yahoo.com) KM44 Litoral. $$$. AE, MC, V. Handicapped Access: No. No children under 10. This exceptional boutique property is geared to surfers, but will satisfy any discriminating traveler with its five spectacular suites. Crafted from the finest imported hardwoods, slates, and tiles, they have been elegantly furnished with wonderful colors, great lighting, and views from the huge windows. Attractively landscaped grounds are centered on a deep blue infinity pool. Across the street is ⊘ **Kayu Surf Bar** (B, L, D; $$), with a walkway down to the sand. Four famous surf breaks are right off the coast, and the owners can arrange lessons and active tours, such as enduro rides, snorkeling, and guided hikes.

⌀ ⌀ ⛱ ❈ 🚗 "🍴" **Casa de Mar Hotel & Villas** (2389-6284, 2223-7966; www.casademarhotel.com, info@ casademarhotel.com) KM44 Litoral. $$$$. AE, MC, V. Handicap Access: No. Spread out across steep and attractively landscaped grounds, 11 unique bungalows offer family-style accommodation. Most have multiple bedrooms, with a separate dining area; the largest are like small homes. All are air conditioned, with hot water baths and private wooden porches where you can enjoy gorgeous views over the beautiful beach and excellent pool area. The onsite, open-air **Café Sunzal** (B, L, D; $$–$$$$) is well known for its creative and rather upscale seafood dishes, and has free Wifi access (rooms do not).

⌀ ❈ 🚗 "🍴" **Las Olas** (2245-2614, 7888-8642 English; www.akwaterra .com, akwaterra@gmail.com) KM45 Calle Litoral. $$$. V. Handicap Access: No. Atop the headlands overlooking Playa Sunzal, this laid-back surf lodge offers cliff-top lodging decorated like your hippy friends' college dorm. Tie-dyed bedspreads and cur-

A HANDFUL OF CLIFF-TOP HOTELS, INCLUDING LAS OLAS NEAR EL ZONTE, MAY LACK SANDY BEACHES BUT DO OFFER REMARKABLE SALT WATER POOLS, REFILLED WITH EVERY HIGH TIDE—PERHAPS WITH SMALL FISH.

tains, Indian arts and crafts, polished wooden floors, and colorful paint schemes all conspire to make this one relaxed spot to chill between waves. Some rooms connect through a shared bath. There's no beach—you're on a rocky point—but they've constructed saltwater swimming pools among the cliffs, which refill at high tide with salt water and colorful fish. A regular pool, restaurant, and hammock-strewn lounge areas are up top. It's owned by Akwaterra, one of the country's best-known tour operators.

Playa El Palmarcito

The village of Palmarcito, with access to a reliable break, has at least two secluded hotels.

El Palmarcito (7942-4819; www.el palmarcito.com; molina_alex@hotmail .com) KM50 Litoral. $–$$. Cash only. Handicap Access: No. A great deal, this spot has clean, basic rooms and a mellow little restaurant right on the sand, with relatively inexpensive packages that include meals and surf tours.

⚲ 🛏 **Hotel Ver Mar** (2335-7318, 7265-2390) KM50 El Litoral. $. Cash only. Handicap Access: No. In the village, this family-owned budget hotel has five cleanish rooms with thin mattresses, shared cool bath, and sketchy-looking pool. The beach is two minutes away, and it's only $5.

Playa El Zonte

La Casa de Frida (7797-3270; www .lacasadefrida.com; info@lacasade frida.com) KM53.5 El Zonte. $. Cash only. Cute little hostel, decorated with reproductions of Frida Kahlo's paintings, offers four-bed dorm rooms and a restaurant.

⚲ 🛏 ✳ 🚗 "🍽" **Horizonte Surf Resort** (7722-3237, 7922-6056, 2323-0099;

www.horizontesurfresort.com, hori zonte@micorreomepaga.com) KM53.5 El Zonte. $$$$. Credit Cards: No. Handicap Access: Challenging. The plushest hotel on El Zonte is fine, if aesthetically a tad odd; cinder-block bungalows have been left unpainted, giving the place a rather unfinished feel. But they're large and comfortable, with air-conditioning and private porches, surrounding landscaped grounds with a wonderful pool. Most people come on multiple-day, all-inclusive surf packages that include meals and surf tours, but you can get better rates.

✪ ⚲ ✳ 🚗 "🍽" **Esencia Nativa** (7737-8879; www.esencianativa.com, esencianativa@yahoo.com) KM53.5 El Zonte. $–$$. Credit Cards: No. Handicap Access: No. This relaxed, colorfully painted surf lodge is your basic tropical paradise, with thatch-roofed buildings, shaded hammocks, above-average dorms, private air-conditioned rooms, great pool, surf shop, and the restaurant is right on the waves. Bilingual owner Alex Naboa, by the way, was recommended to me more than any other surf guide in the country; he's either the best or the friendliest.

Rancho Palos (7525-0047) KM52 El Zonte. $. Cash only. Handicap Access: No. You're here to surf, and this lonely little lodge in the quiet village of El Zonte can help. Follow the signs to the shady, unpaved side street, where you'll find the simple building with four basic rooms and shared cool baths, arranged around a common area with kitchen, hammocks, and shell art.

West of Playa El Zonte

The winding coastal road becomes even more beautiful—Big Sur beautiful—as the beach towns thin, where jungled mountains draw close and steep to the froth-streaked Pacific. There's not much between El Zonte and Acajutla, save a few perfect *playas* in the middle of nowhere.

⫪ ⚐ ❋ ⚑ "⫯" **K59 Surf Lodge** (7894-9466, 2300-5490; k59surftours.com, eschleusz@k59surftours, comreservations@k59surftours) KM59 Litoral. $$$$. AE, MC, V. Handicap Access: Challenging. You'll only be staying at this relaxed pair of beach houses on an all-inclusive package with K59 tours. In addition to the chill, three-bedroom homes furnished for comfort and relaxation, the price gains you boat access to two little-surfed waves, two pools, all your meals, and tours to other surf spots and land-locked sites around the country.

⫪ ⚐ **Wicho Dominguez** (No phone) KM67.5 Carretera Litoral, Playa La Perla. $. Credit Cards: No. Handicapped Access: No. Special Features: Surfing and seafood. At the *bocana*, or mouth, of the Río La Perla, there is a wave. And next to the wave, there is this simple, two-room, wooden hotel, with a small pool, shared bath, and a great seafood restaurant. Smack dab in the middle of nowhere, this might be your own personal paradise. They don't rent boards, but they do make a great seafood soup.

⫪ ⚐ ❋ ⚐ **Mizata Resort** (7890-4751; www.mizataresort.com, info@mizataresort.com) KM86.5, Playa Mizata. $$$. AE, MC, V. Handicapped Access: No. There's really only one reason to come all the way out to Playa Mizata, and that's to surf. A few beachgoers from Sonsonate show up on Sundays, when a handful of stands set up selling seafood; otherwise, it's just you and a few fishing families. Five huge rooms have inspiring surf murals above the two comfortable

queen-sized beds, large bathrooms, Claro televisions, and—fronting the two upstairs rooms—a porch with great ocean views. There's also a deep, raised pool. The onsite restaurant serves international dishes, and staff can arrange fishing trips, surf classes, and other tours. To get here, take Bus 281 "Mizata" from Sonsonate; the resort is about 1 kilometer (0.6 mile) from the highway.

⫪ ⚐ **La Parlama Beach Lodge** (2298-6558; 7883-2700; www.elsalvadorbeachlodge.com, jrrengif070@yahoo.com) Barra Salada. $$. V. Handicapped Access: No. La Palarma is a laid-back lodge on Barra Salada, a lagoon fronted by a sandy beach between the Río Banderas and Río Apancoya. The gray sands are laying grounds for the palarma (olive Ridley sea turtles) and fishermen ply the rich waters for fresh seafood served onsite. Simple, fan-cooled rooms are clean and well maintained, but you'll probably spend most of your time hanging out on the breezy second-floor terrace overlooking the waves, or at the courtyard pool.

Playa Salinitas and Los Cóbanos
South of Acajutla, these neighboring beaches of coarse, golden sand are separated by a vast cultural divide. Salinitas is home to two exclusive resorts, one all inclusive option offering discos, fine dining, and unlimited drinks, the other a great golf course. Just 15 minutes by car (or 10 minutes on foot) is the very traditional, wood-framed fishing village of Los Cóbanos, with brightly hued boats and 25¢ pupusas. Right offshore is the largest, most important coral reef on the Central American Pacific, teeming with sea turtles, migrating whales, and huge schools of fish.

There's an eco-battle brewing, between the caretakers of **Los Cóbanos National Marine Park** and the resorts, over the exploitation of loopholes in new laws designed to protect the fragile marine environment. These luxury properties, however, bring more tourists, and much-needed dollars, into El Salvador than every other business listed in this chapter combined.

No matter where you stay, it's beautiful. **Playa Los Cóbanos**, fronting the rustic fishing village, has a handful of even cheaper hotels, basically dingy cement boxes with sagging beds and fans. The main beach is primarily for boats, so head west on the dirt road, and around jungled **Punta El Faro** to the soft blonde sands of **Playa del Amor**, with a safe swimming hole close to the point. Dirt roads continue to the resort beaches, which are public by law. If you're staying at the resorts, walk east to check out the village and its pretty shore.

✦ ⚐ **Casa Garrobo** (2469-2401; www.casagarrobo.com; hotelanahuac @tikal.dk) Playa del Amor. $. Cash only. Handicap Access: No. Guesthouse on empty Playa del Amor offers a dorm for backpackers, sleeping five, and a private double with bath. It has a cute pool, a community kitchen, and a great covered hangout area with hammocks and sofas. Hotel Anahúac in Juayúa provides inexpensive private transport and tours.

✪ ⚐ ✳ ⚐ ⁱ⁰ Los Cóbanos Village Lodge (2420-5248 7887-1308; www .loscobanos.com.sv) Playa Los Cóbanos. $–$$. AE, MC, V. Handicapped Access: No. In the heart of the fishing village, this airy, sky-blue lodge is constructed of natural materials, with seashell and bamboo décor. Two

top-floor rooms with refrigerators and small living areas offer views over fishing boats bobbing in the bay; dorms downstairs are a good deal. The walled-in courtyard has a great little pool, with banks of shaded hammocks for relaxing, and an onsite restaurant. Or, just open the gate and grab pupusas or fresh fish at any of the rickety stands lining the shore. It's used primarily by **El Salvador Divers** (www.elsalvadordivers.com), and also organizes fishing trips and kayak tours.

⚐ ⚐ ♨ ✳ ⚐ ⁱ⁰ **Decameron** (2209-3100; www.decameron.com, royal .salinitas@decameron.com.sv) Playa Salinitas. $$$$. AE, MC, V. Handicapped Access: Yes. This is El Salvador's premier all-inclusive resort, with a quasi-Mayan theme, nice beach, and 280 perfect rooms. It's not as plush as luxury resorts in, say, Cancún, but the vibe is similar and it's much less expensive. Eleven buildings overlook the pool complex and golden beach, surrounded by palapas, lounge chairs, bars, and several restaurants. Avoid the buffet; instead, make reservations in the morning (inconvenient, as check-in is 3 PM) to dine at Maya Grill Steakhouse or Restaurant Pastafari, with Jamaican and Italian cuisine, but no flying spaghetti. Bring your own cup to the resort—alcohol is unlimited, but served in thimble-sized portions. It offers a full-service spa with a *temazcal*, or Mayan-style steam bath, Jacuzzi, gym, tennis courts, sail boats, kayaks, and a disco to dance the night away. The bilingual staff arranges activities for kids, and tours all over the country, and there's a **dive center** right onsite.

✳ ⚐ ⁱ⁰ Hotel y Restaurante Marsolio (2420-5602, 7493-0981; restaurante.marsolie@yahoo.es) Punta

Remedios. $$. V. Handicap Access: Challenging. At the village entrance, the best restaurant in town now offers five small, recently refurbished rooms, with white-and-rose color schemes, pedestal beds, air-conditioning, WiFi, and porches. Enjoy the excellent seafood ✪ **restaurant** (B, L, D; $–$$$), as owner and chef Margarita Dueñas de Ramírez is locally revered for her *langosta rellena,* shrimp-stuffed lobster, and *filete a la Veracruzana,* fish simmered in a spicy tomato sauce.

✄ ∮ ♨ ❄ ⌂ **Las Veraneras** (2420-5000, 2205-9191; www.veraneras resort.com, info@veranerasresort .com) Playa Salinitas. $–$$. AE, MC, V. Handicapped Access: Yes. You're here to golf the best course in El Salvador. It's world-class in dry season, when the water features of this 7000-yard, par 72 course—rivers, lagoons—sparkle like gems against the lush and varied terrain. It's still good in rainy season, but doesn't always drain well. Villas are also nice, geared to families, with kitchenettes, cable TVs, and private patios; larger cottages have multiple bedrooms and full kitchens. The pools have slides and playground equipment, and you can rent bikes and ponies. The only drawback is the beach, which is only so-so; just stroll a few hundred meters to Decameron's nicer stretch of sand. This is a private club, but non-members are welcome. You must have reservations.

Playa El Metalío
This deep gray swimming beach is a bit scruffy, but surrounded by lush vegetation and popular with Salvadoran families. It's 1 kilometer (0.6 mile) from the Litoral, where buses between Sonsonate and La Hachadura drop you off.

∮ ❄ ⌂ **Hotel y Restaurant Vista al Mar** (2469-9041; vistaalmar2007@ yahoo.com) Playa Metalío. $–$$. Cash only. Handicap Access: No. This basic spot has simple rooms with TV and a private bath; air-conditioning is a few dollars more. The pool is OK, with a few hammocks, and the onsite seafood **restaurant** (B, L, D; $$) outstanding.

∮ ❄ ⌂ **Villa Esmeralda** (2457-5500; www.resortvillaesmeralda.com, gerencia@resortvillaesmeralda.com) Playa Metalío. $$. Cash only. Handicapped Access: Yes. Metalío's best hotel is a modern, two-story stuccoed number surrounded by palm trees, right on the beach. Rooms are simple but clean, with air-conditioning, DirecTV, and private cool bath. Two "suites" are larger, with a living area, dining table, and refrigerator. The pools are nice, and a second-story mirador is a great spot for watching the soft, swimming surf roll in.

Barra Santiago
This long peninsula of dove-gray sand fronting a mangrove estuary is one of the most remote beaches in El Salvador. There's a bus twice daily, though hardier souls could be dropped off on the Litoral and wait for pickup trucks. Bring groceries, as there's not much out here.

Lodging is for the most part in guesthouses, usually arranged through budget hotels on the Ruta de las Flores and in San Salvador, but it's also home to one of the country's very best hotels.

✪ ✄ ∮ ♨ ❄ ⌂ ⁞¶⁞ **La Cocotera Resort & Ecolodge** (2245-3691, 7359-5238; www.lacocoteraresort .com, operaciones.lacocotera@ gmail.com) Barra Santiago. $$$$. AE,

MC, V. Handicap Access: Challenging. This outstanding ecolodge on the endless beach may be a bit upscale for folks really watching their carbon footprint, but it's fantastic. Six spacious palapa-topped bungalows are hewn from natural materials, with exquisitely crafted bamboo detailing and gorgeous solar-heated showers with smooth black rocks all around. Private porches overlook the unchlorinated, palm-shaded pool and wide beach. Prices are steep, but include all your meals. They also work with the local sea turtle preservation program, and in season, you can see mothers lay their eggs in the sand. They also have a reintroduction program for red macaws. The lodge arranges kayak and birdwatching tours, as well as fishing trips.

✳ 🚗 **Capricho Beach House** (2260-2481; www.ximenasguesthouse.com, ximenas.guesthouse@gmail.com) Barra Santiago. $. AE, MC, V. Handicapped Access: No. Long-standing lodge geared to international backpackers is operated by Ximena's

A FUTURE POOL SHARK IN THE VILLAGE OF BARRA DE SANTIAGO GETS AN EARLY START, LEARNING HIS MOVES.

Guesthouse in San Salvador. Though it's located quite close to the bus station, they do not accept drop-ins, so contact them in advance. Rooms are colorful and comfortable, with private bath and air-conditioning; there's a dorm for travelers on a budget, as well as restaurant service and a shared kitchen. Rooms have shared porches, there are plenty of hammocks, and they offer turtle tours, estuary trips, and surf lessons at the tip of the peninsula, with an uncrowded break.

✴ Where to Eat

With the exception of La Libertad and Playa El Tunco, both of which have a small selection of independent eateries, the best restaurants are attached to hotels. Be sure to try the Salvadoran specialty, *mariscada,* a cream-based seafood stew.

Note that there aren't many markets in the beach towns, and finding fruits and vegetables is particularly difficult.

DINING OUT

La Libertad
The classic place to eat is the scroungy Tourist Malecón, serving cold beer, amazing ceviche, and fresh fish cooked to your specification. A dozen sturdier, perhaps cleaner options are scattered among the budget hotels along Playa La Paz. Two blocks inland, the chaotic downtown has market stands, pupuserías, and simple eateries.

The government recently inaugurated a new option, however, the **Complejo Turistico**, unmissable beneath gleaming white tents. Spotlessly clean, with great security, it has a handpicked selection of fairly fine dining options, with gleaming chrome furnishings, colorful tablecloths, and glass stemware. Even if you're on a budget, stop at ✪ **La Michoacana** (2341-0230; L, D; $; cash only), for all-natural fruit *paletas*, or popsicles.

Acajutla Seafood (2346-2110; www.acajutlaseafood.com) Complejo Turistico. $–$$$. V, MC, AE. Cuisine: Seafood, Steak. Children's Menu: Yes. Serving: B, L, D. Handicap Access: Yes. Reservations: No. Excellent seafood chain anchors the Complejo Turistico with exquisite seafood cocktails, *spaghetti la marinera,* seafood pasta, and *cazuela Acajutla,* a sort of seafood casserole, all with awesome views over the pier. The bar is open relatively late, until 11 PM, which makes it the most likely spot for nightlife in town.

There are several other top-end restaurants due to open here as well, including famed **La Pena** (2312-9099; www.lapena.com; L, D; $$–$$$$; V, MC), serving tasty *tortillas con enredo,* stuffed with cheese and loroco, *mariscada,* and shrimp stuffed with mushrooms and cheese. It also has a full bar.

Karla's (2301-4649) Playa la Paz. $–$$$. Credit Cards: No. Cuisine: Seafood, Salvadoran. Children's Menu: No. Serving: B, L, D. Handicap Access: No. Reservations: No. Much loved, two-story restaurant with wonderful ocean views offers excellent seafood at appropriate prices. But show up at lunchtime and you'll enjoy a set meal for $2.50; you can eat it in the restaurant, but will need to order it at the kitchen (right across the street) and carry it to the table yourself.

✪ **Fisherman's Beach Club** (2235-3272, 2262-0246; www.fishermans beachclub.com) Playa Las Flores, 2 kilometers (1.2 miles) southeast of La Libertad, near Playa San Diego. $$$. V, MC, AE. Cuisine: Seafood. Children's Menu: Yes. Serving: B, L (open until 6 PM daily). Handicap Access: Yes. Reservations: No. Beach Club is surrounded with slender Mediterranean arches, which frame the view over San Diego's long, pearl gray beach rather elegantly. Within, lovely gardens cradle three sparkling pools, a tennis court, and a restaurant. Start with La Libertad's signature *ceviche de colores,* fresh fish marinated with purple onions, red tomatoes, and yellow and green peppers. The bar specializes in icy frozen beverages, such as the *tropical de coco,* with coconut and condensed milk. The beach club is open until 6 PM. Day passes cost $3 for adults and are free for kids under

---

MOUNTAIN LODGES

Close to Barra de Santiago, **El Imposible National Park** has excellent cabins, 13 kilometers (8 miles) from the Litoral; see the Western El Salvador chapter.

🚗 **Finca San Jorge** (2284-1353; www.anades.org; alba@anades.org) San Julián, Sonsonate. $–$$. Handicap Access: No. About 6 kilometers (3.7 miles) from San Julián, Sonsonate, this agrotourism project is run by a nonprofit on an old balsam farm where you can watch sap processed into fragrant beauty products. Cabins are small and simple, but offer access to waterfalls, swimming holes, and viewpoints.

12 Monday through Thursday. On weekends, it's $6 per person.

Punta Roca (2346-2110; www .puntaroca.com.sv) Playa La Paz, La Libertad, 4 Calle Poniente and Rotulo de Punta Roca. $–$$$. V, MC, AE. Cuisine: Seafood, Steak. Children's Menu: Yes. Serving: B, L, D. Handicap Access: Yes. Reservations: No. Landmark restaurant sprawls across the shoreline, with two open-air floors overlooking Playa La Paz and surfers doing their thing. Though there are plenty of salads, seafood cocktails, and other light dishes, specialties are geared toward surfers, who'll get their money's worth with fried fish smothered in creamy garlic and mushroom sauce, or the fish pizza, topped with mozzarella cheese, tomato sauce, and fresh oregano. Big breakfasts are also a deal.

El Cocal and San Blas

Bello Sol (2300-4470, 2346-0475; hotelbellosol@gmail.com) Playa San Blas. $$. V, MC, AE. Cuisine: Salvadoran. Children's Menu: Yes. Serving: B, L, D. Handicapped Access: Challenging. Reservations: No. Grab a hammock beneath the palms, and enjoy delectable, traditional dishes, beginning with the *coctel bello sol,* a ceviche of clams, shrimp, and calamari. The specialty is seafood, such as the spicy shrimp-stuffed *filete Veracruz,* but the menu also includes *arrozes* (stir-fried rice), pastas, and *churrasco al carbon,* a grilled meat platter. You can hang out all day, enjoying the beach and two pools, with a $10 day pass, or even spend the night in their simple, smallish, air-conditioned rooms ($–$$), with new beds and cable TV.

La Dolce Vita (2328-0877; www .viaroma.com.sv) Playa San Blas. $$. Credit Cards: No. Cuisine: Italian. Children's Menu: Yes. Serving: B, L, D (closes 6:30 PM on weekdays). Handicapped Access: Challenging. Reservations: No. Next door, this Italian-owned restaurant serves up Mediterranean-inspired seafood dishes. Try the *mariscos gratinados,* seafood prepared in a creamy sauce of white wine and brandy, spiced up with purple onions. Save room for the tiramasu. The restaurant also rents three large, tiled **rooms** ($$), with

FISHERMAN'S BEACH CLUB ON PLAYA LAS FLORES, JUST SOUTH OF LA LIBERTAD, IS A FINE PLACE TO RELAX OVER A DELICIOUS MEAL.

good beds, cable TV, and private cool bath.

Playa El Tunco

Restaurante La Bocana (2389-6238; www.restaurantelabocana.com) KM42, Playa El Tunco. $$. Cuisine: Seafood. Serving: B, L, D. Reservations: No. Popular seafood restaurant overlooking the waves offers fine views of the surfers and good-value cuisine. There's an even nicer one in El Palmar (2323-2840; KM50.5 Litoral), in a breezy palapa also overlooking the sea.

Restaurante Erika and Bam Bar (2389-6054; www.restauranteerika .com) KM42, Playa El Tunco. $–$$. Credit Cards: No. Cuisine: Seafood. Children's Menu: No. Serving: B, L, D. Handicapped Access: No. Reservations: No. At the mouth of the estuary, this palapa-topped spot with fine views from the second floor serves seafood for folks on a budget, as well as huge breakfasts. It stays open until midnight on weekends.

West of Playa El Tunco

✪ **Hotel-Restaurante La Curva de Don Gere** (2389-6297, 2389-6293; lacurvadedongere.ventas@gmail.com) KM45.5 Calle Litoral, Playa El Sunzal. $–$$$$. V, MC, AE. Cuisine: Seafood, gourmet Salvadoran. Serving: B, L, D. Handicapped Access: Yes. Atop a rocky bluff crashed by waves, this well-known seafood restaurant surrounds several fine swimming pools, including a saltwater pool at the bottom of the cliffs. The menu has a few basic items, but specialties such as crab claws, black oysters, river shrimp, and fresh fish prepared several ways are on the pricey side. The restaurant also boasts three of the finest **rooms** ($$$$) on

the coast: The over-the-top Blue Room is the best, its plush half-moon couch facing an entire semicircular wall of windows that invite the ocean in. Heirloom-quality king-sized beds, a huge Jacuzzi tub (but no hot water), air-conditioning, and a large TV complete the flowing scene. The other rooms were smaller, but just as plush; #3 has a private terrace.

Café Iguana (No phone) KM51. $$–$$$. Credit Cards: No. Cuisine: Salvadoran. Children's Menu: Yes. Serving: B, L, D (closes at 5:30 PM). Handicapped Access: Challenging. Reservations: No. At the top of this mirador *turistico*, with trail access to the sea, a handful of simple restaurants take advantage of the view. The sturdiest of these is Café Iguana, with an extensive menu, big screen television, and well-stocked bar. Not a bad place to stop and stretch your legs.

✪ **Costa Brava** (2302-6068; www .costabravazonte.com, info@costa bravapacifico.com) KM53.5, Playa El Zonte. $–$$$. Credit Cards: No. Cuisine: Mediterranean. Serving: B, L, D. Handicapped Access: Challenging. Reservations: For groups. On a bluff overlooking El Zonte's waves, this restaurant gets raves for its delicious Spanish and Italian cuisine. There are several kinds of breakfasts, but the real magic comes later, with dishes such as *papas alli olli,* with homemade mayonnaise, lentil soup, tuna *sofrito,* Spanish omelets, several Mediterranean salads, and of course, paella. They also serve a variety of espresso beverages in the lovely open-air restaurant, as well as big licuados, several wines, sangria, and *tinto de verano,* wine mixed with lemonade. Day visitors can use the tiny pool and hammocks, or head straight for the beach; Costa Brava arranges surf lessons and boards as well. Or stay the night—they also offer seven simple, fan-cooled cement **rooms** ($), freshly painted with wood accents and modern cold bath.

Restaurant K-59 (2323-4445) KM59 Carretera Litoral. $–$$$. Cuisine: Salvadoran. Serving: B, L, D (closes at 6 PM). Handicap Access: Challenging. Reservations: No. This basic roadside restaurant overlooking a stunning stretch of crashing waves and cliffsome coastline is a landmark stop for really excellent seafood. Don't let the open-air construction fool you, dishes such as lobster thermidor, seafood cocktails, fresh oysters, and other excellent dishes are available. Simpler, less expensive offerings are also in abundance, such as the *plato de chorizo,* an appetizer with sausage, avocado, and cheese, which goes perfectly with a beer and the view of the surfers below. Look for it after the first tunnel heading north on the Carretera Litoral.

Hotel y Restaurante Playa Dorada (2415-8973, 7247-7687) KM79 Litoral, Playa Bahía Dorada. $–$$. Credit Cards: No. Cuisine: Salvadoran, Seafood. Serving: B, L, D. Handicap Access: Challenging. Reservations: For rooms. Overlooking a long, broad, smoky-gray swimming beach just half an hour from Sonsonate, this isolated restaurant offers inexpensive seafood, *bocas* (bar snacks), and cold beer in a second-floor dining room with fine views. It's totally local, no surfing waves here, but the relaxed vibe and inexpensive day pass (just $1) make it delightful. They also offer seven surprisingly pretty rooms, painted cool blue, each with a double bed, air-conditioning,

and private (a bit smelly) cool bath. Bus 281 to Mizata from Sonsonate can drop you off at the signed exit from the Litoral; it's about a 1-kilometer (0.62-mile) walk.

CAFÉS Balsalmo Café (7886-0945; balsamocafe@yahoo.com) San Julian. Quiet café in the balsam trees offers $2 tours of the plantation; open Sundays only at 11 AM, or by reservation.

Dalé Dalé Dalé (No phone) Central El Tunco. B, L, D. $. Cash only. Cute coffee shop offers espresso beverages, bagels, breakfasts, smoothies, sandwiches, and other light fare. Closes at 6 PM.

✪ **La Panadería** (No phone) Central El Tunco. B, L, D. $. Cash only. Great Irish-owned bakery and café was still under a tent when I visited, but look for a more permanent "downtown" location for its excellent bread, pastries, sandwiches, and homemade peanut butter and jams.

PIZZA Hotel Mopelia (2389-6265; www.hotelmopelia_salvador.com) KM42 El Tunco. $–$$. Cash only. A gourmet pizzeria at this surf hotel also delivers.

PUPUSARÍAS While it didn't have a name, there was a stand set up close to Los Cóbanos Village Inn selling shrimp pupusas that were out of this world.

✪ **Pupusodromo del Puerto de la Libertad** (No phone) Avenida Simón Bolivar and Calle Gerardo Barrios. B, L, D. $. Cash only. Overlooking La Libertad's clean, kid-friendly central park, this fine pupusodromo, a bank of pupuserías and juice bars, is a great place to eat and is open late.

El Zunzalito (No phone) KM45 Calle Litoral, Playa El Sunzal. B, L, D. $. Cash only. Handicapped access. Small store and restaurant near the break serves pupusas and other inexpensive food.

✱ Selective Shopping

There aren't really any handicraft shops on the coast, though some of the big resorts sell souvenirs. It's best to do grocery shopping in one of the major cities–San Salvador, Sonsonate (see the Western El Salvador chapter), or La Libertad. Otherwise, stores are small, selection is limited, and prices are high. Beach towns also lack ATMs, so have plenty of cash on hand.

Mall El Faro, on the Litoral at the entrance to La Libertad, is the best place to shop before heading to the beaches, with a large SuperSelectos grocery store, an ATM, and even a ghost story; be on the lookout for two shimmering nuns who once lived in a convent onsite. **Dispensa Familiar** (Calle Gerardo Barrios), in the chaotic heart of town, a couple of blocks from the beach and surrounded by **market stalls**, is a cheaper grocer. At the turnoff to Los Cóbanos, on the Litoral, there's a 24-hour **BAC ATM** at the Texaco.

✱ Special Events

International surfing competitions are held throughout the surf season, March through October.

May: **Fiestas Cara Sucia** (May 1–4) Cara Sucia honors its patron, San José.

Fiestas Acajutla (May 22–23) Port town honors the Sacred Trinity.

August: **La Libertad Gastronomic Festival** (last weekend in August) Celebration of seafood in El Salvador's most popular fishing town.

October: ✪ **Procession of the Archangel Raphael** (October 23 and 24) After a devastating 1932 explosion of a dynamite shipment all but destroyed La Libertad, a single unharmed box was discovered in the charred wreckage, containing an image of the Archangel Raphael. Though destined for another church, the Fisherman's Association successfully lobbied to keep him here. Each year, at 4:30 AM on October 23 (the anniversary of the image's discovery), Saint Rafael is taken around the harbor in a procession of boats as fireworks explode.

November: **Fiestas Cara Sucia** (November 3–7) Cara Sucia honors its patron, San Martín de Porres.

December: **Fiestas La Libertad** (December 7–8) Surf spot honors its patron, the Virgin of the Immaculate Conception.

Eastern Beaches 3

Alvaro Calero

EASTERN BEACHES

A WALK ON THE WILD SIDE

Surfers call this the Wild Este, where fishing villages overlook beautiful beaches and fantastic waves. It remains little explored by most international travelers, most of whom head west and miss its sun-drenched sands and mangrove-forested bays.

Salvadorans, however, prize their pretty east coast, and bring their families to long, palm-fringed peninsulas, strung with hotels and hammocks that sway in the salty breeze. Or to explore, in small boats, calm, jade green estuaries and gulfs, protecting islands where birds and sea turtles nest. Of course, everyone is welcome to enjoy these treasures, described in this chapter from west to east.

Begin with the beaches close to San Salvador, perfect for those in a rush; perhaps the upscale resorts of isolated **Playa Pimental** and **Las Hojas**, offering every comfort on an otherwise undeveloped shore.

Or join crowds of capitaleños on the long, festive peninsula of popular Costa del Sol, with its broad, pearl gray beaches lined with hotels and restaurants for travelers on any budget. Its family-friendly surf, perfect for swimming, is only half the appeal; on the other side of the cape is lush **Jaltepeque Estuary**, filled with islands and wildlife galore.

More adventurous souls will continue east, past the busy market town of **Zacatecoluca**, and across the mighty **Río Lempa**, a living border that has divided this country since Mayan and Lenca times. Linguists will notice that place names in the east are remnants of the softer Ulua tongue, such as the region's next major city and department capital, busy **Usulután**. Though these two inland towns have little to offer most tourists, other than their bus terminals, banks and shops, they are ancient places.

To the south, an immense complex of wetlands and tropical forests is being slowly but surely protected. It is centered on **Bahía de Jiquilisco**, Bay of Stars, an important wildlife sanctuary of mangrove islands and long, white, pristine Pacific beaches. Adjacent to the enormous estuary are **Changuantique Reserve** and **Nacuchiname National Park**, where spider monkeys still prowl.

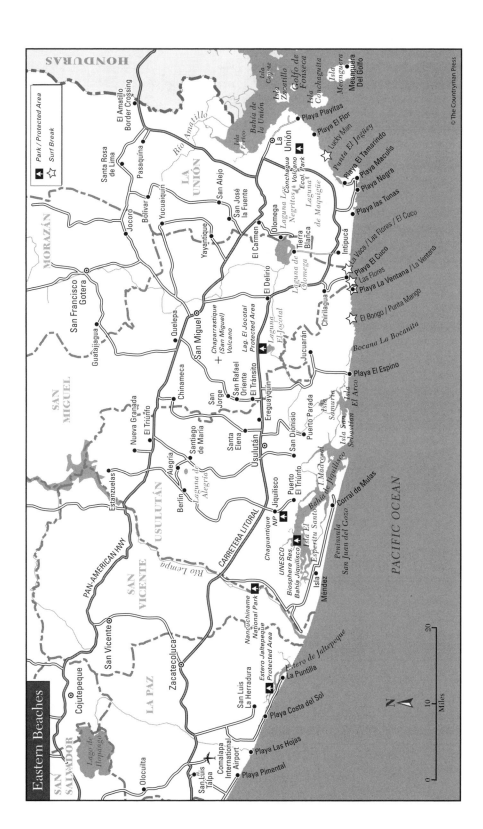

Eastern Beaches

HONDURAS

SAN SALVADOR

MORAZÁN

LA UNIÓN

SAN MIGUEL

USULUTÁN

SAN VICENTE

LA PAZ

PACIFIC OCEAN

Park / Protected Area
Surf Break

Golfo de Fonseca

Isla Coyote
Isla Zacatillo
Isla Conchaguita
Isla Meanguera
Meanguera Del Golfo
Bahía de la Unión
Isla Perico

El Amatillo Border Crossing
Santa Rosa de Lima
Pasaquina
San Alejo
San José la Fuente
La Unión
Río Amatillo

Playa Playitas
Playa El Flor
Lucky Man
Punta El Jagüey
Playa El Tamarindo
Playa Maculís
Playa Negra
Playa las Tunas

Negros / Volcano
Conchagua Volcano
Eco. Park
Laguna de Maquigüe

Bolívar
Yucuaiquín
Jocoro
Yayantique
El Carmen
Olomega

Tierra Blanca
Intipucá
La Vaca / Las Flores / El Cuco
Playa El Cuco
Las Flores
Playa La Ventana / La Ventana
El Bongo / Punta Mango

San Francisco Gotera
Guatajiagua
Quelepa
San Miguel

Chaparrastique (San Miguel) Volcano
Lag. El Jocotal Protected Area
El Delirio
Laguna de Olomega
Chirilagua

Laguna El Jocotal

Bocana La Bocanita

Chinameca
San Rafael Oriente
San Jorge
El Tránsito
Eregüayquín
Jucuarán
Puerto Parada
Playa El Espino

Nueva Granada
El Triunfo
Santiago de María
Santa Elena
Usulután
San Dionisio

Isla Samuria
Isla San Sebastián
Isla El Arco

Estanzuelas
Alegría
Berlín
Laguna de Alegría
Jiquilisco
Puerto El Triunfo
Chaguantique

Isla San Madresal
Bahía de Jiquilisco
Corral de Mulas

Jiquilisco NP
UNESCO Biosphere Res.
Bahía Jiquilisco
Isla El Jobal
Isla Méndez
Península San Juan del Gozo

San Vicente
Nancuchiname National Park
Estero Jaltepeque Protected Area

Río Lempa
CARRETERA LITORAL
PAN-AMERICAN HWY

Zacatecoluca
San Luis La Herradura
La Puntilla
Estero de Jaltepeque

Cojutepeque
Olocuilta
San Luis Talpa
Comalapa International Airport

Playa Costa del Sol
Playa Las Hojas
Playa Pimental

Lago de Ilopango

N
0   10   20
Miles

© The Countryman Press

IT'S POSSIBLE (IF PRICEY) TO USE BOAT TRANSPORTATION ALL OVER EL SALVADOR'S EASTERN PACIFIC.

Scattered through this wilderness are a handful of isolated hotels, some accessible by car, but more scenically by boat, from gritty **Puerto El Triúnfo**.

Continuing east on the coastal highway, called Carretera El Litoral, you'll come to two excellent vacation escapes. The soft, smoky gray sands of **Playa El Espino** seem to stretch endlessly on both sides, with a handful of hotels, and boat access to both Jiquilisco and one of Central America's best waves, Punta Mango. The broad beaches and quiet coves of isolated **El Cuco**, however, offer the widest selection of surf spots, as well as some of the nicest accommodations on the coast.

The Litoral ends at **Golfo de Fonseca**, an utterly volcanic gulf shared between three nations, with fantastic islands and empty beaches accessible through the port city of **La Unión**. This region, at the end of the road, is populated with small Colonial towns and natural wonders, including **Conchagua Volcano** and untrammeled **Laguna Olomega**, a crater lake often compared to Coatepeque.

Its black-sand shores cradle a handful of beaches scattered with just a few small hotels. **Playa Las Tunas**, **Playa Negra**, and **Playa Tamarindo** all occupy a windswept peninsula that curls from the Pacific into the gulf, at the edge of El Salvador and, seemingly, the world.

Crime The cities of Zacatecoluca and Usulután, both transport hubs, evidently have a gang presence. The city centers, however, are perfectly safe for daytime exploration. La Unión is sort of seedy, but a large, visible security presence keeps an eye on things.

Stay on your toes, though, in Puerto El Triúnfo, gateway to Jiquilisco Bay. The port area is safe and policed,

ONLINE RESOURCES
Costa del Sol Online
(www.elsalvadorcostadelsol.com) Limited, bilingual tourism information about the Coast of the Sun.
Zacatecoluca Online
(www.zacatecoluca.tk) Busy little city has useful Spanish site.

but there's no need to wander around. Drivers should definitely pay for guarded parking.

The fishing village of El Cuco can be sketchy at night; definitely avoid the beach after dark. Surf lodges located just outside of town are safer and more comfortable.

GUIDANCE There's only one official tourist information center in this region, semi-helpful **La Unión Turismo Centro de Atención** (2604-0470) 6 Avenida Norte and Calle San Carlos. Open 8–1 and 2–5 daily. Staff recommends hotels, offers transport information, and can help arrange guides to Laguna Olomega and the Mancomunidad del Golfo de Fonseca. Both Zacatecoluca and Usulután have alcaldías with information, but most beach towns don't have municipal buildings. Head to one of the hotels, instead.

GETTING THERE The Eastern Beaches are linked by the Carretera Litoral, which runs parallel to the Pan-American Highway, traversing the major cities of Zacatecoluca, Usulután, and La Unión. Clearly signed access roads run south to the beaches and bays. Bus transport is good, but you'll need to get boats, often pricey, to visit some islands and beaches.

By Car: The Pacific Coast is paralleled by the smoothly paved Carretera 2, better known as Litoral. While it hugs the shore along most of the Western Beaches, on this side of the country it runs well inland, with clearly signed access roads heading several kilometers south to the waves.

Most major roads in this chapter are paved, though some beach access is on good, maintained unpaved roads, still usually fine for a normal car. The little-used road across Peninsula San Juan del Goza in Bahía Jiquilisco is 4WD-only.

The beach communities are small and simple to explore, with an access road meeting a coastal street, and most hotels close by or clearly signed from the

PENINSULA SAN JUAN DEL GOZA IS ONE OF THE LEAST ACCESSIBLE, BUT LOVELIEST, BEACHES IN EL SALVADOR.

crossroads. The Costa del Sol lies along a single paved road, as do Playas Las Tunas, Negras, and El Tamarindo.

Both Zacatecoluca and Usulután are traffic nightmares. It's best to find parking close to the central park and walk. Usulután's wider selection of banks and grocery stores is the more easily accessible of the two from the Litoral. La Unión is smaller and more easily navigated, with the port located 2 kilometers (1.2 miles) east of town.

By Bus: **Costa del Sol** Buses run the length of this coast's only road, Boulevard Costa del Sol, turning around at La Puntilla (The Point), where you can rent boats. Simply wait anywhere on the road and flag your bus down.

San Salvador (495) Every half hour to Terminal del Sur. **San Vicente** (193E) Leaves la Puntilla at 8:30 AM and 3:30 PM. **Zacataluca** (193) Every half hour. **Playa El Cuco** Buses leave to **San Miguel** (320) every half hour. You can disembark in **El Delirio**, and catch buses to **Usulután** and points east. **Playa El Espino** Buses leave from the main crossroads to **Usulután** (351, 358) eight times daily; the last leaves at 2:30 PM. **Playas Las Tunas, La Negra, and El Tamarindo** One road links these three beaches, terminating at Punta Jagüey, and you can flag down a bus anywhere. **La Unión** (383) Every half hour. **San Miguel** (385) Hourly. **Puerto El Triúnfo (Jiquilisco Bay)** The bus stop is three blocks north of the port. **San Miguel** (377) hourly. **San Salvador Terminal Sur** (185) hourly. **Usulután** (362, 363) every 10 minutes. **Zacatecoluca** (185) several times daily.

La Unión A hybrid between the classic Spanish Colonial grid and port town, La Unión has a central park bookended by east-west, one-way roads, connecting the Litoral with the new Puerto Cotuco and Playitas. Most hotels and the Mitur office are within a few blocks of the central park, and the pier with tourist boats is two blocks north.

There are two bus stations within walking distance of each other, the Main Terminal (3 Calle Poniente and 6 Avenida Norte), at the entrance to town, about five blocks northwest of the park, and a Local Bus Lot (4 Calle Menéndez and 4 Avenida Sur), three blocks west of the park. The **Playitas** bus leaves every two hours, two blocks south of the park; the last bus back is at 3 PM. For **Playa El Espino** and **El Cuco**, it's easiest to backtrack to San Miguel, but for the latter, you could go to Intipucá, catch a bus to Chirilagua, then another to El Cuco.

For information on exploring the Golfo de Fonseca by boat, see that section under Other Parks and Protected Areas.

Main Terminal San Miguel via El Carmen (324) Every 20 minutes. **San Salvador** (304) Every half hour. **Santa Rosa de Lima** (342) Every 20 minutes. **Local Buses Conchagua** (382A) Every 15 minutes. **Intipucá** (339) Hourly. **Playas Las Tunas, Negras, and El Tamarindo** (383) Every half hour.

Usulután The department capital and a major city of more than 80,000 people, Usulután sprawls. The main bus terminal is located 1.5 kilometers (1 mile) east of the Central Park, while the San Miguel bus leaves from a west-end terminal. Other important buses stop close to the central park. Most buses originating at either terminal also pass close to the park, but sometimes it's just worth taking a taxi. Unless otherwise noted, these leave from the main terminal.

Alegría, Berlín, and Santiago de María (348, 349,362,) Every 1.5 hours.
Playa El Espino (351, 358) Eight times daily, last bus at 2:30 PM; bus leaves
across from the main terminal. **Puerto El Triúnfo** (362) Every 10 minutes;
leaves from Parada Dispensa de Don Juan, at the entrance to town, east of the
central park. **San Miguel** (373) Every 10 minutes (exit El Delirio for Bus 320 to
Playa El Cuco). **San Salvador** (302, 302C) Every 10 minutes; 302C goes to the
Terminal del Este, via Santiago de María instead of Zacatecoluca. **San Vicente**
(302) Five times daily. **Zacatecoluca** (302) Every 10 minutes. **Zacatecoluca**
The bus terminal is located just south of the Central Park and Iglesia Santa
Lucia, close to two good hotels. **Costa del Sol** (193) Every half hour. **Laguna
de Ichanmichen** (92) Leaves from the central park throughout the day. **San
Salvador** (133, 133A, 133B, 302) Every 10 minutes; the 133 and 133A are faster.
San Vicente (177) Every 15 minutes, from 2 Calle Oeste and 5 Avenida Norte.
Usulután (302) Every 10 minutes.

By Boat: While boats in this chapter are used primarily for recreation rather
than transportation, big-budget travelers can hire private lanchas between towns.
For information about boats around Estero de Jaltepeque (Costa del Sol), Bahía
Jiquilisco, and Golfo de Fonseca, please see those sections under National Parks.

From La Puntilla on the Costa del Sol, it's possible to rent boats to hotels on the
Río Lempa and in Jiquilisco Bay. From Jiquilisco, you could take another boat to
Playa El Espino.

When arranging a private boat, it's always best to talk directly to the captain,
avoiding middlemen (those guys who intercept you on the beach and offer to
help find a boat) who charge a fee, which is passed on to you. The first offer is
rarely the actual price, so bargain. Most captains speak some English. It's best to
find out actual fares, which fluctuate with gas prices, from neutral parties
beforehand.

✳ To See

Neither the Spanish nor the Mayans built many cities on the Pacific, thus sites of
historic importance are generally found inland.

Zacatecoluca, Place of Owls and Herbs, was home to the Nonualco people
when the Spanish arrived. Conquistadors erected **Iglesia Santa Lucía**, but
failed to quell repeated indigenous revolts, most recently the 1833 rebellion led
by Anastasio Aquino, which captured the entire department. An image of the
Virgin Mary, which once stopped a lava flow, is inside, while a statue of José
Simeon Cañas at the entrance marks the spot where the Liberal reformer began
his successful campaign to end slavery in Central America. The **Alcaldía** (2334-
0039; Nicolás Peña and Avenida Narciso Monterrey) may be able to arrange
guides.

Usulután, Place of Ocelots, sprawls with its fine collection of fast food chains
across the Litoral. Look a little closer, however, and you'll find an impressive old
central park presided over by elegant **Iglesia Santa Catalina**, dedicated in
1898, after an apparition of Saint Catherine healed wounded Salvadoran troops.
The monumental **Usulután Palacio Municipal** (2662-0072, 2662-0062; Calle

Grimaldi # 2) may be able to find guides. Both conservative former President Antonio Saca and his FMLN opponent, Schafik Handal, were born in Usulután, to immigrant families from Bethlehem. After the elections, the ideological opposites dedicated Plaza Palestina, in San Salvador, together.

Several inland villages around **La Unión**, members of the **Mancomunidad del Golfo de Fonseca** (see sidebar, later) are Colonial, most impressively **Pasaquina**, its central park framed with slender wooden arcades.

Above La Unión is 1693 **Iglesia Santiago de Conchagua**, its classic façade the backdrop to the region's folkloric dance, *Christians and Moors*. Abandoned railroad tracks connect El Carmen, Conchagua, and La Unión; guides may be able to lead hikes.

✳ To Do

CENTROS TURISTICOS Atlantis Parque Acuatico (2211-4103; www .atlantis.com.sv) KM51 Comalapa Highway. The Biggest Water Park in Central America is just 15 minutes from the airport, with wave pools, water slides, playgrounds, ball courts, and more, plus brick-and-thatch **bungalows** ($$$$) sleeping five.

Oasis del Sol (2354-4732; www.oasis-delsol.com) KM52 Boulevard Costa de El Sol. Open 8–5 daily; admission $5/2 adult/child. Day-trippers on the Costa del Sol could spend the day at this complex of pools, playgrounds, and eateries. There's an even larger one at KM65, **Parque Acuático Costa del Sol** (2338-2050).

MANCOMUNIDAD DEL GOLFO DE FONSECA
The Gulf of Fonseca Commonwealth is a group of charming agricultural towns in the rolling hills between the Gulf and the Pacific. They have food festivals, Colonial centers, and guided hikes to crater lakes, volcanic peaks, and archaeological treasures. But, they don't have much tourist infrastructure. Alcaldías, however, are working together, and can provide guides, camping, horses, and homestays. It's best to call in advance.

Bolívar (2680-7601) Its arcaded 1827 central park is the starting point for hikes to La Torrecilla Hill, with views; Peña del Diablo, with caves and petroglyphs; and La Pedernal swimming hole.

Chirilagua (2680-1208) Lenca for Three Stars, this city is close to hot springs, archaeological sites, and Playa El Cuco.

El Carmen (2680-7331, 2612-2980) Best known for Laguna Olomega, you could also hike La Garrocha and El Piche peaks, or visit Los Ausoles geysers.

Intipucá (2649-4033) Ancient Lenca town is on El Esterón, a mangrove estuary.

Laguna de Ichanmichen (2334–0115) About 1 kilometer (0.6 mile) south of Zacatecoluca, at KM52. Open daily; admission $3/2 adult/child. Used by the Lenca Indians for centuries, the Place of Litle Fish is a relaxed, natural *balneario* with shady picnic spots. Take local bus #92 from the Zacatecoluca central park.

FISHING Fishing is best best from November through April, when the cooler waters bring in trophy blue marlin and sailfish, as well as tuna, wahoo, dorado, red snapper, pargo, pompano, roosterfish, barracuda, and jack crevalle. With fewer tourists than Costa Rica or Panama, you're more likely to score.

The nation's biggest competitions are held on the Costa del Sol (see Special Events) hosted by **Bahía del Sol Marina**, which also organizes fishing tours. **Restaurant Aqua Fun** (see Where to Eat) does as well. You can also organize artisanal fishing trips with independent captains from Playa El Espino and Playa El Cuco; **Las Flores Resort** offers plush yachts. Golfo de Fonseca operators organize volcanic fishing trips.

Blue Sail Charters (2298-2365; 225-763-1349 USA; www.bluesailcharters.com) 1 Calle Nueva #3811, Colonia Escalon, San Salvador. Offers deep-sea fishing trips with top-of-the-line boats and equipment.

Paradise Fishing Lodge (7930-8844 El Salvador; 302-678-3794, 302-734-2538 USA; www.paradisefishinglodge.net; info@paradisefishinglodge.net) KM69 Boulevard Costa del Sol. $$$$. AE, MC, V. Serious fishers stay here, with great lodging and the best boats and tours around.

Pasaquina (2649-7507, 2649-7725) Postcard-perfect Colonial town has beautiful gulf views and hikes to the Río Goascorán.

San Alejo (2615-5232) Arranges boat access to the gulf, hikes, and trips to stone-working factories. The town was once called Queiquin, or Town of Stones. Incidentally, this was probably the first Central American city to rebel against the Spanish, and the first to be wiped out.

San Jose La Fuente (2680-8005) Guided hikes up Cerro de la Cruz, with a monument to a pilot who crashed here.

Yayantique (2283-7650) Hill of Grasshoppers, is half a kilometer from Culquinte Cave, with pre-Columbian paintings of the moon, stars, and serpents.

Yucuaiquín (2680-2391) The Town of Fire is a Lenca center, and still has traditional indigenous dances and fiestas, performed during the Fiestas San Francisco, as well as a couple nice swimming holes.

THE BEAUTIFUL BLACK-SAND COVE JUST WEST OF EL CUCO VILLAGE IS HOME TO EASTERN EL SALVADOR'S MOST FAMOUS WAVE, LAS FLORES.

SURFING Though the Western Pacific gets all the press (and crowds), the Wild Este has plenty of waves. Access is a bit more difficult, but there are several operators who run tours; the Western Beaches chapter has listings. Most surf camps are in Playa El Cuco, with easy access to monumental Las Flores. Another has opened in El Espino, with boat access to Punta Mango. These are just some of the waves:

Las Flores The best-known break in Eastern El Salvador, in a pretty palm-fringed cove, is a fast, mechanical, consistent right with a hollow takeoff at low tide. Less-experienced surfers can ride small to moderate swells, but on big swells at low tide (compare to Jeffrey's Bay or Bells) it is for experienced surfers only.

La Vaca If Las Flores is too crowded, paddle around the point to this fast right.

El Cuco Nearby, this slow, mushy beach break with a sandy bottom is great for beginners.

Punta Mango It's boat access only to this powerful point break with a consistent barrel and hollow takeoff for 100–400 meter (109–438 yard) rides, often called the East Coast's answer to El Sunzal. For experienced surfers only.

El Toro Also accessible by boat, this long, fast, sandy-bottom 150-meter (164-yard) ride is best at mid tide; for intermediate and experienced surfers.

La Ventana 6 kilometers (3.7 miles) from El Cuco, this mellow right is good for beginners.

Luck Man's This least-accessible wave, at the edge of Golfo de Fonseca, needs a big swell for long rides.

NATIONAL PARKS AND PROTECTED AREAS **Chaguantique Natural Reserve** (2273-5755, 2662-0810, 7105-5909) 7 kilometers (4 miles) south of Jiquilisco. Admission $4. Open: 9–4 daily. The Place of Beautiful Springs is a protected area encompassing 955 hectares (2350 acres) of humid tropical forest, where massive ceiba trees reach 60 meters (200 feet) above the streams. It was once part of a huge hacienda; a small museum and restaurant run by Cooperativo Chaguantique occupy the old house. They offer guided hikes, and you can climb a rope ladder 28 meters (92 feet) into the canopy for a better view of El Salvador's rare wild spider monkeys, as well as morpho butterflies, torogoz, ocelots, armadillos, snakes, and other species. Area hotels can arrange tours, or drop by before noon; it's best to call ahead.

Conchagua Volcano Ecological Park (2661-9832, 2680-3334) 6 kilometers (3.7 miles) south of La Unión. Admission: On guided tour only. Volcán Conchagua rises 1242 meters (4073 feet) above the Golfo de Fonseca, to a spectacular panorama of islands and volcanoes. Local operators can arrange guided hikes through the forest, with some 65 species of bird, on two developed trails around the mountain to scenic overlooks. They also offer camping and basic cabins ($). Try **Conchagua Turistica** (2225-1846; comdetur_conchagua@yahoo.com), **Conchaguatur** (2680-3301, 2634-7513, 2680-3433, 7702-8711), or **Complejo Conchagua** (2659-5320; conchagua@hotmail.com). The entrance to the park is 6 kilometers (3.7 miles) from Conchagua, near the town of El Faro, on a 4WD-only road.

Estero Jaltepeque Protected Area Costa del Sol. A mangrove estuary forms the other shore of touristy Costa del Sol, offering easy access to 8000 hectares (30 square miles) of languid, life-rich waters with rare colonies of birds, fish, and other wildlife; Bahía Jiquilisco on a smaller scale. Independent captains at La Puntilla offer the cheapest trips. *Lanchas* (small boats) seat 10, so bring friends. Popular tours run to Isla Tasajera, with a hotel; Isla El Cordoncillo, with virgin beaches; and Isla de las Garzas, with great birding. You can arrange pricier transport up the Río Lempa or into Bahía Jiquilisco. You could also rent kayaks and arrange boat trips at **Restaurant Acajutla** and **Restaurant Aqua Fun**.

Fiesta del Sol (2298-5139, 2224-6550; castaneda_mayte@hotmail.com) runs booze cruises for groups.

✪ UNESCO Biosphere Reserve Bahía Xiriulatique-Jiquilisco Usulután Department. **Bahía Jiquilisco**, Bay of Stars, is a massive mangrove-dominated wetland stretching from the Río Lempa to Playa El Espino. Its shallow, wildlife-rich waters are an important stopover for some 87 species of migratory birds, as well as oystercatchers, screech owls, orange-breasted parakeets, terns, herons, and Central America's last colony of black skimmers. Four types of sea turtles lay their eggs here: olive Ridley, green, leatherbacks, and hawksbills. Their eggs, though illegal, are still collected and sold, but four new sea turtle preservation projects aim to protect their dwindling populations. A handful of hotels scattered throughout the bay can arrange visits to the nurseries, and in rainy season, to see the ladies nest.

Peninsula San Juan de Gozo protects the bay with endless, white, coconut palm-fringed beaches, arguably El Salvador's best. Tilapia and shrimp farms, coconut palm plantations on **Isla Espiritu Santo**, and a handful of hotels and villages are the only businesses within the park, but the peninsula road is being improved, paving the way to much more development.

In the meantime, the easiest way into this luxuriant paradise is by boat. Most people go through **Puerto El Triúnfo**, a gritty port town. Passenger boats ($3) leave when full in the morning, otherwise you'll need to rent a private *panga* to get around the 27 islands and to your hotel. But you can also find boats in **Costa del Sol**, **Playa El Espino**, the **Río Lempa**, and **Puerto Parada**, southeast of Usulután. Persistent Spanish speakers might also be able to find boats in cute **San Dionisio**, 7 kilometers (4 miles) south of Usulután.

You can also drive along the peninsula, on an unpaved 4WD-only road running 60 kilometers (37 miles) past the villages of Isla Méndez and Corral de Mulas to find Barrillas Marina. The exit is at KM108 on the Litoral. Catch pickup trucks as far as Isla Méndez at the Texaco station.

Nancuchiname National Park (2603-5173, 2267-6259) 6 kilometers (3.7 miles) south of San Marcos Lempa. Admission: With a guided tour. This park protects 1175 hectares (4.5 square miles) of delicate humid tropical forest between the Río Lempa and Bahía Jiquilisco. This alluvial ecosystem, prone to both floods and fires, once covered most of the Salvadoran coast. It shelters alligators, boa constrictors, and some of El Salvador's last spider monkeys. There are several trails and basic campsites in the park, as well as a Civil War memorial, cashew farm, and fossils. Local hotels can arrange the tour, while independent travelers should call ahead.

OTHER PARKS AND PROTECTED AREAS **Golfo de Fonseca** Southeastern El Salvador. This immense, island-strewn gulf is shared between three nations, each marked with a magnificent volcano: El Salvador's Conchagua, Honduras' Isla El Tigre, and Nicaragua's sprawling Cosigüina. All three countries are part of the C4 Customs Treaty, so visitors can travel between them freely by

AT PUERTO EL TRIÚNFO, COVERED LANCHAS SEATING 12 ARE READY TO EXPLORE BAHÍA JIQUILISCO WHEN YOU ARE.

boat; bring your passport. The gulf was discovered by the Spanish in 1522, as Gil González de Avila sought the fabled passage between the oceans. Pirates like Sir Francis Drake roamed these parts as well, sacking the town of Conchagüita in 1682. Close to that site is a large petroglyph, apparently a pre-Columbian map of the gulf.

Boats leave La Unión's **Puerto Cutuco** (www.puertolaunion.gob.sv) and **Puerto Corsain** (www.puertocorsain.com), but most tour boats leave from the old pier, three blocks north of the central park. Until about 1 PM, **three-hour boat tours** ($6) leave when full. A **passenger ferry** ($2.50) leaves each day at 10 AM for islands Islas Meanguera and Zacatillo, with lodging, returning from Meanguera at 5:30 AM. On weekends, a **party barge** (2604-2222, 2604-2223, 2604-1155; $10/5 adult/child) leaves Puerto Corsain at 10 AM, returning at 3 PM. A 10-person private lancha costs about $60 an hour; try Ramón Ventura Cruz (2649-5054). Other options include **Velazul** (2243-9559; gio_fabi@hotmail.com), a 10-meter (30-foot) sailing yacht with a kitchen; **Dolphin Tours** (2604-1723), specializing in dolphins; and **La Ruta del Zapamiche** (2228-1525, 7884-5369; www.laruta delzapamiche.com), which operates community-based ecotours all around the islands.

Laguna de Olomega (www.comiteolomega.com) San Miguel Department, 20 kilometers (12 miles) east of La Unión. Eastern El Salvador's largest lake is less developed than famed Coatepeque in Western El Salvador, but it's volcanic, approximately the same size, and you can hire boats to see boiling patches of water, a handful of petroglyphs on the largest island, and birds. Locals call Olomega the Airport of the Birds of the World. Nearby is another lagoon complex, collectively known as **Lagunas de La Unión**, some of them accessible by boat. Take Bus #324 between La Unión and San Miguel, to La Carmen; local buses and trucks head to Olomega.

✳ Lodging

This region, so little traveled by international tourists, lacks a wide range of upscale hotels. Some of the beach towns, particularly those closest to San Salvador, do offer resort-style lodging, and there are excellent hotels geared to surfers on Playa El Cuco and El Espino. Jiquilisco Bay also has a few comfortable options, with boat access only.

Other beaches and towns usually offer mid-range accommodations, geared to Salvadoran families. Most have lovely beachfront restaurants, pools, and playground equipment, which can be enjoyed by day-trippers who purchase a day pass.

However, the vast majority of hotels are pretty basic, from sturdy cement structures with clean, air-conditioned rooms and onsite restaurants, to flimsy budget shacks with fans and saggy beds. Budget travelers can often find hammocks to rent.

Playas El Pimental and Las Hojas
The closest beaches to San Salvador offer two plush properties on otherwise little-developed shores.

✐ ⨍ ♨ ✳ 🍴 **Rancho Estero y Mar** (2270-1172, 7885-9445; www .esteroymar.com, info@esteroymar .com) Final, Playa El Pimental. $$$–$$$$. AE, MC, V. Handicap

Access: Challenging. Day pass $15. On a slender isthmus between an estuary and the sea, this is a beautiful spot. Lush, shady gardens filled with waterfalls and pools are interspersed with hammocks and quiet common areas with beanbags, pool tables, massage room, and more. You could stop in for seafood at **El Manglar Restaurant** (B, L, D; $–$$$), set in palm-thatched bungalows set out over the mangrove-fringed estuary, or stay overnight. The hotel pitches itself as an ecolodge, but I doubt environmentalists will adore those caged monkeys and caimans. And never mind the jet skis. But if you can get past the greenwashing (and they do rent kayaks and offer tours to see nesting sea turtles), it's fabulous. Cheaper rooms have DirecTV, minifridge, air-conditioning, and private cool bath, but are small; spring for a suite instead. Each is unique, with high ceilings and hand-carved furnishings, some with views over the mangroves, others, the crashing Pacific waves. A three-bedroom apartment with full kitchen runs $600 a night. They organize boat tours, fishing trips, horseback rides, and more. Drivers head to San Luis Talpa, between La Libertad and Costa del Sol, from which the hotel is well signed. Public transport is trickier. Take Bus #138 from San Salvador, or any bus between La Libertad and Zacatecoluca, and disembark in San Luis Talpa. From there, pickup trucks run to Final Playa El Pimental.

🛏 🍴 ♨ ❄ 🚗 "❢" **Las Hojas Resort** (2325-7000, 2310-6865; www.lashojas resort.com) Playa Las Hojas, 15 kilometers (9 miles) south of airport. $$$–$$$$. AE, MC, V. Handicap Access: Yes. A great deal on resort-style accommodations (meals, but not beverages, are included) Las Hojas

offers private, pretty bungalows, on a broad, flat swimming beach. Doubles have air-conditioning, hot bath, and television, while two-bedroom family suites have sitting rooms and kitchenette. All have private porches with hammocks and chairs, and access to three pools, one with a waterfall, plus sauna, spa, tennis courts, miniature golf, and even a sad little zoo. Service is great, particularly on weekends, when you should have reservations.

Costa del Sol

This broad, uninterrupted stretch of pearl gray sand and safe, swimmable surf, so convenient to San Salvador, is the nation's most popular playa for families seeking a weekend getaway. Convenient public transport passes rows of hotels, all packed from Friday through Sunday, with crowds evaporating (and prices dropping) as the workweek wears on.

Well-heeled Salvadorans have walled off much of the beach with their posh vacation homes, leaving (by law) narrow public-access alleys from paved Boulevard Costa del Sol. Where the peninsula ends, at **La Puntilla**, the mouth of **Estero de Jaltepeque** (see National Parks), buses turn around at a cluster of ramshackle restaurants right on the sand, catering to those who can't afford a day pass elsewhere.

Or, day-trippers can alight at one of many hotel-restaurants overlooking the coast. A day pass costs between $5 and $40, depending how plush the facilities, with shady restaurants serving seafood and beer in the breeze, with hammocks and pools all close to the waves.

FYI: This place is a madhouse during Semana Santa, and to a lesser extent the Christmas holidays and the

August San Salvador fiestas. Make reservations (which often require multi-day, all-inclusive packages) well in advance, and prepare to party.

🏄 ♨ ✳ 🚤 "♈" **Hotel Bahía del Sol** (2510-7200 reservations, 2327-0300 hotel; www.bahiadelsolelsalvador.com, asistencia@bahiadelsolelsalvador.com) KM80 Boulevard Costa del Sol. $$$. AE, MC, V. Handicapped Access: No. Best known for hosting El Salvador's two most important fishing competitions, this upscale choice has 115 large condo-style rooms and suites overlooking either the mangroves or marina. All are luxuriously outfitted with big flat-screen DirecTV, air-conditioning, and private hot water bath with Jacuzzi tub. More expensive suites have multiple bedrooms and fully separate living areas, others have full kitchens and private plunge pools. Wifi is only available in the lobby for an extra fee. Also on the property are two pricey gourmet restaurants, and a small casino with card tables, roulette, and slots. They offer excursions on private yachts, specializing in sportfishing, and organize other tours.

🏄 ♨ ✳ 🚤 "♈" **Comfort Inn Bahia Dorada** (2325-7500; www.comfortinn.com; hotelhelp@choicehotels.com) KM75.5 Boulevard Costa del Sol. $$–$$$. AE, MC, V. Handicap Access: Challenging. Homesick? This well-run chain offers the comfortable (if cookie-cutter) rooms you're used to, with great beds, big cable TVs, nice furnishings, large pools, restaurants, and a Tiki Bar.

🏄 ♨ ✳ 🚤 **Costa del Sol Residences** (503-2261-0142 USA, 2261-0142 El Salvador; www.playacostadelsol.us; carolinadonan@gmail.com) KM73 Boulevard Costa del Sol. $$$. MC, V. Handicap Access: Challenging. Rents two fully equipped, three-bedroom houses with private pools, complete with maid service and a boat.

🐚 🏄 ♨ ✳ 🚤 **La Curva de Don Gere** (2338-2753; lacurvadedongere.ventas @gmail.com) KM66 Boulevard Costa del Sol. $$–$$$. AE, MC, V. Handicap Access: No. This almost suburban sprawl of modern, condominium-style buildings spreads across a green lawn with three huge, clean pools. It's a great choice for families, but not right on the beach; they have a clubhouse four blocks from the hotel, with free air-conditioned shuttles throughout the day. Regular rooms are small but very comfortable, with big televisions, phones, cool baths, nice furnishings, and a soothing blue color scheme. Family-style rooms are much bigger, with living areas furnished with sofas, a dining table, and refrigerator. All rooms come with breakfast, but do stay for dinner at least one night; the open-air ✪ **restaurant** ($$–$$$) is well known for excellent seafood, steak, and fresh oysters.

THE EASTERN BEACHES ARE WELL KNOWN FOR THEIR ENORMOUS OYSTERS, LIKE THESE AT FABULOUS LA CURVA DE DON GERE.

Cabañas y Restaurante Oasis de Tasajera (2223-9265, 2304-5052) Isla Tasajera. $–$$. Credit cards: No. Handicap Access: No. Day pass $3. Just across the calm waters of Estero Jaltepeque, accessible only by boat (around $15 for up to 10 people; 10 minutes) from La Puntilla, is the Island of Tasajera. Almost-white sands beneath the coconut palms offer beaches on both the ocean and estuary, and this basic, thatch-roofed hotel, along with a few tiny stands offering seafood, snacks, and beer. Three fan-cooled, wooden cabins, two of them large enough for families, surround a pretty courtyard with breezy gazebos, and a **restaurant** (B, L, D; $$) serving red snapper and great shrimp cocktails. Boats provide tours of the estuary and Río Lempa.

✐ ⨍ ♨ ❄ 🚗 **Hotel Izalco Cabaña Club** (2224-3066 reservations, 2338-2006 hotel; izalcocabanaclub@saltel .net) KM65.5 Boulevard Costa Del Sol. $$–$$$. AE; MC; V. Handicap Access: Challenging. Great mid-range option has comfortably furnished, air-conditioned rooms with cable TV and private bath, surrounding the huge pools and palm-shaded gardens. Nice.

✐ ⨍ ♨ ❄ 🚗 "1" **Joya del Pacifico** (2338-2753; www.joyadelpacifico.com, gerencia@joyadelpacifico.com) KM70.3 Boulevard Costa del Sol. $$–$$$$. AE, MC, V. Handicap Access: Yes. Resort-style property on a beautiful beach is built around an amazing complex of pools and fountains, surrounded by private palapas, a great outdoor bar, and coconut palm-shaded gardens. There's no all-inclusive option, but that's the feel of the place, with its fabulous cocktails, upscale dining, and weekend entertainment. This is actually a private club, but allows foreigners (and Salvadorans with foreign residency) to book rooms without the pricey annual membership. You must make reservations in advance; WiFi is an extra fee.

⨍ 🚗 **Mini Hotel Mila** (2338-2074) San Antonio Blancos. $. Cash only. Handicap Access: No. This was best of a cluster of budget hotels in a small, ramshackle-but-cute fishing village toward the center of the peninsula. Mila offers tidy cement rooms with plastic tables and chairs, decent beds, and shared cold-water bath. Air-conditioning costs a few dollars extra.

✪ ✐ ⨍ ♨ ❄ 🚗 "1" **Pacific Paradise Hotel** (2281-2107, 2338-0156, 2281-2028 reservations; www.hotelpacific paradise.com, ventas@hotelpacific paradise.com) KM75 Boulevard Costa del Sol. $$$. AE, MC, V. Handicap Access: Challenging. Day passes $20/12 adult/child ($5 more on Sunday). This is a fabulous family-friendly spot, though rooms in the main building are showing their age. These older rooms are spotless and well maintained, however, with tiny terraces, cable television, air-conditioning, telephone, safety boxes, and a cool freshwater bath. Plusher, newer bungalows are larger and more private, with large terraces overlooking the pools and beach (patrolled by lifeguards, a rarity in El Salvador). It's about $30 more on weekends, when meals are served buffet style (they have an all-inclusive option), and there are free movies on Saturday night.

✪ ⨍ ❄ 🚗 **Princess One Hotel** (2300-2676) KM62 Boulevard Costa Del Sol. $$. AE, MC, V. Handicap Access: Challenging. Special: Day pass $8 per person. Of the many perfectly acceptable mid-range choices available, this was my favorite. Simple, spacious, freshly painted rooms have great beds, private bath, and sleep four easily, all with access to a very nice pool. The restaurant, in a slender three-story building that rises to breezy views above the waves, has hammocks and inexpensive snacks, or go for the pricier seafood dishes, perhaps the $20 shrimp plate for two.

🐾 🍴 ❄ 🚗 "ℹ" **Hotel Paseo del Sol** (2218-1893; www.hotelpaseodelsol .com; hotelpaseodelsol@hotmail.com) KM61.5 Boulevard Costa Del Sol. $$. AE, MC, V. Handicap Access: Challenging. Fifteen spacious, clean rooms with white tiles, private cool bath, and low beds are plain, but comfortable. The grassy courtyard has a small pool, and the thatched open-air restaurant has beach views.

🍴 **Hotel & Restaurant Puri** (No phone) End of Boulevard Costa del Sol. $. Cash only. Handicap Access: No. The road ends at La Puntilla with a chaotic collection of palm-thatched restaurants and fishing boats. You can camp, rent hammocks, or stay in the one cement "hotel," offering grimy little rooms with uncomfortable double beds, loud Latin pop, smelly shared bath, and a great pool . . . but hey, it's $6 for two, right on the beach.

🍴 🛏 ❄ 🚗 "ℹ" **Tesoro Beach** (2328-9765 hotel, 2275-9393 administration; www.tesorobeachhotel.com, tesoro beachhotel@telesal.net) KM67.5 Boulevard Costa del Sol. $$$$. AE, MC, V. Handicap Access: Yes. Day pass $40/30 adult/child, including lunch and unlimited drinks. For more than three decades, the magnificent, 120-room Tesoro (Treasure) has been Costa del Sol's most glamorous option. The soaring arcaded lobby, with its murals, parquet floors, and magnificent views, is furnished with

film noir aplomb, just perfect for a society wedding. The spectacular grounds, the pools interspersed with statues and stone columns, are absolutely decadent. Sadly, however, this place is in serious need of a facelift, and seems to be crumbling away. Despite the obvious disrepair, the air-conditioned rooms are still in good shape, with custom-made wood furnishings, wrought iron accents, polished granite in the modern cool baths, and beautiful color schemes, all with tiny terraces. Suites are more spacious, with cold-water bathtubs; one even has a private pool. All-inclusive packages make it a better deal.

Zacatecoluca

Both of Zacatecoluca's best lodging options are close to the bus terminal.

🛏 **Hotel Brolyn** (2333-8410) 7 Calle Oeste #25. $. Cash only. Around the corner from the bus terminal, this rather nice hotel has rooms with private cool bath.

🛏 **Hotel Primavera** (2334-1346) Avenida Juan Viacortez #23. $. Cash only. Across from the terminal, cheaper spot has clean, festively decorated rooms with private bath and hammock.

Bahía de Jiquilisco

The most important wetland in El Salvador is a UNESCO Biosphere Preserve (see National Parks). It is less accessible and larger than neighboring Jaltepeque, its shallow expanse scattered with 27 seabird-covered islands and a handful of hotels, protected from the Pacific by El Salvador's most beautiful, white-sand swimming beaches. Rising above the calm waters, visible from most hotels, are the volcanoes of the Tecapa-Chinamenca range.

RÍO LEMPA AND ISLA MONTECRISTO

The mighty Río Lempa divides El Salvador in two, forming the ancient boundary between the Maya and Lenca polities, and a modern, less formal border separating Eastern and Western El Salvador. Here, where the river wends to a wide and languid close, **Montecristo Island** (2632-2069 for information in Spanish) faces the sea. There are three simple places to stay along the river.

It's easiest (but expensive) to rent pangas (boats seating up to 12) from Costa del Sol or Jiquilisco Bay, via Nancuchiname National Park. By land, you can head south from the Litoral in San Nicholas Lempa (pickup trucks run from the Texaco station where buses drop you off) to the tiny town of La Pita, to the first option.

Hostal Lempa Mar (2310-9901) $. Cash only. It's lovely, centered on hammock-filled thatch verandas, with simple fan-cooled rooms that can also be rented by the bed. Simple meals are served, and boat service arranged, at the riverfront deck. Boats ($10 or so) run to Isla Montecristo, with the two other hotels.

Cabanas Brisas del Mar (2367-2107) $. Cash only. The nicer of the two has simple, clean private cabins, an excellent restaurant, and hammocks on the dock above the river.

Hostal Juan Lobo (2634-6387) $. Cash only. Even more basic cabins, cement with thatched roofs and thin mattresses, are available at this little hostel, where you can go cheaper by renting a hammock for the night.

While some hotels are theoretically accessible by car or public transport, it's easiest by boat, usually arranged at seedy Puerto El Triúnfo, south of Usulután. For more transport information, see the National Park section.

There are four burgeoning sea turtle protection projects in the region, a nesting ground for several species including the endangered hawksbill and leatherback. People also feed their families with revenue from illegal turtle eggs. This is one area where tourists really can make a difference, by refusing the eggs (Viagra is more effective, anyway) and requesting visits to nurseries and nesting grounds.

⨍ ♨ ✳ 🛏 ❝❞ **Barillas Marina Club** (2675-1134 hotel, 2263-3650 San Salvador; www.barillasmarina.com, informacion@barillasmarina.com) $$$$. AE, MC, V. Handicap Access: No. The poshest spot on Jiquilisco Bay is this sailing club that caters to yacht owners, even processing documents for those who make their way (at high tide only) into the protected waters. It's a private club, but non-members are welcome with pre-paid reservations. Rooms, in cement bungalows and villas, are outfitted with modern kitchens, private hot baths, breezy porches, and attractive, new furnishings. A clubhouse has DirecTV, a great restaurant, book exchange, and access to a nice pool. Tours include boat trips around the bay, visits to area parks and protected areas, or perhaps private plane trips to Guatemala and Honduras. Dahlings.

❋ 🚣 **Hotel y Restaurant El Jardín** (2663-6089, 7840-7086) Calle El Malecón, two blocks from the port. $. Credit cards: No. Handicap Access: No. Puerto El Triúnfo has one hotel, and it's awful. There was a roach on the toilet seat and, worse, the manager just shrugged when I pointed it out. Rooms smell weird. But if you're stuck overnight, they have cable TV, air-conditioning, private bath, and sturdy locks. Offers guarded parking for $5 per day.

Hostal Pirrayita (2610-7142) Isla Pirraya. $. Credit Cards: No. Handicap Access: No. Close to Puerto Parada, this beautiful island far from the Pacific beaches is home to a fascinating ecotourism project. Designed primarily to protect three species of the sea turtle, the olive Ridley and rarer hawksbill and leatherback, the organization has also erected a two-story hotel, with five basic wooden rooms, shared bath, and plenty of hammocks. They organize fishing trips, tours of the mangroves, and there's even a pool nearby, but be sure to visit their sea turtle refuge. There, eggs are hatched in protected sand, for release a few weeks after hatching. In rainy season, you can also do night trips to the beach, and see the lovely ladies nesting for yourself.

❋ **Puerto Escobar Hotel** (7263-5146; puertoescobar.blogspot.com, puertoescobar.bahia@gmail.com) Isla de Mendéz. $. Cash only. Handicap Access: No. With access to both the bahía and broad Pacific beaches, this pretty family-run hotel has five adorable white cottages, with porches, air-conditioning, and private cool bath. Four of the attractive gem-toned cabins, with new beds and colorful accents, are for couples; one is family-sized, sleeping five in two rooms. All surround a very nice pool, though you may prefer to hang out at the covered beachfront palapa where hammocks sway in the breeze. The owners arrange all the boat tours, and you can walk for kilometers (it's not really an island) along the white sands and coconut palms by the waves.

🎣 ❋ **Solisal Centro Recreativao** (2338-4130, 2318-5705; www.hotel solisal.com, guillen_ecotur7@yahoo .com) Corral de Mulas #1, Peninsula San Juan de Gozo. $$. Cash only. Handicap Access: Challenging. Corral de Mulas is the largest town on Peninsula San Juan de Gozo, accessible by car (though boats are highly recommended), with sandy streets that link broad beaches to the bay. On the mangrove-forested side, with views to the mainland's lovely volcanoes, are nine simple wooden cabins with private cool baths. Some are actually over the water, connected to the hammock-hung dock by raised wooden platforms. This place is a party spot on weekends, when visitors fill the large pool. Packages, including transport, tours, and meals, are a great deal. They can also arrange helicopter transport and tours, as well as kayaks, jet skis, and for groups of at least 20, the *Cocoloco*, a party barge perfect for the whole drunken family.

Playa El Espino

This gorgeous beach is an isolated 22 kilometers (14 miles) from the Litoral. En route, be sure to stop at the scenic mirador over the mangrove estuary of La Chepona, part of the Jiquilisco complex.

Someday, this beautiful beach will be a prime destination. For now however, far from any towns save Usulután, you'll usually have the place to yourself, with small crowds on weekends. There are a handful of other budget hotels on this beach, but so flimsy that they might blow away while the book is still in print. These are generally furnished with hammocks or saggy beds, shared bath, and plenty of ventilation, often adjacent to two-table, palm-thatch restaurants serving typical breakfasts and fried fish. All are close to the entrance to town, the cheapest just east of the bus stop and main road.

✳ 🛏 "🍴" **Hotel Arcos del Espino** (2608-0686, 7888-3723) One block east of the access road. $$. AE, MC, V. Handicap Access: No. The best hotel at the El Espino crossroads is downright adorable, as well as clean, secure, and friendly. The basic cement structure has been freshly painted an inoffensive pink, which really works with the pretty pool in the courtyard, and colorful hammocks hanging on the porch outside. It's not right on the beach, but just a few meters away. Rooms are simple, and sleep four—for the same price as one—in two acceptable double beds. Cable television and private bath are also well maintained. An onsite **restaurant** (B, L, D; $) serves everything from seafood to pupusas.

ƒ ✳ 🛏 **Bosque de Mangle Casa de Mar y Surf Camp** (2510-7627; www.grupoamate.com.sv/elespinohotel, fernando.ortiz@grupoamate.com.sv) Isla El Arco, east of main road. $$$$. AE, MC, V. Handicap Access: No. Attractively constructed surf lodge at the western edge of El Espino abuts the mangrove-forested estuary known as La Chepona, part of the protected Jiquilisco complex. The main attraction is easy access to legendary Punta Mango, a 400-meter (437-yard), hollow right break with a barrel that rivals Punta Roca. The lodge offers spacious, air-conditioned, cheerfully painted rooms and bungalows, topped with palm thatch; some have full kitchens. Palm-shaded grounds surround a circular pool, inset into pale flagstones, with banks of shady hammocks where you can relax. Rates seem high, but include airport transfer, meals, and boat trips to area breaks (the only way to get there). They also offer guided hikes, bicycles, fishing trips, and boat tours into the mangroves, with alligators.

ƒ ✳ 🛏 **Hotel y Restaurant Las Cabañas** (2608-0701) At entrance to the beach. $–$$. Cash only. Handicap Access: Challenging. Right off the main road, this simple, clean cement number is a great choice. Individual rooms are tiny, with a microscopic bathroom and fan. Larger, nicer doubles have cable TV, a few more dollars gets you air-conditioning. There's even a "suite" with separate living area. The front porch is right on the waves, with hammocks and food service, while their excellent pool, across the street, is surrounded by lovely gardens.

✪ ⚓ ƒ ✳ 🛏 **Hotel La Estancia de Don Luis** (2270-1851, 2614-1861; laestanciadedonluis@yahoo.es) About 1.3 kilometers (0.8 mile) east of main road. $$$. AE, MC, V. Handicap Access: Yes. It's worth the short drive (or long walk) from town to the finest accommodations in El Espino. Manicured gardens punctuated with pretty palapa-topped hangout spots surround a pool right on a particularly winsome stretch of sand. It's not exactly plush, but rooms are very comfortable, clean, and modern, with mismatched but well-maintained furnishings, excellent beds, modern baths, and faux marble floors. Breakfast is included. Even if you aren't staying here, the open-air **restaurant** (B, L, D; $–$$) is easily the nicest in town, with a bilingual menu featuring cocktails, inexpensive sandwiches, tacos, and pricier dishes such as seared snapper in a sesame seed crust.

✳ 🏠 **Hotel-Restaurante Mirage** (7914-6242) One block east of the entrance. $. Cash only. Across from Los Arcos, this place is mellow. Fishermen untangle their nets in the adjacent seafood restaurant, overlooking the waves. Low beds with thin mattresses, icy air-conditioning, a few rooms with indoor hammocks, all spell low-budget relaxation.

Hotel Real Oasis (2270-2798, 7856-3445; www.realoasisespino.com.sv; donchepe@elsalvador.com) About 2 kilometers (1.2 miles) east of main road. $$$. AE, MC, V. While the Web site reveals beautiful pools and sunny, air-conditioned rooms, it was closed when I dropped by. Make reservations in advance.

Usulután

There are a dozen love motels scattered along the Litoral, some perfectly acceptable for travelers. Ask to see a room (you may be pleasantly surprised) before committing.

✳ 🏠 **Hotel Florida** (2662-0540) 4 Calle Oeste and 6 Avenida Norte. $. Cash only. Handicap Access: Challenging. Large downtown hotel has clean, basic rooms with private cool bath, hammocks, and an onsite eatery.

Playa El Cuco

El Cuco is awesome. Though geographically isolated, it's also home to some of the best surf spots in Central America. Thus, several excellent accommodations geared to international travelers (including one of the nation's best hotels) have sprung up in scenic spots on either end of town.

The scruffy center, where the entrance road hits the sea, is a bustling fishing village with the usual assortment of thatch-roofed seafood stands, colorful fishing boats, Internet cafés, chickens, and dogs, all flooded with Salvadoran families on weekends. A handful of cheaper hotels are clustered here, just east of the main road. El Cuco also has several informal tent camps, private homes, and other inexpensive options that cater to surfers. Check surfing sites and forums for more information.

🏄 🏠 ✳ 🏠 "🍴" **Azul Surf Club** (888-946-2985, 626-487-4863 USA; www.azulsurfclub.com, lissette@azulsurfclub.com) Just 1.5 kilometers (0.93 mile) east of El Cuco. $$$$. AE, MC, V. Handicap Access: No. This classic surf spot is laid back but with plenty of amenities—for instance, check out the pool, with a Jacuzzi and swim-up bar. Rooms are clean and spacious enough for your boards, with modern furnishings and great views from the porch. It's right on the beach, with shady hangout spots to relax. In general, you book multi-day packages including meals (but not alcohol), private transportation from the airport, and guided boat trips to more remote waves, but you can arrange to omit some services for a lower price. They collect items to help local kids; the Web site suggests what to bring.

✦ ❋ ⚲ **Hotel Cucolindo** (2619-9012; www.hotelcucolindo.com; hotelcu colindo@hotmail.com) About 1 kilometer (0.6 mile) east of El Cuco. $–$$. Cash only. Handicap Access: Challenging. A bit away from El Cuco village (which is a good thing), this beachfront property has cheerfully painted cinder-block rooms with air-conditioning or fan, next to a great pool. There's an onsite restaurant.

✪ ✦ ⚲ ❋ ⚲ "⫯" **Las Flores Resort** (2619-9065 El Cuco, 2236-0025 San Salvador; www.lasfloresresort.com, recepcion@lasfloresresort.com) Just 1 kilometer (0.6 mile) west of El Cuco. $$$$. AE, MC, V. Handicap Access: No. Cradled in the cove that gives rise to El Cuco's most famous wave, this excellent hotel is an exercise in elegant architecture, with clean, mod-

ern lines and a minimalist Zen aesthetic. Each of the five junior suites and two master suites is possessed of the same sleek style, with fabulously simple furnishings from Salvadoran designer Mitsuku. Though the vibe is clean and modern, most materials are warm and natural: polished wood, gleaming marble, fresh flowers, woven reeds. The bathrooms, with their elegant ceramic fixtures, are divine. Stroll out into the landscaped grounds, where an exquisite pool has been inset into a gleaming wooden deck, a theme that flows into the open-air yoga studio and outdoor restaurant (B, L, D; $$$). Serving gourmet Salvadoran cuisine and seafood—everything from fish tacos to lobster thermidor—alongside a full bar and solid wine list, this is a fantastic spot for a splurge, with views of surfers taking on those waves. The only thing that might harsh your mellow is booking a room. Most visitors come on pricey surf packages through Wavehunters (www.wavehunters.com).

LAS FLORES RESORT OFFERS ELEGANT LODGING AND DINING IN ISOLATED EL CUCO.

But it is possible to make reservations one week in advance (not sooner), with a two-night minimum.

☀ ✦ ⌂ **Leones Marinos** (2699-9015) KM135, central El Cuco. $–$$. Cash only. Handicap Access: Challenging. Acceptable choice right in town offers dark, air-conditioned rooms with private baths, cable TVs, and in-room hammocks, as well as cheaper, more basic, fan-cooled bungalows. A popular second-floor restaurant (B, L, D; $$) overlooks the ocean, and there are scores of colorful hammocks.

✪ ☀ ⌂ ✦ 🚗 "♪" **Hotel Miraflores** (7890-4751; www.elhotelmiraflores.com, info@elhotelmiraflores.com) Only 500 meters (547 yards) west of El Cuco. $$$. AE, MC, V. Handicap Access: No. Perched atop the stunning headland that separates El Cuco's two main beaches, this surf lodge is exceptional. It's a fairly serious climb down to Las Flores break, but well worth the effort for the astounding 360-degree view over beaches and volcanoes; on a clear day, you can see Nicaragua. The English-speaking Dutch owners have topped their property off with a brilliant gazebo, where you can surf the Internet from your hammock, get a massage, or relax in the perfect pool. Clean, white-tiled rooms are simple and spacious, sleeping five with room for your boards, cable TV and breakfast included. The hotel rents surfboards, arranges lessons, and has a sister property at Playa Mazata, in the Western Beaches chapter.

☀ ✦ ⌂ **Vina del Mar** (2619-2122) KM135, central El Cuco. $–$$. Cash only. Handicap Access: Challenging. Next door to Leones Marinos in the village, this quieter spot definitely has a love hotel vibe, but also a nice

grassy area and huge, deep swimming pools. Rooms are simple but immaculately clean, with cable TVs, private baths, and in-room hammocks; $10 more gets you air-conditioning.

Playas Las Tunas, Negra, and El Tamarindo

There are a few hotels on the warm black sands of this almost undeveloped peninsula. Las Tunas is the major "town," a cluster of seafood restaurants overlooking beautiful tide pools, but lacks a grocery store, Internet café, and most other services.

A good, paved road follows the coast some 12 kilometers (7 miles), from the crashing waves of Playa Negra, to the much calmer surf at El Tamarindo, on the edge of Fonseca Gulf. The road continues to Punta El Jagüey, where a few seafood shacks, specializing in the region's enormous oysters, cluster at the mouth of a mangrove estuary.

☀ ⌂ **Hotel y Restaurante Buenos Aires** (7886-0930, 7239-0298) A half block from the Calle Principal of Las Tunas. $$. Cash only. Handicap Access: Challenging. Simple spot in the heart of "town" has freshly painted rooms with air-conditioning, cable TV, and really smelly private bath. A nice patio has hammocks, and there's a seafood restaurant.

☀ ⌂ ✦ ⌂ **Los Caracoles** (2335-1200, 7786-9949) KM175, Carretera Litoral. $$$$. AE, MC, V. Handicap Access: No. This plush guesthouse, operated by exquisite Los Almendros de San Lorenzo in Suchitoto, is right on the waves on gorgeous Playa Maculis, just north of El Tamarindo. The four-bedroom home sleeps eight very comfortably in an architecturally outstanding abode. Accented with designer kitchenware, bedding, and other luxurious amenities, the setting is divine. There is a full kitchen, and all meals and maid service can be provided. The covered oceanfront deck, with hammocks and other furnishings, is inlaid with a lovely pool, kissed by the waves at high tide. You'll wait right here for a 36-foot Hunter sailboat to pick you up for a tour of Golfo de Fonseca, then return and watch the moon rise.

Hotel y Restaurante Playas Negras (2649-5097; kpq84@hotmail .com) Playa Negra, KM8 Carretera La Unión. $$–$$$. Cash only. Handicap Access: Challenging. Decent hotel in the middle of nowhere has small, air-conditioned rooms with cable TV and private cold bath; request a beachfront room, for the same price. There's an onsite restaurant.

Hotel Torola Cabaña Club (2681-5528, 2681-5529) KM175, Playa Tamarindo. $–$$$. AE, MC, V. Handicap Access: Challenging. Day pass $7. It's hard to do glamour out here in the hinterlands, but the freshly uniformed staff (clearly quite proud of the place) has for half a century kept this two-story beachfront hotel the most elegant option around. Winding staircases past sparkling pools connect 30 immaculate if aging rooms, with excellent beds, faux Oriental rugs, attractive plastic furnishings, creatively folded towels, and rather romantic lighting. Second-floor suites are larger, with private patios, fresh breezes, and beautiful views. Family rooms, with several beds, have niches for some privacy, and large closets. The onsite **restaurant** (B, L, D; $$) serves great seafood, Salvadoran dishes, and even pastas and vegetarian items, and has a

very full bar. There are two regular pools, both lovely, one outfitted for easy wheelchair access. A third fabulous pool (complete with drink service), is carved into a rocky point in front of the hotel, where tiny multi-hued fish get caught at low tide.

Hotel Tropitamarindo (2649-5082, 2682-8675; tropicoinn @yahoo.com) Carretera Tamarindo, 2 kilometers (1.2 miles) before town. $$. AE, MC, V. Handicap Access: Challenging. Relaxed hotel on pretty stretch of sand has six spacious, air-conditioned rooms with private bath and cable TV, overlooking a small pool and restaurant.

Hotel y Restaurante Las Tunas (2681-5515) Just 200 meters (219 yards) east of town. $$–$$$. Cash only. Handicap Access: Challenging. Plain but pretty, brightly painted two-story hotel has a nice pool and simple rooms with air-conditioning and private cool bath. The restaurant is popular on weekends.

La Unión

Steamy, seedy La Unión is a port town, filled with sailors and, well, attractive single ladies. Most budget hotels cater to couples as well as tourists.

Comfort Inn La Unión (2665-6503, 2665-6565; www.choice hotels.com, comfortinn.launion@real hotelsandresorts.com) KM2.8 Calle a Playitas, La Unión. $$–$$$. AE, MC, V. Handicap Access: Yes. Well away from downtown, but close to the port, this hilltop option is an oasis of modern comfort, rather like an upscale business-class hotel, but surrounded by a bay filled with volcanoes. Doubles are laid out like a US-style chain, two beds facing a large cable television, table and chairs, and real hot-water private bath. Spend another $20 for an *ejecutivo*, with a separate living area, sofa bed, microwave, refrigerator, and small dining room table. A small gym is onsite, and there's a pricey **restaurant** (B, L, D; $$–$$$$) serving buffet-style meals, with absolutely fantastic views over the Gulf of Fonseca through enormous windows. The huge pool also takes in that island-studded panorama. They run group (minimum 10 people) boat tours around the bay; make reservations. It's a $4 cab ride to town.

♨ ❄ 🚗 "🍴" **Hotel La Estación** (2665-4300; www.hotellaestacion.com, info @hotellaestacion.com) 3 Avenida Sur and 8 Calle Oeste. $–$$. AE, MC, V. Handicap Access: Challenging. In a historic home in a quieter neighborhood, still close to the city center, this charming hotel surrounding soothing gardens will make you forget you're in La Unión. Sturdy wooden beams, stained dark with age, frame the adobe with Colonial ambiance. Rooms are modern, decorated in soothing earth tones, with handcarved furnishings, nice art, and lots of light. Modern amenities include private hot bath, new mattresses, cable TV, telephone, and air-conditioning. You may not want to leave. If you do, however, they can arrange all the tours.

✪ ❄ **Hotel La Joya del Golfo** (2648-0072; www.hotellajoyadelgolfo .com, correo@hotellajoyadelfgolfo .com) Isla Meanguera. $$$. AE, MC, V. Handicap Access: No. On the fertile Island of Meanguera, City of Small Jade, this graceful, whitewashed hotel on the Gulf of Fonseca truly is a gem. Very comfortable, rather elegant rooms have cable TV and private

bath, decorated in pale, soothing tones with pretty porches overlooking the islands and volcanoes beyond. A good restaurant, popular with day-trippers, serves tasty seafood and cocktails. The island is home to some 5000 people, with a small, festive village and beautiful beaches, particularly El Majuagual (a 40-minute walk, or much shorter boat ride from the hotel) and less accessible Corozal. The island is served by passenger ferry, or the English-speaking owners can arrange private transport. Tours, including fishing trips and visits to more pristine isles, are all arranged. There's apparently another, simpler hotel, on nearby, populated Zacatillo island, called **Paraíso Hotel and Restaurant** (2604-4113), with basic rooms and beach access. Ask around.

❄ 🚗 **Lainez Hotel and Restaurant** (2604-2526, 7899-1938; hotellainez @navigante.com) Block A, Pasaje #1, entrance to La Unión. $$. AE, MC, V. Handicap Access: Challenging. Green, three-story building at the entrance to town has comfortable, rather dark rooms with colorful décor and cable TV. They also rent cars.

Hostal Playitas (No phone) Playa Playitas. $. Cash only. Handicap Access: No. Just 10 kilometers (6 miles) from La Unión on a good dirt road with bus transport, this small, secluded, truly black-sand beach is caressed by the chocolate brown waves of the Gulf. Views are amazing. There's not much here, just a few ramshackle seafood shacks and one place to stay, the home of Adolfo Cruz Fuentes; look for the wall painted *se aquilan habitaciones*. Four small, cement, fan-cooled rooms have double beds and clean, shared bath; the larger "deluxe" has a hammock.

✳ ⌂ **Hotel San Francisco** (2604-4159) Calle General Menéndez. $–$$. Cash only. Handicap Access: Challenging. Though primarily a love hotel, this is a really pretty place, with gorgeous flagstones, balconies, and huge, immaculate rooms with cable TV, telephone, hammocks, romantic piped-in music, and private bath, surrounding well-tended gardens.

✶ Where to Eat

Costa del Sol has several excellent stand-alone options lining its beaches and estuary. Along the Wild East's less-developed shores, however, you'll find that most real beachfront restaurants, with menus and full bars, are attached to the hotels listed earlier. You'll also see scores of simple wood-framed restaurants, with thatched roofs and plastic tables, right on the beach. These generally serve beer, soda, and the day's catch and other simple meals, cheap, and will let customers hang out all afternoon in the shade without charging for a day pass.

Zacatecoluca and Usulután have several inexpensive dining options, from fast food chains and *comida a la vista*, to very good seafood spots. Because they are not really tourist destinations (and space is limited) I haven't covered them here. But ask at your hotel or have a look around—but do it early, as both cities tend to roll up the sidewalks by 8 PM.

DINING OUT

Costa del Sol

Just about every hotel on this strip has a restaurant. In **La Puntilla**, at the very end of the road, there are a dozen seafood shacks serving simpler meals, cheap.

On the way back to San Salvador, be sure to stop in the town of ✪ **Olocuilta,** at KM23 on the Comalapa Highway. The small town is famed as the Cra-

THE SMALL BEACH AT PLAYITAS, CLOSE TO LA UNIÓN, OFFERS TRULY VOLCANIC VIEWS OVER THE GOLFO DE FONSECA.

dle of Rice Pupusas, which are lighter and chewier than traditional corn pupuses. The highway off-ramp (buses will stop) is lined with dozens of green stalls, where competitive cooks busily prepare the treats 24 hours a day. Note that rice pupusas are much better fresh; don't settle for those kept warm for to-go customers.

✪ **Restaurante Acajutla** (2338-0397) Boulevard KM73.5 Boulevard Costa del Sol. $$–$$$. AE, MC, V. Cuisine: Seafood. Children's Menu: No. Serving: L, D; breakfast on weekends only. Handicap Access: Yes. Reservations: On weekends. This popular restaurant is a destination in itself, where well-heeled Salvadorans come to dine overlooking the estuary, surrounded by mangrove trees and water birds. The specialties are top-notch traditional dishes such as their enormous *mariscada*, a creamy seafood and fish stew, or day's catch stuffed with shrimp, cheese, and vegetables. Dine out over the water, in a breezy pavilion or at least stop by for a beer. You're welcome to make a day of it, and they also offer kayaks for $15 an hour.

Kenny Mar (2338-2578; www.res taurantekennymar.com) KM60 Boulevard Costa del Sol. $$–$$$. MC, V. Cuisine: Seafood. Children's Menu: Yes. Serving: B, L, D. Handicap Access: Yes. Reservations: For groups. Right where the San Salvador highway reaches the sea, in Playa Marcelino, there is a cluster of restaurants where day-trippers can enjoy the sun, surf, and seafood without heading farther along the sandbar. Kenny Mar, in a solid rancho with guarded parking and great beach views, is a fine choice. Burgers and other inexpensive snacks are fine, but try the *amor marino,* the catch of the day stuffed with smoked salmon and cheese, or *camarones de mi tierra,* shrimp wrapped in bacon. They also rent three small **rooms** ($$) with tiny private bath and air-conditioning, but they're pretty grungy.

Restaurante Aqua Fun (2305-5297, 7996-2438; www.aquafundelsol.com, info@aquafundelsol.com) Boulevard. KM75.5 Boulevard Costa del Sol. $$–$$$. AE, MC, V. Cuisine: Seafood. Children's Menu: Yes. Serving: B, L, D. Handicap Access: Yes. Reservations: For groups. This isn't just a restaurant, it's a theme park for folks who like water toys. Just inside the mouth of the estuary, the water is calm and perfect for the herds of jet skis and small boats waiting right off the covered pier. Or, just go full bore and organize a fishing charter, $550 to $1,550 for up to five people, all-inclusive, depending on the size of the boat and distance of the trip. You can also just relax and enjoy the action over a large menu of seafood specialties. Seafood cocktails, lobster, fresh fish, and a very full bar can be enjoyed in very scenic environs. You could even try your luck with a fishing rod, or splash around in their good-sized pool.

Restaurant Yessenia (2338-2576; restaurante_yessenia@yahoo.com) KM59.5 Boulevard Costa del Sol. $$–$$$. MC, V. Cuisine: Seafood. Children's Menu: Yes. Serving: B, L, D. Handicap Access: Yes. Reservations: For groups. Next door to Kenny Mar, Yessenia is another great option, offering fine hammocks suspended three stories above the water, as well as dishes including ceviches, seafood cocktails (try the shrimp-stuffed avocado), and *pescaditos,* broiled sardine-sized fish. Big spenders could try the *cazuela con manos gigantes* (seafood stew with large crab claws). At the time of research, they were completing a small hotel with mid-range rooms.

Bahía Jiquilisco

The handful of hotels scattered around Jiquilisco Bay all have restaurants you can visit on day-trips. Puerto El Triúnfo has several seafood stands close to the malecón, the nicest of which is **Restaurante La Mariscada** (7006-0367; Terminal Turiscada; $$–$$$; AE, MC, V) specializing in *mariscadas,* a seafood soup served with heads, shells, claws, and tail intact, infused with a rich, creamy broth. Seafood cocktails, as well as steak and chicken dishes, are also on offer.

Playa El Espino

There are probably a dozen very basic thatch-roofed eateries, serving simple Salvadoran cuisine and fresh seafood, at the crossroads village of El Espino. Area hotels have nicer restaurants. Notably, the ubiquitous **Pollo Campestre** (2608-0640; beach entrance; L, D; $$) chain of fried chicken fast-food restaraurants has opened, but instead of fluorescent lights and molded plastic booths, El Espino's has a sandy, open-air dining room on the shore.

Playas Las Tunas

The lonely road from Playa Las Tunas, past El Tamarindo to Punta El Jagüey, passes palm-thatched restaurants right on the beach, serving seafood and other simple meals. All the hotels have restaurants, while the village of Las Tunas has a few other options.

Rancho Brisas Marinas (7799-9422) Playa Las Tunas. $$–$$$. Credit

Cards: No. Cuisine: Seafood. Children's Menu: Yes. Serving: B, L, D. Handicap Access: No. Reservations: For groups. Overlooking the rocky outcropping of tidepools where many come just to soak, this breezy cement restaurant serves fresh seafood and other Salvadoran favorites next to gently swaying hammocks. Nearby, Rancho Las Tunas and Rancho Rica Mar offer similar options.

La Unión

If you're here on the weekend, head up to the ✪ **Conchagua Gastronomic Fair** (10 AM–5 PM Saturday and Sunday), a few minutes from town.

Amanecer Marino (2604-4645, 2615-6270) 3 Calle Oeste and 9 Avenida Norte. $$–$$$. AE, MC, V. Cuisine: Seafood. Children's Menu: Yes. Serving: B, L, D. Handicap Access: Challenging. Reservations: For groups. Enjoy top-notch seafood and other well-prepared dishes at this popular restaurant overlooking the gulf. There's a full bar, best enjoyed with a beautiful sunset, dipping behind the pretty islands.

El Gran Pelicano (2604-4648) Final Calle Principal. $$–$$$. AE, MC, V. Cuisine: Seafood. Children's Menu: Yes. Serving: L, D. Handicap Access: Challenging. Reservations: Yes. This special-occasion restaurant, close to the turnoff to Conchagua, serves topnotch Salvadoran cuisine, the specialty (of course) seafood.

BAKERIES Pastelería Lorena (Jiquilisco) Excellent bakery at the turnoff leaving the town of Jiquilisco toward Puerto El Triúnfo is a fine place to stock up before heading into the bay.

PUPUSERÍAS **Pupusería Conch-agua** (Central Park) Admire the old church while munching pupusas in the tiny town of Conchagua. There's another pupusería, on the way out of town, with a view.

Pupusería Mena (next to El Cuco bus station; open Thursday through Sunday.) The "best pupusas in El Cuco" are only available on weekends, to cater to the crowds.

Pupusería Eva (Isla Meanguera) Head into the village, where Eva pats out pupusas every evening.

✴ Selective Shopping

BANKS Most beach towns do not have banks, other than **Costa del Sol**, with an HSBC ATM at Supermercado Costa del Sol, right before the highway reaches the sea. Both **Zacatecoluca** and **Usulután** have several banks close to the central park, including ScotiaBank, HSBC, and BAC; Usulután's are much more convenient for drivers. **La Unión** also has several banks, but visit ScotiaBank (central park), in a 150-year-old mansion.

GROCERIES Most beach towns lack grocery stores. Right before Costa del Sol, **Supermercado Costa del Sol** has pricey groceries. Zacatecaluca has a **Dispensa de Don Juan** on the Litoral, while Usulután also has **Superselectos** and a **Dispensa de Don Juan** on the highway. Jiquilisco, the access town to Puerto Triúnfo, has **Dispensa Familiar** (2 Calle Oeste and 1 Avenida Sur). Grab snacks in La Unión at **Dispensa Familiar** (1 Avenida Norte).

MARKETS The beach towns don't really have markets, but **Mercado**

Zacatecoluca covers most of the city center, while indoor **Mercado Usulután** (4 Avenida Norte and 2 Calle Oeste) has everything.

HANDICRAFTS Zacatecoluca is known for its gold and silver filigree jewelry, woven palm products, and cigars. **San Alejo** is known for its stone statues and *metates,* or corn grinders, perhaps not the right choice for travelers. Engraved *morro* cups, made from large seed husks that resemble smooth, thin coconut shells, are also made here.

✴ Special Events

The town of ✪ **Conchagua**, close to La Unión, has a weekend gastronomic fair.

January: **Fiestas San Alejo** (January 13–14) Stone-working town honors its patron, El Señor de los Milagros.

Fiestas Conchagua (January 17–20) Food and folkloric dance honor San Sebastián.

February: **Fiestas Intipucá** (February 20–March 10) Tiny town displays its indigenous heritage as it honors San Nicolas de Tolentino.

March: **Fiestas Meanguera** (March 17–19) Island community in the Fonseca Gulf honors San José.

Fiestas El Triúnfo (March 23–25) Gritty port city pretties itself up for its civic fiestas.

Semana Santa (week before Easter) Holy Week packs the Pacific Coast, particularly Costa del Sol—make reservations.

May: **Fiestas El Triúnfo** (May 10–23) Puerto El Triúnfo honors its patron, the Virgin of Fatima.

July: **Fiestas El Carmen** (July 13–16) El Carmen honors its patron.

✪ **Feast Day of Santiago Apostle** (July 23–25) Conchagua's biggest party is celebrated with food, dance, and alcoholic *chicha,* a corn drink fermented with pineapple. A mellower celebration for Saint James takes place in Nonualco.

September: **Fiestas Yucuaiquín** (September 30–October 5) Colonial town shows its indigenous roots with *La Partesana,* featuring painted dancers and colorful costumes.

October: **Fiestas Bolívar** (October 22–October 30) Civic fiestas honor San Simón Apostle.

Presidential Challenge Fishing Tournament (end of October) Costa del Sol hosts a national fishing tournament.

November: **International Billfish Tournament** (third week in November) Teams from all over the world come to Costa del Sol for blue marlin and sailfish.

December: **Fiestas Chirilagua** (December 1–3) Honors the Virgin of Guadalupe.

✪ **Fiestas La Unión** (December 1–17) Port town pulls out all the stops for the Virgin of Immaculate Conception; tiny Intipucá has lower-key festivities.

Fiestas Zacatecoluca (December 10–13) Festival honors Santa Lucía.

Western
El Salvador

4

Western El Salvador

Park / Protected Area
Archaeological Park

© The Countryman Press

GUATEMALA

HONDURAS

San Salvador

PACIFIC OCEAN

N

0   5   10
Miles

PAN-AMERICAN HWY

CARRETERA LITORAL

TRONCAL EL NORTE

PAN-AMERICAN HWY

Departments:
HONDURAS
CHALATENANGO
CABAÑAS
SAN VICENTE
CUSCATLÁN
SANTA ANA
LA LIBERTAD
SAN SALVADOR
AHUACHAPÁN
SONSONATE

Towns and places:
Chalatenango
La Palma
Santa Rosa Guachipilín
Metapán
Escipulas Border Crossing
Masahuat
Texistepeque
Santiago de la Frontera
San Cristóbal Border Crossing
Chinamas Border Crossing
Tacuba
San Francisco Menéndez
La Hachadura Border Crossing
Barra de Santiago
Ahuachapán
Concepción de Ataco
Atiquizaya
Turín
Apaneca
Chalchuapa
El Refugio
El Porvenir
San Sebastián Salitrillo
Santa Ana
El Congo
Los Naranjos
Juayúa
Salcoatitán
Nahuizalco
San Pedro Puxtla
Guaymango
Jujutla
San Benito
Izalco
Caluco
San Julián
Sonsonate
Armenia
Sacacoyo
Tepecoyo
Jayaque
Colón
Santa Tecla
Quezaltepeque
Ciudad Arce
Suchitoto
Cojutepeque

Lakes and features:
Lago de Güija
Lago Suchitlán (Embalse Cerrón Grande)
Lago de Coatepeque
Lago de Ilopango
Volcán San Salvador
Cerro de Apaneca

Parks and archaeological sites:
Montecristo – El Trifinio National Park
San Diego–La Barra National Forest
Tazumal & Casa Blanca Arch. Parks
Los Volcanes Nat'l Park
El Imposible NP
Santa Rita Protected Area
Cara Sucia Archaeological Park
Cihuatán Archaeological Park
Joya de Cerén Arch. Park
San Andrés Arch. Park

San Pablo Tacachico
San Juan Opico

WESTERN EL SALVADOR

GREAT HIKING AND FINE CUISINE

This region was the heart of Cuscatlán, the Maya-Pipiles' Land of Precious Things. Volcanic highlands, inset with sparkling crater lakes, are echoed by Mayan pyramids. Today, picturesque Colonial towns and coffee plantations are interrupted by national parks, where waterfalls pour to the sea.

The regional capital, **Santa Ana**, is El Salvador's second largest city and architectural masterpiece. Once called Cihuatehuacán, Place of Priestesses, it is still at the center of El Salvador's most important archaeological sites: **Casa Blanca**, **Joya de Cerén**, **San Andrés**, and **Tazumal**.

The **Ruta de las Flores** (see sidebar, next), an impossibly scenic collection of cobblestoned villages, fantastic cuisine, and ecotourism adventures, runs between the bustling city of **Sonsonate** and the quiet Colonial town of **Ahuachapán**. To the west of the Route of Flowers is lovely little **Tacuba**, gateway to **El Imposible National Park**. just east of Sonsonate is **Izalco**, Houses of Obsidian, a Catholic religious center surrounded by indigenous villages and the thermal springs of **Caluco**.

Close by are other gems: stunning **Laguna Coatepeque**, one of the world's most beautiful crater lakes; **Los Volcanoes National Park**, its three volcanic peaks forming El Salvador's most recognizable silhouette; and the cloud forests of **Montecristo-El Trifinio National Park**, rising above the ranching town of **Metapán,** and volcano-rimmed **Lago de Güija**.

Crime This is one of El Salvador's most populated areas, and crime is a concern in the cities, particularly Sonsonate, where you should take cabs when carrying luggage and at night. Stay alert in Santa Ana's Central Park and market area, particularly after dark.

GUIDANCE While Ruta de las Flores has a well-equipped (but inconveniently located) MiTur office, better information is often available through tour operators and at backpacker hostels.

Ruta de las Flores MiTur Office (2453-1082) KM70 Carretera CA-8. Open 8–4 daily. Inconveniently located opposite the exit to Nahuizalco, excellent tour

RUTA DE LAS FLORES

El Salvador's most popular mountain escape, the Route of Flowers connects a collection of cool mountain towns, coffee *fincas,* and the volcanoes of the Ilamatepec-Apaneca Range. Most operators offer day-trips, but enjoy it at a more leisurely pace. Public transport is excellent, or rent a car to enjoy every epic viewpoint, romantic restaurant, delightful handicraft shop, and tasty food festival.

Begin in **Sonsonate**, River of 400 Waters, a congested, none-too-safe city 65 kilometers (40 miles) west of San Salvador with little for tourists, though there's a neat central park. From here it's 9 steep kilometers (5.6 miles) to **Nahuizalco**, with a MiTur information office and dozens of stands selling handcrafted furniture. Make a right to enter the small town, once an indigenous capital, today with lots of handicraft shops, a lovely Colonial church, and the ✪ **Night Market**.

Tiny **Salcoatitán**, Place of Quetzalcoatl, is 6 kilometers (3.7 miles) farther, with a few art galleries and two Colonial churches 1040 meters (3411 feet) above sea level.

It's just 3 kilometers (1.8 miles) more to wonderful ✪ **Juayúa** (why-YOU-uh), River of Purple Orchids. The friendly village, surrounded by 11 volcanoes, is home to the country's most important Gastronomic Fair. On weekends, roads close and the Central Park fills with fantastic chefs serving grilled meats, ceviches, and other exotic meals, surrounded by live music, carriage rides, and an amazing arts market. Nature lovers should stay a while; several great guided hikes lead to waterfalls, hot springs, and crater lakes near town.

You could make a sidetrip 6 kilometers (3.7 miles) east on Route 12 to **San José la Majada**'s delightful coffee museum; 7 kilometers (4.3 miles) farther is misty **Los Naranjos**, another foodie town with famed restaurants and rustic mountain lodges.

The main road winds 10 kilometers (6 miles) through the coffee-covered highlands to **Apaneca**, River of Winds, passing a handful of rustic mountain lodges with restaurants and *viveros,* or flower nurseries, as well as a canopy tour, at 1477 meters (4844 feet).

It's 5 scenic kilometers (3 miles) to **Concepción de Ataco**, Place of High Springs, a great spot with colorful murals, cool cafés, and fantastic handicraft shops. The route ends at the pretty Colonial city of **Ahuachapán**, City in the Pines, surrounded by geysers and hot springs, and just minutes from the Guatemalan border. Or, continue 16 kilometers (9.9 miles) west to **Tacuba**, gateway to **El Imposible National Park**.

office has information, free maps, and brochures. There's also Internet and a
Tourism Police unit.

Caluco Alcaldía (2483-0681) Central Park. Arranges guides to the church and
nearby Mayan ruins.

Oficina de Turismo Izalco (2453-5075) Alcaldía. If this still isn't open, try La
Casona de Los Vega or Restaurant El Chele.

Metapán Alcaldía (2402-7615; www.alcaldiademetapan.org) Avenida Estrada
Valiente and 1 Calle Poniente. May be able to find local guides; Montecristo-El
Trifinio Park has guides there.

ServiViajes Santa Ana (2441-2177; www.annasviajes.com) 3 Calle Poniente and
10 Avenida Sur. Santa Ana has no official tourism office, but this travel agency,
next to Hotel Sahara, can arrange area tours.

GETTING THERE This region is one of the easiest to navigate, thanks to excellent roads with good signage, and frequent bus connections.

By Car: This region is easy and convenient in a car, with smoothly paved, well-
signed roads. Several sites, such as roadside miradors (overlooks), archaeological
parks, and mountain lodges, are time-consuming to visit using public transport. On
the downside, Santa Ana (not to mention Juayúa on weekends) is an absolute night-
mare for drivers; it's better to park as soon as possible, and walk. The route through
Sonsonate is signed to the Ruta de las Flores, but be careful not to miss the turn.

By Bus: Ahuachapán Most buses leave from Calle Menéndez between 10 and
12 Calle Oriente; buses for the border leave from Parque Menéndez, two blocks
south.

Sonsonate via Ruta de las Flores (249), every 15 minutes.

Frontera Hachadura 1 PM only. **Frontera Chinamas** (263) Every 7 minutes,
from Parque Menéndez.

Santa Ana (202, 210) Every 10 minutes.

San Salvador (202) Every 30 minutes.

Tacuba (264) Every 30 minutes.

Metapán While the main bus terminal is right on the highway, trucks to **Montecristo-El Trifinio National Park** leave from the turnoff near Hotel San José.
For **Lago de Güija**, take the Santa Ana bus and have the driver drop you off
the entrance; it's six blocks to the lake.

Frontera El Poy/Citalá, Honduras (463) 5 AM and noon.

Frontera Anguiatú, Guatemala (235) Every 30 minutes.

San Salvador (201A) Every 30 minutes until 4:30 PM.

Santa Ana (235) Every 20 minutes.

Ruta de las Flores Bus #249 runs between **Sonsonate** and **Ahuachapán** every
30 minutes from 5 AM to 6 PM, stopping in all towns except **Nahuizalco**, which
is about 1 kilometer (0.6 mile) from the highway. Bus #R53 from Sonsonate goes
into **Nahuizalco**. Alternately, Bus #R23 runs between Sonsonate and Juayúa. In
most towns, buses leave from the central park.

ONLINE RESOURCES

These Web sites are in Spanish unless otherwise noted; Google Translate can help.

Amuvasan Online (amuvasan.isdem.gob.sv) Covers the Valley of San Andrés, including Armenia, Ciudad Arce, Colón, Sacacoyo, and San Juan Opico, with downloadable maps.

Apaneca Online (apaneca.isdem.gob.sv) Government site has good information but a poor layout.

Chalchuapa Online (chalchuapa.gob.sv) Archaeologically rich town has some tourism information.

✪ **Ecoexperiences El Salvador** (www.elsalvadorexperience.com) Bilingual Web site offers great ecotourism information.

Izalco Piadoso (www.izalcopiadoso.com) Photo-heavy site describes the traditions and festivities of this proudly indigenous, Catholic religious center. Also check **Santo Entierro de Cristo Izalco** (santoentierroizalco.googlepages.com).

Foro Ahuachapanecos (ahuachapanecos.informe.com) Site is packed with photos and videos about Ahuachapán.

✪ **Juayúa.com** (www.juayua.com) Well-organized Web site has photos and other information.

Metapán Turistico (metapanturistico.com) Great site has information about attractions, traditions, and activities near Metapán, as does **Tu Metapán** (www.metapanecos.com).

Santa Ana Municipal Site (www.santaana.gob.sv) El Salvador's second city has this government site with a Directorio Turistico (Tourist Directory).

In **Juayúa**, however, buses to Sonsonate and Ahuachapán leave from the central park on weekdays, but move close to the town entrance, near Scotiabank, on weekends. Buses to Santa Ana via Los Naranjos stop at 5 Avenida Norte and Calle Caceres Oriente, near Hotel Anáhuac.

Santa Ana Most buses leave from chaotic Terminal Francisco Lara Piñeda (Avenida Santa Ana California [10 Avenida Sur] and 15 Calle Poniente), while others leave from Metrocentro and a stop at 16 Avenida Moraga Sur and 13 Calle Poniente. Local Bus #51 runs between the Parque Libertad and Metrocentro. Taxis charge a minimum $4 fare.

Ahuachapan via Casa Blanca (210) Every 10 minutes.

Coatepeque via El Congo (209, 201, 220) Every 30 minutes.

Frontera Candelaria Every 20 minutes.

Frontera San Cristóbal (236) Every 20 minutes.

Juayúa via Los Naranjos (238) Every 30 minutes.

San Salvador via San Andrés and Joya de Cerén (201, 202) Every 15 minutes.

Sonsonate via Los Naranjos (216) $1, every 15 minutes.

Chalchuapa and Tazumal (218) Avenida Moraga.

Metapán (235) Metrocentro, Every 20 minutes.

Sonsonate via El Congo (209) Avenida Moraga.

Los Volcanes National Park (248) Avenida Moraga.

Sonsonate Sonsonate's well-organized bus terminal is an oasis of order in a large, sketchy city. Taxis outside the main terminal can take you to Apaneca ($20), Ataco ($25), Los Cóbanos ($20), and elsewhere.

Acajutla (252) Every 5 minutes.

Los Cóbanos (257) Every 30 minutes.

Frontera La Hachadura via Cara Sucia (235, 259) Every 9 minutes.

Izalco (53A) Every 15 minutes; leaves from Parque Dolores.

La Libertad (287) 3:45 PM.

Mizata (281) Ten buses daily.

Ahuachapán via Ruta de las Flores (249) Every 30 minutes.

Santa Ana via Juayúa and El Naranjo (216) Every 15 minutes.

San Salvador (205) Every 10 minutes.

✳ To See

This is a fascinating region for history buffs, with El Salvador's best archaeological parks and some of its finest Spanish Colonial architecture.

Although El Salvador's human habitation dates from at least 8000 years ago, probably much earlier, its first monumental stone architecture was erected here. The earliest of these cities were probably founded between 2000 BC and the first century (with the earliest definitive remnants displayed at Tazumal Archaeological Park—Olmec-style friezes—dating to 600 BC). Most of El Salvador's oldest and most important archaeological parks are centered on the modern town of Chalchuapa, although the Mayan regional capital of San Andrés is farther south, lying between modern San Salvador and Santa Ana. Nearby, a rare Mayan village—these were made of wood and clay, rather than stone—was preserved beneath volcanic ash in 640 AD, today protected as Joya de Cerén.

ARCHITECTURE The Spanish constructed their first Salvadoran churches during the 16th and 17th centuries, massive brick monuments displaying *Mudéjar*, or Moorish, style. The finest of these, **Iglesia La Asunción** in Izalco, **Iglesia San Pablo y San Pedro** in Caluco, and **Iglesia María Magdelena** in Tacuba,

THOUGH MOST FAMOUS FOR ITS HANDMADE FURNITURE, NAHUIZALCO'S SEVERAL SHOPS SELLING ARTESANÍAS THAT WILL FIT IN YOUR BACKPACK.

were destroyed in the 1773 Santa Marta earthquake that also leveled Antigua, Guatemala. You can still see their evocative ruins.

Santa Ana

El Salvador's most impressive architecture surrounds Santa Ana's central **Parque Libertad**, built during the coffee boom in 1886. The masterpiece is the 1909 neo-Gothic **Cathedral of Santa Ana** (2441-0278; diocesissta.ana@integra .com.sv; central plaza), with an ornate exterior of elegant archways and delicate details, emulating such Spanish masterpieces as the Burgos Cathedral.

You'll see the pale green façade of **Teatro de Santa Ana** (2447-6268; elblogdelteatro.org), on the northwest corner of the park; it is most notable for its richly decorated interior, with neo-Rennaissance and Greco-Romanesque elements, inaugurated in 1910 with a performance of Giuseppe Verdi's *Rigoletto*. It fell into disrepair when coffee prices collapsed in 1930, but has been restored to its former glory. You can tour the interior or, better yet, see a show; check the Web site to find out what's on.

The 1871 **Palacio Municipal** (2447-8080; www.santaana.gob.sv), on the west side of the park, exemplifies traditional Colonial style, with an arcaded façade and tejas roof surrounding a manicured interior garden.

Other notable buildings include the three churches that, along with the Cathedral, formed Santa Ana's historic cross: 1825 **El Calvario** (2447-7689; Calle Libertad Poniente and Avenida José Matías Delgado), recently rebuilt after a 2001 earthquake; Federalist **El Carmen** (2441-1827; 1 Avenida Sur and 7 Calle Oriente), and San Lorenzo (2448-1872; 1 Avenida Norte and 10 Calle Oriente). The Baroque 1896 **Casino Santeco**, today a plush events hall on the east side of the park, is another important building.

Most visitors are disappointed that a large, modern city has enveloped such sites, but this is the price of progress.

Izalco and Caluco

These two towns just east of Sonsonate were important Mayan trade centers and among El Salvador's first Spanish settlements, thanks to fertile soils and Caluco Dehucetat, or Hot River, a rushing thermal spring today lined with centros turisticos. **Izalco** was founded shortly after the Spanish arrived in 1534, when Conquistador Don Alvarado couldn't get his weary troops to leave the hot springs. Settlers constructed three towns, two of which are now modern-day Izalco, marked by two churches, 1586 **Iglesia Dolores** and 1572 **Iglesia Asunción**. Ruins of the orginal Iglesia Asunción are still visible in town.

About 1 kilometer (0.6 mile) away, is the smaller town of **Caluco;** occupied by the Spanish in 1543, it was a cacao-growing center. The 1567 **Iglesia San Pablo y San Pedro**, called El Salvador's finest example of Colonial architecture by William Fowler, author of *Caluco: Arqueología e historia de un pueblo pipil,* is now in ruins, declared a national landmark in 1990. The new church, as well as the spaghetti western-style train station, is also interesting.

Metapán

Metapán, River of Maguey, has been a mining town since around 700 A.D., producing pale lime that inspired the town's Spanish nickname, The White City. Dating to 1734, the **San Pedro de Metapán**, with a Mexican-style façade of arcaded bell towers and Greek columns, houses the famous El Señor Angüe, a

GORGEOUS, GOTHIC SANTA ANA CATHEDRAL SEEMS ENSNARED IN THE CHAOS OF THE MODERN WORLD, YET RETAINS ITS ORNATE SERENITY.

miraculous statue of Christ. There are catacombs you may be able to visit. Other buildings around Constitution Plaza, including the alcaldía, also date from the Colonial era.

Ruta de las Flores

The towns of the Ruta de las Flores were once indigenous centers, occupied early on by strategy-savvy Spaniards advancing on Cuscatlán from the west. The region's first church was built in 1605, Tacuba's original **Iglesia María Magdalena**, an unusual saint (Dan Brown fans take note) for this once very important town. Though the Mujédar behemoth was destroyed in 1773, its ruins lie undisturbed close to the central park.

Other churches on the route have been repeatedly destroyed and rebuilt, including Nahuizalco's 1660 **San Juan de Bautista** (1 Avenida Norte and Calle Oriente), which miraculously stopped a cholera epidemic in 1857, and **San Miguel Salcoatitán**, the "Place dedicated to the worship of Quetzalcoatl," perhaps hallowed ground centuries before the Spanish arrived.

Juayúa's **Iglesia del Cristo Negro**, with its unusual red-and-white façade, is the most striking church on the Ruta de las Flores, revered for the far older Black Christ figure inside. Apaneca's **Iglesia San Andrés Apóstal** was one of the oldest churches still standing, until a 2001 earthquake destroyed it as well. **Concepción de Ataco** displays an almost Byzantine style.

Ahuachapán is an architectural gem, its old adobe Colonial buildings interspersed with newer metal coffee-boom buildings. The wedding cake of a whitewashed church, **Iglesia La Asuncion**, most recently rebuilt in 1904, overlooks pretty Parque Menéndez.

MUSEUMS Many of the Archaeological Parks also have excellent museums. **Via Roca** (Where to Eat) in Izalco and **Aventura El Limo Parque Geotúristico** (Centros Turisticos) in Metapán have natural history museums.

APANECA MEANS "RIVER OF WIND," HENCE THE PATCHWORK QUILT OF COFFEE AND WINDBREAKS DRAPED ACROSS THE VOLCANOES.

Alvaro Calero

THE QUIET COLONIAL TOWN OF AHUACHAPÁN, ON THE RUTA DE LAS FLORES, IS
ESPECIALLY BEAUTIFUL ON THE NOCHE DE LOS FAROLITOS.

⊙ Museo de Café La Majada (2467-9008, 2484-1400; www.cafemajadaoro
.com.sv) San José La Majada, Carretera Juayúa, Santa Ana. Admission: Free with
cup of coffee. Open: 9–5. Tiny museum and café is a bit off the beaten path, on
the road between Juayúa and El Naranjo, but makes a great excursion for folks
who'd like to learn more about the region's rich coffee-growing heritage. The
museum is small but interesting, with two rooms of coffee memorabilia—old
grinders, computers, and demonstrations of how coffee is processed—along with
a few other antiques. Then, enjoy your coffee in their lovely gardens, with hammocks and artsy tables scattered between the flowers and trees with plenty of
room for privacy. From November through February, they offer guided tours of
the coffee processing facilities, including the tasting rooms, for $5/2 adult/child.
Make reservations.

Museo General Maximiliano Hernández Martínez (2250-0330) 3 Avenida
Sur and Calle Mendez Poniente. Admission: Free. Open: Daily. On an active,
150-year-old military base in downtown Santa Ana (bring photo ID), this small
military history museum is named for one of the most unsettling figures in Salvadoran history. An excellent officer by all accounts, Hernández rose through the
ranks from an impoverished rural upbringing to Minister of Defense. Then, with
the backing of wealthy coffee growers, he seized control of El Salvador in a
December 1931 coup. A student of fascism—and a vegetarian, non-drinking
occultist, to boot—his first act as President committed the military to stopping
strikes by mostly indigenous coffee workers. Called the Peasant Uprising, a
movement led by Farabundo Martí was demanding economic justice in the wake
of a global coffee price collapse that had caused massive layoffs. Their protests
were peaceful, until shortly Hernández seized power, when a fight at one strike
line got out of control. The response was quick and complete. By January 22,
1932, Martí's rebellion had been utterly crushed. To avoid further problems,
Hernández rounded up between 10,000 and 40,000 workers, mostly Mayans,
who were systematically shot and buried in mass graves. The episode is called
La Matanza, The Slaughter, and is why El Salvador seems to lack the rich

IN THE COFFEE-GROWING HIGHLANDS, EACH CHILD'S FUTURE REMAINS INEXTRICABLY LINKED TO COFFEE PRICES, WITH TOP-QUALITY GROWERS PAYING WORKERS AROUND 50¢ PER HOUR.

indigenous cultural heritage of Guatemala; survivors quickly abandoned their language and traditional clothing. Hernández' subsequent legacy is mixed. He built a police state and blocked non-Whites from entering the country, but also managed to drag the nation through the Great Depression with its economy intact, building roads, schools, and El Salvador's first Central Bank. A hero to some, a villain to most, he was finally deposed nonviolently in 1944, thanks to a general strike that began in Santa Ana. The museum doesn't go into much detail about any of this, but does a nice job detailing El Salvador's military history. Simple exhibits begin with pre-Columbian stone clubs and obsidian arrowheads uncovered at Tazumal. There's also a vivid pictorial of the 1524 Battle of Acajutla, when Spanish Conquistadors defeated indigenous troops. The museum then blazes through the Colonial era, independence, and the Civil War with a nice collection of uniforms, swords, cannons, guns ("all of them in working order") and paintings, including a portrait of General Hernández, who looks a bit Mayan.

Museo Regional de Occidente (2241-2128; www.indes.gob.sv) 15 Calle Oriente and Avenida Independencia Sur #8. Admission: $1. Open: Wednesday through Sunday 9–noon and 1–5PM. Closed: Monday and Tuesday. In the stately old Banco Central de El Salvador, once the nation's central bank, this good museum's only permanent collection, of Salvadoran currency, remains in the vault. Colonial coins include silver *macacos* (still local slang for coins) and *fichas de fincas,* or hacienda scrip, paid to workers in lieu of legal currency for use at the plantation store. After independence, the government began printing its own fiat bills, but was stopped in 1934, when the privately owned Central Bank took over printing. You can also see the 1992 *Paz Acuerdo* coins commemorating the Chapultepec Accords that ended the Civil War. The upper floors have professional, regularly changing exhibits focusing on El Salvador's cultural and natural history.

✪ Museo Religioso Convento Inglesia Colonial Santiago Apóstol (2244-0554) Chalchuapa, Central Park. Admission: $1. Open: Daily. Perhaps because they were surrounded by awesome Mayan pyramids, the Spanish constructed a real gem in Chalchuapa, the 1650 Church of Santiago Apostal. Its ornate façade, with beautiful wood and gold interior with columns and balconies, houses a small museum with religious statues, books, and relics, most dating to the 18th and 19th centuries.

✳ To Do

BICYCLING **Aventura Apaneca** (2433-0470, 7136-5851; apanecaaventura@yahoo.com) 4 Avenida Norte, Calle Los Platanares, Apaneca. Rents mountain bikes and runs bicycle ($15) and ATV tours ($80–125) to Los Ausoles and Laguna de las Ninfas.

El Imposible Tours (see El Imposible National Park) Offers epic 40-kilometer (25-mile) downhill ride through a mountainous national park to the beach.

Hotel Mirador (2469-2470; www.elmiradorjuaya.com) Juayúa. Rents the best bikes in Juayúa for $3 per day.

CANOPY TOURS **Parque Acuático Apuzunga** (see Centros Turisticos) Near Metapán, fabulous water park has a four-cable canopy tour.

Apaneca Canopy (2433-0554; info@apanecanopy.com; www.apanecanopy.com) Avenida 15 Abril and Calle Central, Apaneca. Admission $30 per person; groups leave at 9:30 AM, 11:30 AM, 2 PM, and sometimes 4 PM daily. El Salvador's best canopy tour is world-class, with 14 cables crossing the rainforest, the longest 280 meters (918 feet).

Hostal Cerro Limón (7871-9783, 2402-1874; info@hostalvillalimon.com) Near Metapán, rustic hostel offers an eight-cable canopy tour.

CENTROS TURISTICOS

Izalco and Caluco
Atecozol Tourism Center (2453-5329) About 500 meters (547 yards) from Izalco. Admission $4/2 adult/child; open 8–5 daily. Popular water park sits on on 19 manzanas (32 acres) of gardens, balsam trees, natural pools, playground equipment, and more. Not relaxed? Close by, **Paint Ball Izalco** (2300-5169; www.paintballizalco.com; admission $10; by reservation) lets you work out your aggressions.

Ecoparque Acuatico Entre Ríos (2483-0673; ecoparqueentrerios.galeon.com) Caluco, 4 kilometers/2.5 miles south of Izalco. Admission $3/2 adult/child; open daily. Tiny colonial town of Caluco, Big Water, is famous for three things: An ancient church, El Salvador's best *gallina de India* (chicken-and-vegetable soup), and a thermal river steaming through the rainforest. This centro turistico has hot and cold pools, water slides, and a restaurant. Nearby, much more basic **Turicentro Shutecath** (No phone; Caluco; admission $1 adult/child; open daily), has several cement and natural pools along the river, and palapa-topped rancheros serving more *gallina de India*. There are Mayan ruins nearby.

Metapán
❂ **Parque Acuático Apuzunga** (2483-8952, 2440-5130; www.apuzunga.com; apuzunga@yahoo.com) KM100 Carretera Metapán. Admission $3/2 adult/child, parking $1; open 7–5. Five gorgeous pools and a great restaurant along a rushing

river have two big bonuses: a four-cable canopy tour ($15, two-person minimum) and whitewater rafting ($50/35 foreigner/Salvadoran) on the Class III Río Guajoyo. Make rafting reservations at least four days in advance. Hourly buses run between nearby Metapán and Masahuat, a tiny town 1.5 kilometers (1 mile) from the highway, dropping you 700 meters (766 yards) from the park.

Aventura El Limo Parque Geotúristico (7392-7688, 2211-3114; cascada _limo@gmail.com) KM122.5 Carretera Frontera Anguitu. Admission $3; open daily. On the misty edge of Montecristo-El Trifinio National Park, this rural tourism operation has waterfall hikes, ancient petroglyphs, orchid gardens, and even a small geology and archaeology **museum**. You can also milk cows. Getting here is a challenge without 4WD transportation, it's a 5-kilometer (3-mile) hike uphill from the bus stop; they arrange transport for groups. You can camp for $3 per person, or stay in a Mayan-style adobe house next to the waterfalls for $6. Simple meals are available.

Ruta de las Flores

Balneario Atzumpa (No phone) About 1 kilometer/0.6 mile from Ataco, toward Ahuachapán. Open 8–5; 25¢ entry; $1 parking. Beautiful, deep cold-water pools set into the forest make a fine place to relax on a hot day.

Polideportivo Municipal Nejapa (2201-0178; polideportivonejapa@hot mail.com) Nejapa. Admission $3; open daily. Pools, slides, playground equipment and more in a tiny town near Ahuachapán.

Around Santa Ana and Chalchuapa

Parque Acuático Galicia (264-5177 y 264-5178; www.galicia.com.sv) KM72 Carretera Santa Ana-Chachuapa. Admission $6/3 adult/child; open 9–6 Tuesday through Sunday. Cool off at this large water park near Santa Ana, with very creative water toys and slides.

Parque Acuático Sihuatehuacán (2222-8000) KM65 Carretera Santa Ana. Admission $3/2 adult/child; open 8–4. Spring-fed Olympic-sized pool (plus several smaller ones) and hiking trails are just minutes from downtown Santa Ana; take city bus #51 from the Central Park.

✪ **Termos del Río** (2340-7756; www.termosdelrio.com.sv) KM39.5 Carretera San Salvador-Santa Ana. Admission $5/2 adult/child; open 8–5. Huge water park with scores of slides, a wave pool, restaurants, and playgrounds, would be spectacular even without the wonderful, warm thermal springs, surrounded by quiet gardens.

✪ **El Trapiche** (2444-0010) KM79 Carretera Santa Ana toward Chalchuapa. Admission $3; open 9–4. In addition to the usual pools and slides, El Trapiche preserves what may be the region's oldest human settlement. Founded around 1200 B.C., this ancient city has an Olmec-style pyramid and ceremonial burial grounds where ceramics, obsidian tools, part of a Mayan calendar, and other artifacts have been discovered.

HORSEBACK RIDING Almost any tour operator or hotel in rural El Salvador can arrange horseback rides with some notice, including **El Imposible Ecolodge** (see El Imposible Park), **Casona de Los Vega** (Izalco), and **Quinta**

El Carmen (Ruta Las Flores). The most professional operation is at **Portezuelo Park** (see Other Natural Attractions), offering guided rides on premium Peruvian steeds. In Juayúa, **El Zorro** (7003-8015) offers pony rides on the plaza; look for the gentleman wearing a mask.

NIGHTLIFE On the Ruta de las Flores, **Juayúa** has friendly **El Cadejo Café** (3 Avenida Norte; open 5 PM–2 AM Thursday through Sunday; $$), half a block from the central park, with live music, a full bar, and gourmet international cuisine, including lots of vegetarian options. Also ask about **Bar y Galería de Arte Jah**, with live reggae and an art gallery.

Ataco has two artsy, intriguing options for live music and great food: **Café El Botón** (see Where to Eat) and **Bar-Restaurant Tayua** (7253-0108; tayuacafe @gmail.com; Avenida Central Norte, #31-A; $$–$$$; AE, MC, V; open Friday through Sunday), with original art, gourmet cuisine, live music, and a relaxed, bohemian vibe. **Posada de Don Olí** (see Lodging) has great food and live Latin music every Sunday afternoon.

In Santa Ana, **Los Horcones** (2484-7511; Parque Libertad), next to the cathedral, is the classic spot for a brew or two, or six. More adventurous travelers could take a cab to **Trench Town Rock** (Desvío Chalchuapa; cover on weekends), with a rowdy college crowd and live reggae, ska, punk, and alternative bands. **Lover's Steakhouse** (see Where to Eat) offers a more sedate bar, while **Monte Carlo Casino** (2440-2877; 10 Avenida Sur and 25 Calle Poniente) has slot machines, blackjack, roulette, and bingo.

THEATER **Teatro de Santa Ana** (2447-6268; elblogdelteatro.org) Parque Libertad. This spectacular theater hosts a wide range of musical and theatrical performances; check the Web site to see what's on.

✷ Green Space

NATIONAL PARKS AND PROTECTED AREAS **El Imposible National Park** (2411-5484, Salvanatura; salvanatura.org) Admission: $6/3 Foreigners/Salvadorans, parking $1. Open: Daily. These dramatic waterfall-streaked mountains and magnificent forests are called The Impossible One for a reason. The intense topography, ranging from cloud-forested Cerro La Campana (1425 meters/4674 feet), to the dry tropical forests of Sector San Francisco Menéndez (250 meters/820 feet) was once the backdrop to a difficult 40-kilometer (25-mile) mule road between the coffee-growing Apaneca highlands and Port of Acajutla. The harrowing trail crossed narrow El Imposible Pass, where a makeshift bridge crossed a steep and deadly gorge; many never returned. Finally, the government constructed a proper bridge with a plaque reading, 1968: IT IS NO LONGER IMPOSSIBLE. The region's formidable landscape continued to dissuade further development, and in 1989 it was formally declared a national park. It is home to 1000 recorded species of plants, 286 birds, 111 mammals, and 50 reptiles. Eight rivers pour down its slopes as massive waterfalls, past fossilized forests, bottomless caverns, petroglyphs, and unexcavated ruins. Despite the name, El Imposible is actually one of El Salvador's most easily accessible national parks. There are two entrances, the official one, close to Cara Sucia, covered in the Western Beaches chapter; and the more accessible "back door," via Tacuba, just off the Ruta de las Flores. Both offer hikes, tours, and lodging.

Salvanatura (2279-1515; salvanatura.org) El Salvador offices at 33 Avenida Sur #640, Colonia Flor Blanca. The park's southern San Miguelito Sector is most easily accessible from the Western Beaches. It's managed by the Ecological Foundation of El Salvador, open 8 AM to 4 PM daily. They offer camping ($5/10 national/foreigner) in three campsites, with latrines, potable water, and grills, but don't yet rent tents. Guides ($10 for up to 15 people) are required to take four different hikes. Two are short, family-friendly hikes, a 1-kilometer (0.62-mile) walk to **Los Engaches**, with swimming holes and picnic areas, and a 1.2-kilometer (0.74-mile) hike to a **Mirador El Mulo**, with fabulous views. **Piedra Sellada** is 3 kilometers (1.86 miles) farther, a massive petroglyph in the Río Venado Canyon, with more than 100 figures depicting butterflies, spiders, and geometric patterns. It was probably carved between 600 and 900 A.D. The most difficult hike is a steep 7-kilometer (4.3 mile) round-trip to **Cerro El León**. Salvanatura also operates neighboring **El Imposible Ecolodge** (2411-5484, 7700-4699; www.elimposible-ecolodge.com; turismo@salvanatura.org; Comunidad San Miguelito; $$; AE, MC, V), 1 kilometer (0.6 mile) from the park entrance. The well-constructed lodge has a great restaurant (B, L, D; $–$$) and five pretty wooden cabins with tin roofs and private solar-heated bath, sleeping six apiece, scattered throughout the forest. They arrange other hikes and horseback tours. **Cabañas Milton** (7545-7110, 7484-2138; $; cash only) is a much more basic option 2 kilometers (1.2 miles) from the park, with two tiny fan-cooled rooms with shared bath, but it's cheap. They also offer horseback tours, hikes, and swimming in a nearby river. The 13-kilometer (7-mile) road from the Litoral leaves at KM116.5, between Cara Sucia and La Hachadura. Microbuses leave from Cara Sucia Terminal de Pica at 11 AM, 12:30 AM, 2 PM, and 3:40 PM.

El Imposible Tours (2469-2109; www.imposibletours.com; contact@imposibletours.com) Tacuba. The back door to the park comes courtesy of this excellent, local tour outfit, headquartered **Hostal de Mamá y Papá** (see Lodging, earlier) in Tacuba. This is a private company that arranges a dozen different tours, all of which can be customized. The most popular are day-hikes, which cost around $25 with a two-person minimum, leaving at 8 AM to ✪ **Las Cascadas**, a series of waterfalls that you'll need to jump down; or more strenuous hikes to **Las Vistas** and **El Cerro Campana**, the highest points in the park. **La Luna** is a mellower hike to the most spectacular waterfalls. There's also a mostly downhill hike (or mountain-bike trek) across the entire park, exiting at Salvanatura and the San Miguelito entrance, close to Barra de Santiago. You can camp in the park or spend the night at the beach, returning via Ruta de las Flores. Other tours include an evening at **Santa Teresa Hot Springs**, or visiting **Santa Rita Protected Area** and its alligators.

Lago de Coatepeque (lakecoatepeque.org) Between the city of Santa Ana and Los Volcanes National Park. Admission: Free. Open: 24 hours. Though this famed crater lake is not currently a protected area, it sparkles alluringly at the bottom of a dramatic volcanic caldera, one of El Salvador's most beautiful natural treasures. The 26-square-kilometer (10-square-mile) lake was formed during a series of eruptions that began 72,000 years ago. Today it is ringed with huge vacation homes that block views from the road with high cement walls, but a handful of festive restaurants and hotels offer public swimming access, boat tours, tasty seafood, cold beer, and mariachi bands. There's a public trail around the lake, by law, but homeowners passive-aggressively block access; expect to get wet going around barriers. It's easier to explore Coatapeque in a *lancha*, a covered, 12-person motorboat, easily arranged at any restaurant or hotel. Rates range from $20 for 30 minutes, to $50 for a whirl around the whole lake. **Los Pinos Coffee Cooperative** (2434-0038; KM55.5 Carretera Cerro Verde; $6) in El Congo offers a two-hour, guided descent from the crater rim down to the lake; hikes begin at 8 AM; you must make reservations. On the western side of Coatepeque, **Isla Teopán**, Temple Island, was once a holy place, where a Mayan calendar and several statues were found. The Salvadoran government has set aside about half the island as a future national park. You can stay at **Quinta Torino** (7860-8244, 2263-7780; 612-605-8542 USA; islateopan.com; coatepeque @islateopan.com; $$$$) a vacation home in the plush Teopán Country Club. A car ferry runs from 6 AM to 6 PM. Other hotels and restaurants are clustered together on the eastern shore.

Restaurante El Gran Mirador (2411-3754, 7269-9322) Lago de Coatepeque. L, D. $–$$. Cash only. Recommended restaurant overlooks Lago Coatepeque from access road into the crater.

Nantal Hostal and Restaurant (2412-7998, 2319-6792; claudia_navarrogomez @hotmail.com) KM53 Carretera Cerro Verde. $–$$. Cash only. Make reservations to stay on the crater rim at this surprisingly nice pink hostel with small rooms, great beds, lovely furnishings, and lots of light. Breakfast is included.

SANTA TERESA HOT SPRINGS' HEALING WATERS POUR THROUGH THE COFFEE PLANTATIONS AND RAINFOREST.

Restaurant Los Ranchos (2441-3754) B, L, D. $. Cash only. Away from the other hotels, this quiet local restaurant and hotel has a dock where you can catch fish yourself, or just enjoy their cooking. Two rooms offer hourly rates but are actually quite spacious and attractive; one sleeps four comfortably.

Rancho y Cabañas Alegre (2441-6071; ranchoalegre@hotmail.com) B, L, D. $–$$. V. WiFi. Popular restaurant, on a floating dock with a pool, offers top-notch seafood, ceviche, grilled meats, and cold beer. Above the bar, five basic rooms with shared cold-water bath have thin walls, fans, and the only WiFi on the lake. There's a covered porch with hammocks overlooking the action.

El 3er Mundo Hostal (2441-6239; 7822-4051; amahuilcohostal@hotmail.com) $. Cash only. Rambling ramshackle spot has friendly owners, an obsession with extraterrestrials, lakefront restaurant, and cheap dorms (one is cheaper because almonds fall on the roof) furnished with cots. Private rooms are pretty, in a bohemian way, but you still may be sleeping on cots. Day passes are $1, and there's a small pool and comfortable common room with cable TV, DVDs, and board games.

Hotel Torremolinos (2441-6037, 2447-9515; www.torremolinoslagocoat epeque.com; hoteltorremolinos@gmail.com) $$. AE, MC, V. The best hotel on the lake has sturdy brick construction, 16 spotlessly clean rooms (family rooms are huge), with excellent beds, local television, private hot baths, and breakfast. Gardens shaded with magnificent trees have lounge areas, several pools, and playground equipment. The **restaurant** (B, L, D; $$) is an architectural marvel, on dozens of stilts suspending it two stories above the lake. Try the *crema de cangrejo,* creamy crab soup.

Varadero Camping (2411-4764; kimmy854@hotmail.com) Calle de Lago, 900 meters (985 yards) from Shell Gas Station. $. Cash only. Camp right on the shore.

Montecristo-El Trifino Cloud Forest National Park (2224-6926; www .marn.gob.sv) 4.5 kilometers (3 miles) east of Metapán. Admission: $6. Open: daily. Closed: El Trifinio (the highest peak) is closed May through October. This enchanted forest of ferns, bromeliads, and huge moss-covered trees is Central America's largest and least-disturbed cloud forest. There are more than 3000 species of plants and animals, at least 48 of them endemic and 50 endangered, but protected since 1987, when the wartorn governments of El Salvador, Honduras, and Guatemala decided to protect their border, together. The epic journey is a 7-kilometer (4-mile) climb through a tunnel of cool green to Cerro Montecristo, 2418 meters (7931 feet) above sea level, where El Trifinio, a triangular cement monument, marks the spot where three countries meet. Nearby, a wooden view tower lets you climb above this giant forest of 30-meter (100-foot) trees, some of them at least seven centuries old. You can also visit the *Jardín de los Cien Años,* an orchid nursery where some 70 species are grown, including the endemic *ponera pelita.* The garden is close to the trailheads for two other hikes, one past the Trees of Love, another to a mirador overlooking Lago Güija. There are three **campsites** ($; cash only). The one closest to the parking lot has potable water, picnic tables, grills, and outhouses, but the others are undeveloped. Two rustic **cabins** ($$$; cash only), each sleeping eight, have gas stoves and bathrooms. Local Spanish-speaking guides hang out near the parking area, and charge around $5 for the Trifinio hike. Visiting the park requires planning. You must make reservations with MARN before visiting the park. Print out the online permission, and present it at the park entrance. If you have a 4WD vehicle, the route is signed from Metapán. If not, pickup trucks wait at the park turnoff, near Hotel San José; it's around $60 each way.

San Diego La Barra National Forest and Lago de Güija (2260-1998; 7871-7443; www.ceprode.org.sv; metapanturistico.com) Between KM104.5, Carretera Metapán. Admission: Free. Open: Daily. Lago de Güija, Lake of Gravel, straddles the volcano-strewn Guatemalan border, and has been a sacred place for centuries. Formed when San Diego Volcano erupted and created a natural lava dam, the blue green expanse is surrounded by dry tropical forest. Many trees shed their leaves in dry season, making it best time for birders to spot cuckoos, parakeets, screech owls, magpie jays, kites, and egrets. In dry season, as water levels drop, you can also hike around the lake to visit a dozen mostly unexcavated archaeological sites dating from 400 B.C., and petroglyphs probably carved around 900 A.D. The most famous artifact was discovered by divers, the Güija Plaque, a slab of green jade with writing and figures carved between 416 and 465 A.D. There are also abandoned Spanish cities, Ostúa and Anguiatú. **Cerro Igualtepeque** has more petroglyphs, as well as several caves and an observation tower. In rainy season, lakeside trails are flooded, so you'll want to rent a boat to see the ruins; there are more on the islands and peninsulas. They're easy to arrange at any lakeside restaurant, one offering lodging.

La Cocina de Metapán (2402-2311, 7730-8877; r_lacocinademetapan@ yahoo.com) KM109 Carretera Metapán. $$. Serves Salvadoran cuisine overlooking the lake, though you may enjoy swimming in the two huge pools instead.

La Perla de Azacualpa (2415-6490; laperladeazacualpa.com; laperlade azacualpa@yahoo.com) $$. AE, MC, V. Lakeside **restaurant** ($$–$$$) serves Salvadoran specialties and fresh fish, or stay overnight in four comfortable cabañas, with two double beds, DVD, air-conditioning, private terraces with hammocks, and panoramic views.

Restaurante Los Remos (2402-1253; reslosremos@navegante.com.sv) KM109.5 Carretera Metapán. $$–$$$. AE, MC, V. Recommended restaurant specializes in shrimp-stuffed mojarra and other Salvadoran cuisine.

✪ **Los Volcanes (Cerro Verde) National Park** (7227-5466; 2222-8000 San Salvador) Admission $1, 69¢ to park. Open: Tuesday through Sunday 9–5.Closed: Monday. Composed of three magnificent volcanoes, this park's stunning silhouette is one of the most recognizable landmarks in El Salvador. The park is part of the Apaneca-Ilamatepec UNESCO Biosphere Reserve. **Cerro Verde** (2030 meters; 6658 feet), its crater easily explored on an hour's worth of trails from the park entrance, is a soft, low volcano filled with the misty greenery of tropical altitudes. **Volcán Izalco** (1910 meters; 6265 feet), once called the Lighthouse of the Pacific, is the most dramatic, its stark cone blackened with two centuries of eruptions that ceased only in 1966, though its gently fuming crater hints at more to come. **Volcán Santa Ana**, (2365 meters; 7642 feet) or Ilamatepec, Mother Mountain, is the largest volcano in the country—just the crater is 4 kilometers (2.5 miles) across and 280 meters (306 yards) deep, paved with a fuming green sulfur lake. Its most recent 2007 eruption left behind fresh lava. Visiting the park, though easily accessible from Santa Ana, San Salvador, and Laguna de Coatepeque, requires some planning. The family-friendly trails around Cerro Verde, with wonderful views, are open throughout the day, with optional guide service. However, you must have police escort and guides to climb the other two. This means that you must arrive by 11 AM in order to join the daily climb to Izalco, a very steep (60-degree), gravelly, four-hour hike that's quite popular on weekends. The Santa Ana trek, a slightly less strenuous four-hour hike from the park entrance (2.5 hours if you have 4WD transportation to the San Blas Sector trailhead), is provided on demand, *if* there are police and guides available to accompany you. Call ahead. It's easy to get here by 11 AM in a car; roads are good and clearly marked. By bus from Santa Ana, take Bus #248/209 from SuperSelecto Colón no later than 8 AM. From San Salvador, take Bus #205 from the Terminal Occidente, leaving no later than 6:30 AM. Have them drop you off at El Congo Bridge, where you can catch Bus #248/209 at 8:30 AM. From Laguna de Coatepeque, take Bus #220 by 7 AM, to El Congo Bridge, for Bus #248/209. The last bus leaves the park at 4 PM. You should be in good physical condition to climb Izalco or Santa Ana, and wear closed-toe sneakers or boots. Dress in layers, as the temperature can drop to 5 degrees C (40 degrees F). Children under 11 are forbidden to climb. Guides for Izalco cost $1, but you should definitely tip. Guides for Santa Ana run $5–8. There's a three-person minimum for either hike.

Deck camping (2279-1515) $$. Cash only. Covered platforms are available for camping in the Andes Sector, 7 kilometers (5 miles) from the park entrance on a 4WD-only road. You can pitch a tent in several other spots. The other two hotels are in the San Blas Sector, 1.6 kilometers (about 1 mile) from the park entrance on a 4WD road.

Cabañas Campo Bello (2271-0853; 2222-1861; www.campobello.com.sv; riciher@hotmail.com) $–$$$. AE, MC, V. Smooth, dome-shaped cement cabañas are cramped, but have private bathrooms, sleep up to six, and are set in a grassy field with views to Izalco.

Casa de Cristal (2483-4679) San Blas Sector. $–$$. Cash only. Nearby, several wooden cabins are set into a coffee plantation that's currently being developed into a full-on tourist center, Las Brumas Ecological Park, with miradors, restaurants, and more.

OTHER PARKS AND NATURAL ATTRACTIONS

Ruta de las Flores

While many of El Salvador's awesome natural treasures are difficult to visit, ecotourism sites along the Ruta de las Flores are easily accessible on great guided hikes, which can be arranged at almost any hotel. Some may require short bus trips, which your guide can help you navigate. In **Juayúa**, operators include **Juayúa Tours** (2452-2167; www.juayuatours.com; juayuatours@elsalvador.com;

6 Calle Oriente #4); **Tours Anáhuac** (2469-2401; www.hotelanahuac.com, 1 Calle Poniente and 5 Avenida Norte); and **Hotel El Mirador** (2469-2470; hotelposada_elmirador@hotmail.com; 4 Calle Poniente and 5 Avenida Sur).

The **Apaneca** Casa de Cultura recommends **Marvin Rosa** (7012-1878), **Jaime Menjivar** (7267-0995), and **Mauricio Posada** (7795-6462). **Nahuizalco** has a new tour operator guiding hikes to La Golondrinera Waterfall; details below.

These are just the most popular destinations; serious hikers can ask about climbing **Cerro Las Ranas**, with a small crater lake, or **Cerro Apaneca**, a nearby volcano. Operators also arrange horseback rides, camping, trips to the **Apaneca Canopy Tour**, and coffee plantation tours, most interesting during the November through February harvest.

✪ **Chorros de la Calera** 2 kilometers/1.2 miles from Juayúa. Popular hike begins in Juayúa, traversing coffee plantations and arriving at an absolutely stunning set of cascading waterfalls and swimming holes. Adventurous travelers can swim through partially submerged tunnels, or leap from the top of the falls into the pools below, which get packed on weekends. (And yes, people have died doing this.) Anáhuac offers a longer Seven Waterfalls tour that visits other cascades as well.

Geysers and Hot Springs Juayúa and Apaneca. Hike through more coffee to a roaring geyser field with a small hot spring for soaking, and mud pots nearby.

La Golondrinera Waterfall Nahuizalco. **Nahuizalco Tours** (2453-1100) 6 Calle Poniente. Admission: $15. Brand new tour offers a moderate one-hour guided hike to this 40-meter (131-foot) waterfall, pouring through a fern-covered canyon to a shady swimming hole. They also tour Nahuizalco's craft shops, San Juan Bautista Church, and **Tatalpa Gardens** (90 minutes; $3) a local botanical garden with spring-fed swimming pools. Ask about guided hikes to other waterfalls, including La Monja, El Salto, and La Flor.

Laguna Verde and Laguna Las Ninfas Apaneca. Two rewarding hikes begin near Apaneca: **Laguna Verde** (4 kilometers/2.5 miles) and **Laguna Las Ninfas** (2.5 kilometers/1.5 miles) both lovely little crater lakes at 1830 meters (6000 feet) above sea level, surrounded by pines and cypress, and bearded with waterlilies. You can stay nearby, at:

Laguna Verde Guesthouse (7859-2865, 2262-0879; www.apanecasguest house.netfirms.com; gpssal@intercom.com.sv) $–$$. Cash only. Dorm beds, cozy private cabins, hot shared bath, and warm meals; or more comfortable **Villas Suizas de Apaneca** (2433-0193) Calle Laguna Verde. $. AE, MC, V. Offers 14 rather overdecorated condo-style rooms, some with full kitchen, and all with hot water bath and beautiful gardens.

LAGUNA LAS NINFAS, OR "LAKE OF THE LILY PADS," LIVES UP TO ITS NAME.
Colin Plant

Mirador Cruz del Cielito Lindo Ataco. Continue up the road signed to Hotel Balcón in Ataco, where you'll reach this overlook. Ask at hotels about hikes to La Cruz de Chico Los Narajitos, Chorros del Limo; El Salta de la Chacala, and Río Matala.

✪ **Portezuelo Park** (2245-2614; www.akwaterra.com) 7.5 kilometers/4.6 miles north of Juayúa. Admission $3, activities cost extra. Open 8–6. Private park on an organic coffee farm offers several guided hikes, horseback riding on beautiful Peruvian steeds, ATV tours, and mountain-bike treks 23 kilometers (14 miles) downhill to Laguna Verde and Juayúa. There's camping and an artsy B&B onsite (see La Escondido B&B; Lodging).

Elsewhere in Western El Salvador

Los Ausoles de Ahuachapán Ahuachapán. Free; open daily. Just outside the Ahuachapán Geothermal Plant, is this small geyser field that's open to the public. You can hike around, but there are no plant tours.

Don Juan Waterfalls (7976-9462, 7414-6971) Jujútla, 6.5 kilometers/4 miles south of Apaneca. Admission $5; open 8–5 Saturday and Sunday. This restaurant and private park has short hikes to a series of cascades and swimming holes, including a 35-meter (115-foot) waterfall, in the chilly Apaneca-Ilamatepec highlands. Enjoy *sopa de gallina,* local coffee, and other Salvadoran specialties in the colorful gardens, decorated with religious statues. Drivers can head south on the road signed to El Rosario, or have Bus #249 drop you off at the exit, and wait for the #278 or #288 to Jujútla.

Jayaque Coffee Tours (2346-5081; www.jayaquetour.com.sv) Southwest of Coatepeque 30 kilometers/19 miles. Small coffee-growing town offers tours of several different *fincas,* or plantations, including transportation and typical meals. You can visit **Finca-Café La Esperanza** (2338-8046; www.fincacafe laesperanza.com) on your own.

Izalco Volcano (2429-8000). Izalco Alcaldía. Though it's much easier to make this climb from Cerro Verde, adventurers who enjoy a real workout can begin from the town of Izalco. The Alcaldía and local businesses can arrange guides. There are other hikes, too, including **Chiche**, a four-hour hike that requires some rapelling; **Cueva de Chinahejcal**, a 10-meter (32-foot) cave usually reached on horseback; and **Cueva del Alemán**, discovered by a German spelunker in the early 1940s.

Mariposario San Andrés (2278-1582; mariposario.sanandres@gmail.com) Admission $2.50/1.50 adult/child; open 8–5 Friday through Sunday. This small *mariposario* (butterfly garden) close to San Andrés Archaeological Park is home to a dozen different species fluttering by, between flowers, guests, and plates of mashed bananas. The delightful owner takes you through every stage of the butterfly's development, and if you're lucky you may see one emerging from its cocoon. Though the mariposario is signed from Carretera Santa Ana, it's tricky. The turnoff is opposite the ruins, 250 meters (274 yards) south of the Río Sucio bridge. Look for the Profetica La Ciudad de Sion church. From there, a dirt road continues west 400 meters (438 yards) to a signed right turn to the mariposario.

ARCHAEOLOGICAL PARKS This is El Salvador's richest region for ruins, but keep in mind that Cuscatlán was something of a backwater, on the fringes of the Olmec and Mayan empires. The most impressive cities, San Andrés and Tazumal, were merely regional capitals, while La Joya de Cerén was a simple farming village. Though fascinating, they do disappoint visitors expecting the massive stone metropolises of Mexico.

Though most of these cities were founded between 1200 and 400 B.C., their early history remains buried beneath several meters of volcanic ash produced by the 260 A.D. eruption of Ilopango Volcano, which left Western El Salvador uninhabitable for more than a century. Around 400 A.D., Nahuatl-speaking Mayans began returning to the area, and re-established villages at San Andrés, Casa Blanca, and around Lago de Güija. Apaneca, Izalco, Metapán, Nahuizalco, Santa Ana, and Tacuba were also re-occupied during this period.

With the exception of San Andrés, inextricably tied to the Mayan capital in Tikal, Cuscatlán weathered the mysterious Classic Mayan Collapse of 800–900 A.D. rather well, forming ties with the Lenca of Eastern El Salvador. Around 1200 A.D., Post Classic Mayans violently re-incorporated the region into the Tikal polity. This system was very much in place when the Spanish arrived in 1524.

These planned cities are constructed in typical Mayan style, centered on a massive central plaza surrounded by important stone public buildings, administrative offices, ball courts, and pyramids. Smaller adobe buildings with thatched roofs and wide awnings, like those preserved beneath volcanic ash in Joya de Cerén, surrounded the plazas, which served as market and festival centers.

In addition to the public parks, there are several other informally accessible archaeological sites in the region, including **Ruinas Izalco** (2 kilometers/1.2 miles north of Izalco), with unexcavated pyramids; at **Santa Leticia Mountain**

AÑIL, OR INDIGO, WAS ONCE EL SALVADOR'S MOST IMPORTANT CROP; TODAY YOU CAN SEE IT PROCESSED AND USED AT CASA BLANCA ARCHAEOLOGICAL PARK.

Resort, near Apaneca, displaying rounded sculptures of women; **Piedra Sellada**, a massive petroglyph in El Imposible National Park; **Centro Turistico El Trapiche**, near Chalchuapa, with an Olmec-era pyramid that may be El Salvador's oldest; and **Lago de Güija**, with numerous structures and petroglyphs.

Casa Blanca (2408-4641; www.fundar.org.sv/casablanca.html) KM74.5 Carretera Santa Ana, toward Chalchuapa. Admission: $3 foreigner, $1 Central American. Open: 9–4 Tuesday through Sunday. This shady park 1.4 kilometers (less than a mile) from Tazumal, preserves five cement-reinforced pyramids peeking out from beneath grassy mounds; another remains covered. Inhabited since at least 3000 B.C., the stone structures were built around 500 B.C. By 600 A.D., this was a major trade center whose extent encompassed the modern city of Chalchuapa. In addition to a pleasant 1-kilometer (0.6-mile) walk through the ruins, the site includes a pretty Colonial-style complex with an excellent museum. Spanish signage describes the artifacts found here: petroglyphs, statues, and polychrome pottery. There's also an indigo workshop that uses Colonial techniques to process añil, the feathery green bush that produces this profoundly blue dye. Beautiful clothing is on sale at the gift shop. Demonstrations run throughout the day, and you can arrange classes with advance notice.

✪ **Joya de Cerén** (2401-5782; www.fundar.org.sv/e_joyadeceren.html) KM35 East Pan American. Admission: $3 foreigner, $1 Central American. Open: 9–4 Tuesday through Sunday. Though this is El Salvador's archaeological crown jewel, a UNESCO World Heritage Site unmatched elsewhere in the Americas, it's not particularly . . . impressive. But forget those pyramids and palaces—those were for the elites who, quite frankly, spent their time making trouble for everyone else. This is the story of everyone else. Blue-collar Mayans lived modest lives, making ceramics, manufacturing tools, fishing, weaving, mining, and farming. Their unfortified villages were built of wood and adobe—materials that do not last as long as stone. Joya de Cerén, sometimes called America's Pompeii, however, preserves a village almost intact, abandoned by residents who fled the 640 A.D. Laguna de Caldera eruption with meals half-eaten and kitchen fires burning. This great volcanic blizzard smothered the earth beneath 8 meters (26 feet) of ash. Though the region was resettled by Mayan Pipiles, they never knew what lay beneath the land they plowed. The village was discovered by accident in 1976. Today, you must visit on a 45-minute, guided, Spanish-language tour, starting every 15 minutes or so at the entrance. Guides lead you through botanical gardens to huge protective structures that shelter the fragile village, with its simple, wood-framed mud huts, storage units, a communal kitchen, and a *temazcal*, or medicinal sauna. Though the complex is connected to the former regional capital of San Andrés by an ancient 5-kilometer (3-mile) trail, it's not yet open for hiking. Visiting the two sites is tricky using public transport; catch a #108 southbound bus from San Juan Opico to San Salvador, and get off at the PanAmericana, where you'll catch the #201 Santa Ana bus to the San Andrés entrance. From Santa Ana, simply reverse the trip. Bus #108 from San Salvador's Terminal Occidente goes directly to Joya de Cerén.

San Andrés (2319-3220; www.fundar.org.sv/e_sanandre.html) KM32 Pan American Highway. Admission: $3 foreigner, $1 Central American. Open: 9–4. Cuscatlán's administrative capital was originally founded around 900 B.C., and functioned until the Ilopango eruption of 260 A.D. It was re-occupied from 400 A.D. to 900 A.D., when it was abandoned in the wake of the Classic Mayan collapse. Though it was periodically occupied afterward, it ceased to function as a city. Today, visitors begin at the excellent museum, with some signage in English, a model of the ruins, and a reproduction of El Lienzo de Tlaxcala's *Battle of Acajutla,* depicting the final battle between the Maya Pipiles and Spanish Conquistadors. There are several ceramic and stone artifacts—check out those wicked obsidian knives—and photo-heavy exhibits about the region's natural and cultural history. Close to the museum is a pyramid-themed playground, auditorium, and the remains of a Spanish indigo factory, which was buried by the 1658 El Playón eruption. Spanish-language tours through the ruins are free. The old central plaza is now a grassy field from which several partially excavated pyramids and public buildings rise, most impressively The Acropolis, a pyramid once topped with adobe structures. Other mounds and perhaps an underground tunnel will soon be made accessible to visitors. Bus #201 between Santa Ana and San Salvador passes the entrance every 15 minutes.

Tazumal (2408-4295; www.fundar.org.sv/e_tazumal.html) Final 11 Avenida Sur and Calle el Cantón, Chalchuapa. Open: 9–4. Admission: $3 foreigner, $1 Central American. This photogenic collection of step pyramids gets a bad rap for its non-traditional reconstruction; think smoothly poured cement rather than exposed stone. This may be similar to the original façade, however, which would have been thickly stuccoed. In any case, the 23-meter (75-foot) main pyramid is

THE KIDS IN CHALCHUAPA MAY HAVE THE COOLEST PLACE TO PLAY BALL IN CENTRAL AMERICA, IN FRONT OF TAZUMAL'S AWESOME PYRAMIDS.

among El Salvador's oldest and most impressive, as are the artifacts uncovered here, displayed at the onsite **Stanley H. Boggs Museum**, named for the archaeologist who did so much work here. The Olmec-style carved figure displayed in front of the museum, called the Stone of Victories, presents real evidence of an ancient link between El Salvador and Veracruz, Mexico. Carved around 600 B.C., it predates the pyramids by 800 years. Other artifacts include huge studded incense burners; polychrome pottery from Guanacaste, Costa Rica; a statue of Xipi Tótec, the God of Spring and Fertility; and horseshoe-shaped stone belts worn by ball players. The city was originally founded around 400 A.D., reaching its political peak of power between 800 and 1200 A.D., and was a functioning city when the Spanish arrived. There are several related archaeological sites in the area, including developed **Casa Blanca**, 10 blocks away, and many less accessible sites, on private land, covered in the museum. You may be able to arrange guides. The San Salvador–Ahuachapán Bus #202 passes close by; ask the driver to drop you off at the *Gasolinero Texaco cerca de Tazumal*, five blocks away. From Santa Ana, take Bus #201, which lets you off close to Casa Blanca. There's one surprisingly nice place to stay in Chalchuapa, four blocks from Tazumal. **Hostal Las Flores** (2408-1098; www.hostallasfloreschalchuapa.com; info@hostallasflores chalchuapa.com; Avenida 2 Abril #13, Barrio Apaneca; $; cash only) offers 11 spotless rooms with private hot bath, cable TV, and air-conditioning, surrounding well-tended gardens. The restaurant specializes in pre-Columbian traditional dishes like *yuca con chicharrón*, mashed yuca served with fried pork and vinegar cold slaw. They organize guided tours of both ruins, area jade factories (shops surround the entrance to Tazumal), hikes up Volcán El Chingo, and trips to Laguna de Cuscachapa, a little-visited crater lake.

✴ Lodging

From hostels to Colonial hotels to mountain lodges and campsites, this region has a range of accommodations. Many mountain hotels lack air-conditioning, as it's cool; bring a light jacket. For lodging near the National Parks and other protected areas, check those sections; many restaurants and centros turisticos offer accommodations as well.

Ahuachapán

Anchoring the northern end of the Ruta Las Flores, close to the Guatemalan border, this Colonial gem is little visited, but has some intriguing options. Book tours all over the region and Guatemala at **Tours Universales** (2422-0016, 2410-1150; www.elsalvadorvacations.com.sv; tours -universales@navegante.com.sv; 2 Avenida Norte #2–4).

✦ ✴ 🛏 "🍴" **Casa Blanca**(2433-1505; www.casablancaahuachapan.com) 2 Avenida Norte #1-5. $–$$. V. Handicap Access: No. Century-old mansion offers eight immaculate, tiled rooms with cable TVs, telephones, desks, and modern hot baths, some with tubs. An antique-furnished patio wraps around private gardens with a pretty pool, and there's a great onsite **restaurant** (B, L, D; $$). They organize hikes up Volcán Chichicastapec, city tours, and trips around Ruta de las Flores.

✦ 🛁 ✴ 🛏 **Hotel Parador** (2473-0331; www.hotelparadorahuachapan.net; hotelparador@navegante.com.sv) KM102.5 Carretera Chinamas. $$.

AE, MC, V. Handicap Access: Challenging. Just outside town, en route to the Chinamas border, 10 aging but acceptable rooms come with cable TVs, telephones, private hot baths, decent beds, room service, and views over the deep pool and highway. It's a $1 mototaxi from town.

🚗 **Hotel San José** (2413-4399) 6 Calle Poniente and Calle 2 de Avril. $. Cash only. Handicap Access: Challenging. Right by the buses, very basic hotel has cleanish rooms, all with soft mattresses, fans, and private baths. For 50¢ more, you get cable TV and a much bigger room. Hourly rates, too.

✪ 🌿 ♨ ❄ 🚗 **Santa Teresa Aguas Termales** (2443-1937, 7786-2550; www.termalesdesantateresa.com, mbatres@confinanzas.com) Finca Batres, Ahuachapán. $$$$. AE, MC, V. Handicap Access: No. This is a truly magical place, where a thermal river flows through a shady organic coffee plantation into a series of enormous pools; a remarkable abundance of water beautifully set into the scenery. Surrounding the steaming springs are a handful of furnished vacation homes, some with separate bedrooms, others with private pools, partial kitchens, and private porches. Meals can theoretically be arranged in advance, but it's better to bring groceries. While this transcendent spot is uniquely beautiful, it could use some work; pool temperatures can be uneven, and there's little management onsite. The rack rate is high. Local hotels arrange evening visits (highly recommended!), and can often get substantial discounts for overnights. Access is 4WD only.

Apaneca

Budget hotels are located in the city center, while nicer lodging lines the highway between Apaneca and Ataco.

🍴 🌿 ♨ 🏨 "❢" **Alicante Montaña Hotel** (2433-0175, 2433-0572; www.alicanteapaneca.com; alicanteapaneca@hotmail.com) KM93.5 Carretera Ahuachapán. $$$. AE, MC, V. Handicap Access: Yes. Very comfortable lodge is geared to large groups, with a huge restaurant and 26 polished wooden rooms featuring flagstone porches, cable TVs, and private baths, on rolling, grassy grounds. It offers a small gym, Jacuzzi, and fabulous pool, with a waterfall and little island in the middle.

♨ 🏨 **Las Cabañas de Apaneca** (2433-0500; www.cabanasapaneca.com; lascabanasapaneca@navegante.com.sv) KM90.5 Carretera Ahuachapán. $$. MC, V. Handicap Access: No. Family-sized cabins, across the highway from the Apaneca entrance, aren't fancy, but comfortable, with cheerfully mismatched furniture, cable TVs, private hot baths, and wonderful private porches in the misty gardens. Breakfast is included the **restaurant** (B, L, D; $–$$) with an unusual brick interior of archways and original art, serving traditional dishes like *sopa de pata* (cow's foot soup) and chicken dinner for four.

♨ 🏨 **Hostal Colonial** (2433-0662, 7948-9277; hostalcolonial_apaneca@hotmail.com) 1 Avenida Sur and 6 Calle Poniente. $. Cash only. Handicap Access: Challenging. Great murals adorn this classic Colonial, its gardens surrounded by nine very clean rooms with mismatched furniture, good beds, cable TVs, and large hot private baths. Breakfast is available.

♨ 🏨 **Finca Los Andes** (2433-0429, 7736-8923) KM92.5 Carretera Ahuachapán. $$–$$$. Cash only. Handicap Access: No. The Ruta de las Flores is famous for *viveros*, or flower nurseries, and this is like staying within one. Four brick cabins sleeping two to six are wrapped within coffee and orchids, with handmade Nahuizalco furnishings, private front porches, and personal barbecues; firewood is included. There's also a restaurant.

✪ ⌂ 🏠 **El Jardín de Celeste** (2433-0277, 2433-0415, 2433-0218) KM94 Ruta de las Flores, between Apaneca and Ataco. $$–$$$. AE, MC, V. Handicap Access: Challenging. Ensconced in misty gardens, Jardín de Celeste is a beautifully rustic

✪ **restaurant** (B, L, D; $$–$$$) filled with fresh flowers, old Spanish saints, cozy fireplaces, and marimba music on Sunday afternoon, when you should have reservations. Specialties include pork loin in plum sauce; grilled rabbit, and steak sautéed with *tenquique,* a local mushroom available only in rainy season. But there are also 10 different-sized whitewashed adobe cabins scattered through the coffee and clouds, with private flagstone porches, antique furnishings, and your choice of cable television or fireplace. One has a full kitchen. There are hiking trails into the coffee plantation, and they arrange tours to Santa Teresa Hot Springs and Cascadas de Don Juan.

⌂ 🏠 **Hostal Magaña** (2433-0268) Avenida Central between 4 and 6 Calle Oriente. $. Cash only. Handicap Access: No. Make reservations for inexpensive rooms with shared bath.

⌂ 🏠 **Hostal Rural Las Orquideas** (2433-0061; hostallasorquideas apaneca@yahoo.com) Avenida Central Sur #4. $. Cash only. Handicap Access: Challenging. Simple rooms with private hot bath, share a ham-mock-strewn patio, orchid gardens, and common area with TV.

✪ 🍃 🍴 ⌂ ❄ 🚗 "¶" **Santa Leticia Mountain Resort** (2433-0357; www .coffee.com.sv, santaleticia@coffee .com.sv) KM86.5 Carretera Ahuachapán. $$$$. AE, MC, V. Handicap Access: Yes. The best hotel on Ruta las Flores offers tranquil respite among the coffee-covered mountains in colorful, high-ceilinged rooms with warm salto tiles, original art, cable TV, and Guatemalan weavings, surrounding two great pools with hammock-hung porches. Newer rooms are larger and more private. The huge lodge-style restaurant (B, L, D; $$) serves espresso beverages, and fine Latin cuisine such as chicken in mole or churrasco steak in front of the huge fireplace. You can also take a 1-kilometer (0.6-mile) hike ($3 for non-guests) to see a rather mysterious archaeological site, unexcavated mounds dating to about 600 A.D. Three rounded stone female figures of Olmec proportions, weighing between 7 and 12 tons each, may be millennia older. From December through February, coffee-harvest tours are offered for $35 per person.

Ataco

⌂ 🏠 **Balcón de Ataco** (2450-5171, 7505-9034; elbalcondeataco@gmail .com) 8 Calle Oriente (Calle El Naranjito), 500 meters (547 yards) above Ataco. $$. AE, MC, V. Handicap Access: Yes. A steep four-block walk from town, this pretty spot overlooks the city from six pretty, light-filled rooms with private hot baths, good beds, and nice furnishings. The double rooms are huge. The fabulous view can also be enjoyed at the **restaurant** (B, L, D; $–$$) serving soups, salads, and Salvadoran specialties.

⚓ ❋ **Casa Quinta El Carmen** (2298-4188, 2450-5146; www.elcarmen estate.com, cafeataco@yahoo.com) KM97 Cerretera Ahuachapán. $$$–$$$$. AE, MC, V. Handicap Access: Challenging. Nestled into the finca that produces well-regarded Café Ataco, this comfortable, Colonial-style four-room villa offers two less expensive rooms that share a very nice hot bath, two nicer private rooms, including a spacious suite. All come with air-conditioning, cable TVs, fresh flowers, flagstone porches, and other extras; coffee tours and horseback rides can be arranged. The grounds are delightful, meals can be arranged, and central Ataco is just a short walk away.

⚓ 🚗 "¶" **Cipi at Ataco Hostal** (7505-9034; www.cipihostels.com; hostel ataco@yahoo.com) 1 Calle Poniente #14, Avenida 3. $–$$. Cash only. Handicap Access: Challenging. Dorms and large, nicely furnished, dark rooms, some with private bath, are geared to backpackers. The gardens are pretty and there's a TV in the common area.

⚓ 🚗 **Posada de Don Olí** (2450-5155; oogomezduarte@yahoo.com .mx) 1 Avenida Sur between 2 and 4 Calle Poniente. $$. Cash only. Handicap Access: Challenging. Two tiny rooms sleeping four each in a well-kept colonial are a good deal, with private hot bath, cable TV, and access to the ✪ **great restaurant**, with live music Sunday afternoon.

Izalco

Just a few kilometers east of Sonsonate, this classic Colonial town is a much more pleasant place to spend the night. Restaurants El Chele and Río Nuevo also offer accommodations.

✪ 🚗 "¶" **La Casona de Los Vega** (2453-5951, 7129-5416; www.lacasona delosvega.com.sv, casonadelasvega@ yahoo.com) 2 Avenida Norte #24. $. Credit cards: No. Handicap Access: Yes. Architecture buffs will be impressed with this 140-year-old whitewashed adobe, complete with tejas-tiled roof, lovely antiques, and ancient dark wood accents, all surrounding a gorgeous interior garden. This is a hostel, not hotel, with real Colonial rooms (read: small and dark), some with shared bath. All are fan-cooled, and the only cable TV is in the lounge. Los Vega arranges unique tours to the area's fascinating indigenous villages and fiestas, where you'll learn about the customs, *cofradías* (communal governments), and cosmology of the Tecpan Izalco people. They also organize guided hikes up Izalco Volcano, and to little-visited eco-attractions including Bosque Centenario, Cueva de Chanehecat, Río Caluco hot springs, and Teshcal.

THE IZALCO ALCALDÍA PLANS TO ERECT THE FIRST PUBLIC MONUMENT IN EL SALVADOR TO THE VICTIMS OF LA MATANZA, WHICH FOLLOWED FARABUNDO MARTÍ'S 1932 PEASANT UPRISING; MARCO TULIO VEGA DISPLAYS THE PLANS.

Juayúa

This is the tourism epicenter of Ruta de las Flores, with the widest range of lodging. Make reservations on weekends. These are just a few of the budget options available; www.juayua.com lists more.

☐ ❝ᴛ❞ **Hotel Anáhuac** (2469-2401; www.hotelanahuac.com, hotelanahuac@tikal.dk) 1 Calle Poniente and 5 Avenida Norte. $. AE, MC, V. Handicap Access: No. This long-standing backpacker magnet is fabulous, with wonderful murals in private rooms and festive five-bed dorms, arranged around two fine interior courtyard gardens. Cozy common areas have a great social vibe, making this a fine spot to meet and greet fellow travelers, exchange books, or cook a communal meal in the shared kitchen. The friendly owners speak English, have an excellent information board, and run quality tours. Make reservations.

☐ ❧ **Casa de Huéspedes Mercedes** (2452-2287) 2 Avenida Sur and 6 Calle Oriente. $. Cash only. Handicap Access: Challenging. Clean, homey, family-run guesthouse has cheerfully painted rooms with excellent beds and fans, surrounding relaxed common areas and a small courtyard with pomegranate trees. Some have shared bath.

☐ ❝ᴛ❞ **Casa Mazeta** (2406-3403, 7421-0782; alex.721@hotmail.fr) $. Cash only. Handicap Access: Challenging. Beautiful new hostel caters to backpackers: Shared kitchen; spacious common areas; WiFi; and big, comfortable dorms with sturdy bunk beds, great mattresses, and private lockers. Private rooms are excellent; the Garden Room, with big windows right onto all the lush, tropical gardens, is one of the city's best.

✪ ❧ ☐ ✳ ❧ **La Escondida Bed & Breakfast** (2245-2614; 7888-8642 English; www.akwaterra.com, akwaterra@gmail.com) Portezuelo Park, 6 kilometers (3.7 miles) north of Juayúa. $$–$$$. AE, MC, V. Handicap Access: No. At the heart of this Portezuelo Park (see Other Parks), this whimsically decorated B&B has five furnished rooms, and common areas are packed with colorful artwork, fireplaces, cable TV with DVD, and much more. Rooms range from the tiny backpackers' quarters to a fine master suite—or rent the whole place. Just be sure to make reservations, particularly on weekends. Portezuelo is run by Akwaterra, a recommended adventure operator with tours throughout the country, and Hotel Las Olas, in Playa Sunzal (Western Beaches).

✦ ☐ ✳ ❧ **Juayúa Inn** (7878-8011) Final 6 Avenida Norte #22. $$. V. Handicap Access: Challenging. A signed, 10-minute walk from the center, this hidden treasure isn't for everyone. Only three unique, bohemian-chic rooms, they have a wonderful little pool and impressive volcano views. The large suite, with oriental rugs, art, and a faux fireplace, is almost elegant in a hippy gypsy way. The other two rooms, in a rickety wooden building next door, have vines growing through the walls, unique furnishings, and private hot baths. The downstairs room has air-conditioning; upstairs is wide open to paradise.

☐ ❧ ❝ᴛ❞ **Hotel Mirador Juayúa** (2469-2470; hotelposada_elmirador@hotmail.com) 4 Calle Poniente. $. AE, MC, V. Handicap Access: Challenging. Simple, clean rooms come with private baths, fans, cable TVs, and access to glass-enclosed third-floor events salon with 360-degree views over the volcanoes. The hotel arranges all the guided hikes, rents mountain bikes ($3 per day) and has a small **restaurant** (B, L, D; $) on the first floor.

Metapán

More options are available at **Lago de Güija**, under National Parks.

✳ 🏨 **Hotel Christina** (2442-0044) 4 Avenida Sur between Calle 15 de Septiembre and 2 Calle. $–$$. Cash only. Handicap Access: Challenging. Three blocks from the bus terminal, at the market, simple spot offers small, clean rooms with private bath, cable TV, and for a few dollars more, air-conditioning.

🍴 📶 ✳ 🏨 **Hotel Centroamérica** (2402-2988; liligloribel_07@hotmail .com) KM106 Carretera Metapán. $$. Cash only. Handicap Access: Challenging. Just outside Metapán, this hotel offers tiled, air-conditioned **cabanas** with private bath and cable TV, within a centro turistico with pools, restaurants, a small zoo, horseback rides, and playground equipment for kids, all connected by a miniature train. Day passes are $2.

🏨 **Hostal Cerro Limón** (7871-9783, 2402-1874; info@hostalvillalimon .com) Cerro Limo, Metapán. $$. Cash only. Handicap Access: No. Three comfortably rustic log cabins are equipped with handmade furnishings, cable TVs, refrigerators, and full kitchens, including a wood-fired stove. They supply the firewood. Amenities include an eight-platform canopy tour, with one 470-meter (1542-foot) cable across a serious valley.

📶 🏨 ✳ 🏨 **Hotel San José** (2442-0556; www.hoteleselsalvador.com, reservaciones@hoteleselsalvador.com) KM113 Carretera Metapán. $$. AE,

THIS FANTASTIC VIEW, FROM THE JUAYÚA INN, ONLY TAKES IN A FEW OF THE ELEVEN VOLCANOES THAT RING THE BUSY TOWN.

MC, V. Handicap Access: No. Metapán's tallest building, conveniently located at the turnoff to Montecristo National Park, houses 27 modern and comfortable (if slightly dingy) rooms with brown carpeting, older furnishings, cable TV, air-conditioning, and private hot bath. It's by far the best hotel in town.

Los Naranjos

Restaurants Paso de Alaska and Kaltepet also offer accommodations in this cool mountain town between Juayúa and Santa Ana.

EcoParque San Bernardo (2430-1985, 7729-6687; ecoparque sanbernardo.spaces.live.com; pedro portillo@hotmail.com) KM93.5 Carretera Los Naranjos. $$. Cash only. Handicap Access: No. Exquisite spot set on 5 manzanas (8.5 acres) of farmland inset with pretty gardens and pools offers spacious, rustic wooden cabins with rustic décor and modern conveniences.

Finca Los Trozos Estancia (2415-9912; www.lostrozos .com; info@lostrozos.com) KM87 Carretera Los Naranjos. $$$$ including all meals. AE, MC, V. Handicap Access: No. This new luxury option near Los Naranjos offers posh yet ecofriendly rooms, with fabulous furnishings, top-quality bedding, TVs and DVD players, organic buffet-style meals, and a pool set in lovely gardens with trails leading throughout the finca.

Shangrila Eco Lodge (2264-4197, 7319-2222; jacolorado@ gmail.com) KM96 Carretera Los Naranjos. $$$–$$$$. Handicap Access: No. Isolated yet comfortable cabin in the misty highlands of the biosphere reserve sleeps up to eight, with a full kitchen, solar-heated bath

(and solar refrigerator), and guided hikes into all this beauty. Access is 4WD-only, and can be arranged.

Santa Ana

Santa Ana's big-city sprawl overwhelms some visitors, who find the chaos and congestion unappealing. But it's a convenient base for exploring the region, and good for the urban adventurer. You can stay downtown, or try a quieter residential neighborhood, at budget Casa Frolaz and Hotel Latino, or upmarket Tolteka Plaza.

Casa Frolaz (2440-5302; www.casafrolaz.com, contacto@casa frolaz.com) 29 Calle Poniente #42-B, between 8 Avenida Sur and Avenida Santa Ana California (10 Avenida Sur). $. Credit cards: No. Handicap Access: Challenging. Exceptional hostel is in a quiet corner of Santa Ana, a 10–15 minute walk from downtown, but close to restaurants and groceries. A spacious and elegant family home has been converted into one of the country's best budget accommodations: one private room, and two comfortable dorms with seven beds and one bath. There's a fabulous full kitchen, sunny garden, and comfortably furnished common area, with cable TV, DVDs, a spectacular collection of ashtrays, and great vibes.

Hotel Latino (2440-5206, 2440-5910) 29 Calle Poniente and Avenida 18 Sur. $. MC, V. Handicap Access: Challenging. In the same quiet neighborhood as Casa Frolaz, this great little hotel has 20 freshly painted, modern rooms with private bath and secure parking. Cheaper rooms, with cold showers, cable TVs, and fans, are tiny but immaculate; pay $5 extra for larger rooms with air-conditioning, and hot bath.

⌂ **Hotel Libertad** (2441-2358) 4 Calle Oriente and 1 Avenida Norte. $. Cash only. Handicap Access: No. One block from Parque Libertad, simple spot offers clean, threadbare, fan-cooled rooms with cold showers and cable TVs. Not bad.

⌂ **Hotel Livingston** (2441-1801) 10 Avenida Sur between 7 and 9 Calle Poniente. $. Cash only. Handicap Access: Challenging. Industrial hotel is cheap, fairly clean, and close to the center of town. Rooms with stained carpets and dated furnishings have fans, cable TVs, and cold showers.

⌂ ❊ ⌂ "¶" **Hotel Sahara** (2447-8865, 2447-8832; hotel_sahara@yahoo.com) 3 Calle Poniente between 10 and 12 (Matias) Avenida Sur. $$. AE, MC, V. Handicap Access: No. Santa Ana's finest downtown option makes a stab at aging opulence with chandeliers, leather sofas, and faux marble; service really is excellent. Head upstairs, where 30 smallish rooms offer high ceilings, nice furnishings, air-conditioning, and modern hot bath. There's a third-floor terrace with views across the city and volcanoes.

✦ ⌂ ❊ ⌂ "¶" **Hotel Tolteka Plaza** (2479-0888; www.hoteleselsalvador .com, tolteka@hoteleselsalvador.com) Avenida Independencia Sur, Metrocentro. $$–$$$. AE, MC, V. Handicap Access: Yes. Modern hotel offers all the amenities of a mid-range chain in Santa Ana, California: Spacious rooms with great beds, attractive furnishings, reliable air-conditioning, and real hot water in the spotless bathroom. You're even fairly close to the mall (but a $4 cab ride to the city center). Fifty rooms surround a sparkling pool, and staff, some of whom speak English, can arrange tours.

Sonsonate

Please take a cab from the bus terminal.

✐ ✦ ⌂ ❊ ⌂ "¶" **Hotel Agape** (2451-7677, 2429-8767; www.hotelagape .com.sv, laura@agape.com.sv) KM63 Carretera San Salvador-Sonsonate. $–$$. AE, MC, V. Handicap Access: Yes. A few minutes (but seemingly a world away) from downtown Sonsonate, this large, grassy compound has flowers, trees, a pool, and rooms that are small and a bit dark, but have great beds, nice furnishings, cable TVs, air-conditioning, and private hot baths. The **restaurant** (B, L, D; $$) serves Salvadoran food and has a full bar, and next door, a **water park** ($2/1 adult/child) has several pools and slides, open weekends only.

✦ ❊ ⌂ "¶" **Hotel Plaza** (2451-6628, 2451-2600; hotelplaza_sonsonate @yahoo.com) 9 Calle Oriente between 8 and 10 Avenida Norte. $$. MC, V. Handicap Access: Challenging. Well signed at the turnoff to Ruta Las Flores, this hotel delivers comfort, security, and cable TV just minutes from the bus station. All of the very standard, clean rooms come with cable TVs, and soft beds, plus access to a small pool and onsite restaurant in the tidy courtyard.

Tacuba

Though not officially part of the Ruta de las Flores, this ancient adobe village is a recommended 16-kilometer (10-mile) side trip from Ahuachapán.

✐ ✦ ❊ ⌂ **Hotel Cabañas de Tacuba** (2260-2627, 2417-4332; hotellacabana tacuba@yahoo.com) Northeast side of town. $$. V. Handicap Access: Challenging. Family-friendly hotel on grassy, rolling grounds is showing its age, but is still comfortable, with

BUSY SONSONATE ISN'T EXACTLY A TOURIST DESTINATION, BUT PARQUE DOLORES HAS A GREAT CHURCH AND LITTLE TOURISTED GASTRONOMIC FESTIVAL ON WEEKENDS.

private rooms furnished with air-conditioning, private bath, and cable TV. Furnishings vary quite a bit, particularly mattress quality, so check out a few. An onsite **restaurant** (B, L, D; $–$$) serves Salvadoran cuisine. It's well signed from the main road.

✪ 🚗 "🍴" **Hostal Mamá y Papá** (2469-2109; www.imposibletours.com, contact@imposibletours.com) Tacuba, west end. $. Credit cards: No. Handicap Access: No. Tacuba seems at the edge of civilization, where coffee plantations give way to the untamed wilderness of El Imposible Park. There are other hotels in town, which work with this basic, well-run hostel to provide amazing guided hikes into "The Impossible" courtesy of bilingual manager and guide, Manolo González (his mama and papa are the owners). Lodging is simple, a few private rooms with shared hot bath, and several freshly painted dorms in an ancient adobe Colonial. The hammock-strewn common area and sec-

ond-story mirador surround steep gardens that have hosted outdoorsy backpackers and National Geographic film crews, all here for uniquely challenging tours; see National Parks, later. An onsite **restaurant** (B, L, D; $) has a few tables on the patio, serving good Salvadoran and international cuisine, with several vegetarian choices. It's three blocks uphill from the bus stop, on the right, across from the gym ($1 day pass) on the corner. They can also arrange lodging at guesthouses in Barra de Santiago.

🚗 🏠 **Las Nubes** (7224–7337) Three blocks north of the central park. $$. Handicap Access: No. Make reservations to stay at this very pretty hotel, whose high walls hide stunning gardens, with antiques set among the flowers and perfect spots for enjoying the awesome views. Rooms and cabins have private machine-heated showers, cable TVs, and mismatched furnishings, while more spacious cabins offer private porches with hammocks.

✳ Where to Eat

While the gastronomic festivals and many of the best restaurants only operate on the weekends, there are several spots open all week long. Santa Ana has a handful of beautiful restaurants and cafés, and lots of cheaper eats, while Los Naranjos boasts some of the finest dining in the country. The Ruta de las Flores is lined with wonderful restaurants within *viveros,* or plant nurseries, many of them also hotels.

DINING OUT

Izalco

✪ **Restaurant El Chele** (2453-6740; www.izalcoelchelerestaurant.com) 3 Calle Oeste #7. $–$$$. AE, MC, V. Cuisine: Salvadoran. Serving: B, L, D. Child's Menu: Yes. Handicapped Access: Challenging. Reservations: For groups. Elegantly rustic restaurant, decorated with antiques and handmade furnishings, is a local institution, serving traditional dishes like baked rabbit and sopa de gallina India, and more creative fare, such as teriyaki shrimp. Better, there's another El Chele 2 kilometers (1.2 miles) from town, located near a mostly unexcavated archaeological site, with the same great menu and three very basic **rooms** ($). In addition to the archaeological site, they can also arrange guides to the surrounding indigenous villages, which have clung to their culture—despite being at the heart of the 1932 massacre—with colorful celebrations and traditions.

Río Nuevo Casa del Campo (2483-3204, 7851-9174; rionuevorestaurant @yahoo.com) Final 9 Calle Oriente, next to Atecozol Centro Turistico. $$. Credit cards: No. Cuisine: Salvadoran. Handicap Access: No. WiFi: No.

On the outskirts of Izalco, this open-air restaurant offers quality Salvadoran favorites such as grilled meats, chicken dishes, and fish from the Río Nuevo (New River). They even have fishing poles you can use to catch your own dinner, which they can prepare with all the fixings. Four cabañas ($$) are also available, with private cool bath, one double bed, air-conditioning, and hammocks.

✪ **Via Roca Restaurante y Museo de Dinosaurios** (2488-3450, 2453-5416; viaroca.com) KM59 Carretera Sonsonate, 300 meters (328 yards) past Izalco turnoff. $–$$. AE, MC, V. Cuisine: Prehistoric, Salvadoran. Serving: B, L, D. Child's Menu: Yes. Handicapped Access: Challenging. Look for the Flintstones-style

STREET VENDOR IN TACUBA DISHES UP NUÉGADOS, SWEET BALLS OF FRIED YUCA, SMOTHERED IN CANE SYRUP.

WEEKEND FOOD FESTIVALS

The ✪ **Juayúa Gastronomic Festival** (10–5 Saturday and Sunday) is the most famous, when thousands of people come for creative cuisine, live music, handicraft shopping, **miniature train rides** (50¢; 20 minutes), and more food. However, there are several other less famous (and less crowded) spots to enjoy a taste of El Salvador.

Apaneca Expo Snacks (8–6 Saturday and Sunday) "El Salvador's most beautiful city" offers artesanías and tasty meals.

Ataco Flower Festival (8–6 Saturday and Sunday) Dramatic Ataco also has a food, flower, and arts exhibition.

Sonsonate (8–6 Saturday and Sunday) The Parque Central comes alive with handicrafts, food stands, and live entertainment.

Nahuizalco Handicrafts Exhibition (8–6 Saturday and Sunday) Weaving, woodwork, and other handicrafts come with indigenous-accented cuisine.

THE FAMED JUAYÚA GASTRONOMIC FESTIVAL SERVES UP THE BEST IN SALVADORAN CUISINE WITH A SMILE.

construction and cement dinosaurs, just past the Izalco exit, to find this unique restaurant, where servers in caveman outfits offer good Salvadoran typical dishes, such as pterodactyl soup and grilled Tyranosaurus rex, as well as pupusas. There are also swimming pools, bumper cars, pool tables, and a kid-friendly paleontology museum with informative displays, fossils, and more cement dinosaurs. A smaller history museum covers local indigenous culture and religious festivals, as well as a sobering exhibit about the 1932 Matanza, when some 30,000 striking coffee workers and indigenous peasants were executed by federal troops. They also offer tours of coffee and cacao farms.

Metapán

There are simple eateries in town, but Metapán's best restaurants are on the Lago de Güija, covered under National Parks. The city is well known for its kettle-cooked sugarcane candies, available at the market.

Ruta de las Flores

Apaneca If you're here on a weekday, eat at **Mercado Saludable Apaneca** on the central park, serving tasty typical food in a flower-filled courtyard with volcano views.

✪ **Cocina de la Abuela** (2433-0100, 2228-0809) 2 Calle Poniente and 1 Avenida Sur, #15. $$. AE, MC, V. Cuisine: Salvadoran. Serving: L, D. Closed: Monday through Friday. Child's Menu: Yes. Handicapped Access: Challenging. Reservations: Yes. This famous restaurant is only open from 10 to 6 on weekends, when it's packed. The old adobe building is a beauty, decorated with period pieces and antiques, and a porch out back has tables overlooking misty gardens with mischevious monkeys. Salvadoran classics, such as grilled meats, hearty stews, and rich coffee harvested right here are all on the menu, each item exquisitely prepared and served with professional aplomb; according to one fan, Kitchen of the Grandmother is the standard by which all other Salvadoran cuisine should be judged. Don't skip dessert.

Ahuachapán Several good comedors surround the central plaza, selling basic breakfasts and *comida a la vista* at lunch. The large market, just down-

hill from Super Selectos, also has basic food stands, and sturdier-looking restaurants.

La Estancia (2443-1559) 1 Avenida Sur #1–3. $. Credit Cards: No. Cuisine: Salvadoran. Serving: B, L, D (closes at 6 PM). Child's Menu: No. Handicapped Access: Challenging. Reservations: No. La Estancia inhabits a gorgeous, century-old mansion dating to the coffee boom, just a couple of blocks from the town square. There's menu service, but your best bet is *comida a la vista* at lunch.

El Gran Rancho (2406-6100, 7226-9522; www.elgranrancho.com) Laguna El Espino, Colonia El Carmen. $–$$$. Credit Cards: No. Cuisine: Seafood, Salvadoran. Serving: B, L, D. Child's Menu: No. Handicap Access: No. Reservations: No. If you fancy a nice meal on the edge of Laguna El Espino, a breezy lake just outside Ahuachapán, El Gran Rancho has lakefront seating and boats for hire. Or, just relax at the pleasant open-air restaurant, serving burgers and sandwiches to steak and seafood, perfect with a cold *cerveza.* They also rent very basic **rooms** ($) with private bath and air-conditioning, by the hour or night.

Ataco Fantastic Ataco has a fine selection of restaurants. Unfortunately, many of the best are open only on weekends. These include **Restaurante Café-Café** (2263-2413; www .cafecafe.com.sv; central park; $$–$$$; noon–4 PM Saturday), serving beautifully prepared Peruvian cuisine; **Restaurante Sibaritas Fusion** (2289-4867; Avenida Emilia and 2 Calle Oriente; noon–8 PM Friday, 8 AM–11 PM Saturday, 8 AM–7 PM Sunday; $$$–$$$) offering gourmet Mediterranean fusion, such as fresh pasta served with locally grown *tenquique* mushrooms and Northern Italian seafood; and **Restaurant-Bar Tayua** (see Nightlife) offering upscale international cuisine on weekends.

✪ **Café El Botón** (2450-5066; el.boton.ataco@gmail.com) Avenida Sur #19. $–$$. Credit Cards: No. Cuisine: French, International. Serving: B, L, D. Child's Menu: No. Handicapped Access: Challenging. Reservations: No. Excellent and absolutely adorable café offers exquisite French dishes using Salvadoran ingredients, such as chicken and loroco crepes. Goat cheese is the house specialty. Also on the interesting menu are quiches, pastries, wines, and fresh espresso beverages. Try to visit Saturday, when there's free live music. Absolutely fabulous.

Juayúa ✪ Restaurante R&R (2452-2083; restauranter_r@hotmail.com) 100 meters (109 yards) north of Central Park. $$–$$$. Credit Cards: No. Cuisine: Gourmet Salvadoran. Serving: L, D. Child's Menu: No. Handicapped Access: Challenging. Reservations: For dinner. Considered the best restaurant in El Salvador's Gastronomic Capital, it's worth a splurge to enjoy Chef Xiomara de Caceres' gourmet takes on classic Salvadoran cuisine and fresh, often organic, ingredients. Take a seat in the murralled dining room to enjoy such delicacies as steak marinated in coffee sauce, huge shrimp sautéed in garlic and served with several different sauces, or vegetarian lasagna. It all comes artfully presented on locally made ceramics, with excellent side salads. Wine, beer, juices, and espresso beverages are served.

Restaurante y Taquería La Guadalupeña (2452-2195; martin machadojuayua@hotmail.com) 2 Calle Oeste. $. Credit Cards: No. Cuisine: Mexican. Serving: L, D. Closed: Monday. Child's Menu: No. Handicapped Access: Challenging. Reservations: No. Simple spot serves excellent, inexpensive Mexican dishes in diner-style comfort. The specialty is tacos, but they also do tortas and burritos, with vegetarian options and five different salsas. The bar offers several types of mescal.

Los Naranjos ✪ Paso del Alaska (2415-6652, 7205-4262; www.paso delalaska.com) Los Naranjos. $$–$$$. Credit Cards: No. Cuisine: Latin American fusion. Serving: B, L, D. Closed: Monday. Child's Menu: Yes. Handicapped Access: Challenging. Reservations: Recommended on weekends. This highly regarded restaurant occupies a rather wintry-looking chalet in the middle of rolling volcanoes, where Chef Oscar René, trained in Minnesota, uses fresh, often organic ingredients to create well-presented Latin American cuisine. Favorites include *venado a la parillada,* grilled venison; Peruvian-style fajitas; and raviolis stuffed with cheese and bacon in meat sauce. The full bar has several wines, mostly Chilean reds. They offer cooking classes, too. In addition, there are also three rustic, family-sized wooden **cabins** ($$$) with hot-water private baths, private porches overlooking the incredible scenery, and separate common areas. Packages including three meals (recommended) make this a better deal.

Restaurant & Cabañas Kal-tepet (7349-5154, 7349-5179; www.kal tepet.com, mtorres1x@yahoo.com) KM83.5, Los Naranjos. $$. Serving: L, D. Cuisine: Salvadoran. V. Child's

Menu: Yes. Handicap Access: No. Reservations: Recommended on weekends. Just outside Naranjo proper, is the considered less-expensive alternative to Paso del Alaska, serving huge *parrilladas* (grilled meat platters) with sausage, Argentine-style steak, rabbit, vegetables, and other fixings for couples and crowds. They also do a great monte cristo sandwich. In addition, they offer three spacious, quite rustic suites with TV and DVD (no cable), small hot bath, and new mattresses. All are different (and oddly shaped), and have private porches; one has a fireplace.

Salcoatitán Los Patios Restaurante y Arte (2401-8590; hectorito_84@yahoo.com.mx) Main Highway, Salcoatitán. $$–$$$. AE, MC, V. Cuisine: Salvadoran. Serving: B, L, D. Closed: Monday through Friday. Child's Menu: Yes. Handicapped Access: No. Reservations: Yes. With its extensive patios surrounded by gorgeous gardens, offering sweeping views over its coffee-processing facilities and half a dozen volcanoes rising to serrated peaks beyond, this restaurant comes highly recommended for its excellent (if pricey) Salvadoran cuisine. The artsy owners also operate a top-notch gallery. Across the road, **Churrascos de Don Raffa** (2401-8570; $$; cash only; L, D) specializes in grilled meats served in open-air environs.

Tacuba Pickings are slim in Tacuba, with a handful of mediocre eateries. Your best bet for a sit-down meal is **Comedor Miraflor** (2417-4746; B, L, D; central park; $; cash only), which also has simple lodging, but was closed when I was there. **Sol de Media Noche** (2417-4074; entrance to Tacuba, Avenida España; open 6:30

AM–5 PM Monday through Friday; $; cash only) has OK vegetarian food, most involving soy meats.

Santa Ana

El Salvador's second largest city has scores of simple comedores, bakeries, and other spots to eat, with every fast food restaurant in the country represented within five blocks of Parque Libertad or Metrocentro Mall. Don't miss **Sorbetes sin Rival** (www.el sinrival.com.sv), a Santa Ana-based chain with its air-conditioned flagship on Parque Libertad, serving all-natural sorbets such as *fresa* (strawberry) and *mora* (blackberry), *nance*, *arrayán*, and *jocote*, in a crisp red *barrillo*, or bowl-shaped cone.

Restaurante Taquería La Tabastieña (2440-1388) Avenida Moraga and Calle 33 Poniente Sur. $. Credit Cards: No. Cuisine: Mexican. Serving: L, D. Child's Menu: No. Reservations: No. Friendly Mexican restaurant close to Casa Frolaz offers fresh, delicious fajitas, tortas, tacos, burritos, and other Mexican classics, with plenty of vegetarian options and homemade salsas. Or just enjoy a

CHEF OSCAR RENÉ, OF PASO DEL ALASKA IN LOS NARANJOS, PUTS THE FINISHING TOUCHES ON HIS DIVINE CHURRASCO, OR SALVADORAN GRILLED MEAT PLATTER.

beer or licuado in the breezy, open-air lounge upstairs, with views over the traffic.

Restaurante La Tertulia (2440-1149) Calle 33 Poniente and Avenida Moraga Sur. $$. AE, MC, V. Cuisine: Salvadoran. Serving: B, L, D. Child's Menu: Yes. Handicapped Access: Challenging. Reservations: No. Recommended as the best *comida típica*, typical food, in town, this pleasant eatery is popular for big breakfasts, and offers a variety of grilled meats, Salvadoran soups, and other traditional meals. It's also close to Casa Frolaz and Hotel Latino.

Restaurant Lover's Steakhouse (2440-5717; www.loverssteakhouse .com) 4 Avenida Sur and 17 Calle Poniente. $$–$$$. AE, MC, V. Cuisine: Steakhouse, International. Serving: B, L, D. Child's Menu: Yes. Reservations: Weekend evenings. Santa Ana's favorite spot for a splurge, this comfortably rustic steakhouse offers a variety of quality cuts: Try the *lomo relleno*, steak stuffed with spinach and cheese, or *punta jalapeña*, in a spicy sauce. Or go for the grilled rabbit, seafood stew, or a number of Italian and Chinese dishes, some of them vegetarian. There's a full bar, and live music on Thursday through Saturday.

Quattro Estaciones (2440-3168; quattroestaciones.blogspot.com) 23 Calle Poniente and 8 Avenida Sur #399. $$. AE, MC, V. Cuisine: Mediterranean. Serving: L, D. Child's Menu: No. Handicapped Access: Challenging. Reservations: No. Sleek, European-style bistro serves elegant international café cuisine, from gourmet sandwiches and delightful salads to sophisticated seafood and pasta entrees, with several vegetarian options. Begin with one of the bruschettas and choose something off the drink menu, with an impressive selection of coffees, infused herbal teas, and the best wine list in town, boasting vintages from Spain, France, Italy, and elsewhere. Desserts are the specialty.

ASIAN El Dragon Comida China & Mexicana (2415-9463) KM113 Carretera Metapán, Metapán. L, D. $$. Cash only. Tiny Metapán has international cuisine, all in one place.

BAKERIES Ban Ban 2 Calle Poniente. B, L, D. $. Cash only. Excellent pastries in Metapán.

✪ **Nekal Cocina Jardín** (2450-5755, 7233-6508) 4 Calle Oriente #8, Ataco. On the Ataco plaza in an old arcaded adobe, artisanal bakery sells different herb and whole wheat bread, with a gallery for local artists and photographers.

El Pan Nuestro y Café Bonsai (2452-2536) Salcoatitán. B, L, D. $. Cash only. Popular spot serves espresso and pastries.

Pastelería El Festival (2462-2269) Juayúa Central Park. B, L, D. $. Cash only. Beautiful cakes and delicious, inexpensive pastries are specialties, but they also serve sandwiches, hamburgers, and more.

CAFÉS This is coffee country, and many spots sell bags of their own homegrown, everyone's favorite souvenir. Laws forbid chipped and cracked beans—even the top-quality organic stuff—from export. Thus, excellent ground coffee is often a much better deal. In addition to these, drop by the **Majada Museo de Café**, between Juayúa and Los

Naranjos, and **Café El Sítio**, within DiConte-Axul in Ataco.

Café La Asunción (7850-7129) Colonia Talamacha #2, Los Naranjos. Artsy café in Los Naranjos has garden seating, spectacular coffee, Salvadoran cuisine, and volcano views.

Café Vivero Flores de Maritza (2453-5187) 5 Calle Poniente #19B, 50 meters (55 yards) north of the market. B, L, D. $. Cash only. Izalco coffee shop, surrounded with flowers, also serves Salvadoran specialties and local handicrafts.

✪ **Expresión Cultural** (2440-1410; www.expresioncultural.org) 11 Calle Poniente and 8 Avenida Sur. B, L, D. $. Santa Ana's sophisticated side comes out at this café, art gallery, and bookstore, serving light meals with a side of local culture.

Rincón de la Quesadilla Típica Café 2 Calle Poniente, Salcoatitán. B, L, D. $. Cash only. Coffee and Salvadoran quesadillas, rich poundcake baked with cheese, are served three blocks west of Salcoitatán's churches.

PIZZA Baking Pizza Ahuachapán (2413-2245) 4 Calle Oriente. L, D. $. Cash only. Popular chain also delivers. There are other locations in **Salcoatitán** (2452-2917; 3 Avenida Oriente) and **Juayúa** (2469-2356 2 Calle Oriente and 4 Avenida Sur).

Pizzería al Forno (2469–2608) Juayúa. L, D. $. Cash only. Cheap, simple, no-frills pizza joint serves pies and slices; delivers.

Pizza Milán (2415-9291) Calle Oriente. L, D. $. Cash only. Nahuizulco loves pizza, too.

PUPUSERÍAS ✪ **Pupusería Esmeralda** Juayúa. In a residential neighborhood (ask for directions), offers unusual pupusas, including several vegetarian options.

Doña Cony Pupusas y Tacos 2 Calle Poniente, Salcoatitán. B, L, D. $. Cash only. Two blocks west of the Salcoatitán churches, serves pupusas and tacos; there's another in **Juayúa** (2 Avenida Sur and 6 Calle Oriente).

Pupusería Las Gemelas 3 Calle Oriente. Look for the fabulous mural on Ataco's Central Park.

Pupusadromo Izalqueño Avenida Morazán and 9 Calle Poniente. Row of pupuserías offers you a choice.

Restaurante Yulmy (2452-2086) 4 Calle Poniente. Next to Hotel El Mirador, serves *comida a la vista* by day, pupusas by night.

✴ Selective Shopping

BANKS AND ATMS Most major towns have banks and ATM machines, including **Ahuachapán** (ScotiaBank and HSBC in the city, BAC at SuperSelectos), **Juayúa** (ScotiaBank near the town entrance, BAC and HSBC at Dispensa Familiar), **Metapán** (ScotiaBank on Avenida Ignacio Gómez) and **Santa Ana**, with ScotiaBank, BAC, and HSBC close to Parque La Libertad, more at Metrocentro. **Sonsonate** has an HSBC ATM on Parque Dolores. There are no ATMs elsewhere on the Ruta de las Flores, at Lago de Coatepeque, or in Tacuba.

GROCERIES Ahuachapán has a large SuperSelectos at the town entrance, close to the bus stop and market. **Izalco** has a SuperSelectos next to Iglesía Dolores, six blocks north of the city center, and also close to a market. **Juayúa** has both a SuperSelectos (1 Avenida Norte and 3

Calle Poniente) and Dispensa de Don Juan (Avenida Daniel Cordon Sur and 2 Calle Poniente). In Metapán, stock up at small **De Todo Metapán**, next to Hotel San José. **Santa Ana** has several large grocers, including two **Dispensa de San Juans**, one on Parque Libertad and another larger, nicer one near Casa Frolaz. There's a **SuperSelectos** at Metrocentro.

MALLS Metrocentro Santa Ana Boulevard Los 44. Just south of town, this huge mall has dozens of restaurants and boutiques, a SuperSelectos, department stores, and Cinemark Theater. Take local Bus #51 from Parque Libertad.

Metrocentro Sonsonate KM12 Carretera Acajutla. New mall has a large food court and lots of shops, a $5 cab ride from town.

MARKETS Most regular markets are close to the Central Park, including those in **Apaneca**, **Ataco**, **Juayúa**, and **Izalco**. Santa Ana's huge market engulfs the main bus terminal (Avenida Santa Ana California and 15 Calle Poniente), while **Sonsonate's** bus terminal is adjacent to a medium-sized market. **Ahuachapán's** large market is just downhill from SuperSelectos, at the entrance to town. All are open from about 6 to 6 daily.

Mercado de Artesanías Santa Ana Santa Ana, 8–6 daily. Small handicrafts market has an anemic selection of souvenirs, as well as the region's *dulces tipicas,* candied fruits and vegetables.

✪ **Nahuizalco Mercado Nocturno** Nahuizalco. Open 7 PM–9 PM weekends. Once known as the Candlelight Market, El Salvador's only night market once catered to folks who worked

the fincas all day. Softly lit stalls still sell basic veggies and grains, handicrafts, and Mayan cuisine, including *gallina en algüashte* (chicken in pumpkin seed sauce), *ticucos* (tiny, bean-filled tamales), *chanfaina* (sweetmeats cooked with raisins), and several types of *atole,* a sweet, warm corn beverage. Juayúa hotels arrange transport, as there's no lodging in town.

SOUVENIRS Ruta de las Flores is lined with handicrafts shops selling everything from delicate jewelry to dining room sets. Many are open only on weekends.

Nahuizalco The highway is lined with stands selling beautiful wood and woven-reed furnishings, but smaller souvenirs can be found in several shops along Calle Principal, which ends at the market and church. Most are open 8–5, and close some days during the week. My favorites include:

Artesanos Salidarios de Nahuizalco (2431-0258) 2 Calle Oriente and Avenida Calvario, Nahuizalco. Jewelry, leather shoes, woven hats, wood carvings, and more by several of the region's best artists.

CEDART (2453-1336; masantos@ conamype.gob.sv) 3 Calle Poniente #3, Nahuizalco. Both a workshop and store, you can watch handicrafts being made.

Metapíl (7533-9824) Calle Principal and Avenida Flores. Nahuatl for Homemade, sells handicrafts from five local artists.

Salcoatitán This roadside strip of a town has a handful of craft shops. **Los Patios Restaurante y Arte** (see Where to Eat) has a fine art gallery, open weekends only.

Juayúa In addition to a few good souvenir shops close to the Central Park, an ✪ **Artesanías Market** sets up just south of the park on weekends, bringing in craftspeople from all over El Salvador and Guatemala.

Apaneca A few great shops cluster on the main highway.

Café Mirador Añil, Hilos y Piedra (7870-8240) KM90.5. Open weekends only. Sells cool jewelry, indigo-dyed clothing, and other local handicrafts.

✪ **Joyería Artesanal Wilfredo Platero** (7870-7707) KM90.5, Apaneca. Open weekends only. Fabulous jewelry is made with local and imported seeds, clay beads, and even coffee beans.

Tienda Solidario (No phone) Central Park. Open 9–5 daily. In town, this tiny shop sells ceramics and crafts made with seeds and jícaro shells, as well as homemade jellies, jams, and *encurtidos* (pickles).

Ataco This town is becoming an arts center, with several galleries and outstanding crafts shops.

✪ **Diconte-Axul Artesanías** (2633-5030; axulartisans@yahoo.com) Central Park, Ataco. Amazing crafts store (look for the murals) sells whimsically painted wooden crafts by artist Cristina Pineda, and handmade textiles—come on weekends to see weavers working the looms. There's a quiet **café** ($–$$) serving coffee, pastries, and light meals in the gardens. They also run **Artesanias Madretierra** (2450-5437, 2450-5130; arte_madretierra@hotmail.com; Calle Central and 2 Avenida Sur), with masks and other crafts, nearby, and have a gallery in San Salvador (2263-3447; Avenida 79 Norte #420).

Galería Izel (7080-7559; izelataco@gmail.com) 1 Avenida Sur between 2 and 4 Calle Poniente. Original jewelry made with semi-precious stones, silver, ceramics, shells, and fossils.

Galería de Arte Contemporáneo Gerardo Cornejo (2450-5017; www.coroflot.com/gc) Calle Oriente y Avenida Central Norte #3. Hallucinogenic work from one of El Salvador's cutting-edge artists.

Tingere Teñidos Naturales (2450-5760) Avenida Central #5 and 2 Calle Oriente, Ataco. In posh La Placita plaza, upscale boutique sells clothing, scarves, and accessories made with natural fibers and dyes. Next door, **La Bohéme** sells exotic candles made of recycled wax, and used books (in Spanish, French, and English) to benefit local children.

✳ Special Events

January: **Juayúa Fiestas** (January 6–15) El Salvador's famous foodie town honors the Black Christ.

Jujútla Fiestas (January 8–18) Also dedicated to the Black Christ.

✪ **Las Primicias Tacuba** (third week in January) Ancient town reveals its Mayan heritage during the First Fruits Festival, when the Church of Mary Magdalene is decorated with fruits and vegetables and beauty queens wear entirely organic outfits made with corn, sugarcane, bananas, palms, and so on. Celebrated throughout the region.

February: **Sonsonate Fiestas** (January 25–February 2) Huge party honors the Virgin of Candelaria.

Día del Agua (Late February) The youth of Metapán enjoys a Batalla del Agua (Water Fight) with squirt guns and water balloons.

YOU CAN'T MISS THE MARVELOUS MURALS OF DICONTE-AXUL ARTESANÍAS IN ATACO, JUST A HINT OF ALL THE WONDERFUL STUFF INSIDE.

March: **Semana Santa** (week before Easter) The Ruta de las Flores is a destination for vacationing Salvadoreños (read: make hotel reservations!), with fiestas throughout the region; Nahuizalco's huge candlelit procession is a highlight.

✪ **Izalco Semana Santa** (week before Easter) The most spectacular Easter celebrations in the country have a distinctively Mayan touch.

June: **Metapán Fiestas** (June 20–29) Cattle town honors San Pedro Apóstol with horse parades, bull-riding competitions, Masses, a parade honoring U.S. President Thomas Jefferson, and fireworks on the 28th.

Caluco Fiestas (June 23–29) San Pedro Apóstal is honored.

July: **Nahuizalco Fiestas** (July 20–25) Handicrafts town honors San Juan Bautista.

✪ **Fiestas Julias** (throughout July) Santa Ana's civic fiestas are among the biggest in the nation, with parades, carnivals, a huge cattle show, and Masses in honor of Saint Anne.

Tacuba Fiestas (July 17–22) Parades, fireworks, and indigenous dances honor María Magdalena.

August: **Izalco Fiestas de Agosto** (throughout August) While Izalco's historic church honors the Virgin of Asunción, neighboring villages hold a succession of much more Mayan celebrations.

✪ **Nejapa Bolas de Fuego** (July 31) Pyromaniacs won't want to miss this commemoration of the 1658 El Playon eruption, with folks hurling balls filled with flaming gasoline down the street. Seriously. There are videos on youtube.

September: **Noche de Farolitos** (September 7) Ataco and Ahuachapán light up the city, and hold parades.

November: **Salcoititán Fiestas** (November 7–14) Civic festival honors San Miguel Arcángel.

Chalchuapa Fiestas (November 25–30) Civic festival honors Santiago Apóstal.

Apaneca Fiestas (November 29–30) Civic festival honors San Andrés.

December: **Ataco Fiestas** (December 11–15) Civic fiestas honor the Virgin of Immaculate Conception.

Inmaculada Concepción de María (December 8–10) Izalco commemorates the Virgin miraculously stopping lava flows during a 1926 eruption.

Suchitoto
and the
Artisan Route

5

SUCHITOTO
AND THE ARTISAN ROUTE

LAND OF THE ARTS

T he rolling hills and fertile valleys north of San Salvador, rising to the nation's highest peaks, are a largely rural place. Small adobe villages and misty mountain towns are scattered along its rivers and lakes, where farmers and craftspeople cultivate their colorful traditions.

At its heart is **Suchitoto**, Place of Birds and Flowers, El Salvador's cultural crown jewel. Its cobbled streets and Colonial buildings house handicrafts shops and art galleries, luxurious hotels and fine-dining restaurants, and plenty of options for budget travelers, who enjoy this comfortable base as well.

Surrounding Suchitoto are accessible cultural routes, historic sites, and eco-tourism adventures. Hike into the marvelous **Cinquera Mountains**, with vol-canic waterfalls and a revolutionary mountain lodge. Take horses through the tropical forests and Civil War battlefields of **Guazapa Volcano**, or boats across serene **Lake Suchitlán**, patrolled by ten thousand flocks of birds. Even farther afield, rural lodges and working farms offer down-to-earth escape from the mod-ern world.

Tour the region's crafts villages, where **Ilobasco**'s ceramicists build colorful pots and clever *sorpresas*, filled with miniature village scenes; and **San Sebast-ian**'s weavers build beautiful hammocks on old looms. These are just part of the Artisan Route, which you can explore on your own. Most famously, the brightly painted crafts and murals of **La Palma** are heir to El Salvador's best-known arts tradition, the simple, joyful abstractions of village scenes and religious themes, pioneered by artist Fernando Llort.

To the east of this artsy village are the cloudforested heights of **El Pital**, the nation's tallest peak. Rising to 2730 meters (8957 feet), its steep and scenic flanks are studded with beautiful lodges in the pines, from which you can gaze across most of the country. The less-visited lowlands of **Chalatenango Depart-ment** are slowly being developed for tourism thanks to community initiatives,

but few travelers yet make their way into its isolated beauty, with waterfalls, hot springs, and rural collectives.

After roughing it, perhaps return to comfortable Suchitoto for a day or two, taking in a gallery or relaxing over a fine French dinner. They call this Slow Tourism, a time to get in touch with El Salvador, and savor every ingredient.

Crime This region is relatively safe in terms of crime, but very poor. While Suchitoto, La Palma, and the El Pital Highlands have tourism police, there's little law enforcement in the rural hinterlands of Chalatenango and Cabañas. Avoid driving at night and drinking alone.

GUIDANCE In smaller towns, the alcaldía, on the Central Park, can often arrange guides and suggest lodging.

PEACEFUL GUAZAPA VOLCANO, OVERLOOKING LAKE SUCHITLÁN, HAS BEEN TRANSFORMED FROM A BATTLEFIELD TO AN ECOTOURISM ATTRACTION THANKS TO GRASSROOTS LOCAL COOPERATIVES.

Asociación de Municipios Cayaguanca (2353-9073; www.ecoturismocaya guanca.com) San Ignacio, 1.5 blocks west of the Alcaldía. Information about Citalá, Dulce Nombre de María, La Palma, San Fernando and San Ignacio.

MiTur La Palma (2335-9076; catilapalma.corsatur@gmail.com) Central Park. Open 8–4 Monday through Saturday, 9–1 Sunday. Exceptionally helpful tour office offers maps, booklets, and brochures for all of Chalatenango, and neighboring Ocotepeque, Honduras. The **Tourism Police** have an office here, and there's another station at Río Chiquito, in the El Pital Highlands.

MiTur Suchitoto (2335–1835; www.elsalvador.travel, cat.suchitoto@gmail.com) Southeast corner of Central Park. Open 8–4 Monday through Friday, 9–1 Saturday and Sunday. Right on the central plaza, convenient MiTur office has lots of flyers, information, and a free city map. There's a 24-hour **Tourism Police** (2300-3229; Avenida 15 Septiembre and 4 Calle Poniente) post nearby.

Suchitoto Municipal Tourism Office (2335-1782; www.suchitoto-el-salvador .com; turismosuchitoto@gmail.com) Open 8–4 daily, but may be closed Monday. Just off the plaza, locally operated tours office arranges tours, reserves hotels, and can book cars, accommodations, and more, nationwide. They also have a book exchange and offer city walking tours, $15 for up to 15 people.

GETTING THERE While Suchitoto, La Palma, and the El Pital Highlands are well signed and easily accessible on good, paved roads and frequent buses, less-traveled destinations can be trickier to visit. Drivers exploring rural Chalatenango and and Cabañas Departments should have a good map, while those using buses should allow plenty of time to reach their destination.

By Car: Most destinations in this chapter are accessible with a normal car, but if you plan to explore the rustic lodges, parks, and protected areas, it's worth renting a 4WD vehicle. From San Salvador to Suchitoto (47 kilometers/29 miles), the route is well signed, but pay attention or you'll miss the San Martín exit. The speedy Troncal Norte highway, running 84 kilometers (52 miles) from San Salvador to La Palma, with paved roads continuing to the El Pital Highlands and Honduran border at El Poy, passes Aguilares, with a 4WD backroad to Suchitoto, and Cihuatán Archaeological Park. Adventurers planning to explore rural Chilatenango and Cabañas Department should invest in a better map than we've provided.

By Bus: Though Suchitoto is at the heart of this region, to reach many other destinations, including La Palma and El Pital, you'll either need to backtrack to Aguilares, a large city with no good lodging (except love motels), or take the ferry across Lake Suchitlán to San Francisco Lempa, where you can get infrequent buses to the transport hub of Chalatenango. From San Salvador, most buses throughout this region depart the Terminal Oriental.

Aguilares: Chalatenango (125) Every 10 minutes.

La Palma via Cihuatán and Colima (119) Every half hour; continuing service to San Ignacio and El Poy.

San Salvador (117, 125, 141, 124, 170) Every 10 minutes.

Suchitoto (107) Every 40 minutes.

Apulo: San Miguel (301) Every 20 minutes.

San Salvador (129) Every half hour.

San Vicente (116) Every half hour.

Suchitoto (129) Every half hour.

Chalatenango: Buses leave from several spots close to the city center. Some leave from El Amayo, on the highway. Take the San Salvador bus out of town and have them drop you off.

Arcatao (508) Every hour, from Iglesia Calvario four blocks from the Central Park.

ONLINE RESOURCES

Cojutepeque Online (www.cojutepeque.org) Spanish-language site has basic information about the city and its weekend Gastronomic Fair.

Ilobasco Online (www.ilobascoweb.com) Small site has Spanish information about the ceramics center; the **Ilobasco Foundation** (www.ilobasco.net) has more information.

La Palma Online (www.lapalma.gang.net) Has English-language articles and lots of photos of the artists and shops.

✪ **Suchitoto Tourism Information** (www.gaesuchitoto.com) Excellent English-language site with photos, videos, links and other information, including a city map.

✪ **Suchitoto Municipal Tourism Office** (www.suchitoto-el-salvador.com) Bilingual site has information, links, and an up-to-date events calendar.

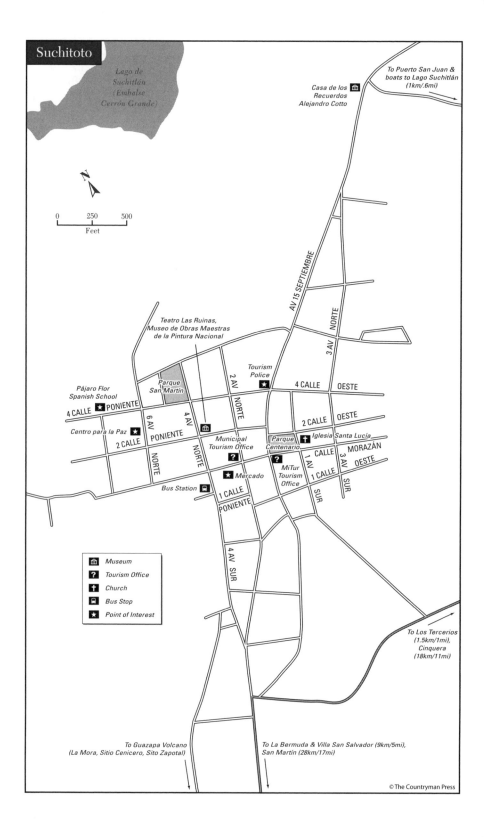

Suchitoto

Lago de
Suchitlán
(Embalse
Cerrón Grande)

To Puerto San Juan &
boats to Lago Suchitlán
(1km/.6mi)

Casa de los 🏛
Recuerdos
Alejandro Cotto

N

0   250   500
Feet

AV 15 SEPTIEMBRE

3 AV NORTE

Teatro Las Ruinas,
Museo de Obras Maestras
de la Pintura Nacional

Tourism
Police

2 AV NORTE

4 CALLE   OESTE

★

Pájaro Flor
Spanish School

Parque
San Martín

4 CALLE ★ PONIENTE

6 AV PONIENTE

4 AV NORTE

2 CALLE   OESTE

Centro para la Paz ★

🏛

Iglesia Santa Lucía

2 CALLE   PONIENTE

6 AV NORTE

Municipal
Tourism Office

Parque
Centenario

✝

1 CALLE   MORAZÁN

3 AV SUR

❓

❓

1 AV SUR

1 CALLE   OESTE

Bus Station 🚌

★ Mercado

MiTur
Tourism
Office

1 CALLE
PONIENTE

4 AV SUR

🏛 Museum

❓ Tourism Office

✝ Church

🚌 Bus Stop

★ Point of Interest

To Los Tercerios
(1.5km/1mi),
Cinquera
(18km/11mi)

To Guazapa Volcano
(La Mora, Sitio Cenicero, Sito Zapotal)

To La Bermuda & Villa San Salvador (9km/5mi),
San Martín (28km/17mi)

© The Countryman Press

Concepción Quetzaltepeque (300A) Every half hour (connecting buses go to Usulután), from 3 Avenida Sur.

Dulce Nombre de María (124) Every half hour from El Amayo.

La Palma and San Ignacio (119) Every half hour from El Amayo.

El Carrizal (542) daily at noon; stops 5 kilometers (3 miles) from La Montañona.

San Francisco Lempa (ferry to Suchitoto) and San Luís del Carmen (542) Daily at 10 AM, 11:30 AM, 1:30 PM, 3 PM, and 5:30 PM.

San Salvador via El Amayo (125) Leaves every 20 minutes; directos 3:30 AM and 3:45 PM; from 3 Avenida Sur and 6 Calle Poniente.

Ilobasco: San Miguel Take bus 111 or 112 to San Rafael Cedros, then 301 to San Miguel

San Salvador via Cojutepeque (111, 112) Every 10 minutes.

San Vicente Take bus 112 or 111 to San Rafael Cedros, then 116 to San Vicente.

Sesuntepeque (112) Every half hour.

Suchitoto via Cinquera (signed) One bus at 11:30 AM daily.

Suchitoto: Most buses leave from behind the Mercado Sur, at the intersection of 1 Calle Poniente and 4 Avenida Sur. Minibuses to **Puerto San Juan** (for boats around Lake Suchitlán) depart the Central Park every 15 minutes (30¢). It's a pleasant but steep downhill, half-hour walk to the lake, and you can take the bus back up.

Aguilares (107) Every 40 minutes.

Cinquera (482) 9 AM and 3:15 PM, with continuing service to Ilobasco; returning from Cinquera at 1:40 PM and 5 AM.

Sitio Zapotal, La Mora (107) Several times daily.

San Salvador (129) 72¢, Every 30 minutes (directos 5 AM and 4:45 PM).

La Palma: Buses stop on either side of the Central Park.

El Poy (119) Every 30 minutes.

San Salvador via Cihuatán (119) Every 30 minutes.

El Pital Highlands (signed) 5:30 AM, 7 AM, 9:50 AM, noon, 12:30 PM, and 5 PM.

San Martín Small town on the Pan-American Highway, at the turnoff to Suchitoto, is a stop for most eastbound San Salvador buses.

Cojutepeque (113) Every 10 minutes.

Ilobasco (111) Every half hour.

San Sebastian (110) Every hour.

San Vicente (116) Every half hour.

Suchitoto (129) Every half hour.

By Boat: Ferry La Luna ($4 car, $1 passenger) makes the scenic 40-minute run from Suchitoto, across Lago Suchitlán (Cerrón Embalse Grande), to San

AWARD-WINNING FILMMAKER ALEJANDRO COTTO SUCCESSFULLY NEGOTIATED WITH BOTH SIDES DURING THE CIVIL WAR TO LEAVE SUCHITOTO RELATIVELY UNSCATHED.

Francisco Lempa, a small town on the northern shore with infrequent bus connections to Chalatenango. The ferry leaves when full. Note that Bus #542 from San Francisco to Chalate-nango only runs at 6 AM, 7:25 AM, noon, and 2:45 PM. You can hire private *lanchas* around the lake as well; see the National Parks section.

✳ To See

SUCHITOTO This is the Cultural Capital of El Salvador, its architecture and scenery a gorgeous gallery for artists who come here to work and show. Its creative civic festivals are worth planning a trip around, particularly February's **Permanent International Festival of Arts and Culture**, with performances every weekend.

Suchitoto survived the Civil War largely intact thanks to the efforts of local writer and filmmaker Don Alejandro Cotto, who somehow convinced both sides that the city was worth saving. Thus, its cobbled streets and harmonious *bahareque* (adobe) homes have been photogenically preserved.

THE CENTERPIECE OF BEAUTIFUL SUCHITOTO IS STATELY SANTA LUCÍA CHURCH.

Some of the architecture is truly Colonial, including La Casona, Pajaro-Flor Spanish School, Tetro de Las Ruinas, and Hotel Los Almendros de San Lorenzo. Most buildings, however, were constructed after Independence, most spectacularly the city's striking centerpiece, 1858 **Iglesia Santa Lucía**, overlooking Parque Centenario. Its whitewashed, neo-Classical façade, with Doric columns and rococo accents, hides a softly detailed interior, with wooden pillars and arched ceilings. The cupolas are lined with reflective porcelain tiles, designed to scatter natural light.

It stands on the site of one of El Salvador's first churches, built atop a Mayan town founded around 1000 A.D., Suchitoto, or Bird-Flower. The Spaniards had built their own original capital nearby in 1528, Villa San Salvador. Local resistance convinced them to move just 17 years later. In the late 1700s, their descendants returned, building haciendas dedicated to toxic indigo production. But, as the 1800s came to a close, synthetic blue dyes destroyed that market.

Wealthy families left their indigo farms for the coffee-growing highlands, abandoning workers to subsistence farming on rented land. The construction of a dam at Cerrón Grande, which flooded the fertile valleys in 1973, displaced thousands, adding to the economic distress.

When the Civil War began sweeping El Salvador, revolutionaries found fertile ground in this impoverished region. Guazapa Volcano was among the bloodiest battlefields of the 1980s, as were the Cinquera Mountains. Most towns in this chapter were were destroyed, though Suchitoto remains, offering visitors the chance to see an older El Salvador. Artists and other creative types have migrated to these inspiring surroundings, opening galleries and businesses.

THE ARTISAN ROUTE The *Ruta Artesanal* takes visitors to handicrafts villages in the mountains around Suchitoto. Most operators offer day-tours, though independent travelers are welcomed into galleries and workshops as well. From Suchitoto, you could begin in bustling **Ilobasco**; a scenic route to the ceramics center threads the Cinquera Mountains, where you'll find **Cinquera**'s 1844 church and the village of **Tenancingo**, known for woven-palm crafts.

Centered on **Iglesia San Miguel de Xilobasco**, Ilobasco is a fairly large city, with banks and other conviences. Several ceramics shops sell bowls, sculptures, and *miniaturas,* tiny detailed figures sometimes hidden in *sorpresas*—surprises. These ceramic vessels are often shaped like eggs or

ARCHBISHOP OSCAR ROMERO'S IMAGE AND WORDS ARE EVERYWHERE IN EL SALVADOR, INCLUDING THE CHURCH IN TINY CINQUERA.

fruit that open to reveal tiny scenes of daily life. *Picantes*, the adult versions, contain couples locked in sweaty embrace.

To the south of Ilobasco is **San Sebastián**, a well-preserved Colonial town famed for its natural dyes and loom-woven hammocks. If it's a weekend, you could stop by the **Cojutepeque** Gastronomic Festival, held atop Cerro de las Pavas. It, too, is an artisan town, producing those cheesy wooden souvenirs (El Salvador-shaped wall plaques, yoyos with flag prints) hawked everywhere.

Continue to Aguilares, where you'll catch the paved Troncal del Norte highway toward Chalatenango Department, past **Cihuatán Archaeological Park** and tiny **Colima**, on the western shore of Lago Suchitlán. You could even cross the lake to **San Francisco Lempa**, with buses to the capital of **Chalatenango**.

If you have time (and a map) you could detour into less-traveled artisan territory. North of Chalate, where utilitarian pottery is produced, is **Concepción Quezaltepeque,** known for its hammocks. Farther north, **El Carrizal**, The Reedbed, specializes in basketry and olive-oil soaps.

Just east, **San Antonio los Ranchos** produces basketry, natural cosmetics, and beautiful indigo clothing. Head south to visit **San Isidro Labrador** and **Potonico**, with their fine cigars and natural soaps. Nearby, **San José Cancasque** is a basketry town. Meandering west, back toward the highway, visit **Dulce Nombre de María**, with a stunning collection of murals, before hitting the Troncal del Norte at **Tejutla**, a basketry town.

LA PALMA You'll know you've arrived when you see the murals on all sides, painted in the colorful and naïve style of Fernando Llort, El Salvador's best-known artist. The Central Park has mosaic-tiled sculptures in his honor, surrounded on all sides by shops selling Llort-inspired handicrafts and wooden

THE TINY TOWN OF DULCE NOMBRE DE MARÍA IS COVERED WITH MURALS, AND SURROUNDED WITH "NATURAL BEAUTY."

LA PALMA'S ARTISANS CREATE A MULTITUDE OF COLORFUL CRAFTS EMULATING THE STYLE OF ARTIST FERNANDO LLORT.

sculptures from **San Ignacio**, churned out by some 300 workshops scattered through the hills.

The town is also known as the *Cuna de la Paz,* Cradle of Peace. Hotel La Palma hosted peace talks between El Salvador and Honduras, while the church witnessed the Civil War's very first peace talks in 1984, between President Duarte and the ERD.

Citalá, River of Stars, boasts neoclassical **✪ Iglesia Pilar-Citalá**, built in the late 1600s, with an elaborate façade and Tuscan columns, protecting several old saints and documents inside.

MUSEUMS There are several other museums in the area, including **La Bermuda 1525 Museum and Art Gallery** (see Lodging), with art and artifacts; **Cihuatán Archaeological Park**; Hacienda Colima's **Museum of Rural Culture** (Other Parks), and **Casa de Hacienda Museo y Parque Acuatico**, a centro turistico near Ilobasco. New Civil War museums are being planned at **La Casona** (Lodging) and **Cinquera** (National Parks).

Suchitoto

✪ Casa Museo de los Recuerdos Alejandro Cotto (2335-1140) Final Avenida 15 Septiembre, near the turnoff to Puerto San Juan. Admission: $4/1 adult/child. Open: Daily; knock to see if Don Cotto is home. This fascinating museum could be best described as El Salvador's Hearst Castle: Sprawling grounds, as yet unfinished, boast exceptional lake views, fountains, glass-inlaid walkways representing Quetzalcoatl, an art collection unrivalled outside San Salvador, a private chapel stocked with ancient saints, and the original Shield of Suchitoto that owner Alejandro Cotto designed himself. It's amazing. Don Cotto, almost 90 years old at the time of research, is Suchitoto's most important arts patron. Knock on the door, and if he feels up to it, the writer, filmmaker, publisher, artist, and activist will give you a tour. Between Cuban dictator Fulgencio Batista's old couch and his father's ancient printing press are numerous photos of Cotto's friends and contemporaries, such as singer María Callas, former President Arturo Arrouco, the stars of his award-winning movie, *Cada Voz Lleva Su Angustia*, and personally autographed photos from King Carlos of Spain and Pope John Paul II. Several rooms hold an important collection of mostly Latin American artwork, with pieces by Diego Rivera, Roger López, Ignacio Varrios, Victor Martínez, and so on. The tour could take hours if you let it (recommended).

Centro Arte para la Paz (2335-1080; capsuchitoto.org) 2 Calle Poniente 5. Admission: Free. Open: Daily. While this architecturally outstanding art center is primarily a place for local kids to learn painting, photography, and folkloric dance, it also offers activities for the general public. Attend exhibitions by local and international artists, performances by students, free films every Friday at 5 PM, yoga classes, and more. Check the Web site to see what's on, or just drop by to see the artwork and building, which from 1917 until 1980, was a Dominican convent and home to the Chapel of San José.

Teatro Las Ruinas and Museo de Obras Maestras de la Pintura Nacional (2335-1909) 4 Avenida Norte. Admission: $1. Open: 8–noon Tuesday through Thursday, 9–5 Friday through Sunday, and for performances. Originally built in the late 1500s by Don Patricio Mejía, this ancient adobe did not survive the Civil War. It became known simply as the ruins, Las Ruinas, a symbol of Suchitoto's lost splendor. In 1990, as fighting wound down, Alejandro Cotto focused his considerable influence on rebuilding it as a center for the arts. A technical restoration salvaged the wooden columns and some adobe walls. The interior was given a pale pastel neo-Classical theme, and in 1991, it re-opened with the first **Permanent International Festival of Arts and Culture**, held every February. Other events are held here regularly; the Municipal Tourism Office (www.suchitoto-el-salvador.com/eventos) lists schedules. The Museum of Master Works of National Painting features the Salvadoran art from Don Cotto's collection.

✳ To Do

CANOPY TOURS **Finca Ecoturística La Montaña** (see Lodging) offers what they claim is the highest canopy tour in Central America, in the El Pital Highlands. In Cinquera Forest, **Parque Agro Ecoturismo** (see Cinquera Protected Area) has a homemade *canopín,* a tiny zip-line across a gully. Hey, it's not Apaneca, but it only costs a quarter. And it's awesome.

HORSEBACK RIDING Just about any rural hotel can arrange horses. The most popular tours are on **Volcán Guazapa**, arranged by several operators.

NIGHTLIFE Suchitoto has a robust nightlife, and is also notably gay- and lesbian-friendly. In addition to the venues listed below, check out the posh bars at **Los Almendros** and **Hotel Las Puertas**.

✪ **Bar El Necio** (2335-1964; www.lacasonasuchitoto.org) 4 Avenida Norte and 4 Calle Poniente, Suchitoto. Get in touch with your inner revolutionary at this cozy, 200-year-old bar, run by former guerrillas and plastered with awesome posters, which will eventually be incorporated into a Civil War museum. The vibe is great, beer cold, and conversation political, in a wonderful space that hosts movie screenings and other events geared toward economic justice, equal rights, and having a good time.

Disco-Café Bar Sánchez (2335-1464) 4 Calle Oriente. At around 9 PM on Friday and Saturday, Suchitoto's premier disco gets started with live DJs and lots of reggae, cumbia, salsa, and even ranchera as the night winds to a close. There's sometimes a $2 cover.

TOUR OPERATORS

Suchitoto has a wide range of tour operators, making it an excellent base. English speakers intent on exploring more remote regions of Chalatenango and Eastern El Salvador could start here.

Tours Los Almendros de San Lorenzo (2335-1200; www.hotelsalvador.com) El Salvador's only luxury tour operator, based at Hotel Los Almendros, offers pricey private day-trips with all sorts of lovely extras; your climb to the caldera of Santa Ana Volcano, for instance, includes a gourmet picnic, complete with long-stemmed wine glasses. Longer trips include fine dining, yacht trips, and stays at El Salvador's best hotels.

El Gringo Tours (2327-2351; www.elgringosuchitoto.com; rbroz@gmail.com) Calle Francisco Moran 27, 1.5 blocks from the Alcaldía. Affable Salvadoran-American Robert Broz, owner of Rincón El Gringo, arranges high-quality tours on backpacker budgets to Guazapa Volcano, Los Terceros Waterfall, and around Lago Suchitlán. You can also enjoy an English-language city tour, nightlife, pupusa-making classes, or trips across the lake to **Sitio Cenizero**, with hiking trails, caves, an organic farm, and very basic lodging.

Suchitoto Adventure Outfitters (2335-1064 x114, 7435-0548; www.suchitoto outfitters.com) Adventure operator based at Posada Suchitlán offers the usual tours around Suchitoto and the country, but specializes in custom kayak trips, treks around wilder Eastern El Salvador, with visits to less-accessible archaeological sites, fossil fields, and remote natural wonders. English-speaking guides can be arranged.

Vista Conga Tours (2335-1679, 7118-1999; www.vistaconga.com; renebarbon @vistaconga.com) Vista Conga Restaurant, Final Pasaje Cielito Lindo 7. Respected adventure tour operator is highly recommended for Cinquera trips, and also offers kayaking, camping in the lakeside town of Culebrilla (best around the new moon), waterfall jumping (June through November), and a hot springs tour, as well as custom tours for $110 per day, including private transport.

2 Gardenias Restaurant Bar (2335-1868; restaurantebar2gardenias@hot mail.com) Avenida 5 Noviembre and 3 Calle Poniente #14. B, L, D. $–$$. Bright pink bar and restaurant has a cozy, colorful interior filled with fine art; serves beer and cocktails, coffees and pastries, and heartier Salvadoran fare.

El Harlequín (2325-5890; harlequincafe@hotmail.com) 3 Avenida Norte #26. L, D. Closed Tuesday. $$. AE, MC, V. Artsy bar and restaurant has a romantic outdoor patio perfect for enjoying homemade pastas and a very full bar that gets packed on karaoke nights, and when big sporting events show on the widescreen TV.

Bar El Torogoz (2335-1079) 3 Avenida Norte #1. Open 4 PM–2:00 nightly. $$. Suchitoto's newest locally owned bar has appetizers and simple décor.

SPANISH SCHOOLS Pájaro Flor Spanish School (2335-1509, 7230-7812; www.pajaroflor.com) Calle 4 Poniente 22, Barrio San José. Why not learn Spanish in a 200-year-old mansion with lake views from some of the open-air classrooms? A week (20 hours) of private classes runs $160, group classes $120, and private teachers can be hired for $8 per hour. The school also arranges hotels and home stays with local families.

THEATER Teatro Las Ruinas (see Museums) hosts local, national, and international performers in its centuries-old audotorium. Several spots show free movies, including **Centro Arte para la Paz** (Friday at 7 PM), followed by discussion and snacks, and **Bar El Necio** (on occasion).

✳ Green Space

NATIONAL PARKS AND PROTECTED AREAS Cinquera Mountains Natural Protected Area (2389-5732 (ARDM); ardmcqr@yahoo.es) Open: 24 hours. Admission: Free. Just southwest of Suchitoto, this 5300-hectare (20-square-mile) expanse of low tropical forest is beautiful, if not pristine. It's a

THE SMALL TOWN OF CINQUERA SURROUNDS ONE OF THE MOST UNUSUAL CENTRAL PARKS IN THE COUNTRY.

mixed-use area with farms and villages, secondary-growth wilderness, and a high point of 754 meters (2473 feet). The protected area is managed by the Municipal Association for Reconstruction and Development (ARDM), headquartered in the town of Cinquera, 18 kilometers (11 miles) from Suchitoto on the well-maintained road through the park. Cinquera's shady central park is centered on the tail of downed military helicopter, held aloft as a monument, and surrounded with machine guns. **Saint Nicholas Church** has been rebuilt since the war (the belltower dates from 1844) and emblazoned with a mural of Oscar Romero. Nearby is the **Memorial to the Fallen of Cinquera**, with the names of those killed during the Civil War, guarded by a bust of Farabundo Martí.

Hostal y Restaurante El Bosque (2389-5765; ardmcqr@yahoo.es) $. Cash only. Has tidy brick rooms packed with new beds, all with private hot baths, and a covered porch almost in the forest, just three blocks uphill from the park. ARDM also runs an attached restaurant, and plans to open a Civil War museum. They offer several guided Spanish-language tours for $8 a day; horses and private vehicles can also be arranged. Ask about Don Pablo Alvarenga, a former guerrilla and gifted storyteller. Lining the road between Suchitoto and Cinquera are several eco-attractions, clearly marked from the main road with cheerfully painted signs. I couldn't visit them all, but most are basic, family-run operations offering inexpensive (25¢ to $3) access to beautiful trails, swimming holes, campsites, cool caves, hot springs, and campsites. **El Caracol Turismo Aventuro** (7962-5592; 25¢), for example, has shady trails to a fairly spectacular waterfall, and a grassy, basic campsite, run by Blanca and Lazaro Sanchez, who also grow corn and can provide meals with advance notice. ✪ **Parque Agro Ecoturismo** (No phone; 25¢) offers covered camping, steep hikes to Cueva del Duende, and a *canopín*, a homemade canopy tour built by owner Santos Ruiz Rivera out of what appears to be a carnival-ride chair and old tow-truck winch. You could also soak in hot springs at **Agua Caliente**, or visit an old guerrilla camp at **Montaña de Cinquera Ecological Park**. It's easiest to visit on a guided trip, offered by Vista Conga Tours and other operators. If you know a bit of Spanish, you can visit on your own; it's easier in a rental car, but many access drives are 4WD-only. Bus 482 leaves Suchitoto for Cinquera at 9 AM and 3:15 PM, returning at 1:40 PM and 5 AM.

Guazapa Volcano Protected Area 11 kilometers (7 miles) southeast of Suchitoto This peaceful, dormant volcano, rising 1438 meters (4615 feet) above the fertile countryside, was one of the country's most intense Civil War battlegrounds, subject of El Salvador's only major motion picture, *Sobreviviendo Guazapa*. The mountain's famously feminine silhouette was pockmarked with bombs and riddled with underground tunnels where guerrillas could survive for months. In 1996, the government set the region aside as a protected area, managed by community organizations based in Palo Grande, La Mora, and Sito Zapotal. It protects dry tropical savannah and lush rainforests, with 260 species of plants, 21 mammals, and several birds and butterflies. You can organize guided hikes and horseback rides into the scenery and Civil War history anywhere in Suchitoto, or with community operators listed below. It's also possible to ascend the mountain from the town of **Guazapa**, a much more challenging hike. The

Alcaldía (2324-0001, 2324-0060; alcaldia_guazapa@yahoo.es; central park) can find guides with advance notice, but there are no hotels in town.

Comité de Ecoturismo Rural Pro-Guazapa (2221-6325, 2323-0814, 7923-9467) Cooperative offers guided tours including transportation from Suchitoto, on horseback trips ($15 per person), foot ($6), or in private vehicles ($25).

Sitio Guazapa (2300-0972, 7924-8886, 7348-0352; www.gaesuchitoto.com/SitioGuazapa; sitioguazapa@gmail.com) Offers horseback tours, hikes, tent rentals, and food service.

Turismo La Mora (2323-6874; www.ecoturismolamora.es.tl) Tours include a 3-kilometer (2-mile) hike to La Escuelita, a former battlefield; El Obraje, a 10-kilometer (6-mile) round-trip to a Colonial indigo facility; and the Tour de Maíz, or Corn Tour, where a local women's collective teaches you how to grow and cook the grain. Tours should be arranged at least one day in advance at the Municipal Tourism Office in Suchitoto.

Lago Suchitlán Spreading scenically from Suchitoto across central El Salvador, this sparkling expanse is more properly known as *Embalse Cerrón Grande,* Big Hill Reservoir, supplying electricity to some half million people. It was created in 1973, and its 135 square kilometers (52 square miles) now cover the once fertile Valley of Almonds. The easiest way to visit is **Puerto Turístico San Juan** (50¢ entrance), a festive spot with eight restaurants and several souvenir stands overlooking the lake, a half-hour walk or 8-minute bus ride from Suchitoto's Parque Centenario. Relax right here or splurge on a trip in a covered *lancha,* seating 10 people in the shade. Boats have set prices: $25 gets 45-minute tour to **Isla de Ermitaño**, with a cave and campsites; $30, an hour-long tour past islands including **Isla de las Pájaros**, absolutely swimming with beautiful seabirds. Other stops include **Copapayo**, with a Civil War memorial; the **dam**, or across the lake to **Hacienda Colima**. **Ferry La Luna** ($4/1 car/passenger) makes a 40-minute trip across the lake several times daily, to the small town of **San Francisco Lempa**, where Hacienda Grande offers swimming pools, restaurants, and hiking trails. A private boat runs $15. From here, you can catch buses to Chalatenango.

ISLA DE LOS PÁJAROS ON LAGO DE SUCHITLÁN IS A BIRDER'S PARADISE.

Around Suchitoto

✪ **Cascada Los Tercios** (1.5 kilometers/1 mile from Suchitoto) Suchitoto's classic excursion is this easy, half-hour stroll to a truly awesome waterfall. It plunges more than 10 meters (30 feet) down a spectacular volcanic formation of hexagonal basalt columns, similar to Giant's Causeway in Northern Ireland. It flows freely through rainy season, (May through December), drying up by January. You can hire a guide, or ask a tourism police officer to accompany you.

Salto Los Limones (23 kilometers /14 miles from Suchitoto) Several waterfalls pour into refreshing swimming holes year-round, at the confluence of the Chalchigue and Los Amates River.

Artisan Route

Hacienda Colima (2235–3149; 2309-3335; haciendacolima@hotmail.com) KM46.5 Tronco del Norte. Just north of Cihuatán, on Lake Suchitlán's western shore, this rural tourism cooperative has hiking trails, agricultural tours, and a **Museum of Rural Culture**. They have a simple **restaurant** and **hostel** ($; cash only) offering fan-cooled rooms with museum-quality antiques, a small pool, and hammocks.

Hacienda Los Nacimientos Indigo Tour (2243-0449; www.elsalvadorazul .com; rhinayolanda45@yahoo.es) Cantón San Lucas, 20 minutes from Suchitoto. Tour a completely organic indigo farm near Cihuatán, or take workshops where you'll dye a shirt.

La Montañona (2301-1955, 2332-0369; www.mancomunidadlm.org) Near El Carrizal, Chalatenango. $. Cash only. High in the mountains along the Honduran border, five villages—Concepción Quetzaltepeque, Las Vueltas, El Carrizal, Ojos de Agua, and La Laguna—have formed a tourism commonwealth. They offer three simple onsite cabins with solar-heated bath, cafeteria, campsites, and hiking trails through the pine and oak forests. The most popular trek visits diesel-fueled Radio Farabundo Martí, a mobile guerrilla radio station stashed 3 meters (almost 10 feet) below the bomb-cratered earth. It's connected to a network of *tatús,* underground Vietnamese-style tunnels with kitchens and hospitals. Other excursions include horseback rides, hot springs, farm tours, visits to undeveloped archaeological sites, and swimming at **Balneario Paraíso Quezaltepeque**, with spring-fed pools and playground equipment. Make reservations with the Spanish-speaking staff; if you can't get in touch, try the Alcaldías in Chalatenango (2301-2964) or Concepción Quezaltepeque (2331-2205).

Parque Ecologico El Manzano (7215-2232, 7914-6596) 8.5 kilometers (5 miles) north of Dulce Nombre de María. $–$$. Cash only. This rural ecotourism outfit offers six simple cabins with private cool baths and kitchenettes. An onsite restaurant serves typical meals. Spanish-speaking guides lead hikes to several miradors (viewpoints) and along the Ereguán River, with 10 pretty swimming holes in the fragrant pine and cypress forest. Close to the cabins are farming plots, orchid gardens, a small zoo with unusual chickens, and the **Museo Historico Héroes de Chalate**, with photos, weapons, and other Civil War relics. Pickup trucks leave for the park from Dulce Nombre de María.

Any tour office or hotel in the region can arrange guided hikes and horseback rides to a number of destinations, most of which allow camping.

Cascada La Laguneta 10 kilometers/6 miles east of Citalá, in Los Planes. Waterfalls, swimming holes, hiking trails, and camping areas are a popular destination close to Mirador Las Cruces, with views.

Piedra Cayahuanaca 4 kilometers/2.5 miles north of San Ignacio. Scenic climb through private farmland, leads to a mountaintop stone marking the border between Honduras and El Salvador, 1550 meters (5084 feet) above sea level. Hotels in San Ignacio and La Palma can arrange guides; camping is possible at the top. This is a place of pilgrimage during Semana Santa.

Río Nunuapa 6 kilometers/4 miles southwest of La Palma. One of the most popular destinations for a hike from town.

Río Sumpul Lago Suchitlán to the Honduran border. Hotels and operators on both sides of this scenic river arrange hiking trips, boat tours, waterfall splashes, and even whitewater rafting, in rainy season only. It was also the site of the first known Civil War massacre of civilians, deliberately targeted as they tried to escape to Honduras. Read more in *Swimming in El Rio Sumpul*, by Elsie B. C. Rivas Gomez.

ARCHAEOLOGICAL PARKS Though this region where the Mayan and Lenca peoples met has important sites, most remain unexcavated. Persistent explorers can find more remains along the **Titihuapa River** (near Ilobasco), with cave paintings and petroglyphs dating to perhaps 7000 B.C.; **Sitio Arcatao** (see Around Chalatenango), an abandoned Lenca village; **Turicentro Agua Fría**, near Chalatenango; and at **La Montañona**, listed under Other Parks.

Cihuatán (2235-9453, San Salvador; www.online.sfsu.edu/~kbruhns/cihuatan) 3.7 kilometers (2.3 miles) north of Aguilares, Carretera Troncal del Norte. Admission: $3. Open: 9–4 Tuesday through Sunday. This massive Salvadoran site is currently being excavated; you may see archaeologists at work (from afar) at The Palace. Only a fraction of the ancient city has been unearthed—note the suspiciously regular hills thrusting up from the fields all around. Currently, only the Western Ceremonial Center and Plaza are open to the public, basically a grassy field with exposed walls and ball courts, and a few partially excavated pyramids, one of which you can climb. Cihuatán means Next to the Woman, a reference to neighboring Guazapa Volcano's unmistakably feminine silhouette, reclining in the distance. A small museum has photos of archaeologists and artifacts, which are displayed at MUNA in San Salvador.

Some 25,000 people lived here between Cihuatán's foundation in 900 A.D., and its destruction by fire in 1150 A.D. Enormous incense burners that once perfumed the temple gates were deliberately smashed, perhaps by enemies seeking to desecrate hallowed ground, or by retreating residents as part of a ritual abandonment. The city, founded right after the collapse of the Classical Mayan empire, had both Pipil and Lenca residents, which may be why it was destroyed during the Mayans' reconquest of Cuscatlán. The site is just north of Aguilares.

AROUND CHALATENANGO

The wilder region around Chalate (Chalatenango city) has several sites that can be difficult for the average tourist to visit. Any operator offering custom tours can help, but if you speak some Spanish, have plenty of time, 4WD transportation, and a good map, you can visit scenic waterfalls, cloud-forested mountains, Civil War guerrilla encampments, and archaeological sites on your own. To find local guides, contact the alcaldías in advance; they can also usually arrange lodging in very basic private homes.

Arcatao (2354-8034, 2354-8017 alcaldía) 32 kilometers/20 miles east of Chalatenango. Close to the Honduran border, Arcatao's original Lenca townsite still crowns Cerro Éramon. Guided hikes visit the ruins, basically unexcavated mounds and stone terraces, as well as area petroglyphs, a guerrilla camp with *tatús,* the Gualsinga River, and Cerro Las Ventanas, with views.

Comalapa (2399-5006, alcaldía) 12 kilometers/7 miles north of Chalate. Crafts town known for its hammocks and baskets is surrounded by pretty waterfalls and mysterious caves.

Concepción Quetzaltepeque (2331-2205, alcaldía) This hammock-making center has several workshops and stores. Hiking excursions include the Olosingo Waterfalls, petrified trees on Cerro El Dragón, and ruins at Caserío la China.

Dulce Nombre de María (2365-9265, alcaldía) 10 kilometers/6 miles north of Paraíso. Beautifully muralled Colonial town is best known for Parque Ecológico El Manzano, but there are other hikes from town. Most begin from the road to San Fernando, including Cerro El Candelero, a steep, naked volcanic plug; Cerro La Conquista, an easier climb; La Cueva del Ermitaño, a bat cave; and deeper and scarier Cueva del Diablo, Cave of the Devil. There are also several waterfalls, including Chorro Blanco, pouring down a climbable granite cliff.

San Fernando (2309-5413, 2309-5419, alcaldía) North of Nombre de María, this tiny town has one hotel, and hikes to the Mirador el Pino, 1 steep kilometer (0.6 mile) to fantastic views over town; the Río Sumpul; and Peña El Malespín, a granite outcropping that may have elves living on it is nearby.

Las Vueltas (2332-0369, alcaldía) 10 kilometers/6 miles northeast of Chalate. Enjoy scenic access to the Sumpúl River, swimming holes along the Tamuscalo River, and hot springs.

Any bus headed north toward Chilatenango (#125), Tejutla (#127) or La Palma (#119) can drop you off 1 kilometer (0.6 mile) from the park entrance.

Villa San Salvador La Bermuda, 9 kilometers (5.6 miles) south of Suchitoto. The original site of Villa San Salvador, the nation's capital for just 17 years, is today preserved as Ciudad Vieja (Old City). The ruins, 9 kilometers (5.6 miles) south of Suchitoto, are not spectacular, basically the foundations of El Salvador's oldest church, a defensive wall, and a few other buildings. This was the Spaniards' second attempt to found their capital in exceptionally hostile territory. The first was built in 1525, but destroyed so completely that no one even knows where it was. On April 1, 1528, the Spaniards gave it another try here. Attacked by Mayans from the West and Lenca from the east, the colonists gave up in 1545. They moved their capital to San Salvador's current site, while Hacienda Bermuda, about a kilometer away, remained. The hotel offers tours.

✎ **Casa de Hacienda Museo y Parque Acuático** (2300-4163; www.lacasa .9f.com) Carretera Tejutepeque-Ilobasco, 500 meters (547 yards) from the Cancha Los Frailes. Admission: $2; open 8–5 daily. Well-signed, kid-friendly diversion has large pools, playground equipment, an onsite restaurant, and a **museum** with old weapons, coins, and musical instruments, as well as a chapel with Colonial art.

Piscina Jupila (22350-9325) KM90 Carretera Troncal del Norte, San Ignacio. Open 7–5 daily; $3. Small centro close to San Ignacio has pools, a simple restaurant, and green spaces.

Turicentro Agua Fría (2335-2059) KM78 Carretera Chalatenango. Admission $2; open 8–6. Two huge swimming pools of very cold spring water are inset into 42 manzanas (73 acres) with a restaurant, trails, and some archaeological relics above the pools.

✷ Lodging

While Suchitoto has a wide range of lodging, from festive backpacker joints to some of the finest upscale accommodations in the country, most small towns lack good hotels. Population centers such as Chalatenango, Cojutepeque, Ilobasco, and Sensuntepeque have very basic accommodations, while Aguilares, Apopa, San Martín, and other travel hubs are without recommendable lodging (though there are love hotels).

La Palma, San Ignacio, and the El Pital Highlands have a few very good mountain lodges, and plenty of cheaper spots. Adventurous travelers will find wonderful rural lodging in the mountains around Chalatenango, Cinquera, Dulce Nobre de María, Lake Suchitlán, and elsewhere. Often run by community-based cooperatives, these usually focus on outdoor adventure, agriculture tours, and Civil War history. Check the National Parks and Centros Turisticos for more options.

Suchitoto
This town may be going upscale, but budget travelers still have plenty of excellent options. **Pájaro-Flor** (see Spanish Schools) can arrange homestays, while **Rincón El Gringo**, **El Obraje**, and **Villa Balanza** (see Restaurants) all have recommended budget lodging.

MUCH OF SUCHITOTO'S CLASSIC COLONIAL-STYLE ARCHITECTURE, WHITEWASHED ADOBE WITH TEJAS-TILED ROOFS, WAS ACTUALLY BUILT AFTER INDEPENDENCE.

✪ ⚲ ⌂ ❄ "🍴" **Los Almendros de San Lorenzo** (503-2335-1200; www.hotel salvador.com, suchitotoplebailly@ hotelsalvador.com) $$$–$$$$. AE, MC, V. Handicap Access: Challenging. This boutique hotel was originally a hacienda, built on a ridge above the Valle de los Almendros by the wealthy Bustamonte family. The city of Suchitoto arose all around them as the fortunes of this indigo city prospered, but when the market fell out beneath the deep blue dye, they abandoned their home for the coffee-growing hills. Their mansion had fallen into deep disrepair when current owner Pascal Lebailley, seeking a relaxed respite from the busy Paris fashion world, rediscovered its thick adobe walls, sunny courtyards, and spacious rooms. He hired Salvadoran architect José Robert Geishman to oversee a 17-month technical restoration, preserving old wooden beams, original ceilings, and a beehive oven now illuminated with candles at sunset. Fountains and flowers fill the formal front courtyard, surrounded with delightful rooms and polished suites. These and the lovely common areas were furnished with local antiques and imports from Marrakesh, Thailand, and Guatemala. Original art, including a gentle mural by Salvadoran painter Luís Lazo, are hung all around, and a deep pool is inset among flagstones in a larger second courtyard. The pièce de résistance is a glass-enclosed fine dining ✪ **restaurant** (B, L, D; $$–$$$$), that overlooks it all. Roundly lauded as one of El Salvador's best, the menu combines local ingredients, French techniques, and a distinct Mediterranean flair, serving recipes originally composed by French Chef Hervé Laurent of the Cordon Bleu. Los Almendros also crafts luxury tours and comfortable day-trips, and operates a plush beach house, El Caracol, on the pearl gray sands of Playa Maculis. Flawless.

⚲ ⌂ ❄ 🚗 **La Bermuda 1525** (2226-1839, 2225-5103; www.laber muda.com, info@labermuda.com) KM34.8 Carretera from San Martín to Suchitoto. $$–$$$. AE, MC, V. Handicap Access: Yes. About 10 kilometers (6 miles) south of Suchitoto, this country inn sits close to the ruins of the original capital, Villa San Salvador. Though those settlers soon moved on, this 1537 hacienda remained, and is still operated by the same family. Today, the sprawling old home has been refurbished with six individually decorated suites, furnished with antiques and local handicrafts, cool ceramic tiles, and original art designed to evoke the Colonial period. All have private, solar-heated baths, cable TVs, and fans. Rates include admission to a small **Museum and Art Gallery** (open 10–5 weekends only; $1), with local handicrafts, Colonial relics, and Mayan artifacts. The **restaurant** (B, L, D; $$–$; weekends only) is highly regarded for its leisurely Spanish cuisine, such as quail in rose-petal sauce, Spanish-style pork loin, and chicken cooked in chicha. Everything is made to order, with many ingredients grown right here on the hacienda. The San Salvador-Suchitoto bus passes every half hour. There are hiking trails, camping can be arranged, and staff organizes tours of the ruins of Villa San Salvador.

✪ ⨍ 🚗 "❢" **Hotel Blanca Luna** (2335-1661; blancaluna21@hot mail.es) 1 Calle Poniente and 5 Avenida Sur #7. $. Cash only. Handicap Access: Challenging. Backpacker mecca is an excellent deal, offering $7 dorms with two beds per room, private baths, cable TVs, telephones (with good rates on international calls), fans, WiFi, and towels rolled up to look like swans. Nice. Get an upstairs room, on the terrace . . . though the downstairs common area has mood lighting and a cool-water Jacuzzi.

Centro de Romero (2335-1049, 7337-4280; www.santaluciasuchi .parroquia.org) Calle 15 Septiembre, Barrio El Centro. $. Cash only. Iglesia Santa Lucía's Romero Center offers simple, spotless dorms, primarily for religious and solidarity groups. Make reservations in advance.

🛏 **Hostal El Patio** (2325-1964; www.lacasonasuchitoto.org; lacasona delnecio@gmail.com) Avenida 4 Norte and Calle 4 Oriente, # 9. $. AE, MC, V. Handicap Access: Challenging. Better known as La Casona (home of Bar El Necio), this 200-year-old Colonial may be a tad too authentic for some. But the dark, barren, fan-cooled rooms are freshly painted and clean, with private cold bath, surrounding a scruffy courtyard where you can camp.

⨍ ⧓ 🛏 ✳ 🛏 **La Pasada del Sol** (2335-1546; www.lapasadadelsol.com; info@lapasadadelsol.com) 2 Avenida Sur #39. $$. Cash only. Handicap Access: Challenging. Great mid-range choice is excellent for families, with lovely gardens, three big pools, lake views, and super clean rooms with air-conditioning, cable TVs, coffeemakers, and private hot baths. (Two rooms with shared bath are $10 cheaper.) There's a good poolside **restaurant** (B, L, D; $$), but no alcohol. Day passes are $2.

✳ **Posada Alta Vista** (2335-1645; www.posadaltavista.com; posadaalta vista@yahoo.com) Avenida 15 de Septiembre #8. $. Cash only. Handicap Access: Challenging. Acceptable hotel has great views from the unfinished third-floor terrace and clean, modern rooms, some sleeping six, with air-conditioning, cable TV, and private bath.

✪ ⧓ ⨍ 🛏 ✳ 🛏 "❢" **La Posada de Suchitlán** (503-2335-1064; www.la posada.com.sv, laposada@suiteslas palmas.com.sv) Barrio San José. $$$. AE, MC, V. Handicap Access: Yes. Surrounded by lush gardens and Suchitoto's loveliest setting, this quiet, faithfully restored old hacienda boasts some of the city's nicest rooms, a wonderful restaurant, and spectacular lake views. The graceful adobe buildings, with ancient wooden columns that support wide tiled awnings, house several types of room, all tastefully decorated in jewel tones, with high ceilings, air-conditioning, telephones, and televisions hidden within handmade Guatemalan cabinets. Those in the older buildings are a bit smaller and less expensive, with two double beds and better bathrooms. The suites, arranged for families as well as couples, are more spacious, with fabulous private patios overlooking Suchitlán. Even if you don't stay here, be sure to drop by their excellent **restaurant** (B, L, D; $$), serving beautifully prepared and very traditional Salvadoran dishes served by waitstaff in period costumes. Breakfast is included.

☕ ❄ ⁖¶⁖ **Hotel Las Puertas** (2393-9200; www.laspuertassuchitoto.com, reservaciones@laspuertassuchitoto .com) Barrio San José. $$$. AE, MC, V. Handicap Access: No. This gorgeous old building above the cobbled city center has undergone an exquisite transformation from jail, to house of ill repute, to one of the country's finest hotels. Above the elegantly arcaded entryway are six spacious, airy, second-floor rooms furnished with whimsically carved lamps and handmade four-poster wooden beds, their new mattresses covered with unique bedspreads handwoven by Don Ciro, for sale in the gift shop downstairs. DirecTV, and marble-

accented bath all add to the ambiance. And the views from your private terrace, over the crafts fair and Iglesia Santa Lucía, are unbeatable. Downstairs, a pretty courtyard and splendid ❂ **bar and restaurant** (B, L, D; $$–$$$$) offers Italian-accented fine dining such as homemade gnocchis and pastas, steak, and seafood. Breakfast is a great deal.

🔧 🍴 ☕ ❄ 🚗 ⁖¶⁖ **El Tejado Restaurant and Hotel** (2335-1769; www .eltejadosuchitoto.com, salvador .eltejadorestaurante@yahoo.com) Avenida 3 Norte #58. $$$. AE, MC, V. Handicap Access: No. Popular, family-friendly spot overlooking Lake Suchitlán fills up on weekends, when kids enjoy the fabulous pools, with a waterfall and panoramic views, next to a good **restaurant** (B, L, D; $$) serving Salvadoran dishes and vegetarian options. Day-trippers can visit for $3.50, but the spacious, spotless rooms are a great choice. Comfortable and modern, rooms with large cable televisions, air-conditioning, big windows, and hot baths, are warmed up with handicrafts. There are also cheaper rooms in an older, cinder-block building, and four new suites, with private terraces overlooking the lake, that were under construction. The complimentary breakfast gets raves.

Hostal Vista Lago (2335-1357, 7889-3076) Barrío San José, Calle 6 Poniente and Final Avenida 2, #18-B. $. Cash only. Handicap Access: No. Suchitoto's cheapest hostel has extra-basic, fan-cooled rooms with shared cleanish bath, a *pila* (like a giant cement sink) for washing clothes, and a dirt floor mirador, with five-star lake views.

Chalatenango

✳ ⚕ **Hotel La Ceiba** (2301-1080) 7 Avenida Norte. $. Cash only. Handicap Access: Challenging. Simple hotel geared to local business travelers has good, basic rooms with cable TVs, air-conditioning, and telephones, plus nice mountain views. Take the road downhill from the Alcadía, it's signed on your right. You could eat at **El Rinconcito Chalateco** (B, L, D; $), across from the massive army barracks, with *comida a la vista* at lunch.

Citalá

⚕ **Mini-Hotel y Restaurante Montecristo** (2502-5133) KM95 Troncal del Norte, half block north of the Alcaldía. $. Cash only. Handicap Access: Challenging. Small cement hotel close to the Honduran border has five fan-cooled rooms with private hot bath, and not much else. Inexpensive typical food is available, or grab pastries and sandwiches around the corner at **Pastelería María José** (2350-9090; 8–5; $).

Cojutepeque

⚕ **Finca La Paz** (2300-6011, 7633-5229; www.fincalapaz.com.sv) $. Cash only. Handicap Access: Challenging. The busy capital of Cojutepeque, Hill of Coyotes, has one great lodging option. About 200 meters (219 yards) from the entrance to town, Finca La Paz is a working farm surrounded by forests, flowers, and trails. Rooms are basic, with fans and private bath, but furnished with rustic antiques, local handicrafts, and hammocks everywhere.

Dulce Nombre de María

Close by, **Parque Ecologico El Manzano** and **La Montañona**, listed in Parks, also offer rustic rural lodging.

🎣 ⚕ ✳ ⚕ **Chalate Country Club** (2301-1321; www.chilatecountryclub .com) KM67 Chalatanango, San José Los Sitio. $$–$$$. AE, MC, V. Handicap Access: Challenging. The region's most luxurious lodging is mainly for members, at a plush lakefront country club with eight pools, expansive gardens, and hiking trails. Non-members can visit for $12/7 adult/child, and arrange sailing lessons; rooms are reserved by special arrangement only.

✳ **Hotel y Restaurant El Mirador** (2356-9512) Barrio Concepción. $. Cash only. Handicap Access: No. Just one hotel resides near the wonderfully muralled city center, with eight clean rooms, foam mattresses, and cable TV; two have air-conditioning. There's a nice mirador over the town, tiny onsite **comedor** (B, L, D; $), as well as a shared kitchen. Upstairs rooms are nicer.

🏊 🎣 ⚕ **Turicentro Manantiales de la Montaña** (No phone) Signed from the Carratera San Fernando. Pools open 8–6. $. Cash only. Handicap Access: Challenging. Small centro turistico has several cement pools of fresh natural water, beautiful views, campgrounds, and six simple cabins.

⚕ **Hotel Río Sumpul** (2309-5408; engupela@yahoo.com) Central San Fernando. $. Cash only. Handicap Access: Challenging. The only hotel in San Fernando is a utilitarian cement structure housing simple, clean rooms with squishy beds and clean private bath, and a simple comedor.

Ilobasco

⚕ **Hotel Ilobasco** (7325-3508) 4 Calle Poniente and Calle al Hospital. $. Cash only. Handicap Access: No. This three-story hotel, five blocks from the city center, has cleanish cement rooms sleeping three on thin mattresses, with cable TV and fan; some have private cold bath. Get a room on the third floor, with great views.

✪ ✐ ∮ ♿ **La Zona Verde** (2310-8000, 7279-2923) KM66 San Salvador-Sesuntepeque, San Isidro. $$. Cash only. Handicap Access: No. Gorgeous centro turistico between Ilobasco and the untouristed (but rather nice) city of Sensuntepeque has several spring-fed pools set into the tropical forest. Six wonderful wood cabins are hidden around the grounds, with polished rustic décor, good beds, and modern cold bath. An onsite **restaurant** (B, L, D; $$) serves pricey fish and steak dinners, but guests can arrange cheaper meals. Daytrippers are welcome ($2.50; open 9–6). Bus #529 between Ilobasco and Sesuntepeque passes every half hour, while Bus #112 to San Salvador runs every 90 minutes.

La Palma and San Ignacio

♿ **Cabañas Lecho de Flores** (2313-5470, 7937-7678; cabana.lechode flores@yahoo.com) $$. Cash only. Handicap Access: No. In addition to rustic private cabins, there are several hiking trails; day-trippers can visit for $2/1 adult child, and campsites (bring your own tent) run $4.

♿ ♿ **Cabañas Prashanti** (2352-9304) KM87 Troncal del Norte. $. Cash only. Handicap Access: Challenging. On the highway between La Palma and San Ignacio, simple spot has three tidy rooms in a wooden structure, with shared kitchen and bath.

♿ ♿ **Finca y Cabañas Pasatiempo** (2300-5251, 7263-0711; www.esmit ierra.com.sv/minisitios/fpasatiempo) KM83 Troncal del Norte, 1.5 kilome-

ters (about 1 mile) from the signed turnoff. $. Cash only. Handicap Access: No. In windswept pines and organic coffee plantations, this spot offers basic, inexpensive cabins and campsites, plus guided hikes to El Cipitio Cave and Río Los Tecomates waterfalls.

✐ ∮ ♿ ❄ ♿ "▮" **Hotel Entre Pinos** (2335-9370; 2263-5623 San Salvador; www.entrepinosresortandspa.com, contact@entrepinos.com) KM87.5 Carretera Troncal del Norte. $$–$$$$. AE, MC, V. Handcap Access: No. The region's most luxurious hotel is enormous, with tennis courts, ponds, petting zoo, gym, spa, horse stables, restaurants, huge pools, hammocks, even a private waterfall, and staff that arrange everything from bicycle rentals to tours all over the country, perhaps in a helicopter. Despite its undeniable charms, the place could use some sprucing up if it plans to market itself to the international luxury crowd. The main lodge is beautiful, with soaring wood-and-stone construction, but the cheaper rooms are only OK—small, with dated furnishings, refrigerators, cable TVs, and phones, and small terraces. Upgrade to a more spacious double deluxe, with better bathrooms, closets, and connecting rooms. The three bungalows, completely separate from the main hotel, have fireplaces. It's isolated, a $3 cab ride into La Palma, so bring groceries unless you plan to dine at the **restaurant** ($$–$$$$) for most meals. Prices almost double on weekends.

♿ **Hotel y Restaurante Montaña Paseo Pital** (2305-9344) KM84 Carretera Troncal del Norte. Handicap Access: Challenging. Though the cheapest option in La Palma proper

looks great from the outside, the spacious, spacious rooms are moldy and gross.

❂ ⌖ ♨ 🚗 "🍴" **Hotel La Palma** (2335-9012, 2305-8483; www.hotellapalma.com.sv, hotellapalma@yahoo.com) KM84 Troncal del Norte. $. Credit cards: No. Handicap Access: Challenging. This lovely little hotel, its whitewashed adobe walls emblazoned with colorful murals, is wonderful. Rooms are simple, with saggy beds, even more murals, fans, and tiny, private hot baths. Out front, porches strung with hammocks overlook the pine forests and a scenic river. A delightful open-air restaurant, serving delicious Salvadoran cuisine on sturdy wooden tables, enjoys the same view. And as you sip your local coffee, you might wonder why the large, deep pool is so unusually shaped. It's an old bomb crater, repurposed for a refreshing swim by owner Salvador Zepeda Carrillo, who managed to keep his hotel operating through two bitter wars. Honduran and Salvadoran diplomats held peace talks right here after the 1969 Football War. During the Civil War, it hosted both guerrillas and federal troops, "who never paid, much less tipped," sighs Don Salvador.

⌖ ♨ ❄ 🚗 **Posada del Reyes** (2335-9318, 2352-9223; www.hotelposadadereyes.com, posada_reyes@yahoo.es) KM87 Troncal del Norte, Calle Principal, San Ignacio. $–$$. AE, MC, V. Handicap Access: Challenging. Right in the center of San Ignacio, this architecturally interesting hotel has lovely gardens plied by flagstone paths. Goood rooms, some with big brick-arched windows, have private hot baths, good beds, and colorful bedspreads; air-conditioning runs $10 extra. The simple open-air restaurant,

overlooking the pool, offers guests all three meals for just $10 a day.

♨ **Hotel y Restaurante Posada Real** (2335-9009) KM84 Carretera Troncal del Norte. $. Cash only. Handicap Access: No. Simple spot behind a modest downtown storefront offers 14 basic, tiled rooms, with fans and private machine-heated baths, surrounding a mossy courtyard. There's an unfinished mirador with great views, and a basic **comedor** (B, L, D; $) in the lobby.

⌖ ♨ 🚗 **Hotel Praderas** (2350-9229, 2350-9331; www.hotelpraderasdesanignacio.com; praderas@navegante.com.sv) KM92 Carretera Troncal del Norte. $$. Cash only. Handicap Access: Challenging. Clean, modern hotel has small but immaculate rooms with private hot baths, good beds, WiFi, cable TVs, fans, and colorful décor. Shared porches have hammocks, and there's a great hangout spot in the gardens, overlooking the pool. The restaurant, **Los Cypresses** (B, L, D; $$), has huge windows and spectacular views, plus top-notch Salvadoran cuisine, grilled meats, and international options.

⌖ ♨ 🚗 **Hostal Quecheláh** (2305-9328) KM79 Carretera Troncal del Norte. $. Cash only. Handicap Access: No. Right on the road to La Palma, this stone and adobe hostel has simple rooms with three meals daily, surrounded by pines.

♨ **Hotel El Roble** (2309-8503) KM79 Troncal del Norte. $. Cash only. Handicap Access: No. Two-story stone and wooden hostel offers rooms and three cabins with private hot bath, and a small onsite restaurant.

♨ **Hostal Ves a Viento** (2305-9368) KM83 Carretera Troncal del Norte, Tierra Blanca. $. Cash only. Handicap

Access: Challenging. Simple adobe hostel has four pleasantly decorated rooms, with lots of locally made woven-reed furniture and ceramic handicrafts, private hot bath, and cable TV.

El Pital Highlands

This area gets *cold*—it even snows up here sometimes. Dress appropriately, particularly if you plan to spend the night.

✪ ⛺ 🚗 **Cabañas y Comedor Norma** (No phone) 13 kilometers (8 miles) from San Ignacio. $. Cash only. Handicap Access: Challenging. Family-run hostel is a great choice for budget travelers using public transport. Right on the main road, it offers two rooms with private hot bath, stuffed with mismatched furniture and art. The relaxed **restaurant** (B, L, D; $), with views over the farms and mountains, has a well-stocked bar.

⛺ 🚗 **Finca y Cabañas El Pinabete** (2276-1852, 7859-8190; www.elpin abete.com; elpinabete@hotmail.com) La Granadilla. $. Cash only. Handicap Access: No. High-altitude finca has five cinder-block and wooden cabins, some large enough for families. There are hiking trails right from the cabins, or they'll arrange farm tours, trips to the Río Sumpul, and private transport from La Palma. Camping and day visits can also be arranged.

🚗 **Las Cabañas del Tío Wicho** (2274-4065) 12 kilometers (7.4 miles) from San Ignacio. $. Cash only. Handicap Access: No. Cheap, downscale option next to posh El Pital Highland Cabañas offers cleanish shotgun shacks with microscopic cold bath, and fantastic surroundings.

✐ 🍴 ⛺ 🚗 **Finca Ecoturística La Montaña** (7886-5057, 7877-7578, 2284-1801 San Salvador offices; www

EL PITAL HIGHLANDS CABAÑAS OFFERS WONDERFUL LODGING IN THE HIGH-ALTITUDE PINE FORESTS.

.lamontanaelsalvador.com, lamon
tana@navegante.com.sv) KM83, Los
Planes. $$–$$$. Credit cards: No.
Handicap Access: No. Special: A
canopy tour. Very comfortable lodge
offers 10 excellent family-friendly
cabins, with great views, private hot
baths, handmade furnishings, and
porches. Staff organizes guided hikes
to Cerro El Pital, the Sumpul River,
and elsewhere, and runs the highest
altitude **canopy tour** in Central
America (open Thursday through
Sunday only). You must have private
4WD transportation to get here; it is
well signed from the main road at Los
Planes.

Mi Casa de Campo (2261-
7828; www.micasadecampo.com.sv;
info@micasadecampo.com.sv) KM105
to Chilatenango, Cantón Los Planes.
Handicap Access: No. My Country
Home offers two very comfortable
full houses sleeping seven, with full
kitchens, solar-heated showers, and
guided tours.

✪ **Hostal Miramundo** (2219-
6251; www.hotelmiramundo.com,
hostal_miramundo@yahoo.com) 15
kilometers (9 miles) northeast of La
Palma, Zona Miramundo. $$. V.
Handicap Access: Challenging. It's
called Miramundo because you can
"see the world," (well, most of El Sal-
vador, anyway) from the top (2450
meters/8036 feet) of a steep
precipice, a pre-montane forest where
bromeliads and orchids thrive. The
glass-enclosed **restaurant** (B, L, D;
$$–$$$) is worth the trip even if you
don't spend the night, with good
international cuisine such as *tiradito
Peruano*, a Japanese-Peruvian fusion
ceviche, Caprese salad, and a half
decent wine list. And karaoke. Rooms
are simple but pretty, with lots of pol-
ished wood, sturdy furnishings,

romantic lighting, and private hot
bath. Packages include meals, trans-
port from San Salvador, and a variety
of tours, such as guided hikes, horse-
back rides, and camping.

✎ **El Pital Highland Cabañas
y Restaurant** (2259-0602, 7739-
0123; www.elpital.com.sv, pital20
@yahoo.com) 12 kilometers (7.4
miles) from San Ignacio. $$–$$$$.
MC, V. Handicap Access: No.
Arguably the best lodging in the highlands, this beauty sits at 2700 meters
(8850 feet), where temperatures can
drop to freezing. Simple rooms are a
bit overpriced, but have good beds
and hot baths. The three cabins in the
trees are fantastic and spacious, sleeping up to six, with huge windows,
kitchens, and fireplaces. There are
several trails from the cabins, and a
river nearby, while guided hikes take
you farther afield. Or, hike to their
campgrounds, about 2 kilometers (1.2
miles) away, and spend the night. The
hotel also offers **paraplaning**, basically jumping off a mountain wearing
a specially designed parachute. Most
people visit on package tours that
include meals, tours, and transport
from San Salvador.

Posada del Cielo (2289-2843,
2512-6737; www.hotellaposadadel
cielo.com; info@hotellaposadadel
cielo.com) Miramundo, 9 kilometers
(5.6 miles) east of La Palma. $$. Cash
only. Handicap Access: No. This sunny
lodge offers nicely furnished rooms and
family-sized cabins with thin mattress-
es, hot showers, and a great restaurant
with views over most of El Salvador.

✴ **Where to Eat**

While Suchitoto offers a wide range
of eateries, serving everything from
fine French cuisine to gourmet

pupusas, pickings are slim elsewhere on the Artisan Route. Most hotels have restaurants, some quite nice, but otherwise it's downscale Salvadoran *típico*.

DINING OUT

Suchitoto
Many of the city's finest restaurants are in its top hotels, including **Los Almendros de San Lorenzo**, **Hotel Las Puertas**, and **La Posada de Suchitlán**, all highly recommended. **Restaurant La Casa del Escultor Miguel Martino**, covered in Galleries, serves outstanding Argentine cuisine on weekends only.

Budget travelers can stop by the tidy **Mercado** (2 Avenida Sur and 1 Calle Poniente), with inexpensive comedors and food stalls.

✪ **Guazapa Café** (2335-1823; www .guazapacafe.com) KM43.3 Carretera San Martín-Suchitoto, near Texaco. $$. Cuisine: Salvadoran. Serving: L, D. Child's Menu: Yes. Handicapped Access: Challenging. Reservations: For groups. It's worth the excursion to this unique outdoor restaurant, 2 kilometers (1.2 miles) south of Suchitoto's city center. Owner Kenia Ramírez Ayala, former guerrilla and outstanding hostess, has created her own personal Eden of gorgeous gardens, strewn with private fan-cooled pavilions hung with hammocks, where you can enjoy excellent Salvadoran cuisine. The specialty is grilled meats (ask for the jalapeño salsa), but there is also lighter fare, including quesadillas, salads and espresso beverages. There's an air-conditioned events room and plans for a pool, and events some weekends. A small exhibit of Civil War materiel is displayed; a museum is in the works.

La Fonda El Mirador (2335-1126) Avenida 15 Septiembre #85. $$. Cuisine: Salvadoran. Serving: L, D (closes at 6:30 PM). V. Child's Menu: Yes. Handicapped Access: Yes. Reservations: Recommended on weekends. On the road to Lake Suchitlán, this local institution has been welcoming guests to its gorgeous flagstone patio, shady gardens, and fine lake views for 15 years. Some come for just a cocktail, but try specialties such as the *boca colorada* (red snapper) served in your choice of sauces made with *mamey, arrayán,* or *tamarindo,* tasty local fruits. Be sure to finish with, *helado epanizado "estilo japonés,"* something like a baked Alaska.

La Lupita del Portal (2335-1429; lupitayeye@gmail.com) Parque Centenario. $–$$. Credit Cards: Yes. Cuisine: Salvadoran, International. Serving: B, L, D. Handicap Access: Yes. Reservations: No. Right on the bustling plaza, this relaxed-spot eatery offers great people-watching and big salads, specialty juices, and lots of vegetarian options. Also try the seafood *sicronizadas*, a type of Mexican sandwich made with tortillas. After 4 PM, a variety of rice and corn masa pupusas are available, with unusual fillings including chipilín, spinach, basil, zucchini, and more.

Restaurant & Hostal El Obraje (2335-1173, 2836-6537; elobraje suchitoto@gmail.com) Next to Iglesia Santa Lucía. $–$$. Credit Cards: No. Cuisine: Salvadoran. Serving: L, D Monday through Friday; B, L, D Saturday and Sunday. Child's Menu: Yes. Handicapped Access: Challenging. Reservations: For groups. Fabulously decorated spot could be described as Colonial kitsch, with its classic interior courtyard decked out in antiques and period pieces, bright colors, and photos by Luís Galmadez. The theme carries over to the menu, where very traditional Salvadoran dishes are named after local attractions; try the *Ciudad Vieja en Alhüashte,* with a sauce made from ayote seeds. They cater to groups; call ahead for multi-course meals serving four ($30) or six ($50). In addition, El Obraje offers five tiny, brightly painted double **rooms** ($) with either shared or private hot bath.

✪ El Rincóncito del Gringo (2327-2351, 2335-1770; www.elgringo suchitoto.com, rbroz@gmail.com) Calle Francisco Moran 27, 1.5 blocks west of the Alcaldía. $. Credit Cards: No. Cuisine: Mexican, Salvadoran. Serving: B, L, D. Child's Menu: No. Handicapped Access: Challenging. Reservations: For groups. Great little restaurant dishes up top-notch Mexican cuisine, including vegetarian options, like huge burritos, tacos, and savory Mexican quesadillas (as opposed to the Salvadoran pastry of the same name). In the evenings, they offer 14 different types of corn and rice pupusas, made with unusual sweet and savory fillings. Original art hangs on the walls, and English-speaking owner Roberto Broz offers some of the best tours around. Behind the restaurant, **Hostal El Rincóncito del Gringo** ($) offers clean, comfortable dorm beds and two good private, fan-cooled rooms (ask for #1) with new mattresses, shared bath, and relaxed common area with cable TV. A great spot.

✪ Villa Balanza Restaurante Hotel (2335-1408; www.villabalanzares taurante.com.sv) Barrio San José 7, next to Parque San Martín. $. AE, MC, V. Cuisine: Salvadoran. Serving: B, L, D. Child's Menu: Yes. Handicap Access: No. Dine within an artistic wonderland at this wonderful restaurant, owned by sculptor Carlos Mauricio Escobar Molina (who also decorated neighboring Parque San Martín). Festive fountains and oversized chairs are introduced with a thought-provoking sculpture above the entrance, balancing a bomb

VILLA BALANZA'S CARLOS MAURICIO ESCOBAR MOLINA WELCOMES YOU TO HIS WACKY, WONDERFUL RESTAURANT WITH THE WEIGHT OF A BOMB MEASURED AGAINST A STACK OF TORTILLAS.

against a stack of thick tortillas. The meals, mostly Salvadoran classics, include pupusas, soups, and a popular $2.50 lunch special, but be sure to save room for traditional *dulces,* candied fruits and vegetables, for dessert. They also operate an outstanding budget ✪ **hostel** ($), just down the (very steep) road. Though not as insanely decorated as the restaurant, it's well on its way, with marvelous little details such as carved doors and columns, and lots of hammocks for enjoying the breeze. Spotless, fairly large rooms come with WiFi and cable TV; most have air-conditioning and private hot bath as well. It also has a shared kitchen, a garden courtyard, and a meditation room.

Vista Conga Restaurant (2335-1679, 7118-1999; www.vistaconga .com) Final Pasaje Cielito Lindo 7. $$–$$$. AE, MC, V. Cuisine: Grilled meats. Serving: L, D, weekends only; closes at 6 PM. Child's Menu: No. Handicap Access: Challenging. Reservations: For groups. Follow the smell of sizzling meats to the grassy, wide-open gardens, with trickling fountains and fabulous lake views. There are salads, soups, and other traditional fare, but you're really here for *la parillada,* your choice of grilled beef, chicken, or chorizo sausage, served with all the fixings. Owner René Barbon also operates recommended Vista Congo Tours.

The Artisan Route

La Palma: This region's most popular destination has more restaurants than average, but they're still pretty average. Hotel La Palma has the best restaurant in town.

Restaurante del Pueblo (2305-8503) KM84. $. Credit Cards: No. Cuisine: Salvadoran, International.

Serving: B, L, D. Child's Menu: No. Handicapped Access: No. Reservations: No. One of the nicer comedores in El Pital, its Llort-style murals are rendered in black and white. The specialty is grilled meats, served with all the trimmings, but they also offer fast food, soups, and more.

Restaurante La Curva de La Palma (2313-6714) KM83 Carretera Troncal del Norte. $–$$. Credit Cards: No. Cuisine: Salvadoran. Serving: B, L, D (closes at 6 PM). Child's Menu: Yes. Handicapped Access: Challenging. Reservations: For groups. Just south of town, this breezy open-air restaurant serves some of the best food in town, including grilled meats, fresh fish, and even a few vegetarian items. But you're really here for the pool and slide, included with your meal.

Típicos y Cocteles María Luisa (2352-1127) KM83 Carretera Troncal del Norte. $. Credit Cards: No. Cuisine: Chinese, Mexican Salvadoran. Serving: B, L, D. Child's Menu: No. Handicapped Access: No. Reservations: No. This very basic comedor just off the main drag offers Chinese food, and it's actually pretty good, if a tad greasy. The specialty is seafood, specifically cocktails and ceviches, but also offers fried fish and seafood fried rice.

Dulce Nombre de María: Restaurant El Roble (2356-9296) Calle Principal. $. Credit Cards: No. Cuisine: Salvadoran. Serving: B, L, D. Child's Menu: No. Handicapped Access: No. Reservations: No. A step above this small town's simple comedores, this festively painted old adobe gets packed. The specialties are grilled chicken and *sopa de gallina India,* chicken soup. Bonus: There's live music on weekends. Also try **Restaurante La Luna** (2356-9416; Barrio San José; B, L, D; $; cash only), serving Salvadoran fast food, pupusas, and snacks; it has an art gallery.

Chalatenango: Restaurante Alemán Piedras Calientes (2264-0147, 2263-8778) Calle Circunvalación and Avenida Juan Ramón Molina #133. $. AE, MC, V. Cuisine: German, Salvadoran. Serving: D. Closed: Sunday. Child's Menu: No. Handicapped Access: Challenging. Reservations: No. Grab a cab to Chalatenango's best restaurant, an open-air eatery on the scenic outskirts of town. The specialty is German cuisine, with sausages, veal, pork roast, and huge mugs of beer. They also offer pastas, seafood, and Salvadoran dishes.

BAKERIES Ella's Cakes (2384-4014) Ilobasco Central Park. B, L, D. $. Ilobasco's favorite bakery specializes in cakes and pastries, but offers savory baked goods too.

✪ **Pan Lilian La Palma** (7305-9482) Gerardo Barrios #130, La Palma. B, L, D; closes at 6 PM. $. Cash only. Popular diner-style eatery specializes in pastries, but also serves pizza, burgers, and other fast food.

Pan Lilian Suchitoto (2335-1114) B, L. $. Across from the Municipal Tour Office, bakery makes beautiful pastries, great cakes, hamburgers, and sandwiches.

CAFÉS Artex Café (2335–1440) Parque Centenario. B, L, D. $. Popular café on Suchitoto's Central Park offers Internet access, coffee beverages, fresh juices, a book exchange, and fairly full bar, including a few wines.

Café D' Café (2335-9190) La Palma Central Park. B, L, D; closed Sunday. $. Cash only. While purusing La Palma's murals, look for the Che Guevara misquote (IF EVERYONE CAN'T HAVE COFFEE, NO ONE WILL HAVE COFFEE!) to find this cute, locally owned café serving espresso beverages, teas, baked goods, and free WiFi.

Fransuchi (2335-1493) Calle 4 Oriente #3, Barrio Santa Lucia. B, L, D. $–$$. Cash only. Simple French-Salvadoran café in Suchitoto serves crepes, waffles, churros, and soft-serve ice cream.

PIZZA Pizzería Fatima Los Planes (7570-4688, 2304-9517) Los Planes. $. Cash only. Even in the El Pital highlands, you can enjoy pizza, plus tacos, enchiladas, and sandwiches.

Pizza Xela (2335-1397) Avenida 15 Septiembre #33. L, D; closed Tuesday. $$. Cash only. Just north of central Suchitoto, on the way to the lake, Xela serves pizzas—try the seafood pie—in a cute dining room or garden with a view. Delivery is $1.

PUPUSERÍAS Suchitoto: Also try **Rincón El Gringo** or **La Lupita del Portal**, both offering a variety of specialty pupusas.

Pupusería Conchita (7387-3619) Calle 1 Poniente, Barrio el Calvario #7. Pats out pupusas every evening.

Pupusería Raquelita (2335-1254) 4 Calle Poniente #1. No-frills pupusería on Parque San Martín offers rice and corn masa pupusas, as well as empanadas, daily.

La Palma: Comedor y Pupusería Tipicos La Palma (7212-2739) KM84, Calle 22 de Junio. B, L, D; closed Sunday. $. Cash only. Just off the main drag, this is a popular spot for pupusas and inexpensive lunch specials.

Pupusería La Palma (2335-9063) KM84 Calle Principal. B, L, D; closed Sunday. $. Cash only. La Palma's favorite pupusería has a log cabin façade rather than the ubiquitous murals, and serves inexpensive *comida típica* throughout the day.

✳ Selective Shopping

BANKS AND ATMS Banks and ATM machines are rare in this region, unlike shopping opportunities. Break big bills before heading to smaller towns, where change is hard to find.

Suchitoto has HSBC and ProCredit ATMs on the central park. **Cojutepeque** has a BAC ATM on its central park. The city of **Chalatenango** has a few ATMs, with an HSBC ATM one block from the central park; **Sesuntepeque** has CitiBank and HSBC near

its park; and **Ilobasco** has CitiBank, BAC, and HSBC ATMs located close to the ceramics shops. **La Palma** has a CitiBank ATM on the corner of the central park.

GROCERIES Suchitoto, Ilobasco, Chalatenango, and Sesuntepeque all have large grocery stores and a variety of shops. La Palma has a mid-sized **MiniSuper La Palma** (Calle Gerardo).

MARKETS Most towns of any size have markets where you can pick up produce and basic items. Usually these are close to the city center; Suchitoto's is by the bus terminal.

GALLERIES

Suchitoto
Like other Spanish Colonial cities co-opted by the arts (I'm looking at you, Santa Fe, Oaxaca, and Antigua) these ancient adobes are packed with shops

THE BEST PLACE FOR FRESH PRODUCE, CHEAP MEALS, BIG SMILES, AND JUST ABOUT ANYTHING ELSE IS THE TOWN MARKET.

ranging from kitschy to sublime. Most hotels and restaurants (notably La Ballanza, Posada Suchitlán, Hotel Las Puertas, and Rincón El Gringo) have gift shops and galleries as well. Many shops close during the week.

✪ **Restaurant La Casa del Escultor Miguel Martino** (2335-1711 Suchitoto; www.miguelmartino.com) 6 Calle Oriente and 2 Avenida Norte #26. Open weekends. Internationally known Argentine sculptor Miguel Martino creates remarkable, organic work, mostly with wood and other natural materials, as well as excellent Argentine barbecue at his gallery's attached **restaurant** (L, D; $$–$$$), with a good wine list.

✪ **Galería Pascal** (2333-1008) 4 Calle Poniente. Fine arts gallery, in a lovely old Colonial, hosts monthly shows by national and international artists. The gift shop has some of the highest quality handicrafts you'll find anywhere in El Salvador.

Galería Shanay 3 Avenida Norte and 2 Calle Oeste. Open Saturday and Sunday. Suchitoto's most famous artist sells his detailed, realistic landscapes and cityscapes, and more affordable work by his students.

Guanacas (2335-1534) 3 Avenida Sur and Morazán. Open daily. In addition to the usual crafts, has a large selection of Spanish-language books about El Salvador.

Espresso Galería Suchitoto (2335-1238) Avenida 15 Septiembre. Artist Victor Manuel Aguilar paints with coffee: portraits, street scenes, and landscapes. The gallery also carries colorful paintings and other handicrafts.

Puros Artesanales (2335-1072) 2 Avenida Sur. Handmade cigars are also works of art.

✪ **Xiquilite** (7860-7731; solazulindigo @yahoo.com) Open Thursday through Sunday. Great spot to get your indigo fix, with clothing, purses, and more; there's also a book exchange.

The Artisan Route
Dulce Nombre de María:
Artesanías y Mas (No phone) Central Park. Open daily. Leathergoods shop sells shoes, belts, embroidered shirts, seed jewelry, and more.

Ilobasco: Most ceramics shops are concentrated on the right fork of KM34, past the Esso Station.

MOJE Casa Artesanal (2384-4770, 2332-0659; www.mojecasaartesanal .com) 4 Avenida Norte, Pasaje El Campo #11. Trains youth to make the city's traditional ceramics. Dozens of shops selling fine pottery, sexy *sorpresas,* and other ceramics line the surrounding blocks.

La Palma: La Palma's most famous resident, Fernando Llort, arrived in 1973, inspired to create his (then) unique acrylics: naïve, childlike landscapes, village scenes, and religious pieces that used indigenous iconography and bright colors to capture El Salvador's traditions, beauty, and optimism. Compared to Miró and Picasso, he became an international sensation, his style synonomous with El Salvador. Llort trained local villagers to create similar work, which kept La Palma afloat through the bitter Civil War and has since transformed it into a popular arts center. Though Llort returned to San Salvador, where he decorated the National Cathedral and opened Arbol de Vida gallery, these beautiful hills are still home to some 300 family workshops. The pieces seem similar at first glance, but you'll soon notice subtle details: some are more intricate, others more richly colored. **La Palma Online** (lapalma.gang.net) has information and photos covering some 50 artisans, but have a look around town before you buy.

San Sebastian: There are several workshops weaving brightly colored hammocks close to the town center; they hang their wares outside. Visitors are welcome, and will probably be treated to demonstrations of dyeing and loom-weaving techniques.

✳ Special Events

Suchitoto is well known for its extravagant fiestas, worth scheduling your trip around. If not, at least try to catch the weekend **Asi es Mi Tierra Artisans Festival**. Also check out the weekend **Ilobasco Gastronomic Festival** (Avenida 1 Sur and Avenida Carlos) and **Cojutepeque Gastronomic Festival** (Cerro de las Pavas). **Cinquera** has a festival market the last Sunday of the month.

January: **Día de la Paz** (January 16) Suchitoto enthusiastically celebrates the signature of the 1992 Chapultepec Peace Accords, with Guazapa starting early, on January 12.

San Sebastian Fiestas (January 24–28) Weaving center honors its patron.

February: ✪ **Permanent International Festival of Arts and Culture** (February) Features painters, singers, dancers, and other performers from all over the country and world on February weekends, most at Teatro Las Ruinas.

Commemoration of the Massacre of Tenango and Guadalupe (February 27 and 28) Communities remember the victims of a 1983 war crime.

Romería (February 18) Suchitoto honors the Virgin of Remedios.

Arcatao Fiestas (February 2) Arcatao honors the Virgin of Candelaría.

March: ✪ **Semana Santa** (March or April; week before Easter) Suchitoto holds an extravagant Holy Week, with elaborate Palm Sunday activities, the Procession of Silence, and a costumed reenactment of the Stations of the Cross, atop beautiful "carpets," or murals made of colored sand, created in the streets.

May: **Day of the Cross** (May 3) Suchitoto is decorated with crosses made of flowers and fruit.

Cojutepeque Fiestas (May 13) Pilgrimage to an image of the Virgin of Fatima atop Cerro de las Pavas.

July: **Anniversary of Suchitoto** (July 15) Parades, traditional dances, early-morning gunfire, homemade hot-air balloons celebrate Suchitoto becoming a city.

San Ignacio Fiestas (July 23–31) San Ignacio honors its patron.

Lantern Procession (July 28) Solemn Cinquera event commemorates the Massacre of San Francisco Echeverría.

August: **Festival of Corn** (August 4) Suchitoto, Dulce Nombre de María, and other towns celebrate the corn harvest with parades, beauty queens, and lots of corn-based snacks.

September: **Parade of Torches and Costumes** (September 14) The run-up to Independence Day, celebrated throughout El Salvador on September 15, includes Suchitoto's festive night parade.

Festival of School Bands (October) Competing teenage marching bands in Suchitoto.

October: **Fiesta Rosario** (First Sunday in October) El Rosario honors its patron.

Halloween (October 31) Suchitoto dresses to impress during this imported holiday, with costume parties around town.

November: **Fiestas San Martín** (November 1) San Martín honors its patron.

Día de los Muertos (November 2) Suchitoto invites tourists to help honor their deceased loved ones, with candles and family festivities in area cemeteries.

El Feriado (First week of November) Suchitoto hosts a fair with rides, games, dancing, an arts festival, and the launch of dozens of homemade hot-air balloons.

December: **Fiestas Citalá** (December 1–9) Citalá honors the Virgin of the Immaculate Conception.

Fiestas Cinquera (December 4–15) Cinquera honors its patron, Saint Nicholas.

Fiesta de Hamacas Quezaltepeque (December 6–8) Concepción de Quetzaltepeque honors its patron, Virgin of the Immaculate Conception.

✪ **Feast Day of Santa Lucia** (December 6–13) Suchitoto goes all out to celebrate its patron saint.

Fiestas Dulce Nombre de María (December 11) Festivities begin on the 7th and move from neighborhood to neighborhood, culminating in the city center of Dulce Nombre de María on the 11th.

Fiestas La Palma (Third week of December) Crafts town celebrates its patron, just in time for Christmas shopping.

Fiestas Chalatenango (December 18–25) Chalatenango honors its patron, the Niño Jesús.

Manger Scene Competition (December) Suchitoto residents compete with elaborate manger scenes.

Eastern El Salvador

6

EASTERN EL SALVADOR

MOUNTAINS AND MEMORIES

Eastern El Salvador's rolling plains, a patchwork of ranches and farms, are interrupted by rumbling volcanoes and tiny whitewashed villages, as yet little explored by travelers. The **Ruta de la Paz**, or Route of Peace, through the ancient mountains and former FMLN stronghold of Morazán, is well known, but there is so much more.

At the heart of this vast expanse is **Chaparrastique Volcano**, one of El Salvador's most active, rising alone to an almost perfect cone 2130 meters (6986 feet) above the regional capital of **San Miguel**. The Pearl of the Oriente is a rather poetic name for this congested commercial city, but perhaps apropos considering such writers as Francisco Gavidia and Juan J. Cañas called it home. More a point in transit than destination for most travelers, it is nevertheless festive, buzzing with life, and famed for its November **Carnival**, El Salvador's biggest fiesta.

To the west, the Route of a Thousand Peaks rolls through the volcanic Chinameca range, centered on the twin towns of **Berlín** and **Alegría**. There, cool green coffee fields and a lovely crater lake are surrounded by a handful of hotels and restaurants. Close by is **Volcán Chichontepec**, often called **San Vicente** for the town below, nestled into the fertile and scenic Jiboa Valley. Though less visited than Alegría, there are old ruins and additional ancient fossil fields just waiting to be discovered.

Most tourists, however, come for the Ruta de Paz, Route of Peace, which climbs into the mountains of Morazán, north of San Miguel. This was the heart of rebel-held territory during the Civil War, and remains El Salvador's poorest and least-populated region. The region is centered on the mountain town of Perquín, Path of Embers in the Lenca tongue. It was the de facto FMLN capital during the 1980s, and its famous Museum of the Revolution has preserved craters of a different sort, alongside the bombs that made them.

Though most famous for its war-related attractions—monuments to the Massacre at El Mozote, the transmitter for the mobile rebel station, Radio

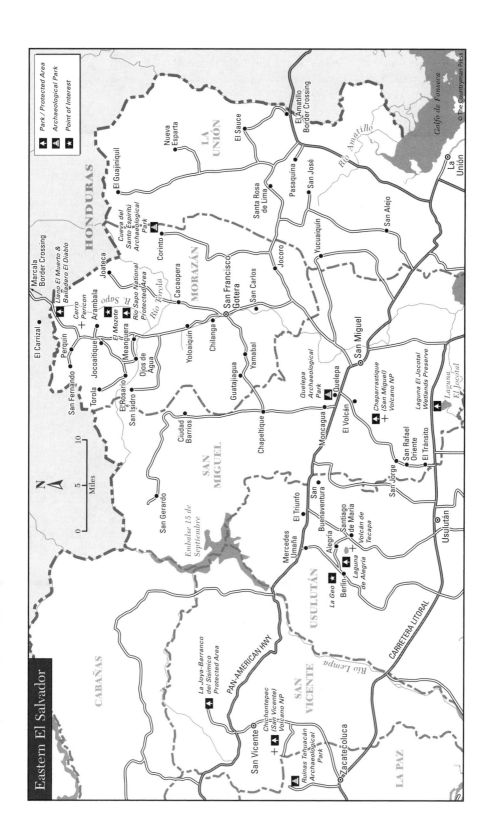

Eastern El Salvador

Legend:
- Park / Protected Area
- Archaeological Park
- Point of Interest

© The Countryman Press

N

0   5   10
Miles

CABAÑAS

HONDURAS

Marcala Border Crossing

El Carrizal

Llano El Muerto & Bailadero El Diablo

Cerro Pericón

Perquín

San Fernando

Jocoaitique

Arambala

El Mozote

Meanguera

El Rosario

Ojos de Agua

Torola

San Isidro

R. Sapo

Río Sapo National Protected Area

Joateca

Cueva del Santo Espíritu Archaeological Park

Corinto

Cacaopera

Caolinga

MORAZÁN

San Francisco Gotera

San Carlos

Yoloaiquín

Chilanga

Yamabal

Guatajiagua

Chapeltique

Ciudad Barrios

San Gerardo

SAN MIGUEL

Embalse 15 de Septiembre

PAN-AMERICAN HWY

La Joya-Barranco del Sisímico Protected Area

SAN VICENTE

San Vicente

Chichontepec (San Vicente) Volcano NP

Ruinas Tehuacán Archaeological Park

Zacatecoluca

LA PAZ

Mercedes Umaña

El Triunfo

San Buenaventura

Santiago de María

Alegría

La Geo

Berlín

Laguna de Alegría

Volcán de Tecapa

USULUTÁN

Usulatán

Río Lempa

CARRETERA LITORAL

Moncagua

El Volcán

Quelepa

Quelepa Archaeological Park

Chaparrastique (San Miguel) Volcano NP

San Miguel

San Rafael Oriente

El Tránsito

San Jorge

Laguna El Jocotal Wetlands Preserve

Laguna El Jocotal

Nueva Esparta

LA UNIÓN

El Sauce

El Amatillo Border Crossing

Río Amatillo

El Guajiniquil

Santa Rosa de Lima

Pasaquina

San José

San Alejo

Jocoro

Yucuaiquín

Golfo de Fonseca

La Unión

Vencermos, and low benches where the 1992 Peace Accords were signed—
Morazán also cradles magnificent wilderness areas of jade green rivers, undeveloped hot springs, splashing waterfalls, and more.

There are many other sites still being developed for tourism, such as the famed black-pottery producing town of **Guatajiagua** and the petroglyph-covered cave at **Corinto**, just one of dozens of caverns bearing the artistry of painters and sculptors whose work is still admired after 8000 years.

Old Colonial villages, with their tejas-topped roofs and adorable plazas, often offer access to still more mountain hikes, historical sites, and swimming holes, though only the most adventurous travelers will find them. Just drop by their alcaldías, where bemused, moustachioed ranchers can help you find guides and guesthouses.

At the border is their commercial capital, the busy market city of **Santa Rosa de Lima**. There, farmers and gold miners gather throughout the week, seeking buyers for their wares.

Crime While this region isn't particularly known for criminal activity, the busy streets of San Miguel, particularly around the bus terminal and downtown, are sketchy at night. You should definitely climb San Miguel and San Vicente Volcanoes with either a guide company or police escort.

GUIDANCE At press time, MiTur was planning to open an office in **San Miguel**, probably close to the central park. Otherwise, you'll find useful, free city maps at hotels and restaurants around town.

Alegría Información a los Turistas (No phone) Central Park. Open 9–5 Tuesday through Sunday. Alegría's tourist "office," a booth at the central park, isn't well organized, but they can arrange guided hikes, and have a small museum with bits of old pottery and a gift shop, plus public bathrooms.

OSCAR, AT THE MUSEUM OF THE REVOLUTION IN PERQUÍN, DISPLAYS THE REMAINS OF COMMANDER DOMINGO MONTERROSA'S HELICOPTER.

Perquín and Morazán Morazán is even less developed than other parts of El Salvador. Anecdotally, this is because conservative governments were loath to spend money on the former guerrilla capital. If this is true, things might change rapidly. Newly elected Vice President Sanchez Cerén is an old-school FMLN guerrilla with deep ties to Morazán; his campaign Web site even ran advertisements for local hotels. Until then, however, your best bet for organizing guides is through the Museo de la Revolución in Perquín, area hotels, or PRODETUR. While I highly recommend seeing this region with a guide, adventurous travelers could try con-

ONLINE RESOURCES

All these sites are in Spanish only, but Google Translate makes them accessible to everyone.

Alcaldía San Vicente (www.alcaldiadesanvicente.gob.sv) City site has solid information for tourists.

Ciudad Barrios Online (ciudadbarrios.isdem.gob.sv) The birthplace of Oscar Romero isn't exactly a tourist destination, but pilgrims will find information here.

La Perla del Oriente (laperladeoriente.com) Has some information about San Miguel; also check **La Web del Oriente** (www.lawebdeoriente.com).

Marcala Perquín Ruta de Paz Lenca (www.marcalaperquin.org) Information about Morazán and the neighboring Honduran regions, with a great photo gallery.

Mi Perquín (www.miperquin.com) Great little site has more information about Perquín and Morazán.

San Francisco Gotera Online (gotera.isdem.gob.sv) City site is mostly nuts-and-bolts government business, but has nice photos.

San Vicente Online (www.vicentinosonline.com) Members of the San Vicente online community posts lots of photos.

Santa Rosa de Lima Online (www.santarosadelimacity.com) Market town has an informative government site.

---

tacting alcadías in Arambala (2680-4109), El Rosarío (2683-9307, 7536-0068) Joateca (2683-0039), Jocoaitique (2680-5619), San Fernando (2683-9516), and Torola (2683-9268).

CORSATUR Ruta de la Paz Lenca Tourist Information (2680-4311; perquintours@yahoo.es) Open 7–5 Monday through Friday. Not completely useless, this sad little tour office arranges guides, and had a few flyers and maps. The **Tourist Police** (2680-4040, 1680-4027) are located a block up from the central park.

Kiosko Información Turístico de El Mozote (2615-5104, 7724-4252, 7891-9691) Open 7–5 daily. Cheerfully painted kiosk has brochures and other information in English and Spanish, and can help organize guided hikes, basic lodging, and transportation.

San Fernando Información Turistico (7450-4991) San Fernando Central Park. May be open when you visit, but don't count on it.

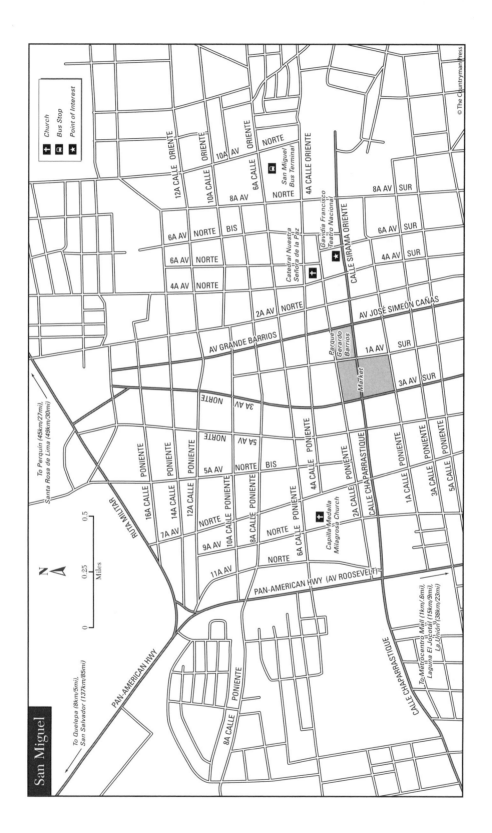

San Miguel

✪ **PRODETUR** (2680-4086, 2680-4311; www.perkintours.ya.st, prodeturper quin.tripod.com; perkintours@yahoo.es, prodeturperquin@navegante.com.sv) Colonia 10 de Enero, Perquín. Open 8–5 Monday through Friday, 8–2 Saturday. PRODETUR manages the Río Sapo Protected Area and operates Perkín Tours, offering energetic adventure trips all over Morazán.

GETTING THERE Because this area is so large and little touristed, getting around can be a chore. San Miguel, Perquín, San Vicente, and the triumvirate of Berlín, Alegría, and Santiago de María, are all easily accessible by public transport or car. More remote destinations, including the Corinto Caverns, El Mozote, and Morazán's rural ecotourism attractions, are time-consuming to explore.

By Car: While major thoroughfares in this region are excellent, there are more unpaved and poorly maintained roads than elsewhere. You can still travel almost anywhere with a regular car, but it can be slow going at times. A 4WD is highly recommended for exploring less developed regions in Morazán.

San Miguel is a large, somewhat confusing city. You'll arrive from San Salvador on the Pan-American Highway, called Avenida Roosevelt as it runs southeast through town, connecting the city to the mall and continuing to La Unión. It forms the western and southern border of the city center, and is lined with many of the city's best hotels and restaurants. If you're driving, it's easiest to stay here. Just before entering town from the west, Ruta Militar exits the Pan-American to the left, heading northeast to Perquín, Santa Rosa, and the El Amatillo border, and forming the northern border of the city center.

The city center is a logical grid, but has lots of one-way streets. It's best to find guarded parking, preferably at your hotel, and explore the center on foot. You can rent a car in San Miguel at **Barrera Rent-a-Car** (2669-8491; barrerarent _car@msn.com; KM137.5 Pan-American Hwy), across from the fire station, or at the **Comfort Inn**.

By Bus: The region's transportation hub is **San Miguel**, with direct bus access throughout the region, including La Unión and many of the Eastern Beaches. There's a direct bus to **San Vicente** from San Salvador, but from San Miguel and elsewhere, you'll need to catch a cab or truck from the Pan-American, which is easy. Things get a bit more confusing once you are in **Morazán**, where pickup trucks leaving from the Perquín Central Park are often the only easy connections to nearby towns. A guide can help you navigate.

San Miguel: This is Eastern El Salvador's transportation hub, with a well-organized **bus terminal** (6 Calle Oriente and 10 Avenida Norte) conveniently located next to a dozen budget hotels. Good city maps are available at hotels around town, and worth finding. The city center is certainly walkable, but sprawls and is sketchy at night, particularly around the terminal. Most local buses stop at the central park; buses 90S and 90B run every few minutes from the park to Metrocentro Mall.

El Amatillo (Honduran border) via Santa Rosa de Lima (390) Every 10 minutes.

Cacaopera Take #328 to San Francisco Gotera then transfer to Bus #337A.

Corinto (327) Every half hour, last bus leaves at 3:30 PM; alternately, Bus #782 from Cacoapera goes to Corinto hourly.

Playa El Cuco (320) Every hour; alternately, take a Chirilagua bus and change buses there.

El Mozote via Joateca (332-C) 5:30 AM and 10:30 AM.

Jucuapa, Chinameca, and Volcán San Miguel (Chaparrastique) (479) Every 10 minutes.

Marcala (Honduran border), via Bailadero del Diablo and Llanos El Muerto (426) 4:40 AM and 11:40 AM, returning from Llanos El Muerto at 8 AM and 2:30 PM.

Perquín and Ruta de la Paz (332) 6 AM, 7:20 AM, 10:50 AM, noon, 12:30 PM, 1:40 PM, 4:15 PM; alternately, take bus #328 San Francisco Gotera and transfer to a pickup truck to Perquín, leaving every 15 minutes.

Playas Las Tunas, Negra, and El Tamarindo (385) Every hour.

San Alejo (331) Every hour.

San Francisco Gotera (328) Every half hour.

San Salvador (301) Every 10 minutes.

La Unión (304, 324) Every 10 minutes.

Usulután (373) Every 10 minutes.

San Francisco Gotera: Cacaopera (337A) Every hour.

Guatajiagua (410) Every hour.

El Rosario via Jocoatique (signed) 9:15 AM, 1:15 AM, and 3:20 PM.

Perquín, San Fernando, and Torola (332) 7:20 AM, 8:30 AM, 10:50 AM, noon, 2:40 PM and 4:15m. The 7:20 AM and 4:15 PM buses do not continue on to Torola. Pickup trucks run to Perquín every 15 minutes.

Perquín Buses and pickup trucks leave from around the central park.

Arambala Pickup trucks every 15 minutes or so.

Llano El Muerto The Marcala–San Miguel bus #426 passes the Las Margaritas exit, about 1 kilometer (0.6 mile) south of town; check with your hotel for times.

El Mozote Pickup trucks leave every half hour or so, but some only go to the Desavio de Arambala, 8 kilometers (5 miles) from El Mozote. It's worth hiring a guide to facilitate the trip.

San Miguel, San Fernando, and Torola (332) Buses run six times daily between San Miguel and Perquín, continuing to San Fernando; some offer service to Torola. Pickup trucks leave every 20 minutes for San Fernando.

San Francisco de Gotera Pickup trucks run every 15 minutes.

San Vicente: This valley town is located 3 steep kilometers (1.8 miles) from the Pan-American, where most buses, including the #301 between **San Miguel** and **San Salvador**, drop you off. From here, you can catch a pickup truck (25¢) or private taxi ($5) into town. Bus #116 from **San Salvador** runs every 10 minutes to the San Vicente bus station, which is also far from the city center; you'll need a taxi ($3) to and from the central park anyway.

Santa Rosa de Lima: Most people come through on their way to the **El Amatillo border with Honduras**. Bus #390 from San Miguel rolls right through.

San Miguel (390) Every 10 minutes, bus 391-C stops in San Juan and El Sauce on their way to San Miguel.

La Unión (336, 342) Every 15 minutes.

Berlín, Alegría, Santiago de María Bus #348 runs every half hour between Berlín, Alegría, and Santiago de María Central Parks.

Alegría buses leave the central park to **San Salvador** at 5 PM; **Usulután** at 6 AM, 8:30 AM, and 4 PM; and **San Miguel** at 5 AM, 5:45 AM; 11 AM; 12:30 AM.

Berlín has buses to **San Salvador** (303) at 4 AM, 5 AM, 1 PM, and 2 PM; and **San Miguel** at 5 AM, 5:45 AM; 11 AM; 12:30 AM.

Santiago de María bus #348 to Alegría and Berlín stops at the central park. Another bus stop, at Símon Bolívar and 1 Avenida Norte, has bus #362 to **Usulután** every 15 minutes; and microbus R-14 to **Ciudad Triúnfo** (not Puerto El Triúnfo), at the intersection of the Pan-American Highway, where you can catch bus 301 to **San Miguel** or **San Salvador**.

By Taxi: **San Miguel** has scores of taxis, easily found at the central park and bus station. It costs about $3 in town, $5 at night, and much more to arrange longer trips throughout Morazán and elsewhere. **San Vicente** also has taxis, which wait at the Pan-American, bus station, and central park.

Santiago de María has real taxis, while **Berlín** only has tiny three-wheeled mototaxis, which can take you to La Geo and even Alegría. Note that **Alegría** does not have taxis, and it's more than 2 kilometers (1.2 miles) to the lagoon.

Transporte Doble R (2634-2770), operated by Casa Mía in Berlín, provides private transportation throughout the country.

There are no official taxis in **Morazán**, but the tourist office, alcaldía, museum, and most hotels can arrange private pickup trucks and air-conditioned minivans for tours around the region.

✳ To See

San Miguel

Though **San Miguel**'s Colonial character may be hard to enjoy amidst all the traffic, the circa 1530 city center does have a few nice adobe buildings, some of which may have conceivably survived all the pirate attacks, earthquakes, and aerial bombing over the years.

The **Catedral Nuestra Señora de la Paz**, with its red steeples and lovely stained glass, was constructed in the early 1900s and most recently rebuilt after the Civil War. The Virgin of Peace, inside, arrived after a 1682 pirate attack destroyed her original chapel near Punta Chiquirín. She survived, however, and local fisherfolk carried her to San Miguel, arriving on November 22, 1682, the *very day* that pirates stopped looting. When a 1787 eruption of Chaparrastique Volcano sent lava toward the city, she miraculously turned the lava safely southward.

More interesting architecturally is the 1909 **Gavidia Francisco Teatro Nacional**, modeled after the Paris Opera House, with neo-Rennaissance frills frosting the elegant exterior. Recently refurbished, it has a small stage and cool, blue, modern interior with neon-accented box seats—very South Beach—and hosts all sorts of performances.

Graceful **Capilla Medalla Milagrosa** (7 Avenida Norte and 4 Calle Poniente; open 8 to noon and 2 to 4) also has lots of neon surrounding the altar, homage to the Virgin's 1830 appearance to Saint Catherine, on a beam of light. The neo-Gothic 1904 church was originally a hospital operated by nine French nuns. Today it is a national landmark, surrounded by a shady park. If it appears to be closed, just knock on the gate.

Berlín

Occupied for some 6000 years, this chilly town was most recently colonized by German and Italian immigrants who came in the late 1800s to grow coffee. Several historic homes with unusual metallic construction date from this period, including **Casa Mía Hotel**, while two private museums offer insight into the region's interesting heritage. German tourists may appreciate that the municipal flag is an echo of your own, and the alcaldía even displays a letter from a Mayor of Berlin, Germany, who liked their coffee.

San Vicente

San Vicente was founded in 1635 by the Spanish, who dedicated the department capital in the shade of **Arból de Tempisque**, a tree that still stands. The 1930 **Tower of San Vicente**, in the central park, is an amazing piece of architecture reminiscent of the Eiffel Tower. Though damaged in an earthquake, the tower was recently rebuilt and you can climb to the top for US$0.50, and enjoy remarkable volcano views.

CAPILLA MEDALLA MILAGROSA, A NEON-LIT OASIS OF TRANQUILITY IN BUSY SAN MIGUEL, WAS ORIGINALLY FOUNDED AS A HOSPITAL IN 1904.

1762 **Iglesía El Pilar** (1 Avenida Sur and 2 Calle Poniente) is a beautiful, white-washed Colonial church with a lovely interior, most notable for its role in the 1833 Nonualco Rebellion, an indigenous revolution led by Anastasio Aquino.

Aquino occupied the town, went to the church, and in front of 3000 rebels, donned the Virgin of Pilar's red robes and declared himself King of the Nonualcos. A huge party followed, which gave federal troops time to surround the town and smash the rebellion. José Simeón Cañas, who successfully led a movement to abolish slavery throughout Central America, is buried here.

Morazán

Morazán Department was leveled during the Civil War; with few exceptions, such as downtown **Jocoatitique**, most Colonial architecture is gone. Even the churches, where villagers would sometimes take sanctuary in the early parts of the war, were specifically targeted in bombing runs. With the exception of a few bullet-riddled original walls, now covered with wonderful murals, almost all the architecture you'll see dates from the late 1990s.

MUSEUMS

San Miguel

Museo Regional del Oriente (2660-2968) 1 Calle Oeste and 4 Avenida Sur. Admission: Free. Open: 8–noon and 2–5 Monday through Friday, 9–1 Saturday. Look for the green Casa de Cultural, two blocks south of the Central Park, to find this ragtag collection of archaeological pieces and donated historic artifacts, as well as photos of San Miguel before the Civil War.

Perquín

Campamiento Guerrilla (2680-4303) Casco Urbano, Perquín. Admission: 50¢, kids free. Open: 7–6 daily. Right behind the famous Museo, this family-run attraction is a model guerrilla camp, furnished with rusty weaponry and other materiel that owner Ángel Recino has collected from the mountains around town. Enter through the beaded curtain, made with old bullet casings, to a park landscaped into a coffee plantation. Bomb art and machine guns are dramatically displayed around earthen fortifications, rope bridges, and *tatús*, or Vietnamese-style underground caverns that were used as hospitals, hideouts, and kitchens, with long tunnels to send smoke plumes several meters away from camp. Very cool.

CAMPAMIENTO GUERRILLA LETS YOU EXPLORE TATÚS, UNDERGROUND HIDING SPOTS, AND TRANSPORTABLE HANGING BRIDGES, JUST LIKE THOSE USED IN THE CIVIL WAR.

○ **Museo de la Revolución** (2610-6737) Casco Urbano, Perquín. Admission: $1.20. Open: 7–6. The most famous museum in El Salvador, operated by former ERD (FMLN) guerrillas, displays the old Radio Vencermos (We Will Win) mobile radio station, where rebels transmitted news, views, tunes, and left-wing soap operas poking fun at government leaders across the mountains, energizing the resistance and pissing the military right off. Commander Domingo Monterrosa, responsible for the El Mozote Massacre, and a frequent target of sharp-tongued Vencermos DJs, hated the programming so much that when he captured the station, he proudly and predictably took the transmitter with him as a trophy. It had been booby trapped by FMLN strategist Joaquín Villalobos, and exploded mid-flight; you can see the remains of the helicopter here, too. The museum has five other rooms of informative displays, with some signage in English. Your guide, a former guerrilla, takes you through the heartfelt collection, displaying amazing political posters, photos of the young rebels and martyrs, maps, articles, and materiel, including weapons manufactured in East Germany, Czechoslovakia, Vietnam, and Belgium. There's coverage of the original 1932 Peasants Rebellion as well, led by Farabundo Martí, for whom the FMLN is named. And outside, surrounded by craters and bombs, are several wooden benches beneath a spreading mango tree. This is where the 1992 Chapultepec Accords were finally signed, bringing peace—if not economic justice—to this beautiful region.

El Mozote Memorial (7534-0383) El Mozote central park. Admission: Free (tours $5–10, depending on the size of the group). Open: 24 hours. They called the strategy *Quitarle el agua al pez,* Take the water away from the fish. This is a reference to a Mao quote: THE REVOLUTIONARY MUST MOVE AMONG THE PEOPLE AS A FISH DOES THROUGH THE SEA. From 1980 through 1984, tens of thousands of civilians were deliberately liquidated by federal troops in Chalatenango, San Vicente, Cabañas, and Morazán Departments. El Mozote is the most famous incident, not because of the body count (900 or so), which was not unusual, but because there was a witness, Rufina Amaya Mírquez. In December 1981, as the war intensified, refugees from across Morazán began seeking safe haven in El Mozote, considered a pro-government town. As their numbers swelled, the elite Atlacatl Batallion arrived. Special forces set up a perimeter, blocked access roads, and reassured everyone that they were finally safe. In the early morning of December 10, everyone was awakened and ordered to the central park, where they were divided into different groups: men, women, adolescents, and children. At dawn, executions began with the men and adolescents. The women and older girls were taken to Cerro de la Cruz and systematically raped, then shot. And finally, 140 children, along with 6 adults presumably left alive to comfort them, were herded into the church. Soldiers fired on them through the windows, then set the building ablaze. Amaya, who had hidden in a tree, went straight to the international media, which broadcast the story all over the world. The Salvadoran government specifically denied that the event had taken place, as did U.S. President Ronald Reagan, who had personally authorized training and support for the batallion. In 1993, the Spanish government sent in a forensics team. Amaya's words were proven absolutely true, skull by charred skull. Townspeople

THE MEMORIAL TO THE EL MOZOTE MASSACRE IS A BEAUTIFUL AND DISTURBING
REMINDER OF ALL THAT HUMAN BEINGS ARE CAPABLE OF.

have rebuilt the church, and covered it with colorful murals of children who are
dancing, playing, studying, falling in love, and "pursuing the dreams we had for
them." The Garden of the Innocents, behind it, has roses above their graves and
another cheerfully mosaic-tiled mural, underscored with the names and ages of
those buried here. A somber memorial nearby lists the names of the adults,
those that are known, anyway. And you can climb to Cerro de la Cruz, a peaceful
spot with pretty views. **El Mozote Asociación Turistica de Historia Viva** (see
the Ecotourism on the Ruta de la Paz sidebar, later) offers tours, and arranges
guided hikes from town.

Museo Shafik Vive! (2680-5509) Comunidad Segundo Montes, Meanguera.
Admission: By donation. Open: Daily. This new museum is named for rebel
leader, unapologetic communist, and perennial FMLN presidential candidate
Shafik Handal. The son of Palestinian immigrants, he devoted his life to organizing for social and economic justice, and though his legacy is (ahem) controversial, he's certainly well loved around here. The museum has displays about his
life, as well as a small collection of weapons, materiel, and photos of the young
martyrs of the war.

Museo Winakirika (2503-2651) Casa Miguel Angel Amaya, Cacaopera. Admission: $1. Open: Daily. The small town of Cacaopera, Chocolate Garden, in the
Ulúa tongue, is home to the Community House Museum, a great excuse to visit
this unique, still proudly indigenous town. It also has a cute plaza and 1660
church where traditional dances are performed during fiestas, including *Los
Negritos, Los Emplumados,* using iconic feather headdresses, and *Los Tapojia-
dos,* which pokes fun at clueless Spanish landowners. The small, stone museum,
located about a kilometer from town, was founded in 1992 to help preserve the
rapidly vanishing culture of the Kakawira people. It features several displays of
indigenous artifacts, including a few pre-Columbian pieces, such as the carved
petroglyph depicting Tata Paikalán, the sun. Most of the photos, dance costumes, wooden masks, grinding stones, hammocks, and other crafts woven from

jarcía, a type of yucca fiber, represent traditions still honored today. The museum also operates a small library, and can arrange classes in Ulúa. They can offer lodging in a very simple **dorm** ($), but you should definitely call ahead. This is also a good place to arrange guided hikes to the Torola and Chiquito rivers, various swimming holes, and most importantly, **La Koquinca Cave**, 30 meters (100 feet) deep and 25 meters (85 feet) high, with dozens of petroglyphs painted in red, green, and violet.

Berlín

Casa Mía (see Lodging) offers tours of the antiques and historic relics in their 80-year-old home. **Alegría** also has a small "museum," basically a few shelves of pre-Columbian pottery, in the tourist information center.

Museo-Restaurante Don Guille (2663-2290; museorestaurante@yahoo.com) 14 Calle Oriente #6. Admission: 50¢. Open: Daily. Friendly Don Guille has been collecting archeological artifacts, old radios, washing machines, and pretty much everything else for 30 years, and invites visitors to drop by and have a look. You may need to ask at the pharmacy next door if no one answers your knock. Most impressive is Don Guille's outstanding coin collection, with everything from Spanish coins dating to 1738 to the local coffee plantations' *fichas,* scrip earned by workers in lieu of money, some emblazoned with swastikas. There are also folios filled with currency from all over the world. Then peruse his beautiful gardens, with cacao (chocolate), nance, papaya, and coffee plants, as well as several unusual ornamentals. You can arrange to eat a typical meal, cooked in a traditional wood *horno* (oven), in his garden gazebo. Give him at least five hours notice, one day for larger groups. The signed museum is located about nine blocks uphill from the town center.

Museo y Gimnasio Don Zelaya (2663-2225) Final Avenida Simón Bolivar. Admission: Free; gym day pass $1. Open: 8–7 daily. You'll have to ask around to find this unsigned museum and gym, a 10- to 15-minute walk uphill from the Alcaldía, just past where the pavement ends. The old adobe hacienda houses an interesting assortment of pre-Columbian pottery, Civil War memorabilia, photos of Berlín before various earthquakes and fires, and an electric guitar played by popular Salvadoran rock band Macizo in the 1970s. Architecture buffs will appreciate the old home, as well. The owner, Ruth Zelaya, also operates Berlín's only gym, with cardio and weight machines.

✳ To Do

BICYCLING Perkín Tours offers mountain-biking adventures in Llanos El Muerto.

CENTROS TURISTICOS There are several others in Llanos El Muerto, listed in the National Parks and Protected Areas section.

San Miguel

Altos de Cueva (2669-5019) 1.5 kilometers/0.9 mile north of San Miguel on the Ruta Militar. Open 9 AM to 6 PM daily. Admission $2/1 adult/child. Stuck in San Miguel? On the north end of town, these natural springwater-fed pools are surrounded by a forested park and little restaurants. Take Local Bus #29-A from the central park.

Aqua Park San Miguel (2619-0114; www.aquaparksanmiguel.com) KM156 Panamericana. Open 9 AM to 6 PM daily. Admission $4/2 adult/child. Farther away, but much fancier, this park has a wave pool (among a dozen others), 10 water slides, horseback rides, even a faux Río Lempa, where you can swim. There's live music on weekends. Take any bus toward La Unión.

Santa Rosa de Lima
Turicentro Obra de Dios (2608-4680) 5 kilometers/3 miles from Santa Rosa. Admission $4. Just outside Santa Rosa de Lima, this spot has natural pools, slides, playground equipment, a petting zoo, and hiking trails to the top of Cerro Los Mapachines. You could even spend the night in a simple **room** ($; cash only) with television and air-conditioning. Take Bus #374 toward La Unión and get off at the El Sauce exit, it's about one kilometer to the centro.

San Vicente
✪ **Laguna de Apastepeque** (2389-7172) Santa Clara, 8 kilometers/5 miles east of San Vicente. Open 8–5 daily. Admission 80¢, parking $1. Less famous than its sister crater lake in Alegría, the similarly golden-tinged lagoon (not to worry, the sulfur odor is mellow) is accessible through a colorful, family-friendly early-1970s-style cement complex of patios, walkways, floating docks, and covered kiosks that have the feel of an original Star Trek set. Kids can check out the squirrel nursery, or hire a small boat around the crater lake. The onsite restaurant specializes in tilapia, farmed right here. Trucks run between the entrance and San Vicente Central Park every 15 minutes or so.

CINEMAS Cinemark (2667-364; www.cinemarkca.com) Watch Hollywood blockbusters at San Miguel's Metrocentro Mall; take bus 90B or 90S from the central park.

COFFEE TOURS Berlín is beginning to develop tours of its coffee plantations, which are particularly interesting during harvest, December through February. Casa Mía can arrange tours, as can Hotel-Restaurante Cartagena in Alegría.
Sociedad Cooperativa de Caficultores de Berlín (2663-2370) Avenida Simón Bolívar #10. 1.5 blocks uphill from the Alcaldía. Open 8–noon and 2–5 Monday through Friday, 8–noon Saturday. Try to arrange tours at least a week in advance. You can stop by any time to watch as coffee is roasted and ground onsite, or ✪ purchase a pound ($2) to take with you.

HORSEBACK RIDING Both Perkín Tours and Cueva del Ratón in Perquín can arrange horseback rides, but ask at any hotel.

NIGHTLIFE San Miguel is the region's nightlife capital, with several bars along Avenida Roosevelt Sur; also stop by Papagallo Bar & Grill (see Where to Eat). In smaller towns, you can always find a local watering hole near the central park.

Febo's Casino (2661-8289) Roosevelt Sur, Plaza Chaparrastique #4. Open 24/7. Small casino has slot machines, card games, booze, snacks, and live music on Saturdays.

Tacos El Paisa (2661-0352) Roosevelt Sur #105. L, D. Festive cantina, plastered with photos of Mexican music and film stars from the black-and-white era, has a very full, air-conditioned bar, live music on weekends, and Mexican food all week long.

El Sarape (2613-5333) Roosevelt Norte. L, D. The other Mexican bar is a bit more upscale, with stage shows, DJs, and a dance floor.

THEATER Gavidia Francisco Teatro Nacional (2667-3706) Central Park. Stately 1909 theater hosts local and national performances. Drop by, or check **Unidad de Comunicaciones** (comunicaciones-fmo-ues.blogspot.com) to see what's on.

✱ Green Space

NATIONAL PARKS AND PROTECTED AREAS For information on Laguna de Olomega, see the Eastern Beaches chapter.

San Miguel

Chaparrastique (San Miguel) Volcano 15 kilometers (9 miles) east of San Miguel. The Colossus of the East is El Salvador's third largest volcano, 2130 meters (6986 feet) tall, though it seems even larger because it stands alone, active, still emiting plumes of sulfur-tinged steam. At the top is a massive crater, its sheer walls plunging 344 meters (1128 feet). There have been eight lava eruptions since the Spanish began keeping records, most recently in 1976. There is a popular, challenging hike to the top, with magnificent views across the Gulf of Fonseca, Jiquilisco Bay, and the Chinameca Range, arranged by several national operators (recommended). But you can do it yourself. You must have a police escort; call Politur (2298-9983) to arrange it, with several days advance notice. There are several trails to the top, but to get to the most popular trailhead, you'll need a 4WD vehicle. Exit the Pan-American just east of San Miguel toward San Jorge, about 10 kilometers (6 miles) from the freeway. From there, you'll take a dirt road to Finca Santa Isabela. From here, it's steep, shadeless, four- to five-hour roundtrip hike.

Laguna El Jocotál 15 kilometers (9 miles) southwest of San Miguel. This popular weekend escape from steamy San Miguel is a RAMSAR wetlands preserve, home to at least 135 species of bird, including emerald toucanets, bar-winged orioles, acorn woodpeckers, blue-and-white mockingbirds, and several types of waterfowl; about 100 migratory birds also nest here. And it's beautiful, covered with waterlilies and the reflection of Chaparrastique Volcano rising majestically above, as well as the peaks of the Sierra Chinameca in the distance. On the weekends, locals operate stands selling tasty ices and fried fish, but on weekdays you'll have the place to yourself. You can take rides in canoes for around $10, depending on how long you'd like to spend on the lake. A taxi from San Miguel runs about $15, or you can take bus #373 to Usulután; the driver can drop you off about 1 kilometer (0.6 mile) from the lakeshore.

Laguna Alegría About 2 kilometers (1.2 miles) south of the Alegría central park. Admission: 25¢ per person, 60¢ per vehicle. Nestled in a lush crater, this cool sulfur lake (but don't worry, the smell isn't too strong) is a popular swimming hole. It's definitely refreshing, and apparently medicinal for skin conditions including rash, acne, and psoriasis. There's plenty of shade, and a few stands selling snacks are reliably open on weekends; otherwise, bring your own picnic. It's a solid 2-kilometer (1.2-mile) walk from the Alegría bus stop, or take a mototaxi from Berlín (Alegría doesn't have taxis) for around $8 for up to three people. Any hotel or restaurant, or the tourist office in the central park, can arrange guided five-hour hikes around the crater rim, for $6-10 per group. **Alegria Tours** (2611-1497; alegriatours.8m.net; alegria-tours@hotmail.com) also arranges the hike, as well as several other treks.

Parque Turistico Geoambiental El Tronador (La Geo) (2211-6850, 2211-6787, 2601-8848; www.lageo.com.sv) About 3 kilometers (2 miles) from Berlín. Open 8–5 daily. Admission: Free. Berlín's local geothermic plant is open to the public, and has a pleasant centro turistico with the usual cold pools, snack bars, and kiosks, as well as a natural sauna. Surrounding it are *ausoles,* bubbling mud pots and tiny geysers, through which you are free to roam. Be careful! The most active fumaroles can be used to boil squash, corn, and other snacks you can bring yourself. Ask the guard to help. Guides offer tours of the geothermic plant ($2) and the trails ($2), which run steeply between smallish animal enclosures holding *tigrillos,* a small Salvadoran wildcat, white-tailed deer, iguanas, and crocodiles. The huge, metallic steam pipes running through the entire complex give it a bizarre sci-fi feel. Plans are in the works to build a public hot spring, cabins, and a taxidermy museum. Take a local bus (25¢) and ask them to drop you off at the "entrada la Geo," then walk the final 2 kilometers to the gate, or grab a mototaxi ($3) all the way there. From Berlín, you can also climb **Cerro Pelón**, a two-hour round-trip to a mountain marked with a cross. Walk to the end of 5 Avenida Sur and ask anyone "*¿Por Cerro Pelón?*"

San Vicente

San Vicente's ecotourism attractions aren't yet developed for easy access, but there's one tour operator in town, **Mini Librería and Tours San Vicente Edgar Luna** (2393-6666, 7931-9809; central park, next to Hotel Central Park) that can help you explore. Look for the sign reading SE HACEN VIAJES to find Edgar Luna, who speaks a little English and guides air-conditioned van trips throughout the region and country.

La Joya-Barranca del Sisimico Protected Area (2223-0453, 2298-3445; www.funprocoop.org) 9 kilometers (5 miles) northwest of San Vicente. Open: Daily. Admission: Free. This newly protected area is 5 kilometers (3 miles) north of Laguna de Apastepeque (see Centros Turisticos), in the skirts of Chichontepec Volcano. Its 434 manzanas (750 acres) of lush humid tropical forest contains one of the most paleontologically rich areas in Central America, with the fossilized remains of several mastodons and other fauna, and at least 54 species of plants. There are also are several steep trails, through a steep ravine with cliffs populated by parakeets, and into premontane altitudes with orchids and bromeli-

THE NAKED GRANITE BALDS AND DWARF FORESTS OF MORAZÁN, INTERSPERSED WITH BLACKBERRY BRAMBLES AND PINE FORESTS, TOP SOME OF EL SALVADOR'S OLDEST MOUNTAINS.

ads. You can enjoy several fine swimming holes and waterfalls, one 15 meters (49 feet) high, and even camp nearby.

Chichontepec (Volcán San Vicente) Southeast of San Vicente. The San Vicente skyline is fantastically dominated by Chichontepec, Mountain of Two Breasts, a dual-peaked volcano affectionately referred to by a number of sexy nicknames. You can hike to the top on a non-technical path through private farms to the 2,173-meter (7029-foot) peak. At the cloudforested top, there are two craters, fumaroles, bubbling mudpots, and other volcanic features. On a clear day, you can see Lago Ilopango and the Río Lempa. You can theoretically do the hike on your own, but it's safer and smarter to go with a guide. Contact the **San Vicente Alcaldía** (2314-2100; www.alcaldiadesanvicente.gob.sv) or Edgar Luna, who specializes in the trip, and can drive you halfway up the mountain. You'll need a 4WD car to do that yourself.

Morazán

Llano el Muerto and Bailadero del Diablo About 5 kilometers (3 miles) northeast of Perquín. Admission: $1 to $2. Open: Daily. Northeast of Perquín, along the road to the Marcala border with Honduras, the landscape opens up into a surreal high-altitude prairie of naked granite rock and sparse trees, marbled with sparkling creeks. Plains of the Dead and Dancefloor of the Devil are covered with pine and oak, dwarf forests, and chaparral, populated with magpies, parakeets, finches, squirrels, coyotes, owls, pumas, and the tepisquitle, a 50-pound groundhog. The Río Negro pours through its dramatically barren, stark white riverbed, becoming a rushing cascade of waterfalls and swimming holes as rainy season pours on. It's easiest to visit with private transport, but there's also the twice-daily Marcala bus from San Miguel, which you can catch at the Las Margaritas intersection. There are a handful of centros turisticos with lodging, camping, small restaurants, and day passes.

Hotel Arizona (2634-8990) $. Cash only. The closest lodging to Perquín, over-looking the naked granite expanse of El Carrizal and Cerro El Pericón, is this hotel decorated with scenes from the U.S. West. It caters to couples, but is expanding to become a real hotel, with cute cabins next to a couple of pools. The other options are several kilometers farther up the road, close to the waterfalls.

Parque Ecologico Bailadero del Diablo (2680-4076) $. Cash only. In a virgin dwarf forest, this centro turistico has camping, trails, a shared kitchen, pool, and access to a large waterfall along the Río Guaco.

Centro Turístico Llano El Muerto (2660-3184; carmenmaria1223@hotmail .com) $. Cash only. A short hike from more waterfalls, these cabins are well con-structed, with three beds in fairly spacious, clean surroundings, private bath, hammocks and a few pieces of furniture. There's a small pool and pool table, and restaurant serving cheap eats all day. Camping is also available. It's open all week.

Turicentro Llano El Muerto (2634-6071, 7736-4980) $. Cash only. Next door, this spot offers camping beneath the pines on weekends only.

Turicentro El Bosquecito (2680-4082) $. Cash only. Across the street, this spot is open weekends only, with simple cabins and a developed campsite, as well as a pool, slides, hammocks, and simple meals.

✪ **Río Sapo National Protected Area** (2680-4086, 2680-4311, PRODETUR; perquinturismo.blogcindario.com, prodeturperquin.tripod.com, perkintours@ yahoo.es, prodeturperquin@navegante.com.sv) About 8 kilometers (5 miles) southeast of Perquín. Admission: Free. Open: Daily. The Río Sapo is a jade green river, coursing through secondary-growth forests, being developed for tourism rather than a proposed dam thanks to **PRODETUR** (Colonia 10 de Enero; open 8–5 Monday through Friday, 8–2 Saturday) with offices in Perquín.

MORAZÁN'S RÍO SAPO FLOWS THROUGH SOME OF CENTRAL AMERICA'S MOST SCENIC SWIMMING HOLES.

ECOTOURISM ON THE RUTA DE LA PAZ

Morazán Department, so hard hit during the Civil War, is the poorest, least populated, and arguably most beautiful part of the country. Its ancient mountains are home to a wealth of fantastic wildlife, where clean, gorgeous rivers cascade with remarkable beauty through the wilderness.

And, thanks to Perquín's position as a point of pilgrimage for every left-wing backpacker who ever owned a Che Guevara T-shirt, it is being developed, through grassroots initiatives, into an ecotourism destination. Forget those five-star, carbon-neutral resorts you'll find elsewhere in Central America, however. This is the real deal.

Most sites are poorly developed, public transport on the 4WD-only roads involves pickup trucks, and you'll be hiking trails used by Lenca Indians for centuries, and little improved since. There are developed campsites, or you can pitch a tent almost anywhere. All but the most experienced adventurers will need a guide.

Several national operators offer Ruta de la Paz tours, but these usually visit the museum, El Mozote, and perhaps a waterfall or two. **Perkín Tours** (see Río Sapo, earlier) offers several day and multi-day treks all over Morazán, as well as mountain biking, rock climbing, and much more. Or, hire a local guide, for $10–15 per day (and please, buy him or her lunch) through the **Museo de la Revolución**, **Perquín Tour Office**, or any hotel, who can help you navigate public transport, or accompany you in your car, to different destinations throughout the region.

Perquín The starting point for all your adventures is Perquín, with several easy hikes from town. You can do **Mirador Cerro de Perquín** (7886-9609; admission 50¢/25¢ adult/child; open daily) on your own; the half-hour hike past Civil War-related displays begins across the street from the museum. Or visit **Quebrada de Perquín**, Perquín Creek, a half-hour walk that begins at the cemetery.

More ambitious hikers could try the steep four-hour hike to **Cerro El Pericón**, with dwarf forest of pine, oak, rose apple, bushes, and views across Eastern El Salvador to Cerro Cacahuatique and the sea; or an even more difficult hike to **Cerro El Gigante**, just south of town, passing several Civil War sites along the way.

San Fernando Just a few kilometers east of Perquín, this quiet village is the starting point for several more fantastic hikes. Some spots have semi-developed campsites and stands selling food, such as **El Chorrerón** (7521-7052), a large waterfall; **Los Manatiales** (7219-6436) , with deep natural pools and camping areas; and **Abejas del Bosque** (7872-8950), an agrotourism destination with farm tours and a small restaurant. Also ask about other destinations, such as the Cañaverales, Pichigua, Secreto del Bosque, and La Golondrina, all with natural wonders that might make fine excuses for escaping into less-traveled wilderness areas.

El Mozote Though best known for the somber memorial, this destination is also home to **El Mozote Asociación Turistica de Historia Viva** (El Mozote Tourism Association of Living History; 7534-0383 Otilla Chicas Díaz), headquartered at the brightly painted Information Kiosk next to the church. The tourism collective offers Spanish-language tours of the monument and town, very basic lodging ($) in cots at the community center, and several guided hikes.

Destinations include caverns such as **Cueva de Eugenio**, where local eccentric Eugenio Ramos provided his cave as a meeting point for war refugees trying to find their families; **Cueva del Murcielago**, which served as a studio for Radio Vencermos; and **Cueva La Ventura**, an ERM (Revolutionary People's Army) base.

There are also several peaks—**Cerro Chingo**, **Cerro Hacha**, and **Cerro Cacalote**—with good trails to the top, most of them strategic outposts during the war. If soldiers stationed there saw federal activity, they would set off a bomb to signal that they were under attack.

Jocoatitique Jocoatique is sometimes called the City of Halls, for the slender wooden columns that surround its graceful, arcaded downtown. It sits atop a dormant volcano, though its Lenca name, Town on the Hill of Fire, suggests it wasn't always so quiet.

There are several crafts shops at the entrance to town, as well as **El Zoocriadero de Mariposas El Almirante de Morazán** (2680-1403, 2680-5574; posada_eltorogoz@gmail.com; open daily; $2), a good-sized butterfly garden behind Posada El Torogoz, with paths that you can wander while waiting for the perfect photo op to flutter by. You could also hike to a popular waterfall and swimming hole, called **Güilisca**, or deep pool, located close to the tiny town of El Rincón.

El Rosario Just 8 kilometers (5 miles) east of Jocoatique, this small circa 1830 town offers steep access to two excellent destinations. **Río Araute**, or Fallen Valley, is a clean river flowing through a 100-meter (300-foot) long canyon bookended by waterfalls, one more than 30 meters (100 feet) tall, with nice swimming holes, La Sirena and Las Piletas.

Or visit the **Aguas Termales**, very hot springs in a cement pool with colorful slime and alleged healing properties. It overflows into the river, making the shore a nice place to bathe. It's a 2-kilometer (1.2-mile) walk downhill from town, where you'll cross the wide river. The spring is about 100 meters (328 feet) uphill from the other side, on your left.

Torola This is the poorest municipality in the country, surrounded by incredible rock formations above steep valleys, offering wonderful views. This was also the site of the Moscarron Battle, one of the Civil War's bloodiest, when the ERD captured the Minister of Defense. It has for centuries been a ceramics center, and women from nearby Ojos de Agua still produce clay vessels sold throughout El Salvador and Honduras.

You must visit with a guide; most people go with recommended **Perkín Tours**, operated by PRODETUR. The river, with waterfalls and fantastic swimming holes, is the starting point for trails through 6000 hectares (23 square miles) of black and white oak, pine, chaparral, and dwarf forests, with coyotes, cats, deer, foxes, squirrels, and the orchids and bromeliads of the moist premontane. You can arrange rock climbing, horseback trips, mountain biking, birding, and camping in developed sites at the park entrance, with lavatories, showers, and grills. You could also stay at **Eco Albergue Río Sapo** ($; cash only), a simple adobe lodge with bunk beds and little else, close to the rushing Río Sapo (River of Scorpions, in Lenca) and its tributaries, with lots of deep swimming spots and waterfalls. Perkín Tours arranges all your meals, but other guides may not, so bring groceries to the campsite. Locals sometimes sell food on weekends. The park is located 6 kilometers (3.7 miles) from Arambala, which has a few very simple shops and eateries, including **Comedor Gloria** (7201-4256; B, L, D; $; cash only), with *comida a la vista* at lunch. Nearby, **Turicentro las Veraneras** (7880-1929; open daily; admission $1) has river access and other small eateries, walking distance from Arambala. Trucks leave Perquín every 15 minutes or so, and there's an hourly bus from San Francisco Gotera.

ARCHAEOLOGICAL PARKS Although this region's ruins and petroglyphs have, for the most part, been left undeveloped for tourism, it is home to the oldest human remains in the country.

Cueva del Santo Espíritu (No phone) Corinto, 1.5 kilometers (0.9 mile) from central park. Open: 8–4 Wednesday through Sunday. Admission: Free. The Cave of the Blessed Spirit is El Salvador's most ancient archaeological treasure, an enormous, shallow cave covered with polychromatic paintings, some partially engraved, that are at least 8000 years old (associated spear points have been found embedded in datable bones), but probably much, much older. Many clearly represent figures, some pregnant, others holding hands, still others with large headdresses very similar to the Feathered Men dancers of indigenous Cacaopera. There are also handprints, perhaps the signature of the artist. There are two other caves within a few kilometers, Cueva del Toro, with more petroglyphs, and Cueva del Duende, with a waterfall. Both are on private land, within an hour of the main cave. Make an appointment (Spanish only) with one of the park caretakers, who can act as private guides: Eustín Argeta (7557-3581) or Argelio Alvarez Villega (2658-1531). The cave is easy to visit, once you've committed to the long trip to isolated Corinto. Bus #327, which runs hourly from San Miguel, takes about 3.5 hours; by car, allow at least 2 hours for the poorly maintained paved road. The cave itself is about 1.5 kilometers (0.9 mile) from town on a good road, just a few hundred meters from the parking lot. Corinto is a fairly large town, with a BAC ATM, and several stores and restaurants close to the plaza. Wednesday and Sunday are major market days. **Hotel Corinto** (7508-0902; three blocks from central park; $; cash only) has clean, basic rooms with shared bath, but for $4 more you get cable TV, private bath, and an in-room hammock. The onsite restaurant/bar is open 24 hours. There are dozens of other painted caves in Morazán that strong hikers can arrange to visit through areas

SOME 8000-YEAR-OLD (AT LEAST) FIGURES PAINTED AT GRUTA DEL ESPIRITU SANTO SPORT HEADDRESSES SIMILAR TO THOSE STILL WORN BY CACAOPERA'S LENCA DANCERS.

alcaldías, most famously **Cueva de Koquinca**, near Cacaopera (see Museo Winakirika), and many others along Río Torola and clustered around the tiny village of Guachipilín, southeast of San Francisco Gotera.

Quelepa (No phone; www.fundar.org.sv) San José, 8 kilometers (5 miles) northwest of San Miguel. Admission: Free. Open: Daily. Though declared a national monument in 1976, Quelepa still has little tourist infrastructure. In fact, most of its 1000 structures have been reburied, to dissuade further looting of its famous artifacts: wax-relief glazed Usulután ceramics, delicately carved obsidian tools, flutes, wheeled toys, and an enormous stone jaguar currently displayed at MUNA in San Salvador. Quelepa means jaguar in the Lenca tongue, but this site was occupied long before they arrived. Its original inhabitants, who founded the city around 400 B.C., apparently had connections with the Olmec Empire. The population exploded around 150 A.D., with refugees from the 260 A.D. Ilopango eruption further expanding the city's extents. Its 10-meter (33-foot) stone pyramids, unusual I-shaped ball stadiums, elaborate tombs, and other structures cover several kilometers, some with stone ramps similar to those in Copán. Around 1000A.D., the site was largely abandoned, although the Lencas, fleeing a still little understood depopulation of northwestern Honduras, arrived shortly before the Spanish Conquest. There's not much too see, although the cooperative that

ALTHOUGH QUELEPA REMAINS LITTLE DEVELOPED FOR TOURISTS, ITS FASCINATING RUINS HAVE YIELDED BOTH RAMPS AND WHEELED TOYS; THE LENCA WERE ONTO SOMETHING.

manages the site can usually find guides and has a small museum. Take Bus #90G from the San Miguel central park to Moncagua, and get off at Quelepa.

Ruinas Tehuacán 10 kilometers (6 miles) southwest of San Vicente. Admission: Free. These little-visited ruins were rediscovered in 1892 in the Valley of the Stone Lion, marked by an ancient sculpture of a puma. There is no tourist infra-structure, so you'll need to arrange a guide; try **Mini Librería and Tours San Vicente Edgar Luna** (2393-6666, 7931-9809; central park) in San Vicente, or the **Tecoluca Alcaldía** (2362-4116; Avenida 14 de Diciembre). Most of Tehua-can, or City of Stone, is located on private Hacienda de Opico. Large stone plazas are surrounded by thick walls, and there is a huge structure, some 60 meters (200 feet) long called La Iglesia, as well as a large pyramid. It probably dates from about 400 B.C., and had trade connections with Quelepa. About 6 kilometers (3.7 miles) north of San Vicente, near the town of San Esteban Cata-rina, there are caves close to Río Titihuapa, with petroglyphs.

✳ Lodging

While there is a wide variety of lodg-ing in San Miguel and a few good mid-range spots just south of Perquín, most towns in this chapter offer only budget hotels, some quite nice. Morazán has some of the best camp-ing in the country, and Perkín Tours rents tents and sleeping bags.

The climate in this vast region varies considerably. For instance, San Miguel and San Vicente are both blis-teringly hot; it's worth springing for a room with air-conditioning. Alegría and Berlín, on the other hand, are refreshingly cool, while Perquín and Morazán can get downright chilly. You'll want pants and a light jacket at times, not to mention a hot shower.

San Miguel

This is Eastern El Salvador's most important city, and it sprawls. If you arrive by bus, it's convenient to stay close to the bus terminal, with more than a dozen budget hotels close by, but the area is sketchy at night. It's more comfortable to stay in outlying areas, with a couple of good options in the quiet residential neighborhood around Capilla Medalla Milagrosa.

The best hotels are on Avenida Roo-sevelt, a strip of highway with most of the city's dining and nightlife. Take a taxi at night, or when carrying lug-gage.

🖋 ♨ ❀ 🛏 "1" **Comfort Inn** (2600-0200; www.comfortinn.com, hotelhelp@choicehotels.com) Final Alameda Roosevelt. $$$. Credit cards: Yes. Handicap Access: Yes. The most com-fortable hotel in San Miguel is far from the city center, but right across from Metrocentro Mall. Beautiful modern rooms, with excellent beds, large TVs, and handmade wooden fur-nishings have all the amenities, including real hot baths. They even have rooms fully equipped for the blind and those in wheelchairs. There's a business center, small gym, onsite bar and restaurant (breakfast is included), and cute little outdoor pool. The desk can arrange several tours and rent cars.

🖋 ❀ 🛏 "1" **Hotel Continental Plaza** (2661-5077; continentalplaza.the hotelesinc.com, continentalplaza@ hotmail.com) 8 Calle Poniente #512. $$. AE, MC, V. Handicap Access: Yes.

MIGHTY VOLCÁN CHAPARRASTIQUE RISES ABOVE BUSTLING SAN MIGUEL.

Solid mid-range choice is well located in a relatively quiet residential neighborhood of town close to the city center, but less sketchy at night than the bus terminal area. The yellow stucco façade brings to mind a California strip mall, while spotless, freshly painted, tiled rooms with generic furniture and floral bed covers have modern bathrooms (alas, no hot water), big TVs, and air-conditioning. A buffet breakfast is included, as is access to a tiny gym and cute pool out by the parking lot. There's even a game room, with foosball and ping pong, and a computer that's free for guests to use. Very friendly.

✦ ✳ 🚗 "¶" **Hotel Floresta** (2640-1549-1550; www.hotelplazafloresta.com; forestahotel@yahoo.com) Avenida. Roosevelt Sur, No. 704, in front of Seguro Social. $$. AE, MC, V. Handicap Access: Yes. On the outskirts of town (but convenient to Metrocentro Mall and several restaurants) solid mid-range choice offers small, clean, tiled rooms with WiFi, phone, cable TV, and private bath, arranged around a parking lot and pool.

✳ 🛎 🚗 **Hotel-Inn El Guanaco** (2661-8026) 8 Avenida Norte, Passaje Madrid #1. $. Cash only. Handicap Access: No. One block from the bus terminal, on a hidden side street, this hotel has a fairly fabulous lobby with a waterfall, and clean, spacious rooms, with desks, phones, air-conditioning, large closets, hard mattresses, cable TVs, and private hot baths. Breakfast is included, and there's 24-hour room service. Cute business card, too.

✳ 🚗 **Hotel Jerico** (2661-4242) 6 Calle Oriente #604. $. cash only. Handicap Access: No. This 17-room hotel next to the bus station isn't bad, with pink rooms, air-conditioning, cable TV, and private bath. Singles are tiny; pay $3 to upgrade to one with space for your luggage.

✪ ✐ ✦ ✳ 🚗 "¶" **Hotel King Palace** (2661-1086; www.hotelkingpalace.com, kingpalacehotel@yahoo.com) 6 Calle Oriente #69. $–$$. AE, MC, V. Handicap Access: Challenging. The best hotel close to the bus terminal is this fine spot, a great deal on tiny but very comfortable, modern rooms furnished with icy air-conditioning, cable

TV, telephone, and modern bath. A great little onsite restaurant ($; cash only) serves typical food, including *comida a la vista* for lunch and dinner, but is closed on weekends. The pool, in the hotel courtyard, is downright spectacular, while the outdoor gym, on the roof, offers fantastic views over the buses, Cathedral, and Chaparrastique Volcano. This hotel is popular with business people, and may be full on weekdays.

❄ 🚗 ((ı)) **Hotel Santa Fe** (2669-0918) Carretera Ruta Militar. $$. AE, MC, V. Handicap Access: Challenging. On the road to Perquín, this excellent, overdecorated mid-range option has huge, tiled rooms with air-conditioning, telephones, cable TVs, big closets, WiFi, modern cool baths, dime-store art, and fake flowers. Common areas scattered throughout the maze of hallways are boldly painted, with overstuffed furnishings and free coffee. You get a complimentary quesadilla at breakfast.

✪ ❄ 🚗 **Hotel El Viajero** (2661-7113) 7 Avenida Norte #403. $. Cash only. Handicap Access: Challenging. Family-run hotel in a quiet, residential neighborhood is a much more relaxed budget choice than the competition clustered around the bus station (a $2 cab ride, or 15-minute walk, away). Arranged around the parking lot in sprawling Route 66 style, simple but spotlessly clean rooms have a shared porch, excellent beds, cable TV, and air-conditioning, but bathrooms are tiny—the shower is almost over the toilet.

San Vicente

There are two hotels in town, and the first one you'll see is right on the plaza.

❄ ((ı)) **Hotel y Restaurant Central Park** (2392-0383) $. Cash only. Handicap Access: No. It seems like a deal—the $15 triples have cable TV, WiFi, and private cold bath. But it was *filthy*. Don't stay unless they've sandblasted the grime away.

❄ 🚗 ((ı)) **Estancia Familiar y Comedor Zayrita** (2393-0276) 1 Calle Poniente #14, 20 meters (22 yards) up from Pollo Campero. $. Credit cards: No. Handicap Access: Yes. The best hotel in town is around the corner and two blocks up from Hotel Central Park, and practically unsigned—look for the Pollo Campero, almost next door. Spotless, tiled rooms have good beds and your choice of air-conditioning and private cool bath, or fan with spotless shared bath. There's a TV in the common area, and a great little restaurant (B, L, D; $; closed Sunday) serving Mexican and Salvadoran dishes, *comida a la vista* at lunch, and pupusas in the evening. In addition, they rent a three-story, four-bedroom house about six blocks away (12 Calle Poniente #25, Barrio San Juan de Dios), arranged through the main hotel. You can rent just one newly furnished room for $20, with excellent beds, great furnishings, private bath and shared kitchen. Views from the top-floor terrace are magnificent, and there are hammocks everywhere.

Alegría

✪ **Casa Alegre** (2211-4132; www.lacasaalegre.org; lacasaalegre.zoomblog.com, lacasaalegre@gmail.com) Half block uphill from Central Park. $. Credit cards: No. Handicap Access: No. The coolest accommodation in Eastern El Salvador is operated by a collective dedicated to helping young

Salvadoran artists, and it exhibits their pieces onsite. The entire downstairs is a gallery and workshop, a warm and whitewashed space accented by thick, wooden beams and colorful hammocks. Three upstairs rooms are sunny but very basic and bohemian, with decent beds, shared bath, and shared kitchen, as well as a shag-carpeted library filled with art books. Rooms are often reserved for artists, so let management know you're the creative type on a vision quest, rather than a normal vacation. Not for you? At least stop by the gallery and adjacent gift shop, with art and crafts made by local kids and world-renowned painters.

🚗 Casa de Huéspedes La Palma

(2628-1012) Central Park. $. Cash only. Handicap Access: No. Right on the plaza, this backpacker hostel's rooms surround pretty interior gardens. Three rooms, with soft beds, cable TVs, and private cold baths are nicer, but I liked the simpler second-story room above the garden—no TV, but more privacy.

Hostal Laguna de Alegría (7594-8956, 7900-0746; afrsamayoa@hotmail.com)

Next to Laguna de Alegría. $. Cash only. Handicap Access: No. Overlooking the lagoon, this peaceful, brand-new, very basic lodge is a bit of a challenge: It's 2 kilometers (1.2 miles) from town, there are no showers (you'll use buckets and pilas), and the only food and potable water is available at a few food stands that aren't reliably open. But, you're actually inside an amazing volcanic crater, right above the water. Rooms are simple, but have a shared porch with lake views and hammocks, handmade wooden furnishings, flagstone floors, and skylights. Staff can also take you on the classic five-hour hike around the crater rim.

Hostal La Montaña de Alegría

(2628-1043) 1 Calle Poniente. $. Cash only. Handicap Access: No. Just east of the central park, this basic budget hostel has simple rooms and a small onsite restaurant.

🍴 🚗 Restaurant y Vivero Cartagena (2628-1131, 7886-2362) Final

NESTLED INTO THE CHILLY CRATER OF TECAPA VOLCANO, LAGUNA DE ALEGRÍA HAS LONG BEEN ATTRIBUTED SPECIAL HEALING POWERS.

Barrio El Calavario, three steep blocks downhill from the central park. $$. AE, MC, V. Handicap Access: Yes. Handicap Access: Challenging. Surrounded by exotic gardens and a coffee plantation crisscrossed with trails, this spot has eight spacious cabins—be sure to get one with magnificent views over Volcán Chichontepec, Río Lempa, and Lago Suchitlán from your private porch. Handmade wooden furnishings, artsy décor, and private cool bath make this the most comfortable spot in town. It costs the same for up to eight people, so bring friends. The **restaurant** (B, L, D; $$), with those same spectacular views, is nationally renowned, and has a rather elegant coffee shop serving espresso beverages, ✪ hot chocolate, and pastries such as a fig-and-apple pie that brings people in from San Salvador. The main, open-air restaurant, decorated with flowering plants and antiques, offers traditional dishes such as grilled rabbit, ceviches, and *sopa de gallina India.* There's an excellent gift shop and bird collection onsite, and they run coffee plantation tours in season (December through February).

Berlín

At press time, two other choices, one a fairly plush boutique hotel and the other a budget hotel boasting a third-floor mirador, were in the works.

🛏🛏 ¹¹ **La Casa Mía** (2643-0608, 2663-2027; www.berlinlacasamia.com, lacasamia05@yahoo.com) 2a Avenida Norte #10. $–$$. AE, MC, V. Handicap Access: Challenging. This historic home, built during the coffee boom of the early 20th century, is one of El Salvador's most beautiful hostels. The exquisitely preserved mansion has high ceilings and scores of historically significant antiques, each of which Don Ramón will explain to you in detail (English or Spanish). Five rooms, each unique but boasting private machine-heated bath and good

AFTER ENJOYING A CUP OF RICH BERLÍN COFFEE AT CASA MÍA, ASK TO SEE THEIR MUSEUM-QUALITY ANTIQUES, SUCH AS PRESIDENT FRANCISCO MORAZÁN'S DINING ROOM TABLE.

beds, surround the museum-quality common areas, outfitted with ping-pong, a large trampoline, and delightful little **café** (open 7 AM–9 PM daily; $), serving gourmet coffee, breakfast, pastries, and great typical dishes ($2-6). Even if you stay elsewhere, stop by for coffee and a tour of the place. They can arrange private transportation and tours all over the region and country.

Perquín

Most basic budget spots are located close to the central park, while nicer hotels are located just south of the entrance to town.

♨ **Casita de la Abuela** (2680-4314) Perquín. $. Credit cards: No. Handicap Access: No. My budget pick is this small hotel in a quiet corner of town a couple of blocks from the buses, fronted by a chaotic souvenir store with a great selection of mostly lefty books, and simple *comedor* (B, L, D; $). Owner Alba Gladys Villalobos will guide you through her overgrown gardens to your very simple, very private room, clean but rather bare. All are different sized, with screened windows and adobe walls, good mattresses and machine-heated private bath.

♨ **Cocina y Hostal Mama Toya** (2680-4158) Entrance to Perquín. $. Cash only. Handicap Access: No. This popular backpacker spot has rooms for just $6 per person, some with private cold bath, and hammocks on the covered walkway. The good onsite **restaurant** (B, L, D; $) serves a daily special.

♂ ⚑ ♨ ⛄ ☈ **Las Margaritas** (2613-1903, 2613-1253; www.hotelyres taurantelasmargaritas.com, hotely restaurantelasmargaritas@yahoo.com)

La Tejera, Perquín. $$. AE, MC, V. Handicap Access: Restaurant only. About half an hour downhill from Perquín on foot (trucks leave every 15 minutes), the Las Margaritas exit toward Llanos El Muerto and Marcala, is named for a locally popular outdoor **restaurant** (B, L, D; $$) serving tacos, grilled meats, nachos, shrimp cocktails, and other eats that go perfectly with a cold beer. For $2, you can enjoy their pools and tennis court, and better, use their 1.5 kilometers (1 mile) of trails, cut into the exposed granite face of the ancient mountain, with views of the pine-and-oak covered countryside. It's awesome. Also onsite are three simple tin-roofed cabins, each perched out on its own rocky outcropping well away from the noise of the bar. The two smaller ones have private hot baths and great porches, with wonderful views from the hammock. A larger cabin sleeps five, with an odd, cramped layout and two small bedrooms, but the porch makes up for it. The restaurant has WiFi access.

✪ ♂ ♨ ⛄ ☈ **Hotel de Montaña Perkin Lenca** (2680-4046, 2680-4080; www.perkinlenca.com, info@ perkinlenca.com) KM205.5 Cerretara a Perquín. $–$$$$. AE, MC, V. Handicap Access: No. Outstanding hotel just outside Perquín is a well-built collection of beautiful wooden cabins and family-sized bungalows set into the steeply pitched, forested slopes. (Read: You'll get some exercise climbing through the grounds.) The simplest rooms are spacious, with excellent beds, fans, modern hot baths, and shared porches furnished with tables, chairs, and hammocks. Cabañas are larger, freestanding, and a bit more stylish, with rustic wood trim, much more private patios, and space for three. Bungalows are relaxingly large, sleeping four easily (extra beds are available) with a small dining area. The restaurant, **La Cocina de Ma' Anita** (B, L, D; $$) is excellent, using fresh, local ingredients prepared traditionally, on a woodburning stove. Breakfast is included. Owner Ronald Brenneman first came to the region as an aid worker in the 1980s, when he watched from the mountaintop refugee camps sprawled along the Honduran border as Morazán collapsed beneath planeloads of heavy artillery. He returned after the war, and remains committed to developing regional tourism, as well as local schools through his nonprofit organization, **Perquín Educational Opportunity Foundation** (www .peofoundation.org).

🦴 ♿ 🛏 **Hotel El Ocotal** (2634-4083, 2669-0587; hotelelocotal@hotmail .com) KM201 Carretera Perquín. $–$$. Credit cards: No. Handicap Access: No. Lovely open-air **restaurant** (B, L, D; $$) with wonderful mountain views is a local favorite, with folks coming from as far as San Miguel to sample their *sopa gallina India* and shrimp dishes on weekends. Follow the flagstone path through the murmuring pine trees and flowers to the cute cabins, all different sizes, with front porches hung with hammocks, hand-carved furnishings, and good beds. There are hiking trails around the property, including to a couple of lookouts, and two large, shady pools below the restaurant.

♿ ⁣🍴 **Posada Don Manuel** (2680-4163; laposadaperquin@hotmail.com) KM206 Carretera a Perquín. $. Cash only. Handicap Access: Challenging. Tucked away on a signed side road

about 200 meters (219 yards) from town, within a cavernous, cement-floored old lumber mill, 14 small rooms have been formed with drywall. A few have private toilet, all have shared cold showers and WiFi. Meals can be prepared with advance notice, and camping is permitted.

🖊 🦴 ♿ 🛏 **Turicentro Cueva de Ratón** (2680-2412) 2 kilometers/1.2 miles south of Perquín. $$. Cash only. Handicap Access: Challenging. Head east at the exit to Marcala (Las Margaritas) to find this centro turistico with pools, horseback tours, hiking trails, a restaurant, and a huge, shallow cave. There are four simple cabins with private hot bath; a neat place.

Santa Rosa de Lima and the El Amatillo Border Crossing

❋ 🛏 **Hotel El Tejano Amigo** (2641-3325; ularios@hotmail.com) 100 meters/110 yards north of stadium, Colonia Altos de Santa Rosa. $–$$. Handicap Access: Challenging. Your best bet for a good night's sleep before crossing the border, this two-floor hotel offers rooms with private cool bath, cable TV, and air-conditioning.

Santiago de María

It's much more pleasant to spend the night in Berlín or Alegría, but if you're stuck:

♿ ❋ 🛏 **Hotel Gramales Inn** (2614-6267) 6 Avenida Sur and 2 Calle Oriente. $. Cash only. Handicap Access: Yes. Geared to couples, this is nevertheless the best place in town, with clean rooms, cable TV, and good double beds.

🛏 **Hotel La Posada del Marqués** (No phone) 3 Calle Poniente and 1 Avenida Norte. $. Cash only. Handicap Access: Challenging. Grimy little hotel surrounding a gated parking lot with chickens has very cheap rooms with saggy beds and private baths.

Around Perquín

The tiny towns around Perquín have a few very basic spots to spend the night.

Casa de Huéspedes la Casona (7273-4201) El Rosario central park. $. Cash only. Make reservations to stay in El Rosario's only guesthouse, private home of Nelson Martinez.

El Mozote Community House (2615-5104; 7534-0383) $. Cash only. Handicap Access: Yes. Make reservations to stay on $2 cots in the El Mozote community house. They also allow camping, but bring your own tent.

Inn Vanessa (7738-1526) San Fernando. $. Cash only. Make reservations to stay at this basic guesthouse, with room for four, in San Fernando.

Posada El Torogoz (2680-1403, 2680-5574; posada_eltorogoz@gmail .com) KM195 Carretera Perquín, Jocoaitique. $. Cash only. Handicap

Access: Challenging. This brick hostel, close to several crafts shops and the exit to Jocoaitique and El Rosario, has fairly modern, simple rooms with private hot baths and TVs. Breakfast is included at the **restaurant** (B, L, D; closed Monday; $) specializing in grilled meats and seafood. There's also a *mariposario*, or butterfly garden ($2).

Hotel San Francisco (2654-0066) Avenida Morazán #29, San Francisco Gotera. $. Cash only. Handicap Access: Challenging. Though San Francisco Gotera has little for the average tourist, this two-story hotel is pretty nice, with clean rooms, good beds, and private cool baths.

✴ Where to Eat

San Miguel, El Salvador's third largest city, boasts a variety of restaurants, including several good steakhouses and just about every fast-food restaurant imaginable. Elsewhere, your choices are much more limited, mostly very basic eateries serving typical

CAMPING

Perkín Tours rents tents and sleeping bags. In addition to Río Sapo Protected Area and Llanos El Muerto (see National Parks, later), there are several other developed campsites in Morazán.

Camping Cerro de la Alegría (7206-7614, 7913-0687) 1 kilometer/0.6 mile from San Fernando. $. Cash only. Has developed campsites with bathrooms and showers.

Camping El Pinar (7580-8739, 7533-0993; meli4083@yahoo.com) $. Cash only. About 3 kilometers (1.8 miles) from Perquín on the road to San Fernando, developed campsite rents tents, serves basic meals, and organizes guides.

Los Manatiales (7219-6436) on the Río Cañaverales; 3 kilometers/1.8 miles from San Fernando. $. Cash only. This beautiful spot, well known to birders, offers deep natural pools, waterfalls, and camping areas.

food, *comida a la vista* at lunch, and of course, pupusas. The hotels just south of Perquín proper have beautiful restaurants, serving upscale Salvadoran fare with fantastic views.

San Miguel

If you stay in one of the many hotels close to the bus terminal, be aware that pickings are slim after 6 PM, save for a few grimy market stalls, and two dueling fast-food places, **Pollo Campero** (2273-6000) 6 Calle Oriente; L, D; $; and **Pollo Campestre** (2228-2228) 6 Calle Oriente; L, D; $. You can take a cab to Avenida Roosevelt, lined with good restaurants, while Metrocentro Mall has several eateries open until 9 PM.

Papagallo Bar & Grill (2661-0400; www.papagallo.com.sv) Avenida Roosevelt Sur, Mall #5. $–$$$. AE, MC, V. Cuisine: Steakhouse Serving: L, D. Child's Menu: No. Handicap Access: No. Reservations: Yes. Not just a restaurant, this is one of San Miguel's favorite nightspots, with a full bar and sometimes live music. They serve steak, seafood, chicken dishes, and pastas, as well as a nice selection of *bocadillos,* or bar snacks. Open late on weekends.

Restaurant La Pema (2661-4915; www.lapema.com) Carretera al Cuco KM142.5. $$–$$$. AE, MC, V. Cuisine: Seafood. Serving: L, D. Child's Menu: Yes. Handicapped Access: Challenging. Reservations: On weekends. Top-notch seafood restaurant with an elegant dining room is a rather romantic spot. Start with one of their oversized ceviches or seafood cocktails, before moving on to entrees that include fish (priced by size) prepared any number of ways: *al vapor* (steamed with vegetables), *frito* (fried), or *relleno con camarones*

(stuffed with cheese and shrimp). They also offer delicious *mariscadas* (cream-based seafood stew) and *langosta* (lobster), which could also be served stuffed with shrimp. The bar is popular.

La Pradera (2661-4915) Avenida Roosevelt Sur #70. $$$. Credit Cards: No. Cuisine: Steakhouse. Serving: L, D. Child's Menu: Yes. Handicapped Access: Challenging. Reservations: For groups. Festive bar and steakhouse, here in the heart of El Salvador's cattle country, caters to cowboys and families with its no-nonsense, delicious meat dishes. Start with something light, such as the *ensalada de palmito*, made with fresh hearts of palm, or perhaps the *crema de camarón,* cream of shrimp soup. It's the aged steak, however, that wins raves, in particular the *punta jalapeña*, in a spicy marinade, and *medallones de novio,* or beef medallions. There's a very full bar as well, including a few Chilean red wines.

San Vicente

There are several basic eateries around town, but both of these, close to the sprawling **Market** (1 Avenida Sur and 2 Calle Poniente), were recommended.

Banquete Acapulco (2393-6386) Calle 4 Poniente and 1 Avenida Sur. $. Credit Cards: No. Cuisine: Mexican, Salvadoran. Serving: L, D. Child's Menu: No. Handicap Access: Yes. Reservations: No. Cozy *comedor* is a step up from the dozens of tiny eateries spilling onto the surrounding streets, with Mexican and Salvadoran platters, as well as *comida a la vista* at lunch.

Comedor Rivoli (2393-0492) 1 Avenida Sur #15. $. Credit Cards: No. Cuisine: Salvadoran. Serving: B, L, D.

Child's Menu: No. Handicapped Access: Yes. Reservations: No. Don't be fooled by this spotless and popular restaurant's fast-food ambiance, orange walls, and plastic booths. Its fresh, tasty *comida a la vista* gets raves from all quarters, as do the made-to-order pizzas. There's also beer, a big TV, and even a cute little courtyard garden.

Alegría

Don't miss Restaurant Cartagena, covered in Lodging.

Merendero Mi Pueblito (2628-1038) Calle Alberto Masterro. $$. Credit Cards: No. Cuisine: Salvadoran. Serving: B, L (closes at 5 PM). Children's Menu: Yes. Handicapped Access: Challenging. Reservations: For groups. This sprawling maze of old tejas-topped adobe colonials and overgrown plant life is a fine place to enjoy a leisurely meal, while the strolling musicians strum through. Take your pick, either a warmer, more romantic enclosed table, or perhaps the deck with a view, then settle in for one this popular restaurant's huge set plates. For $6 take your pick of beef, pork loin, *chicharrones,* chicken, or shrimp ($2 extra), served with all the trimmings.

Bar y Restaurant La Fonda de Alegría (2628-1010) Avenida La Golgata. $–$$. Credit Cards: No. Cuisine: Salvadoran. Serving: B, L, D. Children's Menu: Yes. Handicap Access: No. Reservations: For groups. This town is also famous for its *viveros,* or plant nurseries, and this lovely restaurant is rather like dining inside one. Enjoy quality Salvadoran classics such as grilled meats, mariscadas (seafood soup), and simpler dishes, including pupusas after about 5 PM, when the bar gets going.

Berlín

The tidy little **Market** offers a wide variety of cheap eats. Also consider making reservations for a fantastic

FRESH AGUA DE COCO, OR COCONUT JUICE, IS A GREAT HEALTHY PICK-ME-UP AVAILABLE ALMOST ANYWHERE, INCLUDING THE BERLÍN MARKET.

typical meal in the pretty gardens at **Museo-Restaurante Don Guille**, or dropping into the cute café at **Hotel Casa Mía**.

La Cocina de Doña Silvia (2663-2267) 2 Calle Poniente. $. Credit Cards: No. Cuisine: Salvadoran. Serving: B, L, D. Child's Menu: Yes. Handicapped Access: Challenging. Reservations: Recommended on weekends. Best known for breakfast, this excellent eatery offers great typical food all day long, including the town's best *comida a la vista* for breakfast and lunch—try the *sorpresas*, wheat turnovers filled with sweet plantains and cheese.

Restaurante Mi Ranchito (2663-2889) Calle Principal, on the park. $. Credit Cards: No. Cuisine: Mexican, Salvadoran. Serving: B, L, D. Child's Menu: Yes. Handicapped Access: Challenging. Reservations: No. Right on the central park, this simple spot serves good *lomito de res*, and a solid $2 *comida a la vista* at lunch. Next door, with more of a bar vibe, **Restaurante La Cancha** (2512-0402; central park; L, D), specializes in tacos, burritos, tortas, and sports TV, all perfect with a cold *cerveza*.

Santiago de María

Hey, as long as you're here to get some shopping done, hit the ATM, or catch a bus, why not grab something to eat?

✪ **Restaurant y Pastelería Nataly** (2663-0775) 3 Avenida Norte, near the Market. $. Credit Cards: No. Cuisine: Salvadoran. Serving: B, L, D. Child's Menu: No. Handicapped Access: Challenging. Reservations: No. Everyone's favorite place for *comida a la vista* (7 AM–3 PM) is this local institution that also serves pastries, sandwiches, and other treats to

its loyal customers. After 5 PM, they sell simple set plates for around $3.

Restaurante El Marrua (2369-6328) Parque Central, next to Alcaldía. $. Credit Cards: No. Cuisine: Salvadoran. Serving: L, D. Child's Menu: No. Handicapped Access: Challenging. Reservations: No. Convenient, popular, and pretty, this restaurant occupies an old Colonial home and keeps the ambiance up with cute artesanias, colorful tablecloths, and lovely tilework. The burgers are a favorite of businesspeople in a rush, but the grilled meat platters are the specialty of the house.

Perquín

La Cocina de la Abuela (2680-4002) Central Perquín. $. Credit Cards: No. Cuisine: Salvadoran. Serving: B, L, D, weekends only. Child's Menu: No. Handicapped Access: Challenging. Reservations: On weekdays. When weekend visitors from steamy San Miguel make their way to cool Perquín, this sunny, flower-filled restaurant opens, serving fresh coffee, famous desserts, and excellent Salvadoran specialties. The *desayuno tipo oriente*, or eastern-style breakfast, is rather like the western version, but with pancakes. Other dishes, like churrasco, burgers, and *sopa de gallina India*, are also offered.

Comedor Antojitos Mirasol (2680-4063) Central Park. $. Credit Cards: No. Cuisine: Salvadoran. Serving: B, L, D (closes at 5 PM). Child's Menu: No. Handicapped Access: Challenging. The best restaurant in town certainly won't break your budget, with huge $2–4 set plates. Although there is a menu, savvy customers ignore it and ask what Marisol has cooking. There are usually two or three choices, generally served with rice, beans, and vegetables or salad, and a pile of steaming hot tortillas. It gets packed for lunch, so arrive early or prepare to wait.

BAKERIES Pastelería Lorena (2661-7640) 2 Calle Poniente and 3 Avenida Norte, San Miguel. B, L, D. $–$$. AE, MC, V. Fantastic little bakery in downtown San Miguel serves sweet and savory pastries, sandwiches, and good *comida a la vista* at lunch, in refreshingly air-conditioned comfort. There's another one at Metrocentro, and in **Santiago de María** (2661-5555; 1 Calle Poniente and 2 Avenida Norte), one block from the central park.

La Tartaleta (2660-4983; www .latarteleta.com) Avenida Roosevelt Sur and 11 Calle Poniente, Plaza Jardín. B, L, D. $–$$. Posh bakery and café serves fine pastries, fancy coffees, sandwiches, salads, and other light meals; there's another outlet at Metrocentro.

CAFÉS Arte Café (2660-1302) Avenida Roosevelt Sur, San Miguel. B, L, D. $. Cash only. Art gallery and café serves espresso beverages, pastries, and light meals surrounded by exhibits from San Miguel artists.

✪ **Jugos de Estación** (2663-2004) Berlín, 2 Calle Poniente #10. B, L. $. Cash only. Next to the Berlín market, this sidewalk café serves great *licuados*, fresh fruit juice drinks made with purified water, as well as frozen coffees *(batidos de café)* and great *panes,* submarine sandwiches, filled with chicken and veggies.

PUPUSERÍAS Pupusería Olocuilta (7298-4805) Entrance to Jocatique. B, L, D. $. Cash only. Wheelchair access. About 10 kilometers (6 miles) south of Perquín is this fine eatery, specializing in rice pupusas, cooked fresh all day. The gardens are gorgeous.

Pupusería Eliu (2683-9493) Central San Fernando. B, L, D. $. Cash only. Pupusas are served for breakfast and dinner, and there's *comida a la vista* at lunch. If it's not open, try:

Dining Nohemi (2683-9520) B, L, D. $. Cash only. Serving indigenous Salvadoran dishes nearby.

Pupusería Martita (No phone) Berlín, 2 Avenida Norte, behind Iglesia San José. B, D. $. Cash only. The best pupusería in Berlín gets packed after 5 PM.

✳ Selective Shopping

BANKS AND ATMS San Miguel has half a dozen banks with ATMs near the central park, including HSBC, CitiBank, and Scotia, with more ATMs at Metrocentro Mall. While **Alegría** doesn't have a bank, **Berlín** has a BAC ATM next to the Alcaldía, and **Santiago deMaría** has CitiBank and HSBC ATMs close to the Central Park. **San Vicente** has an HSBC ATM just off the Central Park. There are no banks in Perquín. **Santa Rosa de Lima** has a Scotiabank close to the park.

GROCERIES San Miguel has several large supermarkets, and the most impressive is Dispensa San Juan at Metrocentro. There's a big SuperSelectos on Avenida Roosevelt Sur and 11 Calle Poniente. If you're staying by the bus station, be sure to visit grungy Dispensa Familiar before 7 PM, when it closes.

San Vicente SuperSelectos is right off the central park, next to the cathedral. **Santiago de María** has a Dispensa Familiar, close to the central park, while Berlín, Alegría, and Perquín have small stores with limited selections.

MARKETS San Miguel has an amazing market (Calle Chaparrastique and 1 Avenida Sur), really an attraction unto itself. Part of it occupies an old military base, but it sprawls for several sloppy blocks around Parque Gerardo Barrios. **San Vicente's** large market (1 Avenida Sur and 2 Calle Poniente) is close to Iglesia Pilar. **Berlín** has a ✪ tidy little market two blocks from the central park, with lots of great little stands selling cheap eats.

MALLS San Miguel Metrocentro Avenida Roosevelt. Most stores open 9 AM–6:30 PM; restaurants and theater later. Just outside the city, on the road to La Unión, this large, modern mall has a Cinemark Movie Theater, several banks and ATMs, a huge Dispensa San Juan grocery store, La Ceiba bookstore (2667-5753; www.libros laceiba.com), Radio Shack, department stores, and even a great little souvenir shop, Artesanía El Salvador. The food court has all your favorite fast food. To get here from the city center, take Bus 90S or 90B (25¢) from the Central Park, or grab a taxi (around $2).

HANDICRAFTS Alegría: Both the high-quality handicraft shop at Restaurant Cartagena, and art gallery at La Casa de Alegría (both covered in Lodging) have unique gifts. Artesanías Alegría (2628–1115; central park) sells ceramics, seed jewelry, and other tchotchkies.

Berlín: Artesanías Su Casa Amiga (2663-2789) 6a Avenida Sur and 4a Calle Oriente, Barrio San José. Open daily. Berlín's only handicrafts shop has bowls made of jícaro and morro shells, clothing embroidered by members of a local women's collective; and great belts and other items made with recycled tin cans.

Cacaopera: Best known for creating hammocks from jarcía, a type of yucca fiber (today often strengthened with nylon and/or cotton), craftspeople also produce belts, bags, and other crafts. The museum and Casa de Cultura both sell these items.

El Mozote: El Mozote Asociación Turistica (7534-0383) Central Park. In the colorful information kiosk next to the memorial, an artisanías collective sells handwoven purses, jewelry, indigo-dyed souvenir T-shirts, and traditional Don Gumersindo soap made with local herbs.

Guatajiagua: East of San Francisco Gotera, this small town is famed for its deep, smoky black pottery, made with clay from a single source used since Lenca times. Traditionally hand-formed into comales and other useful vessels, today artists use molds and wheels, and create smoothly finished figurative sculptures. The raw clay forms, once finished, are wood-fired in dome-shaped kilns, with the kindling stacked around them. Once the pieces reach a certain temperature, they are pulled out and doused with a dye extracted from the nacazol seed, then dried. These are then shipped to galleries all over the world, where they command high prices; you can get them much more cheaply here, though the technique means they are relatively fragile. There are several workshops and inexpensive eateries in town, and evidently a good **hotel**; ask around when you get here.

Jocoaitique: At the turnoff to Jocoatique, at KM195 Caraterra Perquín, there are several handicrafts shops including **Artesanías Milita** (2680-5700), with a small restaurant; **Florazul**, run by a women's collective that specializes in indigo-dyed cloth; and **CEFODAR**, another local crafts collective. **ACOPROARMO Cooperative Jocoaitique** (2615-9731; KM200 Carretera Perquín) specializes in hammocks, ceramics, woodwork, and woven goods.

Perquín: Surrounding the Museo de la Revolución are several souvenir stands selling Oscar Romero, Farabundo Martí, and Che Guevara-themed jewelry, keychains, T-shirts, and so on, as well as shrapnel, handmade wooden military helicopters, Civil War dioramas, and other gifts perfect for the history buff in your life. ✪ **Casita de la Abuela** (see Lodging) has a fine selection of leftist books.

Santa Rosa de Lima: Though most travelers just roll through on their way to the border, Commercial Capital of La Unión is a famous *tiangue,* or market town, that trades in livestock, clothing, cheese, leatherwork, and most famously gold, mined from the surrounding hills by families who have worked these claims since around 1200 A.D. Sunday and Monday are huge markets for pig farmers, Thursday and Friday for dairy products, Saturday is for livestock of all kinds. Adventurous types might be able to find guides at the alcaldía for hikes to El Ventarron Hills, La Chorrea waterfall, and Los Ausoles thermal vents.

✳ Special Events

On the last Saturday of the month, San Vicente hosts a Gastronomic Festival, with more than 30 stands selling local cuisine and handicrafts, plus live entertainment.

January: **Fiestas Perquín** (January 21–22) Perquín honors its patron, San Sebastián Mártir; a smaller festival takes place in nearby Guatajiagua.

Fiestas San Vicente (January 23–28) San Vicente also honors Saint Sebastian.

Fiestas Moncagua (January 30–February 4) Moncagua, San Miguel, honors the Virgen de Candelaria.

February: **Fiestas Berlín** (February 15–20) Berlín honors its patron, San José.

March: **Fiestas Verapaz** (March 17–19) Verapaz, San Vicente, honors its patron, San José.

Semana Santa (March or April) Easter Sunday is celebrated with gusto in San Fernando, where Santa Dolores, Holy Wednesday, and Good Friday all merit special events.

May: **Fiestas San Fernando** (May 30) San Fernando honors its patron.

✪ **Festival of Balloons** (Second Sunday in May) San Esteban Catarina, just north of San Vicente creates a huge, colorful balloon made of "papel de China," 3 to 10 meters in diameter. The launch is amidst a festival of music, dance, and food.

June: **Fiestas Corinto** (June 27–30) Corinto honors its patron, San Pedro Apóstol.

July: **Fiestas Santiago de María** (July 19–25) Santiago de María honors its patron, Santiago Apóstol.

August: ✪ **Festival de Invierno de Perquín** (August 1–6) The Winter

Festival is Morazán's biggest event, celebrating the signature of the 1992 Peace Accords, indigenous Lenca culture, local crafts and music, and of course, heavy drinking. Parades, beauty contests, floats, and other activities make this a must.

Fiestas Chinameca (August 8–15) Chinameca honors its patron, San Salvador.

Fiestas Cacaopera (August 12–15) The Ulúa town's civic fiestas are the best time to experience their traditional dance.

Fiestas Santa Rosa of Lima (August 12–30) Santa Rosa de Lima celebrates its patron saint with a huge market.

September: **Fiestas Alegría** (September 26–29) Alegría honors its patron, San Miguel Arcángel.

October: **Feast Day of the Virgin of Rosario** (First Sunday in October) El Rosario honors its patron.

Fiestas San Francisco Gotera (October 1–4) San Francisco honors its patron, San Francisco de Asís.

November: ✪ **Carnival San Miguel** (End of November) El Salvador's biggest party (www.carnavaldesan miguel.net), in honor of Our Lady of Peace, brings in thousands from all over the nation and world for a week of dancing, debauchery, fireworks, parades, floats, beauty queens, carnival rides, and most famously, live music—some 40 bands play annually. The party actually starts October 31 with smaller warm-up fiestas in towns all over the region. Make reservations well in advance!

December: **Fogón Comunitario de Arambala** (December 7) Bonfires set up in the central park to symbolize the burning away of the year's bad vibes.

Fiestas Delicias de Concepcíon (December 4–8) Las Delicias honors the Virgin of Immaculate Conception.

✪ **Fiestas San Vicente** (December 15–31) San Vicente honors its patron with a huge, two-week party.

RECOMMENDED READING AND VIEWING

ARCHAEOLOGY

Fox, John W. Maya Postclassic State Formation: Segmentary Lineage Migration in Advancing Frontiers. 2008. $34.99. The history and politics of the Mayan people.

Kelly, Joyce, and Jerry Kelly. An Archaeological Guide to Northern Central America: Belize, Guatemala, Honduras, and El Salvador. 1996. $19.95. This puts El Salvador's ancient cities into context.

Sheets, Payson D. The Cerén Site: An Ancient Village Buried by Volcanic Ash in Central America. 2005. $39.95. La Joya de Cerén, discovered by Sheets in 1976, was buried beneath a blizzard of ash, preserving a single moment in time.

Sheets, Payson D., ed. Archeology and Volcanism in Central America: The Zapotitan Valley of El Salvador. 1984. $129.99. One of the earliest archaeologists to study El Salvador describes his findings.

CHILDREN

Nickels, Greg. El Salvador: The Land (Lands, Peoples, and Cultures). 1997. $7.95. Aimed at pre-teens, this book looks at El Salvador's geography, natural history, people, and economy.

Argieta, Jorge. A Movie in My Pillow. $7.95. Poems, illustrated by Mexican painter Elizabeth Gómez, recount the life of a young Salvadoran-American caught between his rural childhood in wartime El Salvador and move to the Mission District of San Francisco.

CIVIL WAR

Danner, Mark. The Massacre at El Mozote. 1994. $14.95. This is the definitive, well-written account of the systematic murder of some 900 civilians in Morazán by federal troops in 1981.

Montgomery, Tommie Sue. *Revolution in El Salvador: From Civil Strife to Civil Peace.* 1994. $42.00. This analysis of the war focuses on President Duarte's failed attempts to hammer out a peace accord in 1984, and how militant conservatives exploited those failings and returned to power in 1989.

Sobrino, Jon. *Witnesses to the Kingdom: The Martyrs of El Salvador and the Crucified Peoples.* 2003. $20.00. Few nations have had their modern histories so shaped by the Catholic Church, or rather, by Liberation Theologists who worked for social justice in the 1970s and 1980s. Like Archbishop Romero, shot at point blank range while giving communion, many nuns, priests, and Catholic aid workers were targeted with violence, rape, and execution. This book looks at their sacrifices in the context of historic Christian martyrs.

Stanley, William. *The Protection Racket State: Elite Politics, Military Extortion, and Civil War in El Salvador.* 1996. $34.95. During the 20th century, El Salvador logged more state-sponsored killings than any other country in the Americas. Some 30,000 coffee workers were executed in 1932, during La Matanza, while the first half of the 1980s saw some 1000 civilians per month killed by government forces. This book looks at the government as a protection racket for wealthy clients, not unlike Italian mafias or modern gangs.

Wood, Elisabeth Jean. *Insurgent Collective Action and Civil War in El Salvador.* 2003. $20.56. Based on scores of interviews with the people involved, Wood provides her own analysis of organization during the Civil War.

Vigil, José Ignacio López, Rebel Radio: The story of El Salvador's Radio Venceremos. 1995. $38.85. Collection of oral histories by the DJs of Radio Vencermos, the mobile guerrilla radio station that broadcast news, views, and witty repartee across the mountains during the Civil War, recounts the revolution with the same sense of humor that helped them survive.

GENERAL

Didion, Joan. *Salvador.* 1994. $12.95. Slim, beautifully written book chronicles the Civil War from a left-wing perspective.

Miller, Spring, and James L. Cavallaro. *No Place to Hide: Gang, State, and Clandestine Violence in El Salvador.* 2009. $14.95. This new book takes a look at the gang infestation that continues to plague El Salvador.

Saiers, Danny F. *People of the Sugarcane: The Indigenous People of Northern Cuscatlán, El Salvador.* 2008. $19.95. This memoir of life with "the people of the Church of Santa Lucía," recounts life in the sugarcane fields around Guazapa and Suchitoto.

Shields, Charles J., and James D. Henderson. *El Salvador (Central America Today).* 2008. $9.95. A closer look at the sociology of modern El Salvador from the ground up examines everything from its agriculture and deforestation, to emigration, cuisine, festivals, war, and the continuing influence of the country's wealthiest families and the Catholic Church.

Almeida, Paul D. *Waves of Protest: Popular Struggle in El Salvador, 1925-2005 (Social Movements, Protest and Contention)*. 2008. $75.00. The last century was a tumultuous one for the people of El Salvador, and Almeida examines what he calls "one of the largest and most successful campaigns against globalization and privatization in the Americas."

Boland, Roy C. *Culture and Customs of El Salvador*. 2000. $16.00. This general overview of El Salvador looks at the land, history, people, economy, religion, education, traditional culture and popular entertainment, literature, media, and the arts within the context of disasters both natural and manmade.

Coutin, Susan Bibler. *Nations of Emigrants: Shifting Boundaries of Citizenship in El Salvador and the United States*. 2007. $21.00. The destinies and citizenships of El Salvador and the United States are profoundly intertwined; this book examines this phenomenon's causes and legal challenges.

Dipiazza, Francesca Davis. *El Salvador in Pictures*. 2007. $23.50. This short, colorful "visual geography" text shows off the country with colorful photos.

Gould, Jeffry L, and Aldo A. Lauria-Santiago. *To Rise in Darkness: Revolution, Repression, and Memory in El Salvador, 1920-1932*. 2008. $89.95. This study of the 1932 Peasant Uprising and bloody La Matanza examines the conventionally held belief that the indigenous participants and communist organizers were separate groups using documents from El Salvador, Guatemala, Washington, London, and Moscow, arguing that many proponents of a more socialist state were themselves rural Indians.

Kampwirth, Karen. *Feminism & Legacy of Revolution: Nicaragua, El Salvador, Chiapas*. 2004. $28.00. It's no wonder that joining a revolutionary movement often leads ladies to consider a more feminist perspective; this book examines why.

Tilley, Virginia Q. *Seeing Indians: A Study of Race, Nation, and Power in El Salvador*. 2005. $24.95. The 1932 Matanza (slaughter) of some 30,000 indigenous peasants, followed by the deliberate repression of their culture, language, and traditional dress, has influenced everything from census figures (which significantly underreport El Salvador's indigenous population) to the way Salvadorans see themselves and their country.

White, Christopher M. *The History of El Salvador*. 2008. $40. Historical overview covers El Salvador's history from pre-Columbian times through the Civil War.

MOVIES

Duigan, John. *Romero*. 1989. Raul Julia is at his finest in this masterpiece about Oscar Romero, chosen by El Salvador's elite as archbishop because they thought the bookish priest wouldn't make waves. Instead, his words washed over the nation and all of Latin America, leaving behind ten thousand murals and a new branch of Catholicism, Liberation Theology, still embraced by the poor and downtrodden, who believe that Jesus would have been on their side. Romero certainly was. Highly recommended.

Gomez, Karen. *Sobreviviendo Guazapa.* 2008. El Salvador's first domestically produced major motion picture stars mostly Civil War veterans rather than real actors, and it shows. The plot is predictable as well: a federal soldier and young guerrilla fighter, thrown together on the battlefield of Guazapa Volcano, must work together to save the life of a lost little girl. Regardless, this flick (Spanish with subtitles) is well worth watching for the very realistic firefights, poignant political debate, fantastic scenery, and historically accurate weaponry, uniforms, strategies, and fighting conditions.

Stone, Oliver. *Salvador.* 1996. Director Oliver Stone plays fast and loose with historical facts, but this over-the-top epic, starring James Woods as a feral journalist and James Belushi as his drug-addled sidekick, captures the chaos and horror of the Civil War with a supremely watchable intensity.

WILDLIFE GUIDES

Conant, Roger, and Joseph T. Collins. *A Field Guide to Reptiles & Amphibians of Eastern and Central North America.* 1998. $21. Massive, 640-page guide, with 656 full-color illustrations and photos, should have the information you need.

Komar, Oliver. "Avian diversity in El Salvador." Digital article from Wilson Bulletin. 2005. $5.95. This useful resource is published only online, a comprehensive study of El Salvador's 508 recorded species, including 310 breeding residents, 17 endemics, and 254 endangered species. A list of 73 species not yet officially recorded poses a challenge to adventurous birders.

Reid, Fiona A. *A Field Guide to the Mammals of Central America and Southeast Mexico.* 2009. $45. Comprehensive field guide includes 47 color plates and information about various habitats.

Van Perlo, Ber. *Birds of Mexico and Central America.* 2006. $29.95. Definitive guide for birders lists some 1500 species.

INDEX